A BRIEF INTRODUCTION

To the Playing on the

TREBLE-VIOLIN.

THE *Treble-Violin* is a cheerful and spritely Instrument, and much practised of late, some by *Book*, and some *without*; which of these two is the best way, may easily be resolved: First, to learn to play by *rote* or *ear* without *Book*, is the way never to play more than what he can gain by hearing another play, which may soon be forgot; but on the contrary, he which learns and practises by Book, according to the Grounds of *Musick*, fails not, after he comes to be perfect in those Rules, which guide him to play more than ever he was taught or heard, and also to play his part in *Consort*; which the other will never be capable of, unless he have this *sure guide*.

Baroque String Playing
for ingenious learners

Judy Tarling

Punnett Press

First published 2000

This edition published 2024

Punnett Press

3 North Street, Punnett's Town, East Sussex TN21 9DT, UK

© Judy Tarling 2000 and 2024

All rights reserved

ISBN 978-0-9932810-4-4

Cover illustration from
Michel Corrette, *L'Art De se perfectionner dans le Violon*, (Paris 1782)
by kind permission of Editions Minkoff

Preface to the Second Edition (2013)

Since *Baroque String Playing 'for ingenious learners'* was first published in 2000, more and more players have been attracted into historical performance, and the results of research into a wider chronological field of performance are being seen on the platform. Since 2000 several more generations of students have passed through courses designed to introduce them to period style. The internet revolution had transformed all research, libraries have put their priceless collections of original manuscripts, books and printed editions on-line to be accessed by all, and the search for music of the 17th and 18th centuries has been liberated by the generosity of the individuals and institutions which have made this material available.

In 2004 my second book *The Weapons of Rhetoric, a guide for musicians and audiences* was published, inspired by writing Part One of this book, 'The Rhetorical Style'. *Weapons* attracted readers immediately and filled a very large hole in the performer's armoury. Apart from a break-through in understanding rhetoric applied to musical performance, other research in the field during the last decade means that Baroque groups are now used to playing at a variety of appropriate pitches, not just $a^1=415$, and historical stringing with equal tension has transformed the sound of string bands through the work of Oliver Webber and others. In spite of this, I have kept the original audio examples from CDs by The Parley of Instruments to illustrate points in the book, even though some of the tracks are 20 years old or more. It remains, in my opinion, a useful introduction to 17th-century style which is still less understood than music of the more familiar 18th century, especially in the use and choice of continuo instruments (we still hear anachronistic cellos playing continuo in Monteverdi). To help understand the point we have reached in the period performance field, and the journey which brought us here, I can recommend the late Bruce Haynes's book *The End of Early Music. A period performer's history of music for the twenty-first century* (Oxford, 2007) which should be read by all performers, not only historically informed ones.

Since the publication of *Weapons*, I have had the good fortune to be invited to meet readers of my books in the U.S.A. at Oberlin, Harvard, Bard College, Longy in Boston, Juilliard in New York, and Jacobs School of Music at Indiana. In Latin America I have visited the Universities of Veracruz, Mexico and Sao Paulo, Brazil. In Europe, apart from U.K. universities and conservatoires, I have been invited to teach at Hannover, Lyon, Utrecht, Amsterdam, and Oslo. Everywhere I have found intense interest in the historical, and especially the rhetorical aspects of performance, and I have found students really curious and ready to continue the work of getting to know about rhetoric, which seems to me to have hardly started, although the period instrument movement is already nearly half a century old. Conservatoires are now embracing the idea of historical style for everyone, not just the specialist, and knowing about and applying appropriate style is becoming an essential tool for all performers.

I have updated the bibliography, the section on editions, and made amendments to some of the references (particularly the treatises by Leopold Mozart and Quantz which before only received page numbers of the English translation). A couple of errors which slipped through the original editing process have been corrected.

INTRODUCTION

> *Style is the choice of expressive means. The composer and performer have a choice of expressive means; this choice is style. We apply this thought to the artist's taste. His choice of means will let us know without fail what pleases him, what captivates him, what carries him away. He will be judged on this choice, which results from what he feels. Begin by studying composers of the past.*
>
> Pierre Baillot, *L'Art du Violon* (1834)[1]

The main purpose of this book is to form a guide to the available historical source material about playing the violin, viola, cello and double bass. It is not a 'method' for playing Baroque instruments—these have already been written by 17th- and 18th-century musicians—but a general view of the stylistic conventions of the time with 'how to' technical detail for string players. Treatises written for other instruments such as the viol, lute, flute or harpsichord have been referred to when they contribute to the general stylistic argument.

I do not claim to have undertaken any original research while writing this book, but have drawn mainly on published source material. I hope that this will encourage readers to go and read the complete texts of these sources for themselves. At my elbow throughout has been lurking the spectre of David Boyden, whose monumental tome *The History of Violin Playing from its origins to 1761* has been the 'Bible' for all violinists attempting to re-create a historical style of playing. The organisation of his book in historical periods has meant that as a practical manual it is somewhat awkward to use for the novice needing information on particular topics, for example holding the instrument when starting to play without a chin-rest. The progress that has been made through the use of historical instruments and performance techniques since the sixties means that information about certain subjects such as defining what is meant by the term *violone*, and the use of unequal temperament is scanty. This book is arranged by topic rather than date, so that the historical source material about a particular aspect of style or technique may be considered collectively.

Much of the book has been written as a reaction to the author's observations of current practice, in the hope that players and directors may find the information here to help them to get to grips with the unwritten conventions of the time. Many practices were assumed by Baroque composers, and unless we are familiar with these, we are making serious omissions in our performances. The discussion which appears after the source material (identified as *Practical Application* and *Case Studies*) inevitably reflects my own views developed through practical experience 'in the field', and many subjects such as the use of vibrato, the *messa di voce* and over-dotting have and will continue to generate controversy. Cervantes expressed this author's nervousness in committing ideas to print:

---

[1] tr. Louise Goldberg, p. 12

'an author runs a very great risk in printing a book. For it is the greatest of all impossibilities to write one that will satisfy and please every reader'.[2]

Much has been learned since 1965 when Boyden published his *History*, particularly through the experience of playing newly discovered repertoire, and trying to put into practice the fruits of the research which has taken place since the sixties. As the number of copies sold reveals, there are now thousands of 'ingenious learners' curious to learn about historical techniques and style, but as more generations of period instrument players graduate from the conservatories, I fear that the ethos of playing on what used to be called 'original instruments' has undergone a change. I see the spirit of discovery being lost by attrition as the message gets passed from teacher to pupil instead of being absorbed directly from the sources. These should be under continuous scrutiny as each generation of players comes into contact with the ideas and playing styles of their modern mentors. To be able to study these instruments at all in mainstream conservatories shows that the establishment of historical performance practice is here to stay, and is a force to be reckoned with, whether the player chooses to play a historical instrument or not.

The sources of information from the Baroque period are varied and conflicting, presenting as much of a challenge to today's musician as to the musicians for whom they were written. Peter Prelleur's *The Art of Playing on the Violin* (1731) provided the inspiration for the title of this book:

> Methods of Practitioners are very different; nevertheless it may not be improper for ye satisfaction of ingenious Learners to exhibit some few remarkable Observations on this subject.

Then, as now, creative thinking fashioned individual styles of playing. The fact that many treatises were called 'rules' has led some of today's less well-informed performers to assume that by reading and trying to implement these rules, the player's personal voice will somehow be subverted, and playing music will be transformed into an academic exercise.[3] I hope that this book will show that the exact opposite is the case. The *ingenious learner* approaching historical material should not rely solely upon rules to create a performing style. Expressing his own feelings inspired by the music should form a major part of his interpretation. One of the themes running through the book is the idea of achieving this expressiveness within a suitable historical style created by 'the rules'.

The principal purpose of all music, and particularly of Baroque music, is the expression of emotions. To achieve this, the player should look to the art of rhetoric (manipulating the listener's emotions by persuasive speaking) which was extensively practised and written about during the period, particularly with reference to musical performance. The rhetorical theme will appear throughout the book, showing players how to find clues in the music which will unlock the intended emotional 'affect'.

The type of instrument used, whether a period or modern one, should not be the primary condition on which the use of historical style depends, and I hope that many players who play Baroque music on modern instruments will read this book and apply some of the ideas contained within it to their own performances. The concept, also set out on the title page of Geminiani's treatise (1751), that instrumentalists other than violinists may read and usefully learn from this book may be applied:

> The Art of Playing on the Violin containing All the Rules necessary to attain to a Perfection on that Instrument, with great variety of Compositions, which will also be very useful to those who study the Violoncello, Harpsichord &c.

The sparsity of instrumental methods written for cello, viola and double bass during the period means that relevant information from the violin treatises will need to be transferred to these instruments without additional comment. Readers will find source material about ensemble playing which includes specific instructions for viola and continuo players in Part 5.

Throughout the book I have included the date of the original material. The significance of the date is greater for some points of style than others, which should be apparent from

---

[2] (1605) *Don Quixote*, chapter 3
[3] I have collected some thoughts of contemporary writers on the subject of rules in section 6.3 of this book

the source material I have selected. All writers of the period abhor excessive speed, rushing and any playing style which does not hold the listener's attention. All admire the beauty of the expressive long note and approve of rubato in certain situations. Disagreements occur about details of style, particularly about the use of vibrato and the rule of down-bow.

Basic principles

The main period under consideration is 1600-1760, occasionally extended backwards towards the birth of the violin family, and forwards to include some of the important violin treatises written in the latter part of the 18th century. There are a number of threads woven into the text throughout, leading the performer to consider the following:

- The differences between 17th- and 18th-century music, forms and national styles of playing.
- The various techniques and attitudes required to realise these differences.
- The emotional 'affect' implicit in all the music to be surveyed and how to achieve this in practice.
- Harmonic structure, which is an important pre-requisite for performing Baroque music. The tension of dissonance (strong/down-bow) followed by the relief of resolution (weak/up-bow) is the life-blood of the music. Allied to this is the ability to recognise cadences, which are the punctuation marks of the language of music.

Inequality is OK

One of the main concepts associated with performing Baroque music, in technique and inherent in the music, is the principle of inequality. In playing the violin this is expressed by the bow's natural resistance to gravity. The differences between up- and down-bow should at first be encouraged when learning to use a Baroque bow. By emphasising different parts of the beat, the bar and the phrase, this way of playing has no need of detailed dynamic instructions. Loud and soft are governed by the position of the strong emphases in the music, dictated by rhythm or harmony, and by the player's 'fancy'.

The custom of arranging the stronger stress to occur on the down-bow became known as the 'rule of down-bow' and was used for dance music in the early violin repertoire, but was disliked by Italian violinists as it did not suit their more singing, contrapuntal style of composition. The rule of down-bow became out-dated by the late 18th century as the old Baroque bow gave way to the longer and more incurved model. The Italian 'sonata' style of bowing was always more 'bowed-out' and flowing, to suit the singing style, whereas French music, being more dance-based, relied on the rule of down-bow with more lifted strokes.

Another example of the principle of inequality is found in the tuning systems in use in the 17th and 18th centuries. These are based on a system where commonly used intervals are more in tune than others which are used less frequently. Unequal tuning gives colour to keys, making remote keys (i.e. remote from C major) 'horrible', and keys closer to home 'beautiful' in their perfectly true consonant harmonies. As composers felt the need to use more keys, tuning systems became more equally tempered. Rameau was one of the first composers to advocate more equally tempered tuning as his compositions began to use a wider range of keys. However, key affects inherited from the use of unequal tunings were retained in the musical language.

Equipment

Which came first, the technical advances in the music, or in the instruments? Throughout the life of the violin family from the mid-16th century onwards, the changes in equipment and the musical demands chased each other forward, a process guided by the leading players of the time. Our understanding of the music and how to play it is directly influenced by the equipment we are using, and if this happens to be the most appropriately historic instrument or bow, we will discover things in the music which it is not possible to perceive with more 'advanced' equipment: sonority, fingering possibilities (and difficulties), and choice of bow-strokes. Encountering these problems also helps us to understand why and how developments of violin technique and instrument technology came about.

The text

Source material is all indented to be easily identifiable.

Musical examples from facsimiles of 17th- and 18th- century editions are identified by *f* after the example number.

Clefs: Where facsimile musical material is used, the reader should be aware of the use of unusual clefs, particularly the French violin clef (G on the bottom line).

Audio examples are marked ♪ in the relevant section in the text. They can be downloaded from https://www.hyperion-records.co.uk/dc.asp?dc=D_BSP1.
See the list of tracks on the final page of the book.

References: The original date of the text is followed by the name of the translator where this applies. Unattributed translations are by the author. Fuller details can be found in the bibliography by author, followed by date of publication.

Pitch registers are indicated as follows:

C   c   c¹   c²   c³

Acknowledgements

I would like to thank all my colleagues in The Parley of Instruments, and particularly its director Professor Peter Holman, whose encouragement and advice has been a spur to this project. Also the late Ted Perry of Hyperion Records for his support of The Parley and for the CD tracks of audio examples that can be downloaded from the Hyperion website. Advice from other colleagues has been gratefully received: Elizabeth Wallfisch (part 2), Mark Caudle (parts 5.1, 5.2 and 6.1), Paul Denley (part 6.1), Oliver Webber (strings), Peter McCarthy (double bass), and the late Dr. Bruce Haynes (part 4). The drawings of violins and bows in part 6 were specially commissioned from Martin Bowers and I would like to thank him for the clarity, elegance and care with which these were executed. This book would not have seen the light of day without the generous editorial advice and technical assistance of Peter Lay, who has also prepared this revised edition.

I would like to pay tribute to all the students of the Cambridge Early Music Summer Schools, those who have attended courses at The Benslow Music Trust, and the players of the Essex Baroque Orchestra, whose curiosity and enthusiasm for Baroque music gave me the idea of writing this book. These players have, unknowingly, dictated its form and style. It is dedicated to them.

Extracts from Edith Knocker's translation of Leopold Mozart's *Versuch einer gründlichen Violinschule* are reprinted by permission of Oxford University Press. Extracts from J. J. Quantz, *Versuch einer Anweisung die Flöte traversiere zu spielen* translated by E. R. Reilly are by kind permission of Faber and Faber. Editions Minkoff are acknowledged for permission to use material from the violin treatises by Corrette and L'Abbé le fils and Studio Per Edizioni Scelte, Florence, for musical examples from their facsimile editions of sonatas by Corelli, Piani, Cima, Castello, Veracini, Marini and Bonporti, and from Zannetti *Il Scolaro*, and Marais trios. Facsimile material from the *Concerts Royaux* and *Les Goûts-Réunis ou nouveaux concerts* by François Couperin are from Editions J. M. Fuzeau reprinted by permission of the Bibliothèque Inguimbertine and Gemeente Museum at The Hague. Extracts from the second part of The Division-violin (4th edition) are reproduced by kind permission of the Royal College of Music, London.

CONTENTS

Preface to the Second Edition		v
Introduction		vii
Acknowledgements		xi

PART ONE – THE RHETORICAL STYLE

- 1.1 Baroque rhetoric — 1
  - Emotional communication – Rhythm – Length of note – Intervals – Tessitura – Harmony – Key – Instrumentation – The mute – Pizzicato
- 1.2 Articulation — 9
  - Structure and punctuation – Articulation between individual notes – Articulation signs
- 1.3 Dynamics — 18
  - Which notes are loud and which soft? – Written instructions
- 1.4 Tempo — 25
  - Time signatures – Rubato – Pauses
- 1.5 Ornamentation — 34
  - Ornamentation in ensemble playing – Divisions – Written out ornamentation – The essential graces – Vibrato

PART TWO – TECHNIQUES

- 2.1 Holding the instrument — 63
  - The violin and viola – Bass instruments
- 2.2 Fingering choice and position changing — 72
  - Open Strings – Harmonics – Upward range – When to change position – Sonority – The history of positions and technical advancement – Larger shifts – Audible slides – Range: ensembles – Range: solo repertoire – Highest positions – Position terminology – Thumb position on the cello
- 2.3 Holding the bow — 83
  - The French Grip – The Italian grip – Position of the elbow – Tension of the hair – The cello bow-hold – The double bass bow-hold
- 2.4 The rule of down-bow — 88
  - Orchestral discipline – The rules – Even bowing – Dotted notes
- 2.5 The dance — 98
  - The 17th-century Suite – The 18th-century Suite or Overture – The dances
- 2.6 The slow bow — 122
  - Long notes – The messa di voce – Bow vibrato
- 2.7 Quick notes — 134
- 2.8 The slur — 145
- 2.9 Chords and double stopping — 149

PART THREE – NATIONAL STYLE

3.1	Identifying national style	158
3.2	French style: inequality	163
3.3	Italian style: alignment of mixed note values	170
3.4	Dotted notes	174
3.5	The 17th-century Italian sonata	180
3.6	The consort style	184

PART FOUR – TUNING AND PITCH

4.1	Tuning and pitch	187
4.2	Scordatura	196

PART FIVE – THE BASS DEPARTMENT

5.1	Playing from a figured bass part	203.
5.2	Choice of continuo instrument(s)	208
5.3	Performing recitative	218
5.4	The viola	223

PART SIX – EQUIPMENT

6.1	The Instrument and bow	233
	'On Original Instruments' – A short history of the violin family and its makers – The bow	
6.2	Playing from facsimile editions	248
6.3	Reading the treatises	260

Glossary	267
Bibliography	271
Audio Examples commentary	277
Index	283
List of Audio Examples	Opposite inside back cover

PART ONE
THE RHETORICAL STYLE

1.1 Baroque rhetoric

A commonly held view amongst composers and writers about music in the Baroque period is that a musical performance should resemble a speech.

Quantz:

> Musical execution (or manner of performance) may be compared with the delivery of an orator. The orator and the musician have, at bottom, the same aim in regard to both the preparation and the final execution of their productions, namely to make themselves masters of the hearts of their listeners, to arouse or still their passions, and to transport them now to this sentiment, now to that. Thus it is advantageous to both, if each has some knowledge of the duties of the other.
>
> (1752) XI.1, tr. Reilly, p. 119

St. Lambert:

> A piece of music somewhat resembles a piece of rhetoric, or rather it is the piece of rhetoric which resembles the piece of music, since harmony, number, measure and the other similar things which a skillful orator observes in the composition of his works belong more naturally to music than to rhetoric.
>
> (1702) tr. Harris-Warrick, p. 32

Corelli is said to have asked his pupils *Non udite lo parlare?* (Do you not hear it speak?)[1] This way of playing, which imitates the human voice, is based on the principles of oratory. The three main aims of an orator, according to the principal classical sources, were to inform, to delight and to move. The study of rhetoric and oratory (the art of writing and performing speeches written in the rhetorical style) was part of general education during the Baroque period. It is not surprising therefore, that composers used the forms and devices of oratory for their compositions. The aim of the musician, whether composer or performer (often the same person), was identical to that of the orator—to move his audience.

The two primary ancient classical texts on oratory which were studied throughout the Renaissance and Baroque periods were *De Oratore* by Cicero (106-43 BCE) and *Institutio Oratoria* by Quintilian (35-96 CE). These manuals are full of detailed advice on compositional and performance art, and techniques for moving the audience by the nature of the delivery and attitudes of the performer. In order for the orator to persuade his audience he should understand his subject thoroughly, deliver the speech in an appropriate style, speak with clarity of articulation, fullness and variety, and avoid monotony. It is also important that the structure of the composition is understood. By using clear phrasing and punctuation (articulation in musical terms) the performer should be able to make himself clearly understood, as in speech.

---

[1] J. Wilson, p. 359

1.1 Baroque rhetoric

Emotional communication

> You must imitate the orators who now raise their voice and then abate it, now they gett asleepe the hearer and now they awaken him now they charme him now they amaze him.
>
> Burwell Lute Tutor (1660-72), f.16v

This description of the rhetorical manner of playing from the Burwell Lute Tutor describes the way the audience should be led by the performer from one emotion to another. Quantz:

> You must, so to speak, adopt a different sentiment at each bar, so that you can imagine yourself now melancholy, now gay, now serious etc. Such dissembling is most necessary in music. He who can truly fathom this art is not likely to be wanting in approval from his listeners, and his execution will always be moving.
>
> (1752) XI.16, tr. Reilly, p. 126

During the 17th century, people were very conscious of the connection between their emotions and the physical affects these have on the body. Descartes, the French philosopher, described how the body was affected by the emotions of the soul in his tract *Les Passions de l'Âme* (1649). It is from the word 'affect' (German *affekt*) that an emotional point in the music which affects the body physically is derived, and it is this type of emotional communication which should be sought when performing Baroque music. Points in the music are designed to register specific affects on the listener, and it is up to the performer to discover these in order to interpret the composer's ideas.

There are many clues in the music as to which emotion is intended. Where words are present, these provide an obvious lead, but be careful to find the emotion represented by the words, as sometimes pure word painting in sound will give the wrong impression. For example 'shall laugh them to scorn' (Handel's *Messiah*) is not a happy sentiment. Strong emotional clues may be found in the nature or form of the composition, its function (e.g. church or theatre), the key in which it is written, the type of harmony used (simple home keys, or distant chromatic ones), intervals and rhythms, or tessitura. Any one or a combination of these factors contribute to the emotional framework of a piece of music.

Although any of these elements may represent a particular emotion in one instance, it does not necessarily mean that the same element will always portray this feeling. Mattheson warns us that these elements should not be used like a dictionary:

> One must not use these devices in such a way that one has an index of them and that one treats them, in an academic manner, like a box of inventions. Rather, they should be considered in the same way as the vocabulary and the expressions used in speaking. We do not put these on paper or in a book, but keep them in mind and by means of them we are able to express ourselves in the most comfortable way without constantly consulting a dictionary.
>
> (1739) II.4.17, tr. Harriss, p. 284

I will give some basic principles for identifying emotional points in the music for 'raising and soothing the passions', but Mattheson's advice should always be held in mind: the points of affect should not be used like an index.

Rhythm

Quintilian analyses rhythmic perception from the auditor's point of view:

> The best judge of rhythm is the ear, which appreciates fullness of rhythm or feels the lack of it.
>
> IX. iv. 116

The ancient orators always sought variety in rhythm, as monotony was inimical to holding the audience's attention. In general, slow duple rhythms are found in music of a serious nature such as pavans, grand entrées, overtures and ceremonial music.

Fast triple rhythms, however, are more frivolous and light-hearted, as in jigs. Heavy slow triple music is more serious:

1.1 Baroque rhetoric

Ex. 1.1.1: Corelli, Concerto Grosso op. 6 no. 10

Corelli uses a slow triple molossus rhythm for a serious weighty connecting Adagio movement. The 'Crucifixus' in J. S. Bach's Mass in B minor is in slow triple time and uses this type of affect.

Syncopation shows impatience, but be careful to differentiate between the rebound syncopation which is light and bounces off a strong beat, and the anticipated down-beat syncopation which should be played with a strong emphasis.

Ex. 1.1.2: J. S. Bach, Concerto for harpsichord in D minor

In the above example, two kinds of syncopation are shown in one phrase. In the middle of bar 1, the top d^2 is a rebound off the stronger a^1, while the tied notes should start strongly, showing impatience in anticipating the down-beat.

Length of note

In general, longer notes are serious and shorter ones light-hearted. Quintilian noted the comic effect of using very short syllables.[2] The speed of the bow contributes much to the affect of short notes. A slower speed is more relaxed, and a quicker one more tense. However, heavy short notes represent more serious emotions.

---

[2] IX. iv. 131

1.1 Baroque rhetoric

Ex. 1.1.3: Handel, Concerto Grosso op. 6 no. 8

Heavy staccato for surprise and grief, followed by pathetic falling figures in a minor key.

Ex. 1.1.4: J. S. Bach, Brandenburg Concerto no. 4, Presto

Notes marked with a dagger in the above example give a surprise affect if played strongly, or if played very short and lightly a comic one.

♪ track 17 for a short comic ending.

According to Quantz[3] long notes with a walking bass underneath give rise to sublime, majestic, heavenly feelings, a device often used by Corelli:

Ex. 1.1.5: Corelli, Concerto Grosso op. 6 no. 11, Andante largo

---

[3] (1752) XII.24, tr. Reilly, p. 133

Intervals

Two significant factors control the emotional content of various intervals: the size of an interval and its direction, upwards or downwards. Quantz:

> Flattery, melancholy and tenderness are expressed by slurred and close intervals . . . gaiety and boldness by those forming distant leaps.
>
> (1752) XI.16, tr. Reilly, p. 125

Mattheson:

> Small intervals are for sadness, large ones for joy.
>
> Hope is an elevation of the spirit, and despair a casting down of the same. These are subjects that can be well represented by sound especially when other circumstances (tempo in particular) contribute their share.
>
> (1739) I.3.59, tr. Harriss, p. 105

A summary of the affects of intervals from various sources compiled from Wessel:

Small intervals in the key	lovely, pleasant affects
Ascending 3rd	gaiety, sprightliness
Descending 3rd	sad, mournful, lamenting
Minor 3rd	tender, affecting
Major 3rd	lively, brisk
Ascending 4th and 5th	lively
Descending 4th	pathetic, doleful, solemn
Perfect 5th	bold, commanding
Diminished 5th	pathetic
Minor 6th	lamenting
Diminished 7th	pathetic
Major 7th	supplicative
Large intervals	madness, nonsense

These affects are indications only, remembering Mattheson's warning about not using these devices as a dictionary. It would be possible to find happy descending thirds, or sad perfect fifths, if other factors reinforced that sentiment.

Examples of intervals and their affects

Rising minor 6th: lamenting, mournful (see ex. 1.2.3, J. S. Bach, *St. Matthew Passion*, 'Erbarme dich'). The rising minor 6th at the beginning is pleading and lamenting. The same interval is repeated at bar two in a higher tessitura for emphasis.

Patter and trochaic light-hearted rhythms combined with crazy large intervals can indicate energetic euphoria:

Ex 1.1.6: Corelli, Concerto Grosso op. 6 no. 11, Vivace

Skips along the chord with rapid scales: joy

Ex. 1.1.7: Handel, Concerto Grosso op. 6 no. 1

1.1 Baroque rhetoric

Leaps and scales make a happy affect, even though the following movement starts in E minor:

Ex. 1.1.8: Handel, Concerto Grosso op. 6 no. 1

In the following example, the phrases start with 'normal' intervals, but develop emotional questions (large intervals rising) and answers (falling) with the different intervals at the start of each phrase.

Ex. 1.1.9: J. S. Bach, Sonata no. 4 in C minor for violin and harpsichord, Adagio

Tessitura

A natural result of raising the voice or lowering it gives a clue as to the dynamic levels which can be employed by phrases occurring at different pitches. The general dynamic principle of higher = louder, lower = softer can often be employed when a phrase or fragment of a theme is repeated at different levels. Another factor is the positioning of the phrase within the natural range of that voice or instrument. If the phrase is pitched in the upper register, it is likely to sound bright, excited, or dramatic according to context. In the lower register of the same instrument or voice the same phrase may appear dull, sad, or threatening.

Ex. 1.1.10: Handel, Concerto Grosso op. 6 no. 9, Largo
showing two levels of tessitura for two 'voices' with contrasting (original) dynamics.

Harmony

One of the basic elements of the language of Baroque music is the fluctuation which occurs between consonance and dissonance. Dissonances represent the emotions of trouble, excitement, sorrow, grief and suffering. Consonances have the affect of rest and contentment, pleasure and joy. After a long series of dissonances, the resolution of the harmony into pure consonance provides relief. Strong dissonances may be emphasised by a small articulation beforehand. C. P. E. Bach and many other writers recommend that dissonances should be emphasised, and consonances played weaker. Chromatic movement should express suffering or other deep emotions. Major dissonances represent despair and anger. See figured bass section (part 5.1) for more information about *affekt* from harmony.

Key

Unequal temperaments make some keys more perfectly in tune than others by altering the relative sizes of the semitones for each key (see part 4.1). The colours and characters of the keys were quite distinct before equal temperament became universal, and even after a more even distribution of semitones was in use, composers retained key-colour ideas. Other factors inherent in the nature of the instrumentation limited certain affects to specific keys (trumpet and drums usually in D major, for example). In the 18th century, composers themselves could not agree about whether keys harboured certain affects. Quantz thought that they did, and invited anyone who doubted this to transpose a piece of music into another key to find out. However, Heinichen[4] dismisses any serious emotional key-character association.

A table of key characteristics in Baroque music

Keys not in frequent use: D♭/C♯ major/minor, F♯/G♭ major, A♭/G♯ major, G♯/A♭ minor

	1691 **J. Rousseau**	**1692** **Charpentier**	**1713-19** **Mattheson**	**1722** **Rameau**
C maj	gay, grandeur	gay, militant	rejoicing	mirth, rejoicing
C min	complaints, laments	gloomy, sad	lovely, sad	tender, plaintes
D maj	gay, grandeur	joyful, militant	noisy, joyful	mirth, rejoicing
D min	serious	serious, pious	devout, grand, flowing not skipping	sweet, tender
E♭ maj		cruel, harsh	pathetic, serious	
E♭/D♯ min		horrible, frightful		
E maj		quarrelsome, clamorous	fatal sadness	grand, tender
E min	tenderness	amorous, plaintive	pensive, grieved	sweet, tender
F maj	devotional	furious, quick-tempered	most beautiful, virtuous	tempests, furies
F min	complaints, lamentations	dark, plaintive	calm but with deep despair	tenderness, plaints
F♯ min			languid, love-sick	
G maj	tenderness	sweetly joyful	persuasive, serious and cheerful	
G min	sadness	serious, magnificent	most beautiful, grace & kindness	sweet & tender
A maj	devotional	joyful, pastoral	lamenting, sad, playful, jesting	mirth, rejoicing
A min	serious	tender, plaintive	honourable, calm	
B♭ maj		magnificent, joyful	diverting, sumptuous	tempests, furies
B♭ min		gloomy, terrible		mournful songs
B maj		harsh, plaintive	offensive, hard, desparate	
B min		lonely, melancholic	bizarre, morose	sweet, tender

Compiled from information in Steblin, appendix A, and Cessac, pp. 384, 406-7

Mattheson warns us that

> No key can be so sad or happy in and of itself that one might not compose the opposite.

(1739) I.9.48, tr. Harriss, p. 188

---

[4] (1711) tr. Buelow, p. 283

1.1 Baroque rhetoric

Instrumentation

The instrumental colours used by a composer may give some clues to the emotional affect required. Certain instruments are used for gayer effects: violins, oboes; muted violins may be used for tender, sleepy or gentle music; the lute is a pastoral and sweet instrument; trumpets and drums give a bold triumphal or alarming war-like atmosphere. However, it is possible for almost any instrument to express most emotions, and it is only the combination of instruments and their affects which gives emotional colour to a group.

The mute

The mute for stringed instruments was first used in the mid-17th century by Lully and Purcell. Mersenne (1636) noticed that the effect of placing a heavy object, such as a key, on the bridge was a dampening of the sound. Boyden attributes Mersenne with the first use of the mute,[5] but it seems likely that he merely observed the effect, and the invention of a device to be used whilst playing came a short time later.

The instruction to play *con sordino* applies only to the movement or dance section so marked. An instruction to remove the mute at the end of the section should not be expected in music of the 17th and 18th centuries.

Pizzicato

In 17th-century music, pizzicato usually occurs as an imitative effect. In his *Battalia* (1673) Biber uses pizzicato in the large bass instruments to imitate gun shots, and Monteverdi imitates the clash of swords in *Combattimento di Tancredi e Clorinda*.[6] Whole movements by Farina, Biber and Walther are played pizzicato, imitating lutes, guitars and mandolins. In the 18th century, J. S. Bach often uses a cello pizzicato with flutes, such as in the 'Esurientes' from his Magnificat, and in other 'tender' situations like the 'Domine Deus' from the Mass in B minor (ex. 1.5.41).[7]

Conclusion

The overall affect of any single movement or composition is built up by many details. Identifying the minutest clues for a turn of phrase or a hint of a change of emotion should be the result of constant vigilance and attention in performance to the potential expressive content of the music.

---

[5] *New Grove*, 'Mute'
[6] 8th Book of Madrigals (1638)
[7] see also ex. 1.3.4, J. S. Bach, *St. Matthew Passion*, for pizzicato cello accompanying a solo violin

1.2 Articulation

A fundamental part of the rhetorical approach to performing music of the Baroque period lies in the understanding and demonstration of the structure of a composition. Identifying the smallest elements of the musical structure and building these into larger units is aided by appropriate articulation of individual notes, phrases and sections. St. Lambert:

> Just as a piece of rhetoric is a whole unit which is most often made up of several parts, each of which is composed of sentences, each having a complete meaning, these sentences being composed of phrases, the phrases of words, and the words of letters, so the melody of a piece of music is a whole unit which is always composed of several sections. Each section is composed of cadences which have a complete meaning and are the sentences of the melody. The cadences are often composed of phrases, the phrases of measures, and the measures of notes. Thus the notes correspond to the letters, the measures to words, the cadences to sentences, the sections to parts, and the whole to the whole.
>
> (1702) tr. Harris-Warrick, pp. 32-33

Articulation should always depend on the musical sense. Quantz says:

> The notes must not seem stuck together. The tonguing on wind instruments, and the bowing on bowed instruments, must always be used in conformity with the aims of the composer, in accordance with his indications of slurs and strokes; this puts life into the notes. [Articulation of this sort] distinguishes these instruments from the bagpipe, which is played without tonguing.
>
> Musical ideas that belong together must not be separated; on the other hand, you must separate those ideas in which one musical thought ends and a new idea begins, even if there is no rest or caesura. This is especially true when the final note of the preceding phrase and opening note of the following one are on the same pitch.
>
> (1752) XI.10, tr. Reilly, p. 122

Separating contrasting musical ideas by means of an articulation is described by Mattheson and Tartini among others. Tartini:

> Moreover, since music expresses sentiments, it is important to keep these separated; to avoid confusion, therefore, a short break should be made when the sentiment changes, even though the passage is a cantabile one.
>
> (1771) tr. Jacobi, p. 55

Le Blanc, who defended the viol against the violin's incursion, describes the Lully school of violin playing which was characterised by short bow-strokes:

> ... the bowstrokes were chopped off and the hatchet-stroke marked each bar or at least every phrase.
>
> (1740) tr. Garvey Jackson (1973), p. 71

Mersenne writes in his *Harmonie Universelle*[8] that he loves the violin because of 'its beautiful singing tone'. Leopold Mozart stresses the importance of being able to sing:

> A singer who during every short phrase stopped, took a breath, and specially stressed first this note, then that note, would unfailingly move everyone to laughter. The human voice glides quite easily from one note to another; and a sensible singer will never make a break unless some special kind of expression, or the divisions or rests of the phrase demand one. And who is not aware that singing is at all times the aim of every instrumentalist.
>
> The stops and pauses are the Incisiones, Distinctiones, Interpunctiones, and so on. But what sort of animals these are must be known to great grammarians, or better still, rhetoricians or poets.
>
> (1756) V.14, tr. Knocker, p. 101

---

[8] 4th Book of String Instruments (1636), proposition 1

1.2 Articulation

The clearest example of how to articulate in musical phrases is presented by Mattheson[9] who gives us musical punctuation in the form of commas, colons and even question marks.

Full stops occur at the ends of sections. Observe the lack of rests in his minuet (ex. 1.2.6) used as a case study below. A point of punctuation, where a breath or pause is required, is not commonly represented in the music by notation.

Quantz:

> If there is a cadence and a new idea begins, breath must be taken before the repetition of the principal subject or the beginning of the new idea, so that the end of the preceding idea and the beginning of the one that follows are separated from one another.
>
> (1752) VII.4, tr. Reilly, p. 88

Quantz attributes string players with more sense than wind players and singers on the subject of phrasing:

> Hence you must strive to learn to see clearly and grasp what constitutes a good musical phrase, and what must therefore hang together. You must be just as careful to avoid separating phrases that belong together, as you must be attentive not to link passages that contain more than one phrase, and hence must be divided; for a great part of true expression in performance depends upon this matter. Those singers and wind players (of whom there are a large number) who are not able to divine the intention of the composer are always in danger of committing errors in this respect, and betraying their weaknesses. String players have a great advantage in this matter, provided that they strive after the required insight mentioned above, and do not allow themselves to be misled by the bad example of those who join everything together without any distinction, in the fashion of a hurdy-gurdy.
>
> (1752) VII.10, tr. Reilly, p. 90

Obviously, where words are present, the punctuation and phrasing may be directly transferred to the music, but in purely instrumental works Mattheson observes that

> ... everything would have to be observed with instrumental pieces which the art of composition requires of vocal melodies; indeed, often more. This is emphasized here, as we move on to instrumental melodies and their categories. For here one first looks to the affections, which are to be expressed only with sounds, without words; then to the caesuras of the musical rhetoric, wherewith the words cannot show us the way because they are not used.
>
> (1739) II.13.79, tr. Harriss, p. 451

The articulation question will be examined in three parts: the larger sentence or phrase structure, the separation between individual notes, and the various signs found in the music to indicate different types of articulation.

Structure and punctuation

One of the most important elements of any performance and especially 'historically aware' performance of Baroque music is that of articulation. If music is like rhetoric, then it must include punctuation. Imagine a person reading a text without any punctuation and how nonsensical this would be. If music speaks, it must say something sensible. Knowledge of the structure of the music being performed is essential in order to make the listener aware of the content of the music, and what it has to say.

One of the chief criticisms of so-called 'authentic' performance is that it sounds 'all chopped up', and one of the chief criticisms of a modern performance by Baroque players is that it sounds 'glued together'. How are these two views to be reconciled? The problem of maintaining the thought process of the music through the small elements which make up Baroque musical structure is one of the most difficult for the performer. The performer should first identify the 'points' or figures which characterise any particular movement, and then look at the way they are linked and developed to form the

---

[9] (1739) II.13.82, tr. Harriss, p. 452

1.2 Articulation

long phrase. The manner in which these small elements are joined together gives the listener the musical argument, which leads to cadences marking the ends of sentences.

Articulation is the relationship between notes or phrases, their beginnings and endings, and how these are connected. If the gap is too big, a confused style of performance will emerge which causes the listener to lose patience with the stop/start effect made by the gaps intruding into the rhythmic pulse. Clear rhythmic articulation between notes can be achieved by taking the time from the previous note, but leaving the pulse unaltered. Each musical idea should be separated. 'Leading through' between two ideas or phrases is not compatible with a clear structured musical argument.

However, through the concentration on clear articulation, it is often apparent that many players of Baroque instruments have lost the ability to sing. An articulation after every note, combined with bulging on long notes will often ruin a simple melody line. This fault is particularly prevalent in the performance of contrapuntal consort music of the 17th century where longer weaving lines need to be sustained to carry the structure. Articulation is as much about which notes are joined or connected as about the separation of notes.

To illustrate this point, sing the first phrase from 'I know that my redeemer liveth' from Handel's *Messiah*. The line of the melody is often lost because the sound on the minims sags. In the first bar the minim on the word *know* should be connected to the next word *that* on the third beat, and the minim on the word *my* should be connected to the following crotchet, finally arriving on the strongest point -*deem*. The minims need to be connected to the following note even though there is a large interval between them, which might normally be separated.

Ex. 1.2.1

When the music contains many slurs close together, clipping the slurs results in a hiccuping style of performance. Grading the amount of space between slurs is an extremely fine art. Sometimes a thread of sound needs to be left between slurs to carry the music forward. However, in a very lively movement, clipping can be effective.

The phrase structure 2 + 2 + 4 bars or 1 + 1 + 2 bars are common models for sections of dance movements of various types: the minuet, gavotte, bourée etc. Up-beat bars often occur at the start of minuets, giving an immediate two-bar pattern, which is extended at the cadence to four bars including a hemiola. Only by articulating at the two-bar points can the extended four-bar phrase have its effect.

This 'two short followed by long' structure is all-pervasive in Baroque music. The first two fragments are followed by an extended conclusion, and a consciousness of the effect of the two short ideas which are then extended should be developed. Once you start looking for this device, you will find it everywhere, and will feel less self-conscious about showing the short fragments in isolation, when you know that a longer phrase will redeem and clarify the musical point, developing it in a different direction or taking it to its conclusion.

Ex. 1.2.2: J. S. Bach, St. John Passion final chorus
The two sighing figures (bars 1 and 2) are followed by an extended answer

1.2 Articulation

Ex. 1.2.3: J. S. Bach, St. Matthew Passion, 'Erbarme dich'

Two separate pleading phrases (bars 1 and 2) using the rising minor sixth are followed by a long one, double the length, which contains mostly falling, sobbing figures.

Ex. 1.2.4: J. S. Bach, Sonata for violin and harpsichord no. 6 in G major, Allegro

Short, nervous fragments with semiquavers are toyed with, before finally being extended to a longer phrase with the emphasis on the down-beat of the 5th bar and at the same time changing into a different figure.

Ex. 1.2.5: Vivaldi, The Four Seasons, 'Autumn', Allegro

In this theme, there are emphases in the middle of bars one and two, then the phrase is turned to emphasise the beginning of the third bar. The fourth beat in the first two bars should be weak (the repeated note) in order to reinforce the change in emphasis to a strong down-beat and a weak cadence in the middle of bar three.

CASE STUDY

Mattheson recommends that we analyse the piece of music to be performed, and uses the minuet given below as a simple example, explaining that these ideas should be applied to larger forms.

> As now in the whole of nature and all creation not a single body can be properly understood without analysis: thus I want always to be the first who analyzes a melody and examines its parts in an orderly way. A little minuet is to serve first as an example here, so that everyone may see what such a little thing consists of, when it is not a monster, and so that one would learn to make a sound judgement in moving from trifling matters to the more important.
>
> (1739) II.13.80, tr. Harriss, p. 451

Ex. 1.2.6 *f*

1.2 Articulation

The above minuet is given as an example of articulation and punctuation by Mattheson. Sing or play it through and notice the points of phrasing and articulation marked by him:

a) The ends of the phrases are marked with 3 dots.
b) The final period is marked by the inverted pause sign.
c) The punctuation marks colon, semicolon and commas.
d) Crosses mark the 4 bar phrases.
e) V and . indicate short and long syllables.
f) Vertical lines above the bars indicate rhythmic units.
g) * marks the notes to be emphasised

Notice also the following points:

h) The question posed by the rising figure in bars 1 and 2.
i) Bars 3 and 4 provide the answer, falling and returning to the starting point.
j) Bars 5 to 8 ask a question with a similar beginning followed by the cadential hemiola figure conclusion completing the first sentence.
k) The hemiola (bars 6 and 7) makes a long 3/2 bar and should be performed with emphasis on the start of the hemiola, bar 6, which also happens to be the highest note.
l) Bar 5 is a questioning up-beat bar to the beginning of the hemiola in 6.
m) Emphasis is made either by a gap or by holding back the sound before the note to be emphasised, thus presenting the hemiola bars 6-7 as a single cadential unit.
n) After the strong start to bar 6, the music should fall away without further emphasis to the end of the phrase which ends in the home key of B minor.
o) Avoid the temptation to accent the three minim beats across the bar-line of the hemiola figure. Always think of hemiolas as long 3/2 bars, rather than three equal minim beats bar. This is shown in the final bar of example 1.2.7 below.
p) A breath should be taken at the end of the sentence (at the double bar). The composition has not yet modulated into a different key. We are still in the same key as bar 1.
q) The second part of the minuet is in fact the middle section, as the first part is repeated after it.
r) In the *da capo* form of composition, look for contrasts in character in the middle section (this one is in the relative major and smoother in character).
s) Different types of rhythms and intervals are often used in the middle section to provide contrast to the first section.
t) In this case, the second section begins with a much lower tessitura than the first, and there is a sense of urgency in the first 2 bars, which is answered in the second 2 bars (first rising, then falling).
u) A new figure made up of leaping intervals appears in the final 4 bars of the section, giving an optimistic conclusion to the phrase (in the major).
v) Try not to slow down at the cadence, but take a breath before the *da capo*.

Similar methods may be applied to most dance movements.

Couperin was extremely particular about phrasing and articulation, marking phrases with commas in the music. In bar 7 in the next example, time for articulation should be taken out of the previous note in the treble, as the bass line will not have time to stop on the bar-line. Similar places occur further on where articulation signs are marked after long notes. Obviously these are not 'waiting' places, but breaths while keeping the *tactus* flowing, and the parts overlapping.

1.2 Articulation

Ex. 1.2.7 f: Couperin, 8ième concert, Air Léger

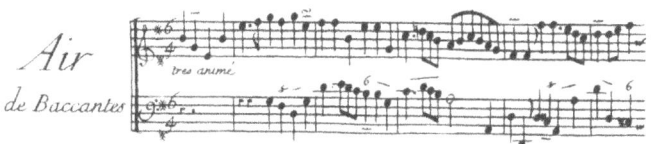

Ex. 1.2.8 f: Couperin, 8ième concert, Air de Baccantes

In the above Air from the same *concert*, 'waiting' places coincide, giving extra emphasis to the next phrase.

Ex. 1.2.9: J. S. Bach, Sonata for violin and harpsichord no. 1 in B minor, Adagio

The violinist may take a large breath out of the long note at the end of bar 2 of the example, and the harpsichordist a smaller one to emphasise the harmony on the downbeat of the next bar, which is reached by a large jump in the bass.

By increasing your awareness of phrase lengths and structure, it will become easier to notice a phrase with an unusual length. Five or seven bar phrases are unusual, so are worth pointing out with especially clear articulation and emphasis.

Articulation between individual notes

Both Quantz and Tartini give us an instruction that says conjunct notes (i.e. adjacent in pitch, or scale-like patterns) should be played smoothly, and notes which leap or are separated by larger intervals should be played detached from each other. Quantz:

> Sustained and flattering notes must be slurred to one another, but gay and leaping notes must be detached and separated from one another.
>
> (1752) XI.11, tr. Reilly, p. 123

This passage appears at the very beginning of Tartini's 'Rules for Bowing':

> In performance it is important to distinguish between cantabile and allegro music. In cantabile passages the transition from one note to the next must be made so perfectly that no interval of silence is perceptible between them; in allegro passages, on the other hand, the notes should be somewhat detached. To decide whether the style is cantabile or allegro, apply the following test: if the melody moves by step, the passage is cantabile and should be performed legato; if, on the contrary, the melody moves by leap, the passage is allegro and a detached style of playing is required.
>
> (1771) tr. Jacobi, p. 55

See ex. 1.2.8 (above), where this rule applies, giving shorter lifted crotchets for the first 4 notes, and on the repeated notes. The quavers are all in conjunct motion so are played smoothly (and unequal in this case).

Ex. 1.2.4 (above): J. S. Bach G major sonata, quavers in arpeggio formation should be played short, but conjunct semiquavers connected.

In the following example, notes which have leaps of an octave or sometimes a fifth may be articulated, but notes in chromatic and conjunct motion played smoothly, following the composer's sostenuto instruction.

Ex. 1.2.10: Corelli, 'Christmas' Concerto op. 6 no. 8

Tartini[10] endorsed legato playing in cantabile passages. The singing style was a feature of Italian violin playing and may be used in the many beautiful slow movements of Italian sonatas, the movements which allegedly were so often ruined by ornaments in bad taste.[11] Corelli asks for *arcate sostenuto e come stà*, meaning long bow-strokes without any added ornamentation, to show off the beautiful melody without interruptions. This instruction implies that adding ornamentation was normal practice, and players needed to be prevented from over-doing it.

Waiting at any point gives emphasis to what follows, and is usually preferable to arriving at a point by means of a crescendo without articulation. Silence can often say more than sound if the listener's attention is held by the manner in which the notes either side of the gap are performed.

Common occasions when an articulation between two notes is required include:
- Before the strong first beat of the bar
- Emphasis of a particular note of interest, harmonic or melodic, such as the highest note of a phrase, a variation in a repeated figure, or an interrupted cadence
- Before a statement of a theme or point
- After a cadence and before the new idea which follows it
- Before a long note
- Before an accented chord
- Before an appoggiatura, *port-de-voix* or other emphatic ornament
- Before the resolution of a trill known as *point d'arrêt*
- Between slurs and at either end of a slur or tie
- After a dotted note and before the small note which follows it (Leopold Mozart: 'in quick pieces the bow is lifted at each dot')

---

[10] (1771) tr. Jacobi, p. 55
[11] see part 3.4 for descriptions of the Italian style of ornamentation

1.2 Articulation

This last instance is particularly appropriate to the French style of violin playing where dotted rhythms abound. Articulation in dotted rhythms should normally be made between the dotted note and the following short note, not between the short note and the dotted note, which are usually linked by a bow change. It is preferable to articulate between notes which are separated by a large interval than a small one.

Articulation signs

The principal signs used in Baroque music for articulation are slurs, dots and dashes. Slurs and their use in performance are covered in part 2.8. From about 1700, when slurs began to be more commonly used, a need arose to mark notes which were to be played short, separate, or emphasised in some way.

J. S. Bach is meticulous in marking particular notes which should either be played short, or not be slurred, with dots:

Ex. 1.2.11: J. S. Bach, Mass in B minor, 'Et in unum'

Dots have come to mean 'short', but in the above example the dots are also a reminder not to slur (an effect saved for the 4th beat of the 2nd violin part). As slurs were added to taste in certain circumstances,[12] dots may often represent an instruction not to slur, as well as just to play short. Repeated notes should normally be played short. Dots over notes in French music can mean simply 'play equally' in music where *inégales* rules apply.[13]

Repeated notes under a slur with or without dots usually means use bow vibrato with a pulsating bow-stroke. Leopold Mozart describes repeated notes under a slur:

> This signifies that the notes lying within the slur are not only to be played in one bow-stroke, but must be separated from each other by a slight pressure of the bow.
>
> (1756) I.III.17, tr. Knocker, p. 45

This technique is often used for harmonic padding (see pp. 129-133, Bow Vibrato). Dashes are used for emphatic purposes or to indicate length. Leopold Mozart:

> A composer often writes notes which he wishes to be played each with a strongly accented stroke and separated from one another. In such cases he signifies the kind of bowing by means of little strokes which he writes over or under the notes.
>
> (1756) I.III.20, tr. Knocker, p. 47

Couperin specifies that a note with a dash over it called *aspiration* should be played 3/4 of the written length.[14]

---

[12] Diego Ortiz (1553) tr. Gammie p. 4, and Leopold Mozart (1756) IV.29, tr. Knocker, p. 83
[13] see p. 166
[14] (1713) ed/tr Halford, p. 13

Quantz:
> If little strokes stand above several notes, they must sound half as long as their true value. But if a little stroke stands above only one note, after which several of lesser value follow, it indicates not only that the note must be played half as long, but also that at the same time be accented with a pressure of the bow. Hence crotchets become quavers and quavers semiquavers etc.
>
> (1752) XVII.II.27, tr. Reilly, p. 232

A sequence of notes with dashes or wedges over them often means that equal emphasis should be given to all the notes. It also usually means play the notes shorter than written. Notes marked with a dash in Baroque music are usually detached from each other by a lifted stroke in the lower half of the bow. The affect of the passage will determine how much lift and weight is given to the stroke.

Conclusion

Articulation gives music life and interest, and without it the listener's attention may be lost. Explaining the structure in the tiniest detail will bring added understanding and maintain the attention of the listener. As in all things, the amount and manner of articulation used is a matter of degree and taste. General rules always need to be considered in the musical context, the affect required, and at the speed of the movement in question. Slow affetuoso movements will be more gentle in articulation than a lively presto, but the principle of speaking clearly and distinctly is the same in both movements.

1.3 Dynamics

Baroque music has few, if any, dynamic markings written in by the composer. What are the implications of this for performers cut off by more than two hundred years from the conventions of the time? There is no doubt that dynamic nuance was used throughout the period for expressive purposes. This chapter describes first the use of dynamics in music where there are none indicated, and then the interpretation of written dynamics as they came into general use in the later part of the Baroque period. Factors which influence decisions to play particular notes loudly or softly are examined: the position of beats in the bar, harmonic emphasis, and the emotional *affekt* produced by playing loudly or softly.

'Good advice to play well' comes from Matteis:

> You must not play allwayes alike, but sometimes Lowd and Sometimes Softly, according to your fancy, and if you meet with any Melancholy notes, you must touch them Sweet and delicately.
>
> (1682), p. 79

Several important points about the use of dynamics in Baroque music are raised by Matteis (above):

  a) The variety of dynamics in the music come from the player's 'fancy' and are not indicated in the music.

  b) The emotional content of the music should be recognised and treated in a suitable manner by the performer.

  c) The implication that to perform well means to play varying the volume as you go, with the rise and fall of the phrase.

Mace reminds the reader that:

> Soft and Loud Play, is a Chief Grace. You will do well to *remember*, (as in all the rest, so in This) to Play *Loud*, and *Soft*, sometimes *Briskly*, and sometimes *Gently*, and *Smoothly*, here and there, as your *Fancy* will (no doubt) *Prompt you unto*.
>
> Then you will find it very Easie, to Humour a Lesson, by Playing some Sentences Loud, and others again Soft, according as they best please your own Fancy, some very Briskly, and Courageously, and some again Gently, Lovingly, Tenderly, and Smoothly.
>
> (1676), pp. 133, 130

Mace links dynamics to the 'humour' of a piece which expresses emotional messages triggered by the music in the player's imagination.

Geminiani refers to the skill of the orator in speaking to illustrate the use of dynamics:

> Of piano and forte. They are both extremely necessary to express the Intention of the Melody; and as all good Musick should be composed in Imitation of a Discourse, these two Ornaments are designed to produce the same Effects that an Orator does by raising and falling his Voice.
>
> (1751), Ex. XVIII, 9th and 10th

Leopold Mozart also leaves it up to the performer to introduce the correct dynamic:

> One must understand how to introduce *piano* and *forte* in the right place and in right measure . . . it follows that the prescribed piano and forte must be observed most exactly, and that one must not go on playing always in one tone like a hurdy-gurdy. Yea, one must know how to change from piano to forte without directions and of one's own accord, each at the right time; for this means, in the well-known phraseology of the painters, Light and Shade.
>
> (1756) XII.5, tr. Knocker, pp. 217-8

North's description of the playing of violinist Matteis in the 1670s includes a tribute to his use of piano and forte:

> The latter was always heard as distinct as the other.
>
> J. Wilson, p. 309, fn. 63

He also describes the manner of using dynamics in a unified ensemble:

> And this soft and lowd is discretionary, falling under no rule, unless it be that in many parts each must conforme, so that some are not lowd when others soft.
>
> J. Wilson, p. 219

Phrases with long continuous crescendos or diminuendos where each note is progressively louder or softer than the last are appropriate only under certain circumstances: a long chromatic line, or a short smooth sequence of notes. The continuous 'Mannheim' or Rossini type of crescendo where each note is louder than the previous one is inappropriate to Baroque style. Hierarchy of harmony or bar-line should still be preserved within a crescendo or diminuendo.

How is the player to decide which notes or phrases are louder and which softer? For a player accustomed to detailed written instructions, this may at first seem an impossible task. To discover how dynamics work 'according to your fancy', many factors have to be taken into account. The musical language of the time would have been so familiar to contemporary players that such a question would seem superfluous. Being used to performances where emphasis by harmonic or rhythmic implication was a natural way of playing, the lack of written dynamic indications would not have been seen as a hindrance to an expressive performance.

The rhetorical approach to performing Baroque music brings with it an imitation of language and the speaking voice in oratorical style as described above by Geminiani. It is impossible to imagine a speech presented without any emphasis or dynamic range. This is the type of loud and soft the player should be seeking: not a violent black and white effect, but a moderated declamatory style with strong and weak emphasis, grading the dynamics with ebb and flow, not just introducing accents at the strongest notes.

Which notes are loud and which soft?

1. Emphasis of beats and rhythm

Leopold Mozart speaks for many writers:

> Generally the accent of the expression or the stress of tone falls on the ruling or strong beat, which the Italians call Nota Buona. These strong beats, however, differ perceptibly from each other. The specially strong beats are as follows: In every bar, the first note of the first crotchet, the first note of the half-bar or third crotchet in 4/4 time; the first note of the first and fourth crotchets in 6/4 and 6/8 time; and the first note of the first, fourth, seventh, and tenth crotchets in 12/8 time. These may be called the strong beats on which the chief stress of the tone always falls if the composer has indicated no other expression.
>
> (1756) XII.9, tr. Knocker, p. 219

Quantz:

> You must know how to make a distinction in execution between the *principal notes*, ordinarily called *accented* or in the Italian manner, *good* notes, and those that *pass*, which some foreigners call *bad* notes. Where it is possible, the principal notes always must be emphasized more than the passing.
>
> (1752) XI.12, tr. Reilly, p. 123

The hierarchy of beats within the bar presents a starting point for dynamic nuance: the first beat is strongest, and thereafter the character and nature of the movement governs what happens next.[15] The basic pattern of strong down-beat may be upset by a syncopated rhythm or a strong dissonance in another part of the bar. Chromatic movement needs to be stressed even if it occurs on a weak beat.[16]

---

[15] for more details, refer to Charpentier's rules (p. 88) and dance characteristics in part 2.5
[16] see part 5.1 for examples of how to use dynamics to emphasise harmony in the bass-line

1.3 Dynamics

In dance music, nearly every first beat will need to be emphasised (enhanced by the application of the rule of down-bow), but in more contrapuntal styles of composition the shape of the musical line will take priority over the bar-line (as in 'consort' style). The strong point in the phrase may be governed by harmonic emphasis, with dissonant harmonies taking precedence over resolutions which are consonances, or by tessitura (although the highest note may not always be the loudest) or a strong rhythmic figure. In most dance music harmonic changes need to be emphasised to a certain degree, whether dissonant or not, with subsidiary passing notes (the bad or *cattivi* notes) and decorative material being underplayed.

Hierarchy within the bar has been discussed, but there is another dynamic shape to look for in certain types of music, which demand a bar to bar fluctuation in stress. In fast movements, particularly, it is not necessary to stress every bar-line equally, so look for important harmonic and rhythmic points to decide which bars are stronger, and which weaker. Many dances (such as the minuet) are based on longer step-patterns than are contained in a single bar.

Where a motif is repeated in a rising or falling sequence, a long crescendo or diminuendo in the music may be achieved by building many short phrases into a long one. Each phrase may fall away, but the next one may start at a higher (or lower) dynamic, until the peak or trough of the phrase is reached.

2. Harmonic emphasis

The importance of the whole ensemble agreeing on the harmonic emphasis of certain notes is pointed out by Quantz in his instructions to those who accompany:

> He [the cellist] must also determine which notes must be stressed and brought out more than the others. These are, first, notes that have dissonances such as the second, diminished fifth, augmented sixth, or seventh above them, or those that are raised irregularly by a sharp or natural sign, or lowered by a natural or a flat.
>
> (1752) XVII.IV.7, tr. Reilly, p. 244

Quantz offers more suggestion for notes which need emphasis:

> The accompanist will often encounter notes that require more emphasis than the others, and thus he must know how to strike them with greater liveliness and force, and how to distinguish them clearly from the other notes that do not require emphasis. The former include the long notes intermingled among quicker ones, also the notes with which a principal subject enters, and above all the dissonances.
>
> (1752) XVII.VI.10, tr. Reilly, p. 253

Quantz suggests a scheme for dynamic levels to emphasise various dissonant chords.[17] He is confident that the player/reader

> will easily be able to divine when to use the Piano, Mezzo Forte, Forte, and Fortissimo without their being written out.
>
> (1752) XVII.VI.14, tr. Reilly, p. 255

3. The emotional affect

It is important to realise that when varying the dynamic, the relevant emotion or 'passion' must match the rise and fall of sound: neither the pathetic or melancholy piano nor the noble forte must sound too agitated. The mood of the music must be matched with the appropriate dynamic level. Quantz:

> To play an Adagio well, you must enter as much as possible into a calm and almost melancholy mood, so that you execute what you have to play in the same state of mind as that in which the composer wrote it . . . you must vary the air in such a way that you provoke melancholy a little more at one time, and subdue it again at another. In this matter the alternation of Piano and Forte may contribute greatly . . . it here forms the musical light and shadow to be expressed by the performer, and is of the greatest necessity. It must be used with great discernment, however, lest you go from

---

[17] see part 5.1 Playing from a figured bass

one to the other with too much vehemence rather than swell and diminish the tone imperceptibly.

(1752) XIV.5-9, tr. Reilly, pp. 163-5

To excite the different passions the dissonances must be struck more strongly than the consonances. Consonances make the spirit peaceful and tranquil; dissonances, on the other hand, disturb it.

(1752) XVII.12, tr. Reilly, p. 254

The manner of playing moods rather than notes may be governed by a number of things, but bow speed is a very important factor. The slower the speed, the less 'fast' the music will sound, and a flowing largo movement may gain a more restful performance by calming the bow than a slower tempo with a faster bow speed, which may produce bulges in the sound. Combined with a soft *dolce* sound, the emotional framework of the movement can be captured purely by the manner of performance. Using fewer emphases can make a movement more restful, whereas more accents produce a more agitated *affekt*. Notes played with separate bows may be articulated gently or more forcefully for varying emotional results. Dynamic nuances should be sought at every rhythmic level: passages with many fast notes should dip and rise according to the musical direction. Passages with continuous slow notes should have gradations of dynamic to match the harmonic and melodic emphases. On long notes the art of swelling and diminishing the sound imperceptibly on a single note—*the messa di voce*[18]—in a crescendo and diminuendo is likened by North to shades in needlework.[19]

Written instructions

Towards the end of the 17th century, composers started putting dynamic markings in the parts. *Forte* and *piano* were at first the only words used (in France *fort* and *doux*). Answering phrases may often be emphasised by a change in dynamic:

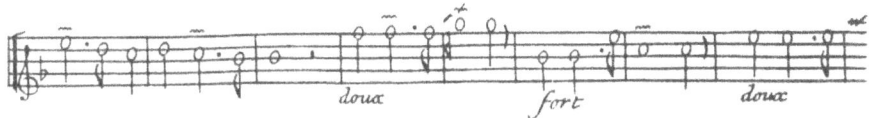

Ex. 1.3.1 *f*: Couperin 8ième concert, Grande Ritournele

The player should continue to do what was expected in the way of detailed nuance as well as fulfilling the general written dynamic instructions. Later, as composers sought finer control over the dynamic nuances, the markings became more detailed:

Ex. 1.3.2 *f*: Piani, Sonata II, Sarabanda

The violin sonatas of Piani (published Paris, 1712), for example, include many detailed instructions for expression, swelled notes and dynamics.

North recognises the tediousness of listening to music at one dynamic level:

> I have allowed soft musick to be usefull in many respects, and now I must conclude it absolutely necessary even in the most pompous entertainments. Every mode, even the very best, by too long continuance grows tedious and demands an alteration, and the

---

[18] see p. 124
[19] J. Wilson, p. 18

1.3 Dynamics

> wider the change is made, the more it sets off either partie. On this account soft and loud in consort or solitary playing is used, and being signed by the words forte and piano, due advantage made of it by every consortiere.
>
> J. Wilson, p. 127

North suggested a novel way of marking dynamics, in red ink for soft and black ink for loud, in order that players would take more notice of the dynamics. Quantz also complains that professional orchestral players do not pay enough attention to the written dynamics.

> The exact expression of the Forte and Piano is one of the most essential matters in performance. The alternation of the Piano and Forte is one of the most convenient means both to represent the passions distinctly, and to maintain light and shadow in the execution of music. Many pieces might have a better effect upon the listeners than they do, if the Piano and Forte were observed by every player in the proper proportion, and at the correct time. One might imagine that nothing could be easier than to play loudly or softly in accordance with the indications of two letters. Yet many pay so little attention to the latter that a further oral reminder is sometimes necessary. Since a good number of professional musicians have little feeling for, and pleasure in, music, however, and devote themselves to it only to earn their livelihood, they often play without pleasure and without the proper attentiveness. Good and reasonable discipline can do much to remedy this evil; and if it is lacking, the orchestra will always remain defective, regardless of the number of able people it contains.
>
> (1752) XVII.VII.19, tr. Reilly, p. 274

North's players must have become accustomed to following dynamic markings, for later he wrote that

> There is a generall ornament of musick, which is an alteration of soft and loud, than which among musitians nothing is better understood and to better effect used. Therefore I need onely say that the cheif vertue of it is consistent in the variety, and is as a *chiaro'scuro* in painting.
>
> J. Wilson, p. 219 fn. 7 (p. 220)

A North family music book contains a *Corant: echo* with markings S and L for soft and loud.[20]

Muffat, in the preface to his concertos, encourages the players to exaggerate the written dynamics, in accordance with Italian style:

> At the direction *piano* or *p* all are ordinarily to play at once so softly and tenderly that one barely hears them, at the direction *forte* or f with so full a tone, from the first note so marked, that the listeners are left, as it were, astounded at such vehemence.
>
> (1701) in Strunk (1950), p. 91

In contrast, according to Quantz, registering the dynamic markings in the performance should not include undue exaggeration 'since the ear will be most disagreeably affected'. He instructs the string player on how to execute the loud and soft sound, and warns against using extreme dynamics except as a special effect, a characteristic of the 18th-century *style galant*:

> The Forte and Piano must never be unduly exaggerated. The instruments must not be handled with more force than their constitution permits, since the ear will be most disagreeably affected, especially in a small place. You must always be able, in case of necessity, to express an additional Fortissimo or Pianissimo . . . It may often happen that you must unexpectedly bring out or soften a note, even if nothing is indicated. And this opportunity will be lost if you always play with the greatest loudness or softness . . . The Fortissimo, or the greatest volume of tone, can be achieved mostconveniently with the lowest part of the bow, playing rather close to the bridge, and the Pianissimo, or the utmost softness of tone, with the tip of the bow, rather far from the bridge.
>
> (1752) XVII.VII.20, tr. Reilly, pp. 274-5

---

[20] J. Wilson, plate 1 facing p. 4

1.3 Dynamics

In ensembles, Quantz points out that the more players there are playing a part, the softer each one will have to play in the *piano* passages. Orchestral technique is here recognised by him as a separate art, in contrast to playing in a solo style. His chapter XVII is full of good advice to 'Those Who Accompany a Concertante Part'. This advice is most welcome, as most treatises concentrate on the solo style of playing.

Frequently, where *piano* occurs, the music should be played moderately louder immediately before the *piano* marking:

Ex. 1.3.3: Corelli, Sonata op. 5 no. 7, Giga

Where no dynamic marking occurs, the mood and affect of the piece will have to be assessed before beginning to play. Usually, the opening of a grand French overture will be loud, an expressive sarabande, softer. Often, the absence of a dynamic instruction means a general level of a moderate forte.

When accompanying, the tutti should play as softly as possible. When the soloist stops, the group should play with a full tone to assert their presence and the musical material, which is either in contrast to the solo music, or in confirmation by re-iteration.

Ex. 1.3.4 *f*: J. S. Bach, St. Matthew Passion, 'Erbarme dich'

In the above example, the solo violin part is marked *forte* (top line), and the accompanying strings *piano sempre*. Where soloists are present, the *tutti* markings often reflect the function of the group: *piano* when the soloist is playing/singing, and *forte* where the solo stops. This instruction serves to provide the players with information about their role as much as the dynamic level. The music should retain the dynamic nuances expected normally, but take into consideration the function of the group, for example whether it is in accompanying mode or not. Where instruments of several types are playing together, consideration should be paid to their relative natural playing level. For example, whenever

1.3 Dynamics

a flute is used, the dynamic level should be monitored, taking into consideration the function of the flute part, and whether it is doubling the violins, or playing a solo line.

The sparse markings of *forte* and *piano* in Baroque music have led some performers to believe that dynamic levels were a minor feature of performance, or used only as 'echo' effects. The evidence shows that dynamics were continually used in conjunction with the player's imagination or 'fancy' to produce an entertaining and moving performance.

Quantz sums up:

> To observe the Piano and Forte only at those places where they are indicated is far from sufficient . . . If . . . you play everything with the same colour or volume, the listeners will remain completely unmoved. If, on the contrary, you express the Forte and Piano by turns, in accordance with the nature of the ideas, and employ them properly in those notes that require them, you will achieve the goal you seek, namely, to maintain the constant attention of the listener, and guide him from one passion into another.
>
> (1752) XVII.VII.25, tr. Reilly, pp. 276-7

1.4 Tempo

One of the most controversial aspects of performances of Baroque music using period instruments has been that of tempo. Usually the criticism is that tempos are too fast. In a performance where articulation and phrasing conform to the music's structure, the more conversational style demands a flowing tempo without making every note in the phrase equally important. If music is to be considered as a language and the rate of speech is too slow, the speaker cannot be understood correctly. Restoring much Baroque music to tempos based on historical principles has been one of the main 'revelations' of the period instrument movement. The speed at which the speaker or musician performs is critical to the listener's understanding and enjoyment.

Various factors contribute to the choice of tempi. These include:

- The speed of the main beat. If this is divided to give a pulse of smaller note values than those indicated in the time signature the beat unit is too slow.
- The tempo instruction at the beginning of the movement. This may be misunderstood in the light of modern conceptions of tempo. Word instructions meant different things to composers during the 17th and 18th centuries (Vivace, Largo, Andante etc.), depending on the period, location and function of the music.
- The rate of harmonic change. If the harmony changes only once per bar, a single bar-beat may be acceptable. If the harmony changes frequently, a slower tempo will be needed for the listener to absorb all the harmonic information.
- The structure and length of movements in classical and romantic works has sometimes influenced the way players view the smaller scale of movements in Baroque music. Musical forms of the 17th and 18th centuries are mainly composed of several related short movements (e.g. in suites of dances), rather than each movement being conceived as a separate unit. The use of relative tempi which operate to connect the short sections of overtures, multi-sectioned works, or short related dance movements should be considered.
- The tendency to slow up at cadences deprives music composed in many short sections of the sense of unity it requires.

The Baroque concept of a beat was a constant, regular *tactus*. It was of moderate speed and is compared by various writers to the human pulse—Quantz says 'at the hand of a healthy person'[21]—the pendulum of a clock, or the walking pace of a man. All tempo markings or time signatures are related to this moderate pulse (the *tempo ordinario* of the Baroque), and quick or slow tempos depart in both directions from this basic *tactus* (imagine walking more slowly or more quickly than your natural pace). North described the inappropriateness of extreme tempos:

> Any regular movement, swift or slow, will doe well in proper place—as after a grave, an allegro, &c. But even there a temper is to be used, and extreams avoided; that is, out of very slow to extream swift, without any interposition . . . especially with fuges which essentially require moderation.
>
> J. Wilson, p. 259.
> The word *temper* here means to modify.

It is important to identify the character of the music, as well as the metronomic tempo, the *tactus*. Couperin reminds us:

> I find that we confuse measure with what is called *cadence*. Measure is defined as the number and length of time beats and cadence is, properly, the spirit and soul which must be added to it.
>
> (1717) tr. Halford, p. 49

Bacilly also alerts us to the two elements which make a tempo: the measure, and the *mouvement*:

---

[21] (1752) XVII.VII.47, tr. Reilly, p. 283

1.4 Tempo

> Many confuse movement with measure . . . Movement is however quite different from what these people imagine; I hold that it is a certain quality that gives soul to a melody, and that it is called movement because it moves [the feelings], that is, because it excites the attention of listeners.
>
> *Remarques curieuses sur l'art de bien chanter* (Paris 1668) in Mather, p. 200

Time signatures

St. Lambert claims that

> The imprecise meaning of the time signatures is a defect in the art for which musicians are not responsible and which may easily be pardoned them.
>
> (1702) tr. Harris-Warrick, p. 45

In 18th-century music, a basic principle is that the larger the lower number the faster the tempo (3/8 faster than 3/4). As time progressed, so did the influence of the word tempo marking, tempering the time signature indication. Here follow some guidelines for interpreting time signatures and tempo indications in various situations:

France

Single figure time signatures common (simply 2 or 3), see ex. 1.2.7.

Georg Muffat (1695) says that **2** was rather slow when used in overtures, preludes and symphonies but faster when used in ballets, and generally slower than ₵. Gavottes with ₵ are not so fast as bourées with the same indication. When **2** is indicated in French music, the notes have the same value as they do in ₵ in Italian music. 3/2 requires a restrained movement, 3/4 a gayer one, yet uniformly somewhat slow in sarabandes and airs, lively in rondeaux, very brisk in minuets, courantes, and many other dances, as also the fugal sections of overtures.[22]

J. Rousseau (c.1690) gives **2** as being quick, and faster than ₵, however his contemporary Loulié (1698) gives **2** the same as ₵. Both writers give ₵ as four beats.[23]

Borin (1722) gives tempo based on '*airs de charactères*':

- Lent: four-beat measures in recitatives of operas, cantatas, and motets, two-beat measures in 'the first part of an opera' (meaning overtures?). Three-beat measures are *fort grave* in recitatives.
- Grave: Three-beat measures in sarabandes, passacailles and courantes.
- Leger: Four-beat measures in allemandes. Two-beat measures in gavottes and gaillardes.
- Three-beat measures in chaconnes.
- Vite: Four-beat measures in *entrée des furies*. Two-beat measures in bourées and rigaudons. Three-beat measures in menuets.
- Très-vite: two-beat measures such in the Lully entrée. Three-beat measures in passepieds.[24]

General Word Tempo Instructions: France

Gravement	slow
Gayement or *vite*	fast
3/2	with 'void' white-note notation—usually slow[25]
Doucement	slow tempo corresponding to *gravement* or *lentement*[26]

---

[22] Strunk (1950), p. 84
[23] in Houle, pp. 19, 36-37
[24] in Houle, p. 37
[25] Examples in Sawkins, p. 365
[26] ibid.

1.4 Tempo

Légèrement	a swift tempo
Gracieux or *gracieusement, modère*	moderate tempo
Rondement	moderate pace with some forward movement[27]
Vivace	found in French music means fast, but also implies that quavers are equal as in Italian style

Ex. 1.4.1 *f*: Couperin, Apothéose de Lully, Sonade en trio

Germany, 18th century

Quantz:

Allegro assai - fastest tempo, the Allegretto twice as slow, the Adagio cantabile twice as slow as the Allegretto, and the Adagio assai twice as slow as the Adagio cantabile.

In common time: Allegro assai, minum beat; Allegretto, crotchet beat; Adagio cantabile quaver beat; Adagio assai, two beats per quaver.

In alla breve time: Allegro, semibreve beat; Allegretto, minum beat; Adagio cantabile, crotchet beat; Adagio assai, two beats per crotchet.

2/4 and quick 6/8 have one pulse every bar in Allegro.

3/4 and 3/8 with six notes per bar have one pulse per bar. Presto must be faster. In a fast piece with continuous triplet quavers, take a faster tempo.

Adagio assai, Mesto or Lento have two beats per crotchet.

Summary of ideas from (1752) XVII.VII.49-50, tr. Reilly, pp. 284-5

Leopold Mozart:

Presto, means quick, and *Allegro Assai* is but little different.

Allegro, which, however, indicates a cheerful, though not too hurried a tempo, especially when moderated by adjectives and adverbs, such as:

Allegro, ma non tanto, or *non troppo*, or *moderato*, which is to say that one is not to exaggerate the speed.

Allegretto is rather slower than *Allegro*.

Vivace means lively .. the mean between quick and slow.

Andante: walking.

Lente or *lentemente*, quite leisurely.

Adagio: slow.

Largo: a still slower tempo, to be performed with long strokes and much tranquillity.

Grave: sadly and seriously, and therefore very slowly. One must, indeed, indicate the meaning of the word *Grave* by means of long, rather heavy and solemn bowing and by means of consistent prolonging and maintaining of the various notes.

Selected from list (1756) I.III. 'Termini Technici', tr. Knocker, pp. 50-1

---

[27] ibid.

1.4 Tempo

England, last part of 17th century

Matteis by way of explanation of the time signatures in his *Ayres for the Violin, The Third and Fourth Parts*, gives the following information:

C	slow time called common time
¢	faster
¢ (slashed)	very swift called 'retort'
3 or 3/4	slow triple
3/2	slower
3/8	quick according to the French curr[ant]t
6/8	swift
6/4	very swift
6/8	very swift

Purcell gave us clear tempo instructions in two sources: *Choice Lessons for the Harpsichord or Spinet*, and the *Sonnata s of III parts* (1683). In the *Choice Lessons*, Purcell describes various time signatures and the corresponding speeds which should be adopted:

C	very slow
¢	a little faster
3/2	very slow
3	slow
6/4	faster, used for brisk tunes[28]

Purcell's *Sonnata's of III parts* are written in 'just imitation of the most fam'd Italian masters'. In order to help us understand Italian style, he defines in the preface the Italian tempo markings which he used in this set:

Adagio and grave	a very slow movement
Largo	a middle movement
Allegro and Vivace	a very brisk, swift or fast movement

The English word 'movement' is used here in the sense of speed, not as in the French 'mouvement' to 'move' the feelings as in Bacilly (above).

It is interesting to note that Largo is not a very slow tempo.

Ex. 1.4.2 *f*: Purcell, Sonnata's of III parts (1683) no. 9

---

[28] (1698) in MacClintock, p. 156

Choosing a tempo

Quantz observes the danger of allowing the players to decide the tempo amongst themselves:

> It is well known that in many places where people play carelessly, a Presto is often made an Allegretto and an Adagio an Andante, doing the greatest injustice to the composer, who cannot always be present.
>
> (1752) XVII.VII.55, tr. Reilly, p. 288

There are two factors which govern the choice of tempo in a piece of music: the time signature, and written word description. During the first part of the Baroque period, there were no tempo word descriptions; the time signature gave all the information needed. The type and style of composition could provide another clue as to the tempo, especially in dance music (entrée, allemande, gigue etc). In fugues, canzonas and music in the middle style, *tempo ordinario* is most usual, especially when there is no word indication. Later on in the period, word instructions were added to moderate or enhance the mood and tempo affect (the French *mouvement*), but were still secondary in importance to the time signature. Other factors such as speed of harmonic movement are very important when selecting a tempo. If very fast notes are found in the music, these may only be written-out decorations, and should be performed as such, maintaining the larger pulse as pillars around which the decorative element is hung. It is important that the *tactus* adopted is neither extremely slow, nor extremely fast. As pointed out by North above, the nature of the composition should indicate a quickening or slowing of a moderate tempo, rather than a random choice of an extreme slow or fast speed.

Early Baroque music is often written in large note values which appear to be slow to the modern musician. If the *tactus* is in semibreves or minims, a musician unused to reading large note values might mistakenly assume a tempo which is too slow by a factor of two. Modern editions often attempt to ease this misapprehension by halving the note values into more familiar crotchets and quavers, rather than minims and crotchets. Look out for editorial changes such as this, and try to identify the original time signature which may give a clue about the tempo. Large note values such as minims and semibreves may indicate a faster tempo, with one tactus per bar in a triple-time movement which follows a duple section. The proportion 2:3 called *sesquialtera* is frequently found in early Italian music. Triple movements following the duple movement should have a related pulse.

The time signature should be carefully noted when playing Purcell's music with three minims to the bar. The tempo of the Largo above (which implies one beat per bar) should be faster than a movement notated in 3/2. A suitable tempo and character for ex. 1.4.3 should be closer to a slow minuet than a sustained adagio.

Ex. 1.4.3: Purcell, Hail Bright Cecilia (1692), 'In vain the am'rous flute'

England, early 18th century

North

> Adagio very slow, Grave somewhat faster.
>
> Largo is strong and bold.
>
> Allegro is easy and lighthearted, and twice as quick as Adagio.
>
> Presto is fast, and Prestissimo even faster.
>
> J. Wilson, p. 100, fn. 9

1.4 Tempo

North relates the word andante to its equal stepping nature, rather than a speed. Later the word is connected to other words to indicate tempo (Andante largo, Andante allegro).[29]

Alexander Malcolm, an English theorist, relies on Italian words for tempo (1721). He gives six Italian tempo indications in ascending order of speed: Grave, Adagio, Largo, Vivace, Allegro, Presto and sometimes Prestissimo. Note that Vivace is slower than Allegro, and Largo faster than Adagio, contradicting the later Leopold Mozart, with Grave the slowest.[30]

Italy, 18th century

Muffat in the preface to his concertos enjoys the effect of extreme Italian tempos:

> In directing the measure or beat, one should for the most part follow the Italians, who are accustomed to proceed much more slowly than we do at the directions *Adagio, Grave, Largo*, etc, so slowly sometimes that one can scarcely wait for them, but, at the directions *Allegro, Vivace, Presto, Piu presto*, and *Prestissimo* much more rapidly and in a more lively manner. For by exactly observing this opposition or rivalry of the slow and the fast, the loud and the soft, the fullness of the great choir and the delicacy of the little trio, the ear is ravished by a singular astonishment, as is the eye by the opposition of light and shade. Though this has often been reported by others, it can never be said or enjoined sufficiently.
>
> (1701) in Strunk (1950), p. 91

Vivace in Italy meant fast as well as lively. Andante meant 'with equal steps'.[31] In Corelli's *Concerti Grossi* opus 6, andante is in every case combined with the qualifying tempo word: andante largo. See ex. 1.1.5 (Corelli) and 1.2.11 & 1.5.47 (J. S. Bach).

Recommended text for further discussion of the meaning of time-signatures and tempo markings: George Houle, *Meter in Music*, 1600-1800 (Indiana, 1987).

See also: dance indications for tempo (part 2.5 The Dance).

Rubato

In many performances in the 17th and 18th century (until the late 18th century in France), tempo was imposed on the performer by a *batteur de mesure*, not necessarily the director, who beat time audibly with a stick.[32] A constant tempo is, of course, most desirable for dance movements, even when dancers are not present. The character and structure of dance music demands that the tempo be held reasonably constant. However, in other types of composition where extended movements contain contrasting ideas, there is no reason why the performer should not use a slight fluctuation in the tempo to give character to particular points or themes, especially when words are present to reinforce the musical ideas. The danger with this approach is that the tempo flags and is difficult to recover in performance. If players agree in rehearsal on moments when the music may languish and when it must move forward, this should not be too much of a problem.

Frescobaldi gives permission for this type of performance

> The manner of playing, just as in the performance of modern madrigals, should not be subjected to strict time. Although such madrigals are difficult, they are facilitated if one takes the beat now languidly, now lively, or holding back, according to the affection of the music or the meaning of the word.
>
> (1614) Preface to *Toccate e partite d intavolatura*, book 1, in MacClintock, p. 133

---

[29] J. Wilson, pp. 194-6
[30] Houle, p. 39
[31] Brossard (1702) and North above
[32] Carse, p. 103

North likened the practice of using rubato in solo music to a grace, which he described as

> dwelling upon some notes too long and coming off others too soon; that is, breaking time and keeping it, which Sigr. Tosi sayd was the chief art of a performer.
>
> J. Wilson, p. 151.

(Tosi was the author of a famous singing treatise *Observations on the Florid Song*, Bologna 1723, tr. Galliard 1743)

However, North's opinion of rubato used in consort music was very different:

> Nothing in time keeping will prosper, without an habit contracted by much exercise in consort, otherwise all endeavours are weak and shufling . . . there may be inconveniences, but of very different quallitys. One is when any of the company for infirmity break time; for that discomposeth the rest that attend. And the other is for too much abillity, when any out of peevishness or pride affect that which is called 'breaking and yet keeping time', and thereby disorder the rest, who for their measures are apt to depend on them; as coachman and postillion that doe not agree have tricks to dismount one and other.
>
> J. Wilson, p. 105

North is pointing out that music with parts which move contrapuntally and contain a variety of rhythmic figures should be played in very strict time, with few expressive liberties. This type of music is democratic, and needs no heroic soloists.

Mace gives detailed instructions on how to make a pendulum which is used to practice 'True Time-keeping'. However he wagers that

> There is *scarcely One Artist, (of the Highest Form) among Ten, (I mean, a Very Master) that shall be able to keep an Exact True Time, (by This Infallible Rule) for 20 Semibreves together, (His Back being Turned towards the Pendent, for That Time.)*
>
> (1676), p. 81

He then excuses this human failing by remarking that

> when we come to be *Masters*, so that we can *command all manner of Time*, at our *own Pleasures*, we Then *take Liberty*, (and very often, for *Humour, and good Adornment*-sake, in certain Places) to *Break Time; sometimes Faster*, and *sometimes Slower*, as we perceive, the *Nature of the Thing Requires*, which often adds, much *Grace*, and *Luster*, to the *Performance*.
>
> (1676), p. 81

Burney relates how Geminiani's free use of *rubato* when leading an orchestra resulted in his being banished to the viola section:

> [after studying with Corelli in Rome] he went to Naples, where from the reputation of his performance at Rome, he was placed at the head of the orchestra; but, according to the elder Barbella, he was soon discovered to be so wild and unsteady a timist, that instead of regulating and conducting the band, he threw it into confusion; as none of the performers were able to follow him in his *tempo rubato*, and other unexpected accelerations and relaxations of measure. After this discovery, the younger Barbella assured me, that his father, who well remembered his arrival in Naples, said he was never trusted with a better part than the tenor, during his residence in that city.
>
> (1789) vol. 2, p. 991

Certain indications in the music give the player license to play freely. When the bass is static, or ceases to play, the soloist or upper part may adopt an attitude of 'free time' or fantasy until the bass starts moving regularly again. A held pedal note in the bass indicates that a soloist may play with certain rhythmic freedom.

When accompanying a soloist who takes liberties with the rhythm, Quantz recommends that the accompanist should stick rigidly to a constant pulse, around which the soloist may wander.[33] Rhythmic freedom between main beats can work well if the soloist arrives on the main beats at the same time as the accompanying group.

---

[33] (1752) XVII.VII.36, tr. Reilly, p. 280

Pauses

The pause sign can mean several things in 17th- and 18th-century music. Sometimes it means a pause, and sometimes it merely signifies the end of a section, without necessarily prolonging the note over which it is written. In the following example, it is a licence to stretch the time spent on the two bars 'intro' before the faster strict tempo section which starts in bar 3:

Ex. 1.4.4: Locke, Broken Consort suite in C major

Ex. 1.4.5: Handel, Messiah, 'Thou shalt break them'

When a pause is written at the end of a movement on a short note, it means 'the end' and it is unnecessary to spend longer on the final note than the time written. If the final note falls on a weak beat, as in the above example, the value may even be shorter than written.

Ex. 1.4.6 *f*: J. S. Bach, St. Matthew Passion, 'Gebt mir meinen Jesum wieder'

When a pause sign is written at the end of the 'A' section of a *da capo* aria, as above, it signifies the end of the section, and does not indicate any lengthening of the note over which it is written. The 'B' section should continue without a pause. When the 'A' section is repeated, apply the same rule as in the Handel example above.

The cadenza point, often marked with a pause sign, indicates that the soloist may play a short flourish.

Repeats

The question of whether to vary the repeat of any particular section of music may include the variation of the tempo according to Quantz:

> It is common knowledge that a piece repeated once or more times consecutively, particularly a fast piece (for example, an Allegro from a concerto or sinfonia), is played a little faster the second time than the first, in order not to put the listeners to sleep.

(1752) XVII.VII.55, tr. Reilly, pp. 288-9

Playing for dancers

It is frequently assumed that there is a single correct tempo for dances. However, many factors other than musical ones may influence the tempo, as explained by Quantz, who is obviously experienced in this field:

> Each type [of dance] requires its own tempo, however, since music of this kind is very circumscribed, and is not as arbitrary as Italian music. If, then, both the dancers and the orchestra can always arrive at the same tempo, they will avoid much ill humour. It is well known that most dancers understand little or nothing of music, and frequently do not know the correct tempo themselves; for the most part they regulate themselves only by their mood at that moment, or by their ability. Experience also teaches that dancers rarely require as lively a tempo at rehearsals that take place in the morning before eating, when they are calm and dance collectedly, as they do at the performance, customarily in the evening, when, partly because of the good nourishment taken beforehand, partly because of the multitude of spectators, who stimulate their ambition, they become more ardent.
>
> (1752) XVII.VII.56, tr. Reilly, p. 289

1.5 Ornamentation

The structure of Baroque music dictates that a large part of the business of performing this type of music involves ornamentation of various types. The music demands that most of the notes which connect and surround the harmonic essentials have the function of ornamentation. The ornamentation may be written by the composer or added by the performer, and today's performer needs to be able to recognise the circumstances under which ornaments should be added, and of which type. It is necessary to identify the style of the music in order to select appropriate additions. A limited repertoire of stock ornaments which are added to any piece of music of the 17th and 18th centuries will not do. The range of expression which is opened up by the possibilities in ornamentation is infinite, and I will demonstrate that a limited range of ornamentation rules applied to all Baroque music is inappropriate. Each ornament should be selected and played in a manner which matches the style of the composition and the specific rhetorical affect.

I shall examine and explain how to perform ornaments indicated by signs, and how to recognise and perform ornamentation which is already written in the music. Examples of written-out ornamentation should be our guide to the performer's own version of this type of free elaboration, and of the division type.

How much the performance of the written-out type and the signed type of ornamentation over-lap is debatable. Throughout his comprehensive and thorough survey *Ornamentation in Baroque and Post-Baroque Music* (1978), Neumann provides examples of written-out ornaments which he argues demonstrate the manner of performance of the signed type. On the other hand, he also argues that because a particular ornament is written out, it is contradicting the normal practice (he cites J. S. Bach as an example of this). As most of the structure of Baroque music consists of harmony decorated with melody and rhythm, it is extremely difficult to separate the ornamental element from the melodic, however it is notated.

Baroque ornamentation should be rhythmically free, should sound improvised, unregulated, and above all express the various 'passions' contained in the music being enhanced: the length and weight of an appoggiatura, for example, or the speed of a trill. C. P. E. Bach instructs us to 'play from the soul, not like a trained bird!'[34] The one possible exception to this is the division style of ornamentation used in the 16th and 17th centuries for display purposes. Instructions on how to ornament in this style may be found in Italian and Spanish treatises by Ganassi (1523), Ortiz (1553), Dalla Casa (1584), Virgiliano (c. 1590), Bassano (1591) and Rognioni (1592).[35] The English viol treatise by Simpson (1659) is a good guide for violinists to the later 17th-century division style. In sets of divisions, long notes are divided into notes of shorter value, while the harmonic pattern is repeated. By its very nature, where a definite number of fast notes in the time of one slow one are performed, a certain mathematical style of performance is appropriate. However, the main purpose of the division style was to dazzle the listener with the *extempore* use of fast notes.

Much ornamentation was left to the player's discretion, and in certain prescribed places, assumed. This chapter presents the basic guidelines to perform the 'essential' ornaments. Players who wish to follow up these basic tools with more study are referred to the original treatises, many of which are available in facsimile, and the books specifically dedicated to this subject (a list is provided on pp. 57-58). As many composers produced a tailor-made set of ornaments to be used for their own music, the amount of detailed information covering this subject is enormous.

The information contained in written-out decorative passages and signed graces specified by many composers will guide us to the right choice where there is nothing written, and show where the performer is expected to supply their own *extempore* additions.

---

[34] (1753) tr. Mitchell, p. 150
[35] Bruce Dickey 'Ornamentation in Early-Seventeenth-Century Italian Music' pp. 247-254 in Carter (1998) contains details of some of these division treatises

1.5 Ornamentation

C. P. E. Bach:

> No-one disputes the need for embellishments. This is evident from the great numbers of them everywhere to be found. They are, in fact, indispensable. Consider their many uses: they connect and enliven tones and impart stress and accent; they make music pleasing and awaken our close attention . . . let a piece be sad, joyful, or otherwise, and they will lend a fitting assistance.
>
> (1753) tr. Mitchell, p. 79

Metaphors abound for the decorative use of ornamenting the harmonic foundations of Baroque music. North's 'carving the fabric', and 'lace adorning the form' are two of the more charming examples. Mace makes the comparison of the addition of ornaments with the decoration of a building:

> *for your* Foundations being *surely* Laid, *and your* Building well Rear'd, *you may proceed* to the Beautifying, *and* Painting *of your* Fabrick.
>
> (1676), p. 102

C. P. E. Bach says they are

> spices which may ruin the best dish or gewgaws which may deface the most perfect building.
>
> (1753) tr. Mitchell, p.81

In most books about the performance of music since the 16th century, many pages are taken up with rules and ornament tables, examples of embellishments, and intricate instructions for the realisation of every trill and grace. In the early 18th century North complained:

> It is the hardest task that can be, to pen the manner of artificiall Gracing an upper part. It hath bin attempted, and in print, but with woefull effect. One that hears, with a direct intent to learne, may be shew'd the way by notation, but no man ever taught himself that way. The spirit of that art is incomunicable by wrighting, therefore it is almost inexcusable to attempt it. But when it is done not for practise but speculation, and to aid a practise, as reason is always a friend to art, it may, for the pure good will, be indulged.
>
> To sett them downe in the musick book is such paines, and for the continuall use and smallness of them, so intricate, puzzling and unintelligible, that with the best musitians they are altogether omitted.
>
> J. Wilson, pp. 149-50

The height of bad taste in 18th-century performance was to overload the music with too many ornaments. This is commented upon by many writers including Quantz:

> Some persons believe that they will appear learned if they crowd an Adagio with many graces, and twist them around in such fashion that all too often hardly one note among ten harmonizes with the bass, and little of the principal air can be perceived. Yet in this they err greatly, and show their lack of true feeling for good taste.
>
> The rarest and most tasteful delicacies produce nausea if over-indulged. The same is true of musical embellishments if we use them too profusely.
>
> (1752) XI.6, VIII.19, tr. Reilly, pp. 120, 99

Marpurg observed of north German performers in 1750:

> A special distinction of Berlin music is that it makes very sparing use of manners and embellishments; but those that are used are the more select and the more finely and clearly performed. The performances of the Grauns, Quantz, Benda, Bach, etc., are never characterised by masses of embellishments. Impressive, rhetorical, and moving qualities spring from entirely different things, which do not create as much stir, but touch the heart the more directly.
>
> *Der Critischer Musicus an der Spree*, in C. P. E. Bach ed. Mitchell, p. 81 fn. 4

But how and where is the player to learn all this good taste and correct application? Many composers leave ornament choice to the performer. Matteis observes:

> To set your tune off the better, you must make several sorts of Graces of your one Genius, it being very troublesome for the Composer to mark them.
>
> (1682), p. 79

1.5 Ornamentation

Ornaments should not disrupt the flow of the piece. St. Lambert:

> The *agréments* must never alter the melody or the rhythm of the piece and that therefore in pieces of a lively tempo the *coulés* and *arpéges* must go by faster than when the tempo is slow; that one must never hurry in making an *agrément*, no matter how fast it must be played; that one must take his time, prepare his fingers, and execute it with boldness and freedom.
>
> (1702) tr. Harris-Warrick, p. 99

An understanding of the harmony is essential to realising the function of the ornaments. Dissonances are often accentuated by the addition of an ornament, and consequently the presence of an ornament often signifies a stressed beat. North advises all musicians to

> informe themselves of the first principles of harmony, plain and artificiall; for knowing the source whence all the ornaments flow, they will not use them improperly nor want the use of them out of ignorance.
>
> J. Wilson, p. 150

This instruction applies particularly to the written out type of ornamentation, as players can often be so excited and misled by seeing so much on the page, that the harmonic structure gets hidden in a confusion of notes.

Corelli's sonatas opus 5 in Roger's edition (Amsterdam c. 1710, and reproduced by Walsh soon afterwards in London) contain graces claimed to be *composez par Mr. A. Corelli comme il les joue*. These were regarded as spurious by many contemporary musicians, including North, who wondered

> Upon the bare view of the print any one would wonder how so much vermin could creep into the works of such a master. And nothing can resolve it but the ignorant ambition of learners, and the knavish invention of the music sellers to profit thereby. Judicious architects abominate any thing of imbroidery upon a structure that is to appear great.
>
> J. Wilson, p. 161

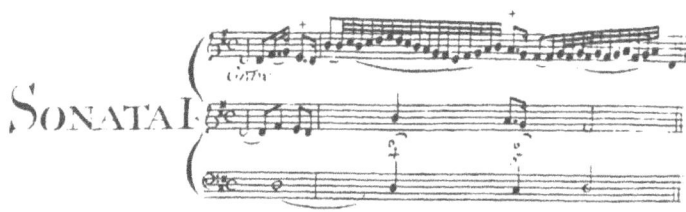

Troisieme Edition ou l'on a joint les agréemens
des Adagio de cet ouvrage, composez par
Mr A. Corelli comme il les joue.

Ex. 1.5.1 *f*: Corelli, Sonata op.5 no.1, Grave

Zaslaw has argued that these ornaments may indeed have been written down by Corelli for the Amsterdam edition, since the handwriting has been authenticated.[36]

Ornamentation in ensemble playing

18th-century writers disagree as to whether players should insert ornaments (including vibrato) into ensemble music, particularly where there is more than one player per part. Quantz maintains that when two play together, the second part should imitate the first with regard to added ornaments, but if the parts move together in parallel motion, the addition of embellishment would be inappropriate.

---

[36] Zaslaw (1996)

1.5 Ornamentation

The general principle seems to be, as in the use of vibrato, that the larger an ensemble or number of parts, the fewer ornaments should be inserted. In 1705 Fuhrmann wrote of Buxtehude's practice of forbidding any ornamentation or deviation from the prescribed bowings:

> Whoever does not like this should hear sometime the incomparable Mr. Buxtehude perform at Lübeck. He puts not two or three violins on a part, but twenty and thirty and even more. But all these instrumentalists must not change a single note or dot, or bow otherwise than he has directed.
>
> Quoted in Snyder, p. 383

Cadential trills maintain their essential status in ensemble music however, and may be the only ornament admitted into fugues or similar contrapuntal compositions (see trill section below).

Extempore additions when playing music in more than three parts were regarded as being in bad taste and expressly forbidden by Quantz and other mid-18th-century writers. Quantz recommends that in a quartet where there are four separate parts, there should be much less freedom to add *extempore* graces than in a trio.[37] He also advises ripienists (in all parts) to refrain from ornaments, which should be reserved for concertante parts:

> The violoncellist must take care not to garnish the bass with graces, as some great violoncellists were formerly in the habit of doing; he must not try to show his skill at an inappropriate time . . . Besides it is absurd to make an upper part of the bass, which should support the embellishments of the other parts and make them harmonious. . . the notes of the bass must be executed entirely without extempore ornaments. If, however, the bass imitates some phrases of the principal part, the violoncellist may repeat the same graces used in the principal part.
>
> (1752) XVII.IV.3, tr. Reilly, p. 242

In the following example, the bass could add an appoggiatura before the second note in imitation of the top part, as recommended by Quantz, as these two parts move in canon.

Ex. 1.5.2: J. S. Bach, Suite no. 2 for flute and strings

North maintains that inner parts and basses should play plain to enhance the harmonic effect:

> For an accompanying part, which is to maintaine the harmony, to trill, and upon the low notes whereon it most leans, unless it be upon a little *ritornell* or solo, is senceless and destructive to the musick. But that is the fault of our English masters who, accompanying a voice, will clatter trills at bottome to make one wild.
>
> J. Wilson, p. 19

Corrette on the subject of ornamentation by viola players asserts that while cadences, martellemens, port de voix, and coulés are rarely played on the viola, the former two embellishments (i.e. trills and mordents) sound very satisfactory on the high string.[38] However, Quantz says that a good violist must shun all *extempore* embellishments in his part.[39]

---

[37] (1752) XVI.26, tr. Reilly, p. 202
[38] (1738), p. 132
[39] (1752) XVII.III.6, tr. Reilly, p. 238

1.5 Ornamentation

Doubling a soloist

A dilemma which frequently occurs when accompanying singers or other soloists is the question of whether to double ornaments in the solo line. In other words, if the soloist has an appoggiatura written into their line, should the tutti double exactly every ornament of the soloist's part? If the tutti are to be regarded purely as a 'backing group', they should maintain their subsidiary function and play softly, while the soloist is allowed every freedom, including that of ornamenting whether written or not. The differences between the parts often appear in the score, and should not necessarily be neatly tidied up. Probably, the soloist will be playing or singing on a much louder level and with more projected tone than the tutti.

Summary of Quantz's guidelines for ornamentation in ensembles:[40]

- When imitation occurs, small graces should be copied by the inner and bass parts. XVI.24, 25 (pp. 201-2)
- If a passage is in unison, all parts should adopt any trills which appear in the upper part. XVI.24 (pp. 201, 230)
- If all parts are trilling in unison with the bass, it is recommended that all players should trill at a slower rate than if they were playing solo. XVII.II.24 (p. 230)
- The bass part should refrain from trilling as a general rule, but support the upper decorated part in a plain manner. XVII.IV.3 (p. 242)
- Intrusive or competitive ornamentation when accompanying a solo is to be avoided. XVII.VII.15 (p. 272)
- Where there is more than one player per part, the players should refrain from adding appoggiaturas etc. XVII.VII.15 (p. 272)
- Ritornellos in particular must be played entirely without extempore additions. These are permitted only to the performer of the concertante part. XVII.VII.15 (p. 272)

Divisions

The earliest type of ornamentation on stringed instruments was a rhythmic division of long notes, breaking them into smaller notes which added up to the original long note value. The first string treatises contained comprehensive instructions and exercises for the breaking of a melody into divisions, for decorating cadences and filling the space between two notes:

Ex. 1.5.3: Diego Ortiz, Tratado de glosas sobre clausulas, Rome (1553)
divisions on the interval of a falling 2nd

---

[40] Page number references are to (1752) tr. Reilly

Ex. 1.5.4 *f*: Simpson, The Division-viol (1659), divisions on a perfect cadence in the bass

A very popular form in the 17th century was the breaking of divisions over a ground bass of four or eight bars, which was repeated many times while the treble part made variations which fitted the harmonic pattern of the bass line. Many popular tunes were based on grounds such as *Ruggiero, Bergamasca* and *Romanesca*. The tune 'Greensleeves' is based on the *Passamezzo antico* ground.

Simpson's *The Division-viol or The Art of Playing Ex tempore upon a ground* is one of the principal instrumental tutors of the 17th century. It is divided into three sections: how to play the viol, how to play a descant, and the method of playing divisions to a ground. Playing divisions *extempore* is an art in itself separate from improvising other embellishments, and there is plenty of material to study in order to understand and learn that art. Playford published two collections of divisions entitled *The Division-violin*, and there are many early Italian variation sets on the above-named ground basses. 16th- and 17th-century composed divisions may also be found in works by Virgiliano (*Il Dolcimelo*, c.1590), Dalla Casa (*Il Vero Modo di Diminuir*, 1584), Giovanni Bassano (*Diminuiti per Sonar con ogni sorte di Stromenti*, 1591), Richardo Rognioni (*Passaggi per Potersi essercitare nel Diminuire. . .* 1592), Schop (*'T Uitnement Kabinet*, 1646), and van Eyck (*Der Fluyten Lust-hof*, 1646). These works contain many dance tunes and melodies with variations which demonstrate a range of divisions which may be used to build a vocabulary of figures to be used *extempore*.

Ex. 1.5.5 *f*: Playford, Division-violin (1684)

The well known ground bass in the above example was also used by Corelli in sonata op. 5 no. 12, variations on 'La Follia'. Later in the 17th century, the fast notes of the composed division form became study material for left-hand technique. Matteis labelled his Aria (ex. 1.5.6) *semplice* with divisions *per far la mano* (for exercising the hand).

However, Locke warns in the preface to his *Little Consort* (1656):

> I desire in the performance of this Consort you would do yourselves and me the right to play plain, not tearing them in pieces with division, (an old custome of our Countrey Fidlers, and now under the title of A la mode endevoured to be introduced).
>
> Locke *Chamber Music* vol. II, ed. M. Tilmouth, Musica Britannica 32, p. xix

1.5 Ornamentation

Ex. 1.5.6 *f*: Matteis, Ayrs for the violin, Third Part, p. 84

Simpson divides ornaments into 'smooth graces' and 'shaked graces'. He instructs that shaked graces should be played

> with one motion of the bow which would not have that grace or ornament if they were play'd severally.
>
> (1659), p. 11

His table of ornaments in *The Division-viol* is a useful guide to the type of embellishment suitable for mid-17th-century string music, and is reproduced (in the treble clef) by Playford in *The Division-violin* (1674).

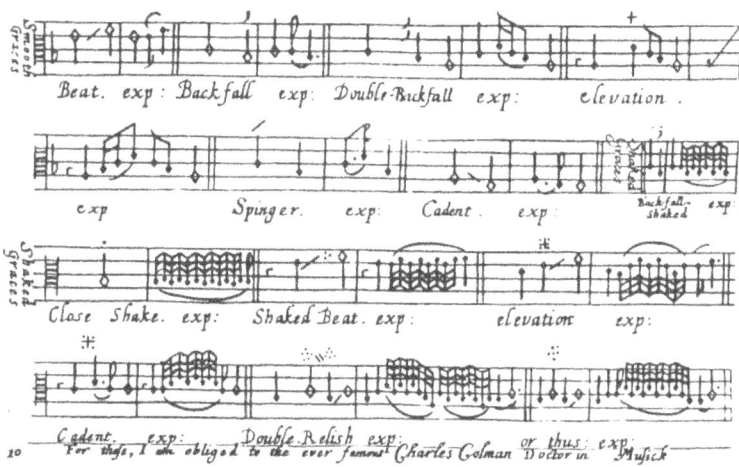

Ex. 1.5.7 *f*: Simpson (1659)

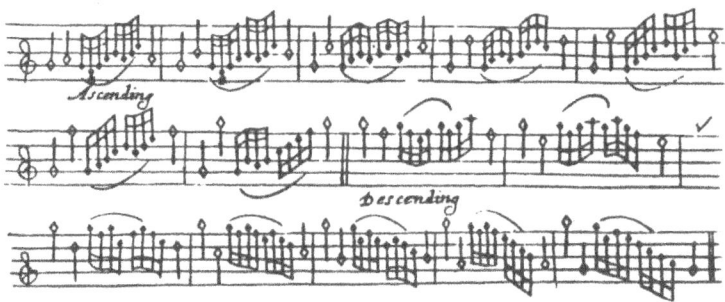

Ex. 1.5.8a *f*: Simpson (1659)

1.5 Ornamentation

Ex. 1.5.8b: Quantz (1752)

It is interesting to compare the style of these two sets of ornaments (ex. 1.5.8a & 8b) by Simpson and Quantz, written approximately a century apart. Both use simple ascending and descending figures to demonstrate the possible variations.

The use of divisions

In spite of Locke's exhortation above to avoid 'tearing' the music into divisions, the most appropriate type of ornament to use in early 17th-century string music is the regular divided type as illustrated above by Simpson and Ortiz. However, beware of using this type of ornament in late 17th-century French music, or English music in the French style, which should have small graces such as trills, mordent, slides etc. added, rather than rhythmic divisions (Lenton's tutor (1694) gives examples). At cadences, it is mandatory to do some sort of division or trill, even if not indicated in the music. Ornaments of the division type and rhythmic trills should normally be played with separate bows. However, trills starting on the note are also acceptable slurred as normal (Simpson, 1659) example above.

♫ tracks 7 and 10 for written out sets of divisions by Rognoni and Notari; tracks 1 and 2 for *extempore* ornamented divisions by the performer; track 11 ends with a lament based on the four note descending bass pattern.

Written out ornamentation

Any ornaments, written or extemporised, should normally be played without affecting the basic pulse of the music. Playing the music without any ornaments is to be recommended in order to feel the harmonic points and the phrasing, before adding any graces. Where the music is heavily ornamented with written notes (J. S. Bach's preludes for unaccompanied violin, or early Italian sonatas in the *stile concitato* for example) try to identify the bare harmonic structure underneath the mass of black notes in order to give the movement shape. In this type of movement, the fast-note ornamentation should not dictate the chosen tempo.

Ex. 1.5.9: J. S. Bach, Sonata in G minor for solo violin, Prelude

The pillars of harmony (observe the chords or position of the figures in the bass) should be the outline for the basic shape and pace of the piece. Ornaments should not dominate the movement, but fit into the main structure, leading towards or away from unusual or important harmonies. Where fast notes double or show an increase in speed, try to give the impression of a smooth acceleration through the two note values. Tartini's example (see below in trill section) of an accelerating trill implies this. This type of figure often

1.5 Ornamentation

leads to a change of harmony. Flourishes containing many fast notes will sparkle when the notes are clearly heard.

Ex. 1.5.10: Handel, Sonata in A major

In performing this movement, the written out ornamentation should not hold up the constant quaver movement in the bass. The players should arrive at the half-bar point together, without the bass player having to wait excessively.

Ex. 1.5.11: J. S. Bach, Sonata no. 3 in E major for violin and harpsichord, Adagio

In this sonata, the first seven bars maintain the same pedal note while the violin and the right hand of the keyboard player weave and pirouette around the re-iterated tonic chord with elaborate written-out decorations.

Ex. 1.5.12 ƒ: Bonporti, Inventione VII

The written-out flourishes should sound improvised, and so a certain degree of rhythmic freedom is to be encouraged, as long as the basic rhythmic structure is not affected. Rubato within large beats adds to the improvisatory effect, starting a run slowly and accelerating towards high points, or approaching interesting chords by holding back the tempo, or making a small articulation.

Ex. 1.5.13 ƒ: Corelli, Sonata op.5 no.1, Allegro

The flourish written by Corelli to end the fugue in his sonata op. 5 no. 1 (from the 1st edition, Rome 1700) is not so different in style from the ornaments purported to be *comme il les joue*. Roger North's conservative English taste in embellishments which condemned Corelli's ornaments as 'vermin' might have prevented him from appreciating the brilliance of the customary Italian flourishes.

1.5 Ornamentation

Ex. 1.5.14 *f*: Veracini, Cappricio Primo 1744, Allegro

The practice of embellishing slow movements in Italian sonatas was normal, and indeed, expected. Critics of Italian taste (including Roger North) usually condemned these as only serving to obscure the harmonic structure. The 'show-off' competitive element in Italian performances must have been a considerable encouragement to this practice. The type of embellishment commonly used would have been similar to that printed in Roger's edition (ex. 1.5.1), and probably even more elaborate when unconstrained by notation. The printed runs and roulades are worth trying to play as a basis for similar free running embellishment in typical Italian-style slow movements. Simple minim-based melodies are to be found in many solo and trio sonatas, and provide opportunities for experimentation. Other composer violinists used Corelli's simpler dance movements for extensive sets of variations to show off their developing left-hand and bow technique. Geminiani wrote an ornamented version of the opus 5 sonatas which is a useful model for a later style of ornamentation, and the same composer also made an arrangement of some of Corelli's sonatas in *concerto grosso* form.

Ex. 1.5.15: Corelli, Sonata op.5 no.9 with ornaments by Geminiani

See *Early music* February 1996 for several articles on the performance and ornamentation of Corelli's opus 5 sonatas.

The essential graces

These graces are indicated by signs above the notes. Some composers give detailed instructions in the music where to play these graces, and others leave most of the decisions about adding essential graces to the performer. Quantz reminds us that:

> French composers usually write the embellishments with the air, and the performer thus needs only to concern himself with executing them well. In the Italian style in former times no embellishments at all were set down, and everything was left to the caprice of the performer.

(1752) XIV.4, tr. Reilly, p. 163

It is for this reason that Quantz suggests learning about French ornaments first, because they are all specified in the music by the composers. The principal sources for the performance of French ornaments are the keyboard works by: Chambonnières (1670), Lebègue (1677), d'Anglebert (1689), St. Lambert (1702) (who includes in his treatise discussion of the ornaments of d'Anglebert and Lebègue), Couperin (1717), Rameau (1724). All these volumes contain ornament tables to be used in the performance of these composers' works, and may be transferred to contemporary music by other composers and for other instruments where information is not supplied.

1.5 Ornamentation

Ex. 1.5.16 *f*: from Couperin, L'Art de Toucher le Clavecin, Paris (1717)

Three examples of the execution of ornaments in the French style. When the player has understood the correct use of these by playing repertoire where ornaments are marked, he may play any unmarked movement and understand the correct places for using the small ornaments to enhance the harmony or melody.

Matteis, an Italian violinist, uses a combination of a general sign for trills and small graces, and written out flourishes for ornamentation. The flamboyant Italian style allowed roulades and other flourishes to be freely added at the whim of the performer.

Ex. 1.5.17 *f*: Matteis, Ayrs for the Violin (1680s), Third Part, p. 2

A consensus of opinion about the essential graces gives us a short list as follows:

- Trill
- Appoggiatura
- Turn
- Mordent

These four ornaments will be examined in detail below.

Several writers list vibrato (also called the close shake), swelling of the sound (*messa di voce*) and slurs as ornaments. These three subjects are dealt with separately in this book. Other ornaments such as beat, backfall, tirade, slide, ports de voix, batteries, etc. will be found in tables of ornaments in other sources listed at the end of this chapter. The confusion is compounded by various composers using the same word or symbol for different ornaments or signs for articulation, or different words for the same ornament.

Several writers (including Couperin himself) agree that it is a good idea to play French music to learn the correct use of each ornament. The *Concerts Royeaux* by Couperin would be a good start:

Ex. 1.5.18 *f*: Couperin, 2ième Concert

Play a piece quite plainly several times, at first inserting only the obligatory cadential trills, before venturing with additional graces. Listen to and play many different sorts of music, to acquire a feel for the different styles (see part 3, Identifying Style). Be wary of applying just one or two familiar trills, with the same length of upper note, to every situation, or imitating what you hear on recordings. Experiment in private in order not to feel inhibited in public.

Ex. 1.5.19 *f*: Matteis, Ayrs for the violin, First Part, p. 6

Trills

Markings include tr, +, x, a comma beside the note and a double stroke above the note (as in ex. 1.5.19). Any of these signs are used as general indications for any small grace consisting of a few notes. Quantz says that trills

> ... add great lustre to one's playing ... and are quite indispensable.
>
> (1752) IX.1, tr. Reilly, p. 101

North claims in his usual sardonic manner that

> ... the trill, being rightly used is a great beauty, but otherwise rediculous in musick.
>
> J. Wilson, p. 19

Five elements are to be considered when performing trills:

- Approach
- Starting note
- Speed of re-iterations
- Stopping point of re-iterations (*point d'arrêt*)
- Ending or termination

Contrary to popular opinion, there is no absolute rule about whether to start trills on the main note, or the one above it. 17th-century trills may sound better starting on the note for melodic emphasis, particularly if the note is long. Allow the main note to register before commencing to trill. However, Purcell in his 'rules for graces' gives an upper-note trill illustrated on a crotchet. North also gives an example of an upper-note trill. Later trills are usually from the upper note, especially if the upper note forms a dissonance with the bass, and for this reason the start of the upper note should coincide with the bass note. A small articulation is necessary when approaching this type of trill, for emphasising this dissonance. The upper note may be quick, or lingering in the manner of an appoggiatura. The rhythmic pulse and affect of the movement should be taken into consideration when deciding on the length of the upper note, and different speeds and number of re-iterations practised for different situations. In a quick movement, four notes would often be enough on a crotchet or other short note. Where two trills or similar ornaments appear close together, it is advisable to vary the length of the upper note. If this occurs when approaching a cadence, try passing quickly over the first trill, giving the final cadential trill (on the dominant) a long upper note.

Towards the end of the 17th century, trills could be started either on the written note or from the note above, depending on the harmonic or melodic circumstances. This is apparent from both French and Italian evidence. The pull both ways lasted into the next century until ultimately over-ridden by the rules of the Berlin School laid down by C. P. E. Bach and Quantz.[41]

Trills starting on the note

Geminiani shows us (Essempio XVIII no.5) a held main note before starting the trill.

---

[41] see Neumann (1978), p. 183

1.5 Ornamentation

Ex. 1.5.20 *f*: Geminiani, The Art of Playing on the Violin (1751)

Leopold Mozart shows another type of trill starting on the main note at the end of a dotted note. The main note is played first, and the trill comes just at the end. This would be used when a particular note needs emphasis:[42]

Ex. 1.5.21: Leopold Mozart

Ex. 1.5.22: Tartini, Traité des Agréments de la Musique (1771)

The above example by Tartini illustrates a similar point, with the trill starting from the note and before the beat when it is in the middle of two or three slurred notes, especially at speed.[43] It is executed with a single re-iteration. The written-out execution shown below by L'Abbé le fils confirms the practice of trilling before the beat when the trill occurs between two falling notes which are slurred. The first note acts as a written-out appoggiatura. When the falling notes are separated, without a slur, the upper note is re-iterated:

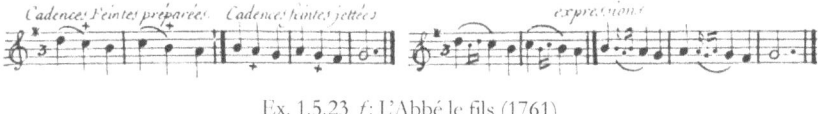

Ex. 1.5.23 *f*: L'Abbé le fils (1761)

Chains of trilled notes are given by Tartini with the trill starting on the written note, and to be executed 'by gliding the finger'.[44] The same fingers will be used for all the trills, sliding up and down the strings (a string crossing is unavoidable in this example).

Ex. 1.5.24: Tartini, Traité des Agréments de la Musique (1771)

Summary—Possible situations in which to use trills starting on the written note:
- Where the instruction 'tr' is shown halfway through a long note
- Where the note is tied over from a previous note
- Where the trill occurs in the middle of a slur (also could be before the beat)
- To emphasise the arrival on a particular note, for example a pedal point or the bottom of a precipitate run of notes
- To emphasise a line of chromatic motion
- When there would be no time to fit in more than three-note re-iteration
- Where a chain of trills ascends or descends

---

[42] (1756) X.19, tr. Knocker, p. 194
[43] (1771) tr. Jacobi, p. 81
[44] ibid., p. 78

1.5 Ornamentation

Cadential trills

The most common place in a phrase to use a trill is at the cadence. In fact, the French word for trill is *cadence*. North notes that

> Custome, as in cadences, hath made it expected.
>
> In common cadencys, and passages, it is left to the performer, who is supposed to understand so much.
>
> J. Wilson, pp. 19, 27

Playford abhors trills and thinks in singing

> ... there being nothing more contrary to Passion than they are ... but in final cadences, some short Points of Division may be used.
>
> (1674), p. 39

The strong dominant chord should automatically have a trill placed over it, whether indicated in the music or not. Even cadences which are momentarily brushed over in the middle of a movement should have a cadential trill added. Following the cadential trill, the resolution in the middle of a movement should usually be played weak, and short if another idea or theme follows on immediately. Recognising these cadence points is an essential skill for the understanding of harmonic structure in a movement.

Ex. 1.5.25: Corelli, Concerto Grosso op.6 no.2

The fugue subject above needs a cadential trill to be added on the b^1 in the third bar, to be imitated by each entry where applicable. The resolution c^2 in bar 4 should be weak. Trills could also be added to e^2 in bar 5 and b^1 in bar 6 (2nd part down).

Ex. 1.5.26: Purcell, Sonatas of 3 parts (1683), no. 7

In the above example by Purcell, one or possibly two cadential trills should be added in the penultimate bar. The upper part should trill on the dominant, the $f\sharp^1$, and then the second part could play a short trill on the $d\sharp^1$ before both parts resolve on to the tonic in the final bar. If the second part leaves a trail of plain sound into the final bar, a dissonance is produced against the e^1 anticipation in the upper part, which should be played long for the most effect from the delicious clash.

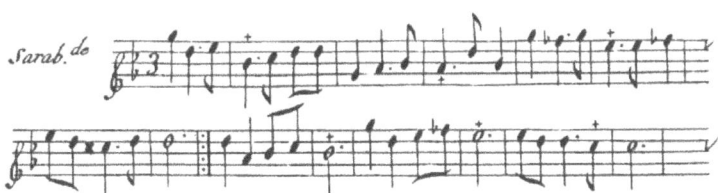

Ex. 1.5.27 *f*: Marais, Pièces en trio, 1er Dessus p.68

In the above example, the cross sign marks trills, but this is conspicuously absent from the dominant ($e\natural^2$) in bar 7 where a trill is assumed, so a sign is deemed unnecessary. Note

1.5 Ornamentation

the use of French violin clef: G on the bottom line. The last sign is slightly misplaced and should be over the dotted note.

Speed of trills

There are so many different occasions for using the trill that the scope for expression is almost without limit. Tartini suggests

> ... a slow trill for serious, pathetic and sad pieces; the moderate trill in moderately gay ones; the fast, in pieces which are gay, lively and swift. A good player must practise and master trills at all these speeds; it is clear that a trill in a cheeky swaggering *allegro* must not be the same as in a *grave* or an *andante malinconico*, nor one on the E string the same as one on the G string.
>
> (1771) tr. Jacobi, p.76

Tartini favours the accelerating trill for use at cadences where the player is not 'tied to the beat'.[45]

Ex. 1.5.28: Tartini, Traité des Agréments de la Musique (1771) tr. Jacobi, p.138

In conjunction with the acceleration, he suggests starting softly and increasing the sound as the speed of the trill increases. Couperin endorses the idea of acceleration:

> All the ornaments ought to be very precise, and those which are made up of repercussions should be played evenly with an imperceptible speeding up.
>
> (1717) tr. Halford, p. 70

Quantz maintains that:

> If the shake is to be genuinely beautiful, it must be played evenly, or at a uniform and moderate speed.
>
> (1752) IX.5, tr. Reilly, p. 102

His idea of the perfect trill is slightly at odds with other writers, unless he is merely condemning the sporadic and jerky re-iteration of notes. Quantz advises:

> All shakes do not have to be struck with the same speed; in this matter you must be governed by the place in which you are playing, as well as by the piece to be performed. If playing in a large place which reverberates strongly, a somewhat slower shake will be more effective than a quicker one; for too rapid an alternation of notes is confused through the reverberation, and this makes the shake indistinct. In a small or tapestried room, on the other hand, where the listeners are close by, a quicker shake will be better than a slower one. In addition, you must be able to distinguish the character of each piece you play, so that you do not confuse those of one sort with those of another, as many do. In melancholy pieces the shake must be struck more slowly, in gay ones, more quickly.
>
> (1752) IX.2, tr. Reilly, p. 101

Tartini in the letter to his pupil Lombardini writes that the trill is the third essential part of a good performer on the violin (after the use of the bow and the left hand):

> I would have you practise it slow, moderately fast, and quick; that is, with the two notes succeeding each other in these three degrees of adagio, andante and presto; and in practice you have great occasion for these different kinds of shakes; for the same shake will not serve with equal propriety for a slow movement as for a quick one; but to acquire both at once with the same trouble, begin with an open string, either the first or second, it will be equally useful; sustain the note in a swell, and begin the shake very slow, encreasing in quickness, by insensible degrees, till it becomes rapid, but you must not rigourously move immediately from semiquavers to demisemiquavers, as in this example, or from these to the next in degree, that would be doubling the velocity of the shake all at once, which would be a skip, not a gradation.
>
> (1760) in Tartini (1771) tr. Jacobi, p. 137

---

[45] (1760) in Tartini (1771) tr. Jacobi, p. 138

This reference (ex. 1.5.28) suggests that one would not use third position just to avoid an open-string trill, but remain in first position, unless other considerations force the move. Quantz, however, does give an example of a trill on c^1, to be played *mezzo manico* (in 2nd position), because

> ... the shakes are generally better made with the third rather than the little finger.
>
> (1752) XVII.II.33, tr. Reilly, p. 235

St. Lambert extols the virtues and beauties of an accelerating trill:

> When the tremblement must be long, it is more beautiful to strike it slowly at first, and to speed it up only at the end, but when it is short it must always be quick.
>
> (1702) tr. Harris-Warrick, p. 77

Trills on long notes

A long note with a trill must be regarded in the same manner for bowing purposes as a plain long note: try to avoid changing the bow, as by that means the shape of the long trilled note will be lost. Quantz:

> If several notes are tied together on the same pitch and a shake is indicated above the first, the shake must be sustained to the end, without repeating the bow-stroke.
>
> (1752) XVII.II.24, tr. Reilly, p. 229

Several writers (C. P. E. Bach, Mattheson and Tartini) give trills accelerating in a dotted rhythm, a device normally associated nowadays with the trills of earlier composers such as Monteverdi. Tartini likens the trill to salt in cookery:

> Too much or too little salt spoils the result and it should not be put into everything one eats.
>
> (1771) tr. Jacobi, p. 74

However, his instructions for the use of the trill, in common with most writers, include compulsory cadential trills. North, writing as an old-fashioned viol player, did not like the fast unmeasured trill at all, and maintained that the sounds became confused and ruined that thing which should over-ride every other, namely harmony. He describes his dislike of the fast trill

> Like a squirrell scratching her ear, but swifter or slower, without government as to measure. Now it seems that a trill is but a species of devision, and ought to keep time, and fall in with that of the consort.
>
> J. Wilson, p. 166

The difficulty of acquiring a good shake or trill in one's repertoire is described by the lutenist Mace:

> Some there are, (and many I have met with) who have such a *Natural Agility* (in their *Nerves*) and *Aptitude*, to *That Performance*, that before they could do anything else to purpose, they would *make a Shake, Rarely Well*. And some again, can scarcely *ever Gain a Good Shake*, by reason of the *unaptness of their Nerves, to that Action*; but yet otherwise come to *Play very well*.
>
> I, for my *own part*, have had occasion to *break both my Arms*; by reason of which, I cannot make the *Nerve-Shake well*, nor *Strong*, yet, by a certain *Motion of my Arm*, I have gain'd such a *Contentive Shake*, that sometimes, my *Scholars* will ask me, *How they shall do to get the like*? I have then no better *Answer* for Them, than to tell Them, They must first *Break their Arm, as I have done*; and so possibly, after that, (*by Practice*) they may get *My manner of Shake*.
>
> (1676), p. 103

His description of the 'nerve shake' is interesting in that it describes a type of trill which sounds stiff and uncontrolled. It is very important for the control of the trill that a finger movement is used on the violin and viola, not a wrist or arm pulse (as in vibrato). The larger movement needed on the cello gives rise to some eminent players using the whole hand to trill. The acceleration and slowing down of the trill and its termination need very subtle gradations of nuance to express the various affects in hand, particularly in slow movements. The superiority of the controlled finger movement over the wrist movement

1.5 Ornamentation

opens up more possibilities of controlled expression. However, if the player is looking for the 'nerve shake' effect there is a two-finger vibrato described by Tartini which would create approximately the effect described by Mace above (described in the section on vibrato pp. 60-61).

Leaving a trill

The final sound of a trill (Couperin's *point d'arrêt*) is usually the written note, and at cadential trills it is tasteful to make this note sound before moving onto the resolution at the cadence, not in a snatched way, but gracefully. Mace described this process as follows:

> For you must know This, That whatever your *Grace* be, you must, in your *Fare-well* express the *True Note perfectly*, or else your *pretended Grace* will prove a *Disgrace*.

(1676), p. 105

This method is particularly elegant when the next note is the anticipation to the final note of the phrase. Where a termination is played, either written or added by the player, the trill continues into the termination without *point d'arrêt*. Terminations to trills are appropriate in some situations, either in the measured 17th-century (separate bows) or free 18th-century (slurred) trill shown below. Tartini says that the termination is essential when the melodic line rises as in this example.[46] Very often, the termination is written out. The trill plus ending should normally be slurred in later music.

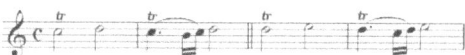

Ex. 1.5.29: Tartini, Traité des Agréments de la Musique (1771) tr. Jacobi, p. 80

If there is no termination, all that is necessary is an articulation before the resolution, anticipation of the resolution, or whatever happens next, leaving the main trilled note with a trail of sound as described above by Mace, before placing the final note resolution.

Trillo

The early 17th-century *trillo* described and used by Caccini and Monteverdi in both written-out and signed forms consists of a repeated note, re-iterated at various speeds, accelerating or de-accelerating towards a cadential resolution. To confuse the issue, 'tr' can mean *trillo* or *tremolo* (a normal trill with re-iterations of two adjacent notes), or even *tremoletto*, a short trill with only one re-iteration. *Tremolo* also may mean vibrato with the bow (see pp. 129-133). Brossard writes about the '*Trillo à L'Italienne*'[47] describing the normal re-iterated sort on two notes but also:

> Tr . . . is very often, in Italian music, the sign that one must beat several times on the same note, at first somewhat slowly, then ending with as much lightness and rapidity as the throat can make.

tr. Neumann (1978)

Ex. 1.5.30: Giulio Caccini, Le Nuove Musiche (1602)[48]

Writers describe the vocal form as sounding like the bleating of a goat. Written out examples are found in early 17th-century violin sonatas by Castello and others.

---

[46] (1771) tr. Jacobi, p. 80
[47] (1702) p. 192
[48] (1602) ed. Wiley Hitchcock, p. 50

1.5 Ornamentation

Ex. 1.5.31: Mealli, Sonata secunda, opus 3 (1660), Adagio

The written 'tr' above is probably describing the effect of the repeated notes, and is not an instruction to add extra ornamentation. This ornament is described by Monteverdi in the preface to his 8th book of madrigals (1638), and is a feature of the new *stile concitato* (excited style). The *trillo* is often found in music together with the *gruppo* (ex. 1.5.32), a trill ending with a turn-like decoration also to be found at cadences in English 17th-century divisions.

Ex. 1.5.32: Castello, Sonate Concertate, Venice (1629), sonata prima a sopran solo

A typical cadential *gruppo* in Castello's sonatas written in *stil moderno*.

Appoggiaturas

Quantz: 'in French *ports de voix*'.[49] The main use of the appoggiatura is 'to arouse tenderness and melancholy'.[50] The appoggiatura is indicated in the music by a small note which may be written as a quaver or semiquaver. Whichever way it is written, the mid-18th-century rule advocated by Quantz[51] and C. P. E. Bach[52] is that the appoggiatura takes half (two- thirds of a dotted note) the value of the main note when the note is long, and the appoggiatura should be swelled if time permits.[53] It should always be slurred onto the main note.

Ex. 1.5.33: Quantz (1752) VIII.7-8, tr. Reilly, p. 95

Tartini gives a musical example which complies with the normal 'two-thirds' rule for dotted notes:

Ex. 1.5.34: Tartini, Traité des Agréments de la Musique (1771), tr. Jacobi, p. 67

If, by playing a long appoggiatura, the main note falls into a rest, this is permissible.[54]

Ex. 1.5.35: Quantz (1752)

---

[49] (1752) VIII.1, tr. Reilly, p. 91
[50] ibid. VIII.16, p. 98
[51] ibid. VIII.8, p. 95
[52] (1753) tr. Mitchell, p. 90
[53] Quantz (1752) VIII.4, tr. Reilly, p. 93, Leopold Mozart (1756) IX.8, tr. Knocker, p. 171, Tartini (1771) tr. Jacobi, p. 66
[54] Quantz (1752) VIII.11 tr. Reilly, p. 96

1.5 Ornamentation

If another grace note is added to an existing appoggiatura it should be played fast, crushed before the beat, to avoid spoiling the dissonance desired by the clash of appoggiatura and bass:[55]

Ex. 1.5.36: Quantz (1752)

Ex 1.5.37: Leopold Mozart (1756)

Ex. 1.5.38: Leopold Mozart (1756)

But Leopold Mozart denies players the right to 'befrill' an appoggiatura (ex. 1.5.38) as this sounds 'exaggerated and confused'.[56]

Appuyé

The essential nature of an appoggiatura is its leaning quality. It usually leans (French *appuy*) on a dissonance, so gains weight and strength from this fact. If the upper note is held over until the bass moves onto the next chord in the French style before starting to trill, it is said to be a *cadence lié* (linked or slurred). A long dissonant appoggiatura is said to be *appuyé*.

Ex. 1.5.39 *f*: L'Abbé le fils, cadence appuyé (1761), p. 14

As most dissonances should be prepared, a small articulation before an appoggiatura is mandatory (in the above example, on the bar-line). Quantz and Leopold Mozart recommend changing the bow so that the appoggiatura is on a down-bow, as it occurs in the place of the principal note.

Quantz warns players against the excessive use of the appoggiatura and *extempore* embellishments in general:

> They allow hardly a single note to be heard without some addition, wherever the time or their fingers permit it. They make the melody too weak through an excessive load of appoggiaturas.
>
> (1752) VIII.19, tr. Reilly, p. 99

Neumann calls Quantz and C. P. E. Bach 'the Berlin School', and pleads that their rules should not be applied to music of all periods indiscriminately, and particularly not to music of a previous generation.[57]

Often, appoggiaturas (or indeed other small graces) need to be played before the beat. An example of this may occur where a dissonance is formed by the main written note and the bass, in which case the appoggiatura needs to be crushed on or played before the beat (ex. 1.5.36, 37, 38 above). An appoggiatura preceding a trill or turn (a common occurrence in Vivaldi) would also need to be crushed in order to give a strong rhythmic pulse.

---

[55] Quantz (1752) VIII.6, tr. Reilly, p. 94, Leopold Mozart (1756) IX.2, tr. Knocker, p. 167
[56] (1756) IX.3, tr. Knocker, p. 168
[57] (1978), pp. 183-4

Ex. 1.5.40 *f*: Vivaldi, Concerto op.11 no.6, Allegro non tanto

It has been pointed out by Neuman[58] that J. S. Bach tends to write out long appoggiaturas in the music, and when he gives the small sign for one, he would often prefer it to be played short. This would contradict the 'half the length' rule.

Ex.1.5.41: J. S. Bach, Mass in B minor, 'Domine deus'

The many pairs of falling notes in this extract are precisely notated in order to avoid any misunderstanding. If the first of each pair was written as an appoggiatura, what difference might it have made to the performance? The written crotchet in bar 2 might not have had its full length. The semiquaver pairs might have been performed crushed or played before the beat (as they do indeed appear in a later source).

Ex. 1.5.42: J. S. Bach, Partia in D minor for violin solo
(see ex. 2.5.56 for a facsimile version)

The long appoggiatura in bar 4 is written out as a crotchet.

Tierces coulés

When appoggiaturas are written between notes a third apart, they may be played unaccented and lightly slurred onto the note following. Leopold Mozart says the short appoggiatura is to be played (in an allegro between descending intervals of 3rds) 'quickly in order not to rob the piece of its liveliness'.[59]

Quantz says they should be

> ... touched very briefly and softly, as though, so to speak, only in passing ... [they] must not be held, especially in a slow tempo; otherwise they will sound as if they are expressed with regular notes. This, however would be contrary not only to the intention of the composer, but to the French style of playing, to which these appoggiaturas owe their origin. The little notes belong in the time of the notes preceding them.
>
> (1752) XVII.II.20, tr. Reilly, pp. 227-228, musical example VIII.6, p. 93

Ex. 1.5.43: Quantz (1752)

---

[58] ibid., pp. 124-164
[59] (1756) IX.9, tr. Knocker, p. 171

1.5 Ornamentation

Note that he says they must not sound like regular notes, but like ornaments.

Tierces coulés (appoggiaturas between notes a third apart) should be played in such a weak and ambiguous way that no-one can tell whether they are on or before the beat.

Ex. 1.5.44 *f*: L'Abbé le fils (1761), p. 16

L'Abbé le fils shows the dynamic expression which should accompany the *tierce coulé* and the appoggiatura. The first example above shows shading off on the weak resolution and the second example shows the way in which the dynamic should lead to the strong appoggiatura on the downbeat.

Ex. 1.5.45 *f*: J. Rousseau (1687)

J. Rousseau shows weak *tierces coulés* on to cadences, played before the main beat.

Ex. 1.5.46 *f*: L'Abbé le fils (1761)

Trills starting before the beat, and without terminations (*cadence subite*), on weak beats and rising intervals.

Ex. 1.5.47: J. S. Bach, Suite no.3

1.5 Ornamentation

Ex. 1.5.48: Purcell, Chacony

In music written in the French style by J. S. Bach and Purcell, above, weak appoggiaturas between notes a third apart (two in bar 2: J. S. Bach, one in bar 4: Purcell) give the music an elegant French accent. This ornament may be inserted in appropriate situations in French music where few ornaments are written.

Performers' views differ about the exact placement of this type of ornament, but as long as the affect is unaccented, light and tripping, the exact point in the beat where they sound is not important.

Turns

The simple turn consists of four adjacent notes forming a circle around the main written note. They may start below or above the main note. Sometimes, they have to be executed quite fast, with an articulation on either side, particularly when the written note is short. At other times the turn is incorporated into a compound ornament as at the end to a trill, bringing it to an elegant close. The turn is used more often in later Baroque music in the *galant* style, and hardly at all in French music.

C. P. E. Bach describes the turn as making melodies both attractive and brilliant.[60] When played in adagio, he recommends playing the start of the turn faster than the end, for expressiveness. In a faster movement such as presto, the four notes should be equal.

Ex. 1.5.49: C. P. E. Bach (1753)

Tartini describes the effect of the turn as making the main note more lively, bold and fiery. He says that the turn is

> . . . more suited to quick, light music than to smooth strains . . . [and] should never be used in slow, sustained and mournful strains.
>
> (1771) tr. Jacobi, p. 89

Tartini suggests that

> . . . it is easy to judge where to place it, for the turn is a kind of accent and percussion, occasioned by the emphasis needed by the main note.
>
> (1771) tr. Jacobi, p. 89

Ex. 1.5.50: Tartini (1771)

Tartini does not approve of the use of a turn at all on an up-beat (because it is a weak note not requiring emphasis) or on the first note of a melody (which might be confusing).[61]

---

[60] (1753) tr. Mitchell, pp. 112-3
[61] (1771) tr. Jacobi, pp. 90-1

1.5 Ornamentation

The Mordent

The *pincé* meaning pinched, or *battemens* in French, is used in a short and long form. When short its character is that of a bite, and it adds zest to the note to which it is attached

> ... to enliven the notes and make them brilliant.
>
> Quantz (1752) VIII.15, tr. Reilly, p. 98

When used long, its affect can be emphatic and annoying, with its many re-iterations. It uses the written note and the one below. For a short 'bite', only three notes are necessary. When approaching the written note with a single note from below (a sort of inverted appoggiatura) this is described by many writers as port de voix. Some writers insist on a mordent to finish off a port de voix, a device particularly effective at cadences. Both J. Rousseau and Hotteterre rule out the use of the mordent when playing *inégale*. Geminiani calls the mordent *mordente* or beat and says it

> is proper to express several passions; as for Example, if it be perform'd with Strength, and continued long, it expresses Fury, Anger, Resolution, &c. If it be play'd less strong and shorter, it expresses Mirth, Satisfaction, &c. But if you play it quite soft, and swell the Note, it may then denote Horror, Fear, grief, Lamentation, &c. By making it short and swelling the Note gently, it may express Affection and Pleasure.
>
> (1751), p. 7-8

The variety of expression available through the use of one ornament is here wonderfully described, and illustrates the possibility of more than one repercussion from the written note. When written over a long note, the repercussions may extend for a good portion of the written note value. When the chevron sign for a mordent (or trill) appears within a slur, it may be performed before the beat (see also trill section).

Coulé du doigt

Finally, a word about an ornament described by Danoville in his *L'art de toucher le dessus et basse de viole* (1687).[62] This ornament is used on slurred chromatic movement by sliding the finger (*glissant insensiblement*) between two notes. He claims that the viol is the only suitable instrument for this effect, as the strings on the violin are too taut (*trop tendues*).

J. Rousseau (1687) also describes an ornament to be used in particularly languishing chromatic passages called *la plainte*. This is executed 'by sliding the finger over the string from one fret to the adjoining one without raising it'.[63]

There appears to be no good reason why violinists shouldn't borrow this ornament for particularly anguished chromatic movement. Obviously, there is a danger in its overuse, and it should be saved for occasional enhancement of particularly strong emotional passages.

Summary

The perceived current position of on-the-beat ornaments in all Baroque music has been challenged by Neumann among others, and players are beginning to realise that the 'Berlin rules' as written down by C. P. E. Bach and Quantz are what Neumann terms 'downstream' from composers such as J. S. Bach, and therefore applicable only to music written by their generation and school of composition, and not to composers of previous vintage. It is true that many composers (particularly J. S. Bach) write out long appoggiaturas, leaving no doubt as to the length and placing of the start of the note. Many appoggiaturas of J. S. Bach which are indicated by a sign are more suitably played short, which goes against 'the rules'.

---

[62] reprinted in *Viole de Gambe - Méthodes et Traités* (pub. Fuzeau), p. 16
[63] ibid., p. 48

Neumann also argues for many written graces to be played *before* the beat for various reasons:

- Source evidence, particularly in French vocal and viol treatises (e.g. J. Rousseau).
- When time does not permit a multiple or compound ornament to be executed within the beat, it must overflow in front of the beat.
- When an ornament occurs within a slur.
- When the main note forms a dissonance which should not be hidden by a consonant ornamental note.
- When the position of the ornament on the beat would create obvious-sounding consecutives.

All of these examples are situations where ornaments are of passing interest only, and not placed at strong points, melodically or harmonically. They are therefore subsidiary to the main feature, be it the line of the melody, or a strong harmonic dissonance. Ortiz proposes a sensible course of action in the introduction to his book on ornamentation for any player unsure about using and inventing ornaments:

> He who wishes to take advantage of this book must consider what ability he has and accordingly choose the embellishments which seem best suited to him; because even if the division is a good one, it won't seem good if the hand cannot manage it, and the fault will not be in the music.
>
> (1553) tr. Gammie

Ornament information

Primary sources available in facsimile or modern editions

Diego Ortiz	*Tratado de glosas sobre clausulas y otros generos de puntos en la musica de violones* (Rome 1553)
Giulio Caccini	*Le Nuove Musiche* (Florence 1602)
Christopher Simpson	*The Division-viol* (London 1659)
Marin Marais	*Pièces de Violes, 1er livre* (Paris 1686)
Jean Rousseau	*Traité de la Viole* (Paris 1687)
Saint-Lambert	*Les Principes du Clavecin* (Paris 1702)
François Couperin	*L'Art de Toucher le Clavecin* (Paris 1717)
Jean-Philippe Rameau	*Pièces de Clavecin* (Paris 1724)
Michel Corrette	*L'Ecole d'Orphée: l'art de se perfectionner dans le violon* (Paris 1738, 1782)
Francesco Geminiani	*The Art of Playing on the Violin* (London 1751)
Johann Joachim Quantz	*Versuch einer Anweisung die Flöte traversière zu spielen* (Berlin 1752)
Carl Philipp Emanuel Bach	*Versuch über die wahre Art das Clavier zu spielen* (Berlin 1753)
Leopold Mozart	*Versuch einer gründlichen Violinschule* (Augsburg 1756)
L'Abbé le fils	*Principes du Violon* (Paris 1761)
Giuseppe Tartini	*Traité des Agréments de la Musique* (Paris 1771)

1.5 Ornamentation

Secondary sources

Howard Mayer Brown	*Ornamentation in 16th century music*
Bruce Dickey	'Ornamentation in Early-17th-Century Italian Music', chapter 13 in Carter (1997)
Robert Donington	*The Interpretation of Early Music* (Chapters XIII to XXV)
Frederick Neumann	*Ornamentation in Baroque and Post-Baroque Music* (contains a comprehensive glossary of ornament symbols and signs and their use)
Hans-Peter Schmitz	*Die Kunst der Vierzierung im 18. Jahrhundert* (contains many musical examples)
Robin Stowell	*Violin Technique and Performance Practice in the Late 18th and early 19th Centuries* (contains glossary of ornaments from treatises)

Vibrato

One of the myths which has crept into modern folklore about playing the Baroque violin, is that the use of vibrato is frowned upon. This is a very big misconception as will be demonstrated. Vibrato was used as an ornament for particular emphasis or expression and its appearance in tables of ornaments justifies this approach. Musicians of all types must have used vibrato at least since the invention of the violin, in imitation of the human voice, as Agricola describes below. The existence and technique of vibrato is well documented by several violin tutors. However, discussion concerning its frequency and use has been the subject of endless debate, in modern times as well as in the early years of violin playing. Agricola:

> One also produces vibrato freely to make the melody sound sweeter
>
> (1529) tr. Hettrick, p. 103

This description of the use of vibrato occurs in the method for 'the fretless Polish fiddle tuned in fifths'.[64] The absence of frets distinguishes this type of fiddle from the viols, and the added factor of the tuning in fifths suggests that the instrument which used vibrato is an early form of the violin. Mersenne claimed that the use of vibrato was one the great attributes and attractions of the violin:

> . . . particularly the ornaments and vibrato of the left hand, which compel those who hear it to confess that the violin is the king of instruments.
>
> (1636) Livre Quatriesme, p. 177

Geminiani lists vibrato or 'the close shake' in his catalogue of 'ornaments of expression': He tells us that:

> . . . this cannot possibly be described by notes as in former [ornament] examples. To perform it, you must press the finger strongly upon the string of the instrument, and move the wrist in and out slowly and equally, when it is long continued swelling the sound by degrees, drawing the bow nearer to the bridge, and ending it very strong may express majesty, dignity etc. But making it shorter, lower and softer, it may denote affliction, fear etc. and when it is made on short notes, it only contributes to make their sound more agreable and for this reason it should be made use of as often as possible.
>
> (1751), p. 8

An opposing view is presented by Leopold Mozart. He calls vibrato 'the tremolo' (not to be confused with the use of the same word for bow vibrato):

> The tremolo is an ornamentation which arises from Nature herself and which can be used charmingly on a long note, not only by good instrumentalists but also by clever

---

[64] (1529) tr. Hettrick, p. 95

1.5 Ornamentation

> singers. Nature herself is the instructress thereof. For if we strike a slack string or a bell sharply, we hear after the stroke a certain wave-like undulation (*ondeggiamento*) of the struck note. And this trembling after-sound is called tremolo, also tremulant.
>
> Take pains to imitate this natural quivering on the violin, when the finger is pressed strongly down on the string, and one makes a small movement with the whole hand; which however must not move sideways but forwards toward the bridge and backwards toward the scroll. . . . For as, when the remaining trembling sound of a struck string or bell is not pure and continues to sound not on one note only but sways first too high, then too low, just so by the movement of the hand forward and backward must you endeavour to imitate exactly the swaying of these intermediate tones.
>
> Now because the tremolo is not purely on one note but sounds undulating, so would it be an error if every note were played with the tremolo. Performers there are who tremble consistently on each note as if they had the palsy. The tremolo must only be used at places where nature herself would produce it; namely as if the note taken were the striking of an open string. For at the close of a piece, or even at the end of a passage which closes with a long note, that last note would inevitably, if struck for instance on a pianoforte, continue to hum for a considerable time afterwards. Therefore a closing note or any other sustained note may be decorated with a tremolo.
>
> (1756) XI.1-3, tr. Knocker, p. 203

He continues with a description of when to use vibrato, and it is indeed only on longer note values, and especially at the held note before a cadenza:

> . . . the stroke must commence softly and gather strength toward the middle, in such fashion that the greatest strength falls at the beginning of the more rapid movement [of the vibrato]; and finally the stroke must end again softly.
>
> (1756) XI.7, tr. Knocker, p. 206

Another reference to vibrato relates the strength of tone to speed:

> The finger must move forward towards the bridge and backward again towards the scroll: in soft tone quite slowly, but in loud rather faster.
>
> (1756) V.5, tr. Knocker, p. 98

North writing of the 'tremolous graces' was much influenced and impressed by the playing of the violinist Matteis who introduced the new Italian style of violin playing to England:

> The Italians have brought the bow to an high perfection, so that nothing of their playing is so difficult as the arcata or long bow, with which they begin a long note, clear, without rubb, and draw it forth swelling lowder and lowder, and at the ackme take a slow waiver; not a trill to break the sound or mix two notes, but as if the bird sat at the end of a spring (and) as she sang the spring waived her up and downe, or as if the wind that brought the sound shaked, or a small bell were struck and the sound continuing waived to and againe - so would I express what is justly not to be shewn but to the ear by an exquisite hand.
>
> . . . to superinduce a gentle and slow wavering, not into a trill, upon the swelling the note; such as trumpets use, as if the instrument were a little shaken with the wind of its owne sound, but not so as to vary the tone, which must be religiously held to its place, like a pillar on its base, without the least loss of the accord.
>
> J. Wilson, pp. 164, 18

He describes a very gentle, glowing type of vibrato designed to warm the sound, rather than a violent aggressive one. He particularly mentions that the pitch (he calls it the tone) should not be affected by the wavering. North was an amateur musician and mainly a viol player, although he did try to play the violin in later life. One surmises that the style of violin playing he had been used to hearing would have been very plain and on a fairly basic technical level. Although he was aware of vibrato as an ornament, he was obviously astounded at its use in the hands of a master (possibly Matteis) as described above.

Mattheson also describes the vibrato as being on the same pitch:

1.5 Ornamentation

> ... on instruments merely bending the finger tips without yielding the positioning accomplishes this very thing to some degree, especially on lutes, violins and clavichords, which sufficiently illustrates that nothing more is required for it than a single pitch.
>
> (1739) II.3.27, tr. Harriss, p. 270

North warns against using the vibrato (or wrist shake) too much:

> I must take notice of a wrist shake, as they call it, upon the violin, which without doubdt is a great art, but as I think injured by overdoing; for those who use it well never let a note rest without it, wheras it ought to be used as the swelling wavee, coming and going, which would have a much better effect.
>
> J. Wilson, p. 165 fn. 21

Muffat observes the detrimental effect vibrato can have on intonation:

> When we use vibrato or similar tricks on notes played uncertainly, we do great harm to true intervals, to the flow of melody, and to the harmonic relationships ... and ... One should avoid playing with those who would do more to spoil the ear than to improve it.
>
> (1698) tr. Cooper & Zsako, p. 223

Other instrumental treatises of the 17th and 18th centuries, for the viol and woodwind instruments in particular, describe other sorts of vibrato. On the viol, Marais marks places where a two-finger vibrato is to be used with a wavy line. Marais uses a separate sign for fourth finger vibrato, from which we may deduce that two fingers were used for the vibrato based on the first three fingers, which he calls *pincé* or *flattement*.[65] One may assume that the notes marked with vibrato signs are stronger or more expressive than those not marked.

The *flattement* for wind instruments is another type of close shake similar to vibrato. This is achieved by using the keys to produce a different pitch (often as much as a quarter tone) achieving a larger wavering than normal vibrato, but smaller than a semitone trill. It is also possible on a flute to produce a type of vibrato where the pitch does not alter by covering an open hole. Quantz describes a long note with vibrato:

> If you must hold a long note for either a whole or half bar, which the Italians call *messa di voce* ... you begin pianissimo, allow the strength of the tone to swell to the middle of the note, and from there diminish it to the end of the note in the same fashion, making a vibrato (German *bebung*, French *flattement*) with the finger on the nearest open hole.
>
> (1752) XIV.10, tr. Reilly, p. 165

J. Rousseau (1687), Marais (1686) and Simpson (1659) describe a two-fingered vibrato/shake to be used on the viol. Rousseau calls it *le battement* and describes it as an ornament that

> ... imitates a certain sweet agitation of the voice
>
> (1687), p. 100

and instructs the player to use it on all notes whose length encourages it.

Simpson:

> Close-shake is that when we shake the Finger as close and near the sounding Note as possible may be, touching the String with the Shaking finger so softly and nicely that it make no variation of Tone. This may be used where no other grace is concerned.
>
> (1659), p. 11

Playford describes the same type of shake for the violin (still with frets on for the beginner):

> For the usual graces, the Shake is the principal; of which there are two, the close shake and the open shake; the close shake is when you stop with your first Finger on the first Fret, and shake with your second Finger as close to it as you can;
>
> (1674), p. 104

---

[65] preface to *Pièces de Violes, 1er livre*, p. 4

A two-fingered vibrato is also described by Tartini:

> There is another kind of trill that is best performed on the violin. The two notes that make it up join in such a way that the two fingers never quite leave the string. It is not done, like the others, by raising the finger but by using the wrist to carry the whole hand, and thus also the finger in a rippling motion, so that this kind of trill is 'rippled' and not 'struck'. It sounds well in playing *con affetto* and when the two notes are only a semi-tone apart.
>
> (1771) tr. Jacobi, p. 78

The technique he is describing is halfway between a trill and vibrato. Lenton also differentiates vibrato with one finger from the 'close shake':

> . . . when you make a Shake let it be from the motion of the Finger alone, and not from any Squeeze of the Body or Wrist (except) it be a close Shake which is done by the content and operation of all the Fingers.
>
> (1694), p. 11

The effect of the two-fingered vibrato is quite dramatic when used at a particularly strong emotional point in the phrase, as a gesture of violence when played loudly, or horror when soft. Some 18th-century parts have wavy lines over long notes of special harmonic interest, which may indicate the use of a trill or two-fingered vibrato according to context.

Geminiani lists the sign for his 'tremolo' in the table of ornaments of expression (no. 14), but it is not indicated at all in the following compositions, whereas the swelling of the sound *is* indicated (p. 125). I take this to mean that he intends it to be used 'as often as possible' especially in conjunction with 'the swelling of the sound' and that it is otherwise up to the performer to use vibrato according to the rules of good taste. The player then has a choice of various effects obtainable by using different speeds of vibrato, combined with the *messa di voce* for certain expressions of the grander type, and the use of vibrato on short notes. Geminiani does not specify how short is short, but he does not say quick notes, and one may deduce from this that he means notes that are quite separate from one another, needing emphasis. The puzzling instruction 'as often as possible' implies that if the use of vibrato is not continuous and this might mean notes of longer duration only, where the vibrato would have time to register as an effect. In his table of ornaments of expression vibrato is illustrated on minims.

If it is agreed (and this is a matter of individual taste) that vibrato on the violin family is mainly used on long notes, strong beats or notes that require extra emphasis or expression, contra-indications for vibrato, or places where its use is inappropriate are as follows:

VIBRATO SHOULD NOT BE USED at the following points:

- Up-beats of any sort.
- Short quick notes.
- Continuous passages of quick notes.
- Resolutions of dissonances where the resolution is shorter and weaker (e.g. passing cadences).
- Any passing notes, or notes on weak beats where the harmony is unexceptional.
- Long notes in accompanying passages, except where the harmony becomes important by way of a dissonance.
- Shorter accompanying figures, in quavers.
- The last note in a slur, except as a special effect.

VIBRATO SHOULD BE USED at the following points:

- Any *messa di voce*, particularly final long notes (in the middle).
- To emphasise strong harmonic points.
- Long notes, suspensions or tied notes which lead to dissonance (at the end).
- At the beginning of long notes marked *sf* or *fp*.
- On shorter notes with marked separation marked *sf* or *fp*.

1.5 Ornamentation

Whenever vibrato is used, it should be combined with a bow-stroke which matches the affect required: slow, swelling bow-strokes with vibrato in the middle; a fast bow-stroke combined with vibrato at the beginning of a note; a quick vibrato on a short emphatic bow-stroke, etc. The increase in sound, and the speed of vibrato should match each other, and similarly, with the decrease in sound the vibrato should subside.

Vibrato in ensembles

All the above descriptions of vibrato and its use apply to solo performance. It is a debatable point whether vibrato should be used at all in orchestral playing, or when accompanying a soloist. If vibrato is classed as an ornament, the use of ornamentation where more than one player is playing the same part is open to question. The logical progression of this argument is that as the size of an orchestra grows, the use of vibrato should diminish. Certain mandatory trills are taken for granted, such as those at cadences, but otherwise, the use of ornaments by orchestral players was not expected.

Bremner was an 18th-century musician and pupil of Geminiani, who was aware that this subject had not yet been written about when he wrote his observations on performance. He distinguishes between solo and orchestral style, pleading that the sound with many players vibrating (evidence that they did indeed vibrate in ensembles, a habit unpalatable to him) distorts the tone and harmonic meaning of the music, and also affects the tuning. He points out that as soon as vibrato is absent from the playing, the resultant improvement in quality of sound made by the bow is apparent. Bremner uses the term *tremolo* for vibrato but explains that it is indeed his teacher Geminiani's close shake:

> Many gentleman players on bow instruments are so exceeding fond of the *tremolo*, that they apply it wherever they possibly can. This grace has a resemblance to that wavering found given by two of the unisons of an organ, a little out of tune; or to the voice of one who is paralytic; a song from whom would be one continued *tremolo* from beginning to end. Though the application of it may, for the sake of variety, be admitted, at times, on a long note in simple melody; yet if it be introduced into harmony, where the beauty and energy of the performance depend upon the united effect of all the parts being exactly in tune with each other, it becomes hurtful. The proper stop is a fixed point, from which the least deviation is erroneous: consequently the *tremolo*, which is a departure from that point, will not only confuse the harmony to the hearers who are near the band, but also enfeeble it to those at a distance; for to these last, the performance of him who is applying *tremolo* is lost.
>
> (1777) Zaslaw (1979), p. 48

He continues with a plea for the pure sound without ornament (including vibrato) when practising, in order to improve the quality of playing:

> Would gentlemen lay aside the graces of the finger, for some time, even when playing alone, and attend to the plain sound, it will soon gain their affection; being of so bewitching a nature, that the more it is practiced, the more it will be admired. The bow hand too will thereby improve exceedingly. Those who feed upon the graces of the finger, seldom pay attention to the bow; in the judicious management of which, all power, taste, and expression, chiefly consist.
>
> (1777) Zaslaw (1979), p. 53

Bremner's idea of vibrato-less practice is to be thoroughly endorsed and can reveal the bare bones of intonation and the sound quality upon which it depends. Many players use vibrato in such an habitual way that they are unaware of when they are using it. Only when a player has become accustomed to hearing the true plain sound of his playing, does he realise the usefulness of vibrato to enhance that which the bow expresses. The player also becomes more aware of how few occasions there are when vibrato is an essential ornament. All this is, of course, a diversion on the journey to the Parnassus of good taste.

PART TWO
TECHNIQUES

2.1 Holding the instrument

There is no area where the 'methods of practitioners' differ more than in the manner of holding the instrument. A brief study of paintings and drawings from the earliest times of the violin family will reveal a large variety of holds and positions for the violin and viola against the neck, shoulder or ribs, often in the same picture. For bass instruments, a mixture of supported and unsupported positions are seen. From our vantage point of the 21st century, it is difficult to ignore the development of technique and the accumulated experience of generations of violinists who have contributed to the present state of violin playing over the last 400 years. The biggest obstacles to be overcome when attempting to put ourselves in the position of a Baroque player are the chin-rest for violin and viola players, and the long metal spike for cellists. These inventions gave the 20th-century playing position a standard aspect which had hitherto been lacking. After the invention of the chin-rest (Spohr calls it 'the violin holder'), the chin was used constantly, not just for position changing but to steady the instrument continuously. As frequent position changing into the higher registers of the instrument on all strings became more common, this method of supporting the instrument became a practical necessity.

The violin and viola

Throughout the 17th century and for most of the 18th, violinists did not use a chin-rest. The chin, when it was needed, rested on the right (E string) side of the tail piece, or on the tail piece itself. Today's Baroque violinists use a number of solutions to the problem of holding of the instrument without *post facto* mechanical aids. They put their chin on the instrument on the left-hand side of the tail piece (the G-string side), on the tail piece, or to the right-hand side of it. Some players opt for a more radical approach and have given up using their chin at all, and a few players hold the violin lower down against the chest, where using the chin is not an option.

The chin-rest was supposedly invented by L'Abbé le fils whose violin treatise was published in Paris in 1761. This early device may have been merely a sliver of wood attached to the violin to prevent the chin slipping off. The chin-rest proper came into use at the beginning of the 19th century having been invented by Spohr. With this aid it was possible to hold the violin steady and place the chin on the violin without bending the head forwards.[1] Spohr's chin-rest was designed to be used over the centre of the tailpiece, and many violinists use a similar model today. The shoulder-rest as we know it is a 20th-century phenomenon, and many different designs and models have been hailed by their inventors as being the perfect solution to the problem of holding the violin. A shoulder-rest or pad should not be disregarded entirely as an aid to Baroque violin playing, as it must be remembered that 18th-century dress would have been, for the men at least, much bulkier around the shoulders, and facilitated the positioning of the instrument nearer to the chin than a thin shirt. Many players today use a piece of chamois leather on the shoulder to prevent the instrument from sliding about, and also to protect the varnish. If the player uses the chin for position changing, a small pad filling the gap

---

[1] for Spohr's description and use of his invention see Stowell (1985), pp. 29-30

2.1 Holding the instrument

between shoulder and under-side of the violin can be useful to prevent the shoulder being raised.

The factors to be taken into consideration when deciding how to hold the violin and make the 'chin on or off' decision will be followed by a survey of contemporary descriptions of how to hold the violin.

Factors affecting the method of holding the instrument:

- Descriptions and pictures of violinists
- The repertoire to be played
- How exclusively this position is to be used in the player's day to day music making
- Conquering the difficulties the chin-off position presents if this method is chosen
- How far the player is willing to go to make technical changes

Remember that for every difficulty encountered, there is knowledge to be gained: fingering and articulation details will have to be re-thought in the light of the new position without any mechanical support at the chin end of the violin. The new position will also affect the way the bow is placed on the string, and the position and use of the bow arm. Here are some descriptions from contemporary writings and violin tutors of how to hold the violin. They are arranged chronologically:

1556 Jambe de Fer

> The Italians call this instrument the *violone*, or *violon da braccio* because it is supported by the arm, although some people use scarfs, cords and other things to aid in holding them.
>
> Riley (1954), p. 60
> [the last comment probably refers to the bass instruments of the violin family]

1615-20 Praetorius

> The *viola de bracio*, or *violino da brazzo*, otherwise the violin, is known to ordinary people as 'fiddle'. It is called de bracio because it is held on the arm.
>
> tr. Crookes, p. 56

1640 Trichet

> One holds it resting against the left shoulder.
>
> ed. Lesure, p. 170

1674 Playford

> The violin is usually plaid above-hand, the Neck thereof being held by the left hand; the lower part thereof is rested on the left breast, a little below the shoulder.
>
> Secondly, for the posture of your left hand, place your Thumb on the back of the Neck, opposite to your Forefinger, so will your Fingers have the more liberty to move up and down in the several Stops.
>
> p. 114

1677 Prinner

> If you want to play the violin properly you must . . . hold the violin so firmly with your chin that there's no reason to hold it with the left hand otherwise it would be impossible to play quick passages which go high and then low or to play in tune like that unless one were to hold the violin with the right hand so that it shouldn't fall down. Nevertheless, I have known virtuosi of repute who irrespective of this put the violin only against the chest, thinking it looks nice and decorative, because they have taken it from a painting where an angel is playing to St. Francis and found it more picturesque: but they should have known that the painter was perhaps more artful with his paintbrush than he would have been with the violin bow.
>
> tr. Charles Medlam, *Early music*, vol. 7 no. 4, Oct. (1979) pp. 562-3.

2.1 Holding the instrument

1688 Falck

The violin is to be held between the left thumb and the ball of the first finger, however, not too tightly, so that it is possible to shift in case of a high note, and then back. The instrument is to be placed against the left breast so that it will tilt toward the right side. Both arms are to be kept away from the body to allow freedom of movement.

Riley (1954), p. 244

c.1690 Matteis described by North

He was a very tall and large bodyed man, used a very long bow, and rested his instrument against his short ribbs.

He was a very robust and tall man, and having long armes, held his instrument almost against his girdle . . . and I have found very few that will beleeve it possible he could performe as he did in that posture.

J. Wilson, p. 309 and fn. 63

1694 Lenton

As I would have none get a habit of holding an Instrument under the Chin, so I would have them avoid placing it as low as the Girdle, which is a mongrel sort of way us'd by some in imitation of the *Italians*, never considering the Nature of the Musick they are to perform; but certainly for *English* compositions, which generally carry a gay lively Air with them, the best way of commanding the Instrument will be to place it somewhat higher than your Breast, your Fingers round and firm in stopping, not bending your joynts inward.

p. 11

1695 Merck

Hold the violin neatly below the left breast, leaving the arm free and not resting it on the stomach. Also acquire a good stance, avoiding a hunchbacked, crooked posture. The legs, too should be straight and not bowed.

Riley (1954), p. 260

1701 Playford

Hold your *Violin* somewhat above half an inch from its Head, or Nut, and keep it close between the Root of your Thumb and forefinger, then begin to play off the Notes of the *Gamut* . . .

[Instructions p. 3]

1711 Monteclair

The neck of the violin to be placed between the thumb and the adjoining finger. The fingerboard should be grasped loosely to avoid stiffening the fingers and the wrist. To hold the violin securely, the tail-piece is placed against the neck just under the left cheek. The elbow should be held directly under the violin. The fingers are to be curved so that the tips, not the nails, are placed on the strings. The left wrist is to be bent.

Riley (1954), p. 92

1731 Prelleur

Hold the *Violin* with your left Hand about half an inch from the bottom of its Head, which is usually termed the *Nut*, and let it lie between the Root of your Thumb and that of your forefinger: then you may proceed to the playing off of the Notes specified in the *Scale* of the *Gamut*.

p. 2

1738 Corrette

Take the fingerboard of the violin in the left hand and hold it with the thumb and the first finger without gripping with the hand, rounding the first, second, third finger and holding the little one stretched out. It is necessary to put the chin on the violin when one changes position which gives complete freedom to the left hand mainly when returning to first position.

p. 7

2.1 Holding the instrument

1740 Crome

Take the fiddle and hold it in your Left Hand. Let the Neck lie between your fore Finger and Thumb, turning your Wrist, that your Fingers may lie over the Finger Board to be in readyness when you want them: then let the back part rest on your left Breast. The best way is to stay it with your Chin, that it may remain steady.

Riley (1954), p. 204

1751 Geminiani

Ex. 2.1.1

B shews a Method of acquiring the true Position of the Hand, which is this: To place the first Finger on the first string upon F; the second Finger on the second string upon C; the third Finger on the third String upon G; and the fourth Finger on the fourth String upon D. This must be done without raising any of the Fingers, till all four have been set down; but after that, they are to be raised but a little Distance from the String they touched; and by so doing the Position is perfect.

The violin must be rested just below the Collar-bone, turning the right-hand Side of the Violin a little downwards, so that there may be no Necessity of raising the Bow very high, when the fourth String is to be struck. Observe also, that the Head of the Violin must be nearly Horizontal with that Part which rests against the Breast, that the Hand may be shifted with Facility and without any Danger of dropping the Instrument.

Example 1B pp. 1-2

1756 Tartini (probably written pre-1756 but first published in French 1770)

As regards changing position, it is impossible to give any hard and fast rules. The student should adopt whatever method he finds most comfortable in each case, and he should therefore practise the hand shifts in every possible way so that he is prepared for every situation that may arise.

tr. Jacobi, p. 56

1756 L. Mozart

Fig. 1　　　　Fig. 2

Ex. 2.1.2

The first way of holding the violin has a rather pleasant and relaxed appearance (Fig. 1). Here the violin is quite unconstrained; held chest-high, slanting, and in such fashion that the strokes of the bow are directed more upwards than horizontal. This position is undoubtedly natural and pleasant to the eyes of the onlookers but somewhat difficult and inconvenient for the player as during quick movements of the hand in the high position, the violin has no support and must therefore necessarily fall unless by long practice the advantage of being able to hold it between the thumb and index-finger has been acquired.

2.1 Holding the instrument

> The second is a comfortable method (Fig. 2). The violin is placed against the neck so that it lies somewhat in front of the shoulder and the side on which the E (thinnest) string lies comes under the chin, whereby the violin remains unmoved in its place even during the strongest movements of the ascending and descending hand.
>
> II.3, tr. Knocker, p. 54
>
> The "handle", or rather the neck of the violin, must not be taken into the whole hand like a lump of wood, but held in such a manner between thumb and index-finger that it rests on one side on the ball at the base of the index-finger, and on the other side against the upper part of the thumb joint, but in no way touching the skin which joins the thumb and index-finger together. The thumb must not project too far over the finger-board, for otherwise it would hinder the player and rob the G string of its tone. The lower part of the hand (namely, where it joins the arm) must remain free, and the violin must not lie on it, for in doing so the nerves which connect the arm and fingers would be pressed together and so contracted, and the third and fourth fingers prevented from stretching. We see daily examples of such clumsy players, who find everything difficult because they restrict themselves by an awkward position of the violin and the bow.
>
> The scroll of the violin is then held on the level of the mouth, or, at the highest, level with the eyes; but it must not be allowed to sink lower than the level of the chest.
>
> II.4, tr. Knocker, pp. 57-8
>
> The violin must remain immovable. By this I mean that you must not allow it to turn backward and forward with every stroke, making yourself laughable to the spectators.
>
> II.6, tr. Knocker, p. 61

1761 L'Abbé le fils

> The violin should be placed on the collar bone, placing the chin on the side of the 4th string, it is necessary to lower the side of the top string a bit. The hand should be at a similar height to the collar. The neck should be held without gripping between the thumb and the 1st joint of the index finger, the part of the neck found on this side of the thumb must be put on the plump prominence of the 1st joint. One must observe the position of the thumb with regard to the open bottom string.
>
> p. 1

PRACTICAL APPLICATION

Several points are raised by this catalogue of holds. The exact parts of the body described as ribs and chest are somewhat vague. The instruction by Crome to hold the violin against the breast, but to use the chin is rather confusing. The breast is a large area extending from the ribs to the neck, and where are the 'short ribs'? I know where the 'girdle' is, and it is an unlikely place for holding the violin to play Italian music, although it appears probable that Matteis did exactly that, much to the disapproval of Lenton.

The general progression of the violin position from low to high holds obviously runs parallel to the musical and technical developments during the period 1650-1750. However, at no period does the hold appear to have been at all standardised, and high holds against the neck are pictured very early in the violin's life, and throughout the 17th century. The bulk of dance music played by violin bands before 1700 would have remained in first position or used a fourth finger extension on the E string to c^3, making the low hold against the chest easy to manage. The small sized violins and *pochettes* used to play for dancing are easier to play held against the chest than larger violins and violas. Only the virtuoso solo repertoire would have moved far out of first position (Uccellini in Italy and Biber and Schmelzer in Bohemia both used positions above third).

Most of the music contained in tutors written before 1700 were for gentlemen amateur players who would have been content with playing fairly simple music in low positions. Even Corelli's solo works, which are in other ways more technically advanced, using double stops and fast bow patterns of *bariolage*, do not go above e^3, an extension from third position, or modern fourth position.

2.1 Holding the instrument

Neck thickness

Another factor to be taken into consideration when holding a Baroque violin is the different thickness of the neck, which is fixed at a lower angle to the main body of the instrument. Violins made before the mid-17th century would have had a thick, short neck. Dance music played on these instruments would have been easy to play with the violin held low against the body.

The thicker and shorter neck lies much more comfortably in the hand than a long thin one, which brings the hand into a more closed position and is designed to facilitate moving up and down the fingerboard with the violin held higher up on the shoulder. It is certainly easier to hold the earlier model violin without the chin, either on the shoulder or lower down against the body, and with the left wrist in a more relaxed inward position. The shorter flatter-angled neck gives a different balance to the whole instrument, bringing the left hand nearer to the body of the instrument, and consequently closer to the other end which is being balanced on the shoulder or held against the ribs.

The Chin

The two holds described by Leopold Mozart are interesting in that they describe the problem of which side of the tail piece to place the chin. He recommends the treble side of the tail piece as being the more secure position, which is the hold adopted by most players of the Baroque violin today. If the chin-rest is discarded and the chin stays on the bass side of the tail piece, the instrument is extremely insecure and is likely to slip away forwards if the chin is not used almost continuously. By positioning the instrument in a flatter position on the shoulder the balance of the instrument is altogether more stable. Holding the violin with an axis pointing in from the neck of the instrument down the line of the fingerboard and tail piece towards the player's collar-bone is a 'half-way house' which is a good starting point for someone who has just discarded their chin-rest (see Monteclair's solution, above). As this becomes more comfortable, the player may gradually move the body of the violin to the left, bringing the scroll round to the front of the body. Try not to grip the instrument at either end, but support it with a relaxed hand, and by a balanced (although loose) position on the shoulder.

The left-hand position as described by Geminiani may help to clarify Monteclair's instruction that the left wrist should be bent. He does not specify which way it is to be bent, but the Geminiani grip is impossible to achieve unless the wrist is relaxed inwards towards the violin. When the elbow is brought round to the front of the instrument, the little finger is in a better position to stretch over onto the G string for the final position to be set. The left thumb should be encouraged to develop an independent life, separate from the fingers, and to be mobile regardless of the position of the left hand. Geminiani's exercises for position changing (see below) are designed to facilitate this.

Playing without the chin to steady the violin is easier when playing music which does not move out of first position. 'Chinless' novices should volunteer to play second violin or viola parts, where position changing is less likely to be needed, while they are gaining confidence in this new technique (Baroque viola parts seldom move out of first position). The player should find a comfortable position for the violin where the instrument is balanced firmly without having to resort to steadying it with the chin. Aim for the instrument to be in a flatter position, placing the scroll towards the front of the body rather than at the side, with the chin positioned over the treble side of the tail piece. When accustomed to the idea of playing without the chin, moving positions upwards should not present a problem as the violin may be raised and pushed slightly towards the neck as the hand moves into the higher position (pushing in this way with the chin over the *bass* side of the tail piece results in the instrument sliding away down the front of the body). However, descending from a high position is another matter as gravity is working against you, and without support the violin may fall away from the shoulder.

2.1 Holding the instrument

The technique of creeping around the fingerboard by small degrees from one position to its neighbour a semitone away should be practised, as large shifts are obviously more impractical than smaller ones. Downward shifts are achieved by moving the thumb separately from the rest of the hand whilst tilting the instrument upwards to defy gravity. This unfamiliar manoeuvre will be difficult at first. However, shifting can be helped by the choice of fingering, and this is where the resourcefulness and imagination of the player comes into play. Look for points where free left-hand time is available to make the shift, such as when playing open strings. Points of articulation should be keenly sought to obtain that extra moment to move into another position, and the 'in-between' positions (half and second) should be more frequently used.

As you develop a chin-off technique, there may be occasions in later music where it is impossible to maintain. Many players adapt their left-hand technique for different periods of music and repertoire. The 18th-century first violin part which moves continually up and down the fingerboard may result in your chin being restored to the violin for certain passages. In earlier music, however, the high passages are often contained within one phrase, so you are not continually moving up and down, but will ascend for a time and take your chin off completely whilst in the high position before descending to stay in first position for a while until the next high passage. The points at which you move will become fairly obvious once you are used to looking for opportunities at which to ascend or descend. Even if you decide to play using your chin occasionally, remember the difficulties of playing without, and try to use a fingering which will reflect the left hand's handicap in this area. For example, sequences where the same fingering may be repeated in different positions.

Position of the thumb

Many contemporary paintings of drinking and domestic scenes depict the violinist's thumb curling round the neck on to the G string. This might be accounted for by the fact that much 'tavern' music would not have required the player to use the bottom string very often, if at all, so the thumb wouldn't have been in the way. This hold also precludes the possibility of using the fourth finger. North observes Jenkins' unusual use of the thumb when playing the bass viol:

> He was once carryed to play on the viol before King Charles I, which he did in his voluntary way, with wonderful agillity, and odd humours, as (for instance) touching the great strings with his thumb, while the rest were held imployed in another way.
>
> J. Wilson, p. 295

Whether this technique was used on the violin and under what circumstances is still open to question, and shouldn't be completely ruled out.[2]

Interaction with the bow

The position of the bow must not be forgotten. When the violin is moved so that the chin is over the treble side of the tail piece, and the scroll of the violin is brought forward to the front of the body instead of being to the side, the angle of the bow must be adjusted to match. The bow should be kept at a right-angle to the strings at all times. Players who alter the position of the instrument often neglect to work on the complementary changes that must be made to the angle of the bow to the string. The bow arm must be brought back closer to the side of the body to achieve the ideal right-angle to the string position. Practising in a mirror can be advantageous at this stage to avoid the 'windscreen wiper' bow-stroke where the bow disappears behind the player's left ear. Watch the right wrist to see that it gives way in order to keep the bow straight. If the wrist is stiff in the lower half of the bow, the bow will continue to be crooked.

See also Penny Schwarz, 'Two aspects of Baroque Violin Technique, Part II: The Low Hold.' *Journal of the Violin Society of America*, Summer 2007, pp. 185-203.

---

[2] for further discussion and iconological observations about the position of the left thumb see Walls (1998) pp. 3-17

2.1 Holding the instrument

Conclusion

To sum up this knotty problem, my advice is that every player should seek their own way of holding the violin, and learn to cope with the difficulties presented. Whatever method the player uses, it is important to take into account the old ways of fingering, when the left hand had sole responsibility for holding the violin, unsupported by the chin, in order to reproduce the fingering patterns and thought processes dictated by old techniques.

Bass instruments

Compared with the violin, there are very few early references to methods of holding the cello and double bass.

Jambe de Fer (1556):

> The bass [member of the violin family] is very difficult to carry because of its weight, for which reason it is sustained with a small hook in an iron ring or other thing, which is attached to the back of the said instrument very exactly so that it does not interfere with the player.
>
> tr. Boyden (1965), p. 32

Corrette's cello tutor *Methode, théoretique et pratique. Pour Apprendre en peu de tems le Violoncelle dans sa Perfection* (1741) contains instructions for holding the instrument:

> He directs the student to seat himself on a chair or stool of suitable height so that he can hold the instrument without sitting too far forward. The violoncello is to be placed between the fleshy portions of the thighs. The neck of the violoncello is placed in the left hand and leaned slightly toward the left side. The violoncellist's body should be held upright and head erect. The feet are to be turned out, never inward. The instrument should not touch the floor as this would deaden the tone. Sometimes when the violoncellist plays in the standing position, an end-pin is put on (*baton au bout*). But this position is not the most desirable, since it is not convenient for performing difficult passages. Corrette continues that the neck of the violoncello should be held between the thumb and the second finger of the left hand. The curved fingers should not clutch the fingerboard too tightly, for they must be free to move on the strings. They must strike the strings firmly, or harmonics like those from the tromba marina will result. In the first position the hand can negotiate two octaves and one tone, or from C on the fourth string to d^1 on the first string. The movement of the hand from its regular place is called shifting.
>
> Riley (1954), p. 118

Most players today play the Baroque cello without a spike, a device which was invented at the end of the 19th century (popular legend relates that the first performance of the Dvorak cello concerto was given without a spike). However, during the 17th and 18th centuries support mechanisms as mentioned above were occasionally used, particularly for the larger bass instruments. Small stools are often seen supporting the larger members of the bass family (bass violins, small violones). Occasionally a short wooden prop is seen. Sometimes bass instruments are seen resting on the floor or a stool, with the player standing.

To play a bass instrument without a spike, try holding the instrument more vertically and lower to the ground, supported in the middle of the lower bouts by the calves. The left foot should be slightly further forward than the right, and the feet (which should rest flat on the ground) closer together than the knees which should be splayed slightly outwards. The instrument may then be held without gripping, balanced vertically on the calves (Riley translates Corrette's position as between the 'thighs'). There is pictorial and other evidence that small bass instruments were supported by a scarf or rope around the player's neck while standing up or walking about in processions or street bands, as described by Jambe de Fer above.

Summary

Playing on the arm (*braccio*) or the leg (*gamba*), there is no 'correct' way of holding the instrument. This is confirmed by a cursory examination of pictures and written descriptions. Various schools of Baroque playing have emerged, with proponents of each fiercely defending their right to a particular way of playing. However, I would like to defend the right of each player to continue to experiment with various types of hold (violin and bow), with each person finding the way which works best for them, perhaps using a different hold for earlier repertoire. Groups of string players seen in paintings reveal a variety of holds, even within the same ensemble. It is very rare in any picture to see players holding the instrument in the same way as their colleagues. While not providing conclusive proof that a standard hold did or did not exist in practice in any one place or period, the pictorial evidence does not encourage us to adopt any suitable alternative conclusion. The modern need to standardise and regulate has overtaken the old way of individual personal preference.

2.2 Fingering choice and position changing

The previous section surveyed the problem of holding an instrument without mechanical support in the form of chin- or shoulder-rest. Now we will examine the way in which this apparent handicap should influence the choice of fingering and positions used, even if the player decides to retain the use of the chin to assist in position changing. It will be necessary to re-think the common 'first to third' position habit in the light of new factors, the most important of which are sonority and phrasing. Trills may be executed on open strings, so moving into position just for an ornament is unnecessary. Lack of mechanical support will mean more creeping around the fingerboard in 2nd and 1/2 positions. The thumb and fingers will need to move separately quite a lot of the time if no support mechanism is used.

In general, until the mid-18th century, low positions are used except when playing high notes, when it is not customary to move the hand higher than necessary, whether in first position or 6th.

Playford:

> When you have any high Notes, which reach lower than your usual Frets or Stops, there you are to shift your fingers; if there be but two Notes, then the first is stopt with the third finger; but if there be three Notes that ascend, then the first is stopt with the second finger, and the rest by the next fingers.
>
> (1674), p. 115

By 'lower' he means higher up the fingerboard. He recommends the use of frets on the violin for the beginner only.

After describing the placing of the 1st, 2nd and 3rd fingers on the G, D and A strings Playford describes the extension of the 4th finger on the E string:

> *Ela* must be struck open, *Ffaut* with the fore finger stopt close to the Nut, *GSolreut* with the second finger an Inch from the first, *Alamire* with the third finger about an Inch from the second, *Bfabemi* with the fourth finger about half an Inch from the third, *CSolfaut* with the same fourth finger stretch'd forth a quarter of an Inch more forward then it was before, which may be done more conveniently by easing your hand at the Neck of your Violin.
>
> (1701), [Instructions p. 3]

Leopold Mozart:

Ex. 2.2.1: (1756) VIII.II.8, tr. Knocker, p. 143

The main reason for playing in low positions is to increase the string length used, and thus the resonance of the instrument. The decision to use vibrato only on certain notes, not continuously, also encourages the choice of low position fingering. Where vibrato is being used continuously, the open string will stick out, having no vibration. If vibrato is less commonly used, the open string will fit into the general sound more easily. Open strings and low positions are much more commonly used than in modern fingering which favours an even covered sound.

The tenüe

Notes should be left to ring without the vibrating string being damped (especially before rests or at the end of a movement). Increased resonance is also gained from holding down the fingers until they are forced to be removed. This technique, similar to the viol tenüe, where holding down the fingers contributes to the ringing of the note after the bow has moved to another string, is recommended in viol treatises by Mace (1676), Simpson (1659), Danoville (1687) and J. Rousseau (1687). Simpson's 'A rule for Holding on the Fingers':

> When you set any Finger down, hold it on there; and play the following Notes with other Fingers, until some occasion require the taking it off. This is done as well for better order of Fingering, that the Fingers may pass smoothly from Note to Note, without lifting them too far from the Strings, as also to continue the sound of a Note when the Bow hath left it.
>
> (1659), p. 5 para 9

Leopold Mozart, nearly a century later, notes that

> It must be observed, as an important rule, that the fingers, once placed, must be left unmoved until the constant change of the notes necessitates their being lifted, when they must be left hanging exactly over the note just played. One must guard against stretching out one or several fingers into the air; contracting the hand when the fingers are lifted; or sticking the little finger or even others under the neck of the violin. The hand must always be held in the same postion and each finger over its note, in order to achieve both certainty in placing the fingers, and purity and velocity in playing.
>
> (1756) II.6, tr. Knocker, p. 60

The *tenüe* technique is particularly important during passages which are conceived on a harmonic basis. Any double stopping or *bariolage* across the strings will require the fingers to be kept down for as long as possible for the 'ring' of the harmony. Vibrato is not used on fast notes, and the player will find that the restricted use of vibrato and the habit of holding the fingers down are complementary.

The string length which is left to resonate after the finger has depressed the string should in general be kept as long as possible. In other words, low positions should be maintained for most of the time on the lower three strings. It is not necessary to go into third position merely to avoid playing open strings, even for a trill. To avoid awkward string crossings, second position is used to accommodate situations where the music only goes one note higher than the next string (a trill on $e^{\flat 2}$, for example, should be played in 2nd position on the A string).

Ex. 2.2.2: Schmelzer, Sonata V

In this example from Schmelzer sonata no. 5, the 4th finger on d^3 should be kept down to 'ring' while the lower notes are played.

In the following example by Geminiani, the group of notes before the chord has a two finger instruction, implying that both 3rd and 4th fingers are to be put down together whilst playing these notes:

2.2 Fingering choice and position changing

Ex. 2.2.3 *f*: Geminiani, Essempio XII, Prestissimo

Note also in the above example that in the last bar a 'creeping' fingering is recommended, descending from 3rd position to 1st in easy stages, via 2nd position. Whilst playing the top $c\sharp^3$, the 1st finger should already be stretching back for the lower $g\sharp^2$, producing a smooth position change without making a bumpy large movement.

Open strings

The use of open strings is recommended but qualified by most writers by the warning that they are only to be used if they are in tune. North recommends the new practice of stopping all the notes, not using open strings as in the old way. He describes

> ... certein late manners of touch ... which are of admirable efficacy and improvement. Of the first sort the cheif is the sounding all the notes under the touch, and none with the strings open; for those are an harder sound than when stopt, and not always in tune, which the stop (assisted by the ear) effects with utmost niceness; so that upon instruments so handled, all the semi-tones, whatever the keys are or however they change, are in tune to the most scrupulous test of the ear. And besides all this, the power of the finger in giving temper and commixture to the notes, hath a superlative effect of sweetness; and by that means the violin hath growne upon the voice, whose prerogative that excellence, as well as the former, hath been esteemed. To perform this [finger-stopping] well is a soveraigne skill, but seems more abstruse than really it is; for among us the old way of using the open strings hath a prepossession, and it is not easy to leave it off. But in time, beginners will take into it, and then comon practise will make it familiar.
>
> J. Wilson, pp. 233-4

Leopold Mozart thought that

> Open strings are too loud compared with stopped notes, and pierce the ear too sharply.
>
> Where the notes fall on an open string note, they must at all times be taken by the fourth finger on the next lower string; particularly when they are to be flattened. If a # stands before an open string note it can, it is true, be taken on the same string with the first finger, but it is always better to take it by an extension of the fourth finger on the next lower string.
>
> (1756) I.V.13, I.III.14, tr. Knocker, pp. 101, 44.

Quantz agrees with North's sentiments regarding risky intonation, but reminds us that although string players can move their fingers up or down to adjust intonation and avoid out of tune open strings, the lowest strings cannot be avoided.[3]

Chords with open strings at the top should be particularly relished for the greater ring they provide. Similarly, any open string possibilities in passages of string-crossing *bariolage* or arpeggiation should be welcomed, as the open string sound increases the resonance and brilliance of such passages, facilitated by the lower arching of the Baroque bridge.

Violinist composers consciously exploited the use of the open strings. A movement or fugue subject might start with the notes a^1-e^2, for example, and this seems to be a clear indication for the use of open strings, especially at the beginning of a piece when they are likely to be perfectly in tune. The opening of *Sonata quarta* by Schmelzer re-iterates the trumpet call figure d^1-a^1 three times before moving into more melodic mode. Many 17th-century canzonas start with a simple rising fourth or fifth where an open string would

---

[3] (1752) tr. Reilly, p. 266

sound clearer and simpler than a stopped note (Roger North's 'old way' as used in consort music). We can learn much about this subject by examining the works for violin in scordatura (part 4.2). Where 'hand-grip' notation is used, this shows the player exactly which notes are to be played with open strings, thus demonstrating their constant use. In 17th-century consort and dance music, North's 'old way' of using open strings was common, and contributed much beauty of resonance to the old-fashioned sound which had more in common with viol sonority than the more advanced technique of the developing Italian school of violin playing.

Zannetti's *Il Scolaro* (1645) gives simple dance tunes in violin tablature, showing the 4th finger only used on the top string, or for a flattened note on the string below ($e^{\flat 2}$). The conclusion that the 4th finger was never used on the lower strings is a dangerous one to draw from this evidence, as this material was designed to be played by beginners. However, Mersenne in his description of the performance of fast divisions describes the use of:

> . . . the three fingers of the left hand, that is the index, the middle, and the third fingers, must be placed so close to the string that one wishes to play on, that they only lack a half-line till they touch, so that this small distance does not impede the velocity of the fingering and ornamentation at all.
>
> *(1636) Livre Quatriesme*, pp. 183-4

Does he omit to mention the 4th finger deliberately, or would the figuration for this type of division not include the fourth finger? It is quite possible that many 'fiddlers' using popular tunes and their divisions as their main repertoire would not have used the fourth finger. Complicated figuration in fast division or written out ornamentation passages, such as found in sonatas by the virtuoso violinists of the first part of the century Castello and Uccellini, would seem to demand the use of the 4th finger where the passage ascends only as far as the 5th above the string being played upon. It would certainly be needed where the hand needed to ascend into the higher positions.

Trills are perfectly acceptable on an open string. Indeed, Tartini (whose music contains much technically advanced material) gives us an exercise for just this technical problem. The exercise (ex. 1.5.28) is for the improvement of the trill at various speeds, starting on an open string:

> Begin with an open string, either the first or the second, it will be equally useful; sustain the note in a swell, and begin the shake very slow, encreasing in quickness, by insensible degrees, till it becomes rapid.
>
> (1771) tr. Jacobi, p. 137

Quantz recommends avoiding open strings when playing in unison with other parts, 'particularly the fifths on the violin.'[4] The risk of them being out of tune is obviously uppermost in his mind.

Harmonics

These are not generally used in Baroque music, and only then towards the end of the period. Leopold Mozart describes the

> . . . intermingling of the so-called flageolet . . . a really laughable kind of music and, owing to the dissimilarity of tone, one fights against nature herself and which becomes at times so faint that one must prick one's ears to hear it.
>
> (1756) V.13, tr. Knocker, p. 101

A footnote (1) to this paragraph recommends that

> . . . he who wishes to make a flageolet heard on the violin, will do well to write his own Concerto or Solo thereon, and not to mix them with the natural violin-tone.

Le Blanc also mocks the use of an effect which produces such a feeble tone:

---

[4] (1752) XVII.VII.3, tr. Reilly, p. 266

2.2 Fingering choice and position changing

> What is this imitation of the Flageolet by the Violin in the uppermost regions or even beyond the heavens, if not sounds without resonance, whose tinyness does not correspond at all to the roundness of the tones of the lower positions.
>
> (1740) tr. Garvey Jackson (1975), p. 25

Naturally, these statements reveal the fact that players did indeed use harmonics. However, they were clearly regarded as being in bad taste. However, Mondonville states that most violinists dread the higher positions, and advocates the use of harmonics to avoid moving the hand, marking the positions of the hand in first position to find the resulting high notes.[5]

Upward range

Corelli's *Sonatas* opus 5, published in 1700, although a milestone in the solo violin literature, have a limited range upwards. He frequently uses d^3 in third position, but on only three occasions goes further to e^3 in the *sonate da chiesa*, and never further than d^3 in the *sonate da camera*. Burney reports a conversation with a friend of Geminiani's who relates that Corelli

> was desired to lead in the performance of a masque composed by Scarlatti, which was to be executed before the King; this he undertook, but from Scarlatti's little knowledge of the violin, the part was somewhat aukward and difficult: in one place it went up to F; and when they came to that passage, Corelli failed, and was unable to execute it.
>
> (1789) vol. II, p. 439

English gentlemen musicians such as Anthony a Wood were astonished at the playing of the north German immigrant Baltzar (c1630-63) when

> playing in consort or division he would run up his fingers to the end of the fingerboard of his violin and run them back insensibly.
>
> Shute, p. 13

Geminiani gives a variety of position changing exercises on all the strings. The use of higher positions on the lower strings is now encouraged.

Ex. 2.2.4 *f*

Geminiani:

> E contains several different Scales, with the Transpositions of the Hand, which ought to be made both in rising and falling. It must here be observed, that in drawing back the Hand from the 5th, 4th and 3rd Order to go to the first, the Thumb cannot, for want of time, be placed in its natural Position; but it is necessary it should be replaced at the second Note.
>
> (1751), Essempio 1D

In other words, the fingers descend to the new position (order) first, and the thumb follows. The position of the thumb when ascending always remains behind the fingers:

---

[5] *Les Sons Harmoniques, Sonates à violon seul avec la basse continue* op. 4 (1738) quoted in Riley (1954) p. 139

2.2 Fingering choice and position changing

> After having been practised in the First Order, you must pass on to the second, and then to the third; in which Care is to be taken that the Thumb always remain farther back than the Fore-finger; and the more you advance in the other Orders the Thumb must be at a greater Distance till it remains almost hid under the Neck of the Violin.
>
> (1751), Essempio 1C

When to change position

Le Blanc recommends that:

> The proper shift of the hand has the same effect as the taking of a breath, when the sense of a phrase is managed without interruption.
>
> (1740) tr. Garvey Jackson (1974), p. 40

The best places to change position include:

1. **When an open string is being played.** Recommended by Leopold Mozart:

    > If, however, one is no longer constrained to remain in the position, one must not instantly run headlong down, but await a good and easy opportunity to descend in such fashion that the listener does not perceive the change. This can be most conveniently achieved if you wait for a note which can be taken on the open string, when the descent can be made quite comfortably.
    >
    > (1756) VIII.I.16, tr. Knocker, p. 138

2. At a convenient point of articulation, e.g. during a dotted note.

    > After a dot, too, the descent can be made very conveniently. At the dot the bow is lifted, during which the hand is moved and the note F taken in the natural position.
    >
    > (1756) VIII.I.19, tr. Knocker, p. 139

    Ex. 2.2.5

3. At the start of a pattern which is being repeated in a sequence, either rising or falling.

    > If several notes be written above the note E, then the hand must be moved. With even notes ascending consecutively tone for tone, beginning with the first finger on A, the changes of position must be made each time with the first and second fingers. For example:
    >
    > (1756) VIII.I.9, tr. Knocker, p. 135

Ex. 2.2.6: from (1756) VIII.III.4, VIII.II.5, VIII.I.9, tr. Knocker, pp. 150, 143, 135

2.2 Fingering choice and position changing

> And if there be ascending notes, one of which, however, descends previously each time by a sixth, then such notes should usually be taken with the first finger. [Last example above].
>
> But look carefully whether the passage progresses still farther into the heights or whether perchance it returns again; and whether the first finger has to be moved up once more; or whether the highest tone can be reached by the fourth finger. It would be an error if in the first [which follows] example the note G (*) were taken with the first finger, for it can be foreseen that the third and fourth fingers can, in any case, reach the highest two notes.
>
> (1756) VIII.I.9, tr. Knocker, p. 135

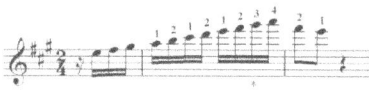

Ex. 2.2.7

Geminiani's Essempio XII shows fingering patterns for sequences in 4th, 3rd and 2nd positions, showing the phrase structure.[6]

Ex. 2.2.8 *f*

4. Between two notes of the same pitch. Leopold Mozart:

   > When two similar notes occur consecutively, they afford very good opportunity for descending. The first note must be taken in the upper position while the second note is played in the natural position. For example: [the last two notes] *

Ex. 2.2.9

   > In this manner the note, already heard in the higher position, will not be so easily played out of tune in the ensuing change, but on the contrary, the fourth finger will in its course be placed the more certainly on the second B, in consequence of the second finger having previously indicated its place in the whole position.
   >
   > (1756) VIII.I.18, tr. Knocker, p. 139

5. Between slurs. It is not good practice to change position during a slur. The result would be an interruption of the smoothness required when slurring notes together. A string-crossing is usually preferable to a position change under a slur.

Sonority

Playing in low positions with maximum vibrating string length gives greater clarity and resonance.

This example from Geminiani shows the use of third position for a special *piano* effect.

---

[6] (1751) p. 17

Ex. 2.2.10 f

The history of positions and technical advancement

The nomenclature for the various positions used in ascending the fingerboard of the violin varies considerably, and can be somewhat confusing. Prelleur's 'half-shift' (1731) is the same as 2nd position, and the whole shift is to 3rd position. Falck instructs the player to place the 1st finger on a^2 when the notes cannot be reached in the ordinary position.[7] Obviously in Nürnberg, where this treatise was published, the violin literature was more challenging at this early date, (see table p. 81) with the Bohemian school of violin playing providing a rich and technically advanced source of material to study. Tessarini calls the positions changes 'transports or transpositions' of the hand, by a 3rd, 4th or octave.[8] Geminiani also uses the term 'transposition' in his tutor. Tartini recommends to his pupil in a letter that any violin part be practised entirely in one position, presumably to familiarise the player with the fingering patterns and intonation adjustments needed for playing in various positions, including the lower strings.[9]

Musical solutions to the position changing problem can usually be found by seeking various clues in the music which offer an opportunity to shift cleanly without the listener being aware of the manoeuvre. These indicators are described above. As the 17th century progressed, the range of solo music extended upwards and made more frequent use of the G string as string technology improved. Unfortunately there are few examples of very early fingering which extend beyond the basic hand position (these mainly in tablature and written for beginners), but as violin technique developed through the 18th century, more elaborate instructions may be found.

CASE STUDIES: LARGER SHIFTS

Larger shifts where the whole hand moves at once may only be accomplished when the fingers are not required, for example when playing open strings, during rests, or at points of phrasing. Otherwise, use small position changes wherever possible.

Ex. 2.2.11: Schmelzer, Sonata no. 3

Ex. 2.2.12: Schmelzer, Sonata no. 4

Ex. 2.2.12a: J. S. Bach, Christmas Oratorio, 1st chorus

---

[7] *Idea Boni Cantoris* (1688) quoted in Riley (1954), p. 245
[8] *Gramatica di Musica* (Urbino 1741) quoted in Riley (1954), p. 308
[9] (1760) in (1771). tr. Jacobi

2.2 Fingering choice and position changing

Audible slides

The practices of using portamento and changing positions using an audible slide do not come into use until after the period under discussion.[10] Sliding the finger between two notes a semitone apart may be used occasionally as a special effect in a particularly tormented chromatic passage, as described by J. Rousseau (see p. 56). Quantz prefers to emphasise chromatic movement with the bow, and use the adjacent finger (normally the second note in a slur would be played more quietly).

Range: ensembles

During the first half of the 17th century the range upwards and downwards for contrapuntal ensemble music was fairly limited, and the use of the violin G string unusual. The top violin and viola parts in consorts and most orchestral music seldom moved more than one note out of 1st position (c^3 on the violin, f^2 on the viola). It is not good practice to play in a position higher than necessary. Leopold Mozart (1756) recommends the half position (our 2nd position) for pieces or passages in C or F where the top note is c^3. An extension 4th finger or 2nd position is recommended if only one note out of 1st position occurs. In consort or contrapuntal music, where no specific instrument is specified (or even where it is), parts of the consort fall within the middle to upper range of the instrument. If a player finds himself constantly playing on the lower strings, it is likely that another instrument of a lower tessitura would be more suitable for that part. However, in five-part 'French' orchestral writing, the three viola parts which make up the middle harmonic part of the ensemble are confined respectively to the upper, middle or lower part of the instrument. Most viola parts of this type, as found in the music of Lully, will only use two strings for most of the time. The smallest sized violas therefore need to be placed at the top of the viola band, and the largest at the bottom. In this way the instruments are being used for the range where their sounds are most resonant and efficient. Only the first viola part will ever go out of 1st position, and then usually only to f^2, in which case 2nd position should be used, not 3rd. The early models of violins and violas, with their thicker shorter necks make moving into 3rd position much more inconvenient than a semitone shift to 2nd.

Range: solo repertoire

In the solo violin repertoire, however, the range was much bigger. In Italian solo sonatas pre-1650, for example, the G string is exploited for special effect (*Sonata 2* by Castello), and occasionally the range reaches 5th position:

Ex. 2.2.13: Uccellini, Sonata Decima, book 5 (1649)

By the time of Biber (1644-1704), Schmelzer (*c*.1620-1680) and Walther (*c*.1650-1717), the range is frequently up to g^3. By the 1720s, Vivaldi and Locatelli take the left hand to the end of short Baroque fingerboard in order to exploit all the brilliance of the top of the instrument. In this example by Locatelli all the notes are available whilst remaining in one position. The finger on the top d^3 should be held in place to 'ring' with the open string:

---

[10] For details see Brown (1988)

2.2 Fingering choice and position changing

Ex. 2.2.14 *f*: Locatelli, L'Arte del Violino

The surviving music by Baltzar (which may be judged to illustrate his technique) only goes up to e^3, and the extremely showy prelude by him published in the second part of *The Division-violin* does not even go out of first position, although the figuration and frequent double stopping show an adventurous style. One may conclude that the reason that the technically limited gentlemen players were so impressed by his playing, depended more on his extrovert style than the written difficulties.

Highest positions

Riley summarises the advancement of highest positions used from tutors in this table:

1636	Mersenne	4th
1655	Playford	4th
1688	Falck	6th
1695	Merck	4th
1732	Prelleur	7th
1738	Corrette	7th
1740	Tessarini	7th
1751	Geminiani	7th

Riley (1954), p. 352

Position terminology

Riley's table of position nomenclature reveals the potential confusion which may arise when reading different treatises:

Position	Prelleur	Tessarini	Geminiani	Tartini
1st			1st order	
2nd	1/2 shift	terza	2nd order	1/2 shift
3rd	whole shift	quarta	3rd order	whole shift
4th	double shift		4th order	double shift
5th			5th order	the 4th position of the hand
6th			6th order	
7th	last shift	ottava	7th order	

Riley (1954), p. 352

Leopold Mozart also calls 3rd position the whole position and 2nd, the half position.

From the latter part of the 17th and through the first half of the 18th century, technical advancements led the violinist further and further up the fingerboard. As may be seen above, the 18th-century tutors published around 1750 give exercises up to 7th position. Wagenseil's *Rudimenta Panduristae, oder: Geig-fundamenta* published in Erben in 1754 gives scales starting on the 1st finger from 2nd to 7th positions.[11] Geminiani's scalic exercises go up to a^3. However, the musical compositions in Geminiani's tutor only once go as far as f^3, and the normal range is up to d^3 in 3rd position. Obviously these tutors are trying to push the technical facility ahead to keep up with the requirements of the

---

[11] Riley (1954), p. 274

2.2 Fingering choice and position changing

violinist virtuosos such as Locatelli and Vivaldi who had already scaled these heights in their concertos published in the 1720s.

Thumb position on the cello

Thumb position was already in use in a few compositions from about 1720,[12] a fact acknowledged by Corrette in his cello tutor published in 1741 (Vivaldi's cello writing goes into this region). Corrette gives notes up to $b^{\flat 1}$, but suggested that higher notes than this were used with thumb position. Walden suggests that this technique became established in the 1730s. Lanzetti took the range to b^2 (*Sonatas* op. 1, 1736).[13] As the practice of playing violin sonatas on the cello must have taken the cellist's left hand into the higher ranges of the fingerboard, it would be a natural progression of technique to use the thumb to stabilise the hand in the higher positions. Because it is shorter than the other fingers, Corrette describes the limited possibility of using the 4th finger in lower positions even if the thumb is used instead of the index finger, but with the thumb in 4th position, the 4th finger can play notes above the half-string harmonic.[14] The use of the fourth finger in thumb position was limited at first.[15] If, however, the 5-stringed model of instrument was being used (with an additional top string tuned to e^1), higher notes would be within easy reach without leaving the normal area of the fingerboard.

Conclusion

Fingering choice should always be governed by musical considerations, never convenience. Rarely do musical factors need to be sacrificed to convenience if the player looks hard enough for a satisfactory solution. This frequently means moving to a new position in advance to avoid a particularly awkward shift. The habitual use of 1st-to-3rd position change on the violin should be re-thought in the light of musical factors involved in making choices about where to place the left hand on the fingerboard.

---

[12] *New Grove*, 'Violoncello - playing technique'
[13] Walden, p. 61
[14] Walden, p. 127
[15] W. Jos D. Wasielewski tr. Isobella S. E. Stigand (1894)

2.3 Holding the bow

Most of today's players of instruments of the early violin family hold their bows exactly as they would a modern bow, and there is no significant reason not to do so. However, the grip which became known as 'French' with the thumb placed on the frog or on the bow hair was commonly in use in the 17th century, particularly by dance bands. The Italian manner of holding the bow with the thumb on the stick only became universal as the Italian influence spread abroad at the end of the century.

Examination of iconographical evidence reveals a variety of holds, with the hand on the bow at various distances from, and adjacent to the frog. Thumbs are wrapped around the hair, and are placed on the stick. Little fingers go flying or are tucked under the stick as in the French grip. By the time of Leopold Mozart's 'error' (1756) which shows the hand some way up the stick with a protruding first finger, the method of holding the bow, more or less as modern players do now would have been almost universal.

Leopold Mozart's 'correct' position seems relaxed—the bow in a rounded hand with the thumb slightly bent. He instructs the player to hold the bow

> ... at its lowest extremity, between the thumb and the middle joint of the index finger, or even a little behind it ... The little finger must lie at all times on the bow, and never be held freely away from the stick, for it contributes greatly to the control of the bow and therefore to the necessary strength and weakness, by means of pressing or relaxing
>
> ... The first, namely, the index-finger, must however not be streched too far over the bow or too far from the others. One may, at times, hold the bow with the first or second joint of the index-finger, but the stretching out of the index-finger is at all times a serious error. For in that way the hand stiffens because the nerves are taut, and the bowing becomes laboured and clumsy; yea, right awkward, as it must then be performed by the whole arm.
>
> (1756) II.5, tr. Knocker, p. 58

> The bow is grasped in the right hand at the lower part (not too far from the nut attached below at its extremity) by the thumb and the middle joint of the index-finger, or even a little behind it; not stiffly but lightly and freely.
>
> (1787) in (1756) II.5, tr. Knocker, p. 58 fn. 1

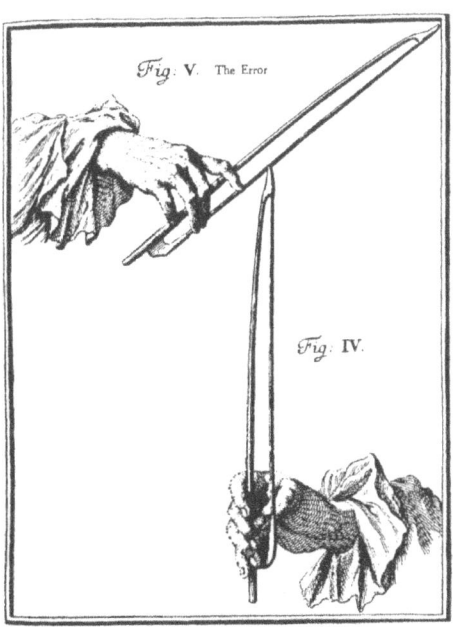

Ex. 2.3.1 *f*: Leopold Mozart (1756)

The importance of the index finger in controlling the tone by pressing and releasing is stressed.

2.3 Holding the bow

Geminiani on the other hand recommends that the bow

> ... be held at a small distance from the nut, between the thumb and fingers, the hair being turned inward against the back or outside of the thumb ... The bow must always be drawn parallel with the bridge, (which can't be done if it is held stiff) and must be pressed upon the strings with the forefinger only, and not with the whole weight of the hand.
>
> (1751), p. 2

The distance of the hand from the frog is also disputed by viol players using the underhand grip as may be seen by Mace's comments:

> I must confess, that for *my own Part*, I could never *Use It so well* as when I held It 2 or 3 *Inches off the Nut* (more or less) according to the *Length or Weight of the Bow*, for *Good Poyzing of It*.
>
> (1676), p. 248

The French grip

Playford:

> The bow is held in the right hand, between the ends of the Thumb and the three first Fingers, the Thumb being staid upon the Hair at the Nut, and the three Fingers resting upon the Wood.
>
> (1674), p. 114

The French grip must have been in common use in England in the 17th century. Lenton also describes the French grip:

> Hold it [the bow] with your thumb half under the nutt, half under the hair from the nutt, and let it rest upon the middle of the first joynt, place all your fingers upon the bow, pretty close (or for the better guiding of it) you may place the out-side of the first joynt of the little finger against the wood.
>
> (1694), p. 11

This must have been the custom in England until the great Italian violinist Matteis arrived and changed things. North tells us that

> he taught the English to hold the bow by the wood onely and not to touch the hair, which was no small reformation.
>
> J. Wilson, p. 309

Matteis was using a much longer bow than the English had been accustomed to, and this probably had a strong influence on the English violinists of the early 18th century. The sonatas of Corelli were in circulation soon afterwards, and must have helped to persuade players to accept the advantages of the new grip and the longer bow.

The French grip was used for heavily accented dance music, and this hold was in use well into the next century for this style of playing. Considering its limitations, it is surprising that the French bow-hold was still in use when Corrette published his method in 1738. The restrictions of this hold are evident to anyone who attempts to play using it, but to do this is a valuable exercise in understanding the way dance music was played. The French grip is most effective when used with a very short bow, with the hair under quite high tension to take the heavily accented strokes. When the violin is held on the shoulder, the French bow-hold restricts the arm and it is interesting to experiment with the violin held lower down against the breast, the position adopted by most dancing masters. Lifting the bow off the string is quite difficult anywhere except very near the frog, demonstrating that very short bow-strokes were the common currency of the dancing master.

In his description of the French grip, Muffat uses the word *serrant*, which can be variously translated as pressing or squeezing the hair. Some readers have interpreted this 'pressing' of the hair as evidence of a technique to increase the tension of the hair with the thumb (as is possible with the fingers in the under-hand bow-hold), but if Corrette's diagram (below) is examined, the position of the thumb is more or less on the frog, where pressing the hair to obtain extra tension is not an option, as it is already lying fixed in the open frog channel. Muffat describes the French grip being used in Germany:

> The majority of German violinists and other players of upper string instruments hold the bow as the French [Lullists] do, pressing the hair with the thumb and resting the other fingers on the stick of the bow; the French hold it the same way when playing the bass. The Italians, among others, differ in playing these upper instruments, in that they never touch the hair.
>
> (1698) tr. Cooper & Zsako, p. 223

Ex. 2.3.2 *f*

Corrette describes both the French and Italian violin bow-holds by means of the above diagram.[16] The instruction for the French hold shows the first three fingers placed on the stick (CDE) and the fourth under the stick in opposition (G). The thumb is placed on the hair which lies freely in the open frog (F). This bow-hold necessarily means that the hand is at the lower extremity of the bow in order that the little finger may be placed in the position indicated. For the Italian hold, the position of the thumb is opposite the first finger (BA), and the whole hand is placed 'three-quarters of the way down' the bow. He says 'these two ways of holding the bow are equally good depending on the teacher'. The bow should be angled a little towards the fingerboard.[17]

L'Abbé le fils differs from the above in that he recommends that the thumb be placed opposite the middle finger 'for sustaining the weight of the bow'.[18]

See also Penny Schwarz, 'Two aspects of Baroque Violin Technique, Part I: The Frog Hold.' *Journal of the Violin Society of America*, Summer 2006, pp. 189-207.

The Italian grip

It is clear from the frontispiece of Geminiani's method and from Corrette's bow-hold diagram that the Italian hold was a short distance away from the frog. This is surprising as the Italian *arcata* (the long bow stroke) was much praised and admired and it might be expected that every inch of the bow would be used. Geminiani states that 'the best performers are least sparing of their bow'.[19] If the bow is held some distance from the frog, its length is reduced considerably. Both Leopold Mozart and Geminiani emphasise that pressure emanates from the forefinger, and only L'Abbé mentions the middle finger

---

[16] (1738), p. 7
[17] (1738), p. 7
[18] (1761), p. 1
[19] (1751), p. 2

for controlling the bow. The normal bow-hold used today is similar to the Italian hold described by Geminiani and others in the 18th century.

Position of the elbow

Leopold Mozart recommends:

> One must, however watch the right arm of the pupil unremittingly; that the elbow, while drawing the bow, be not raised too high, but remains always somewhat near to the body.
>
> (1756) II.3, tr. Knocker, p. 57

Tension of the hair

The tapering design of the Baroque bow means that the focus of tone production is nearer to the middle than in a Tourte-style bow which is designed to even out the sound all the way to the point. As the player will be using more pressure and a slower bow-speed to make a full-bodied sound, it may be necessary to use more tension with the Baroque bow than the player is accustomed to when using a modern bow. The inward curvature of the modern bow means that the hair is still quite close to the stick when under tension. A Baroque-style bow will need a greater distance between the hair and stick in the middle to attain the tension needed to accommodate for the extra weight and pressure used in playing.

The cello bow-hold

The cello bow-hold was influenced by the variety of bass instruments in use. The under-hand bow-hold (as used by viol players) must have been used by many cellists, sometimes alongside the new Italian hold and both may have been employed by players to suit different types of music. Corrette describes three ways of holding the bow: the Italian hold with the hand a little way from the nut, the thumb on the hair, and the thumb on the nut.[20] Burney describes a visit to a church in Padua where 'the famous old Antonio Vandini' was playing. He comments:

> It is remarkable that Antonio, and all the other violoncello players here, hold the bow in the old-fashioned way, with the hand under it.
>
> (1770) *The Present State of Music in France and Italy in Dr. Burney's Musical Tours in Europe*
> ed. Scholes vol. 1, p. 104

Smith in his article 'The Cello Bow held the Viol-Way; Once Common, But Now Almost Forgotten' suggests that Burney implies that the under-hand way of playing was the normal old-fashioned way of holding the bow. Vandini had been cello master at the Pietà in Venice where Vivaldi was employed in 1720-21, and was Tartini's accompanist for many years, proof that this hold was not only used by dance musicians, but also by great soloists, possibly also to perform concertos. The main disadvantage of the under-hand grip is the difficulty of lifting the bow off and replacing it on the string. In putting the bow on the string with the under-hand hold, the assistance of gravity, combined with the fine finger control balancing the stick available with the over-hand method is missing. However, the under-hand method gives a continuous sound capable of delicate nuances in a slightly different way from the type of pressure exerted by the arm and hand in the over-hand way. Fast string crossings often found in Italian arpeggiated bass lines are easier with the under- hand hold, as the forward bow on the bottom string propels the bow towards the top strings in a simpler movement.

Today, many Baroque cellists hold their bows at some distance from the frog (Corrette's Italian hold), to give extra articulation, but with this method precious inches of bow are

---

[20] (1741) quoted in Riley (1954), p. 120

thereby lost. If the Italian *cantabile arcata* technique is required, the hand should retreat further towards the frog to free the whole bow length.

Factors which should be taken into account when playing with the over-hand grip are: the length and balance of the bow, the music to be performed and its demands for the long or articulated stroke. Certainly, for the performance of a convincing *messa di voce*, the whole bow length is required, as the soft beginning followed by a swelling of the sound demand fine control of pressure which is difficult to achieve if the stroke starts too far from the frog.

The double bass bow-hold

There are still several methods of bow-hold in use today in the double bass department. The over-hand French method with a short, heavy violin or cello type design of bow is common in England, France, Italy and parts of Scandinavia. Players in Germany, Austria, U.S.S.R. and most of the U.S.A. prefer the German bow with a deeper frog which is held in the hand.[21] Examination of the iconography of the Baroque period reveals a mixture of bow-holds, over- and under-hand. In Italy a strong outward curved bow developed in the late 18th century, held from the side in the present day Czech and German style. The down-bow is the strong stroke with this type of bow, and because of its greater volume it was championed by Dragonetti who was famous for his large sound.

---

[21] *New Grove*, 'Double Bass'

2.4 The rule of down-bow

Charpentier's rule of strong and weak beats suggests that the inequality of the down- and up-bow should match the hierarchy of beats in a bar:

> Note that there are strong and weak beats in music. In a measure with four beats, the first and third beats are strong, the second and fourth are weak. In a measure with two beats, the first is strong and the second is weak. In a measure with three beats, all the beats are equal; if desired, the second and third can be weak, but the first is always long.

(1692) in Cessac, p. 398

Ex. 2.4.1 ƒ: Corrette, L'Ecole d'Orphée (1738), p. 34

The natural pull of gravity combined with the varied emphasis required to perform Baroque music is responsible for the evolution of a system of bowing rules which follows the 'strong down-bow, weak up-bow' principle. The above example shows the use of the basic rule of down-bow. T for *tirer* (down-bow) and P for *poussez* (up-bow) were the commonly used bowing signs in France.

Ex. 2.4.2 ƒ: Zannetti, Il Scolaro (1645), pp. 42, 10

The above examples show some of the earliest printed bowing instructions. The elementary tutor for the violin by Zannetti uses the French signs to indicate bow direction, and by so doing, the strong and weak beats. Even without bar-lines, we can tell from the bowing instructions that the first example starts on a main beat, with a tucked-in up-bow on the weak crotchet marked 'P'. The second example starts on a weak *poussez* up-beat. This approach to bowings was probably in use for all music for bowed instruments since the viola da braccio family came into being in the early 16th century, and continued in use as the main method of choice of bow direction right up until the mid-18th century. As a result of the demands of the music, the development of the bow towards the Tourte model evened out the natural differences between up- and down-bow strokes. Notes were referred to as *buono* or 'good' (for the strong down-bow notes) and *cattivo* or 'bad' (for weak up-bow notes) by many writers, up to and including Geminiani.

Orchestral discipline

During the 17th century several orchestra directors (notably Lully, Corelli and Buxtehude) developed a sense of responsibility for the strict uniform enforcement of conventional bowing rules in their orchestras. Burney, the musical historian, describes Corelli's ensemble discipline, related to him by Corelli's pupil, Geminiani:

> Corelli regarded it as essential to the ensemble of a band, that their bows should all move exactly together, all up, or all down; so that at his rehearsals, which constantly preceded every public performance of his concertos, he would immediately stop the band if he discovered one irregular bow.
>
> (1789), p. 443

Buxtehude's discipline was probably essential in a violin band of twenty to thirty players:

> but all these instrumentalists must not . . . bow otherwise than he has directed.
>
> Snyder, p. 386

Lully's performances were legendary throughout Europe. Muffat describes the effect they had on him:

> The style of playing *airs de ballets* on string instruments in the manner of the late, most famous Monsieur Battiste de Lully, here understood in all its purity and acclaimed by the best musicians in Europe, is so ingenious a study that one can scarcely imagine anything more precise, more agreeable, or more beautiful.
>
> (1698) tr. Cooper & Zsako, p. 222

The rules

Muffat wrote down the rules which Lully had codified, and they remain the model for most basic Baroque bowing practices in dance music. The influence of these rules extends to all types of music which are dance-based, but they should not be applied universally without thought, and particularly not to music with a contrapuntal flavour, or in the Italian style (see part 3.1 Identifying national style). In naming the down-bow *nobile* and the up bow *vile*, Muffat may have been responsible for the signs n and v used today to indicate bow direction.[22] Muffat's bowing rules are very clearly explained:[23]

> Muffat rule 1: The first note in each measure, where there is no rest or breath should be played down-bow, regardless of its value. This is the principal and almost indispensible rule of the Lullists, on which almost the entire secret of bowing depends, and which differentiates them from the others. All subsequent rules depend on this rule. In order to know how the other notes fall into place and are to be played, one must attend to the following rules.

Ex. 2.4.3: Muffat on the Lully style of performance

The above example shows what should happen when there is a rest on the strong beat.

> Muffat rule 2: In common time, which the theorists call 'tempus imperfectum', the measure is divided equally in half. Notes on odd parts of the measure (1, 3, 5, etc.) are

---

[22] Snyder, p. 386
[23] *Premieres observations sur la maniere de jouër les airs de balets a la françoise selon la methode de feu Monsieur de Lully*. All Muffat's bowing rules (1698) quoted here are tr. Cooper and Zsako from *MQ* (1967) pp. 222-230. Other translations may be found in MacClintock (1979), pp. 297-303, in Strunk (1998), pp. 140-147 and in Muffat's writings trans. D.K. Wilson. The complete text (in French) may be consulted in Lully: complete works preface to *Les Ballets*, vol. 1 (*Ballet de l'Amour Malade*), pp. xxvii-xliii.

2.4 The rule of down-bow

played down-bow, and those on even parts (2, 4, 6, etc.) should be played up-bow. The rule applies also in triple meter, or any meter where the beats are diminished equally in half. I call diminutions all those notes that are faster than those values indicated in the time signature. This way of counting equal divisions of beats is similarly observed if rests of the same value appear instead of notes. All the finest masters agree readily with the French on this second rule.

This last comment introduces a hint of doubt about the universal acceptance of these rules, suggesting that there may have existed some masters who did not entirely agree with certain of them, and that there was some dissention from the Lullists' position. The English violinist Lenton may have been one of the dissenting masters:

> It would be a difficult undertaking to prescribe a general rule for bowing, the humours of Masters being very Various, and what is approved by one would be condemned by another.
>
> (1694), p. 7

Playford:

> *The Method of Bowing in* Common Time
>
> The different opinions of Masters concearning this point, renders it extreamly difficult to lay down any certain Rules for this purpose, never the less for the Encouragement of learners it may not be improper to produce some few that have been Generally receiv'd.
>
> (1701), [Instructions p. 6]

Playford (1701) differs from Muffat by taking another down-bow for any groups of four quavers starting on a weak beat, where Muffat would *craquer* with two up-bows (ex. 2.4.5)

> because the first of an even number of Quavers must be with a down
>
> (1701), [Instructions p. 6]

He gives tucked-in down-bows for short notes after dotted notes (contradicting Muffat, ex. 2.4.7), however, Playford does use the lifted down-bow retake in triple time, as in Muffat (ex. 2.4.4). He is happy to bow out consecutive triple-time bars in crotchets because

> ... 'twill be smoother to play 'em down and up
>
> (1701), [Instructions p. 6]

Prelleur's tutor, also published in London, is equally luke-warm about slavish adherence to the rules, however he does give his own rule which follows basic weak/strong beat emphasis:

> It is difficult to lay down any certain rules for the use of the bow by reason the direction of divers Masters and the methods of Practitioners are very different ... At the beginning of many Lessons you will meet with an odd Note excluded from the others by the first bar, which must be always struck with an up Bow.
>
> (1731), p. 8

Prelleur continues with the rule of down-bow following fairly closely the rules as written by Muffat, including the use of the double down-bow in triple time (see below, rule 3). The French school of playing, which followed the rules without question (or by disciplined enforcement) was regarded with a certain amount of circumspection by other violinists of the time. Different bowing customs evolved in the rest of Europe and in Italy in particular, where the Italian style of composition was less dependant on dance forms, which by their nature make use of a strong down-beat accent. French influences, and with them the French bowing practices, reached Germany and England, infiltrating the music of Purcell, J. S. Bach and Telemann. Let us continue for the moment with Muffat's rules:

> Muffat rule 3: Since, according to the first rule, the first note in the measure is down-bow, the second of three equal notes (which comprise a complete measure in triple time) is always up-bow, and the third is once again down-bow, at least when one plays rather slowly; therefore in beginning the measure following, one must play down-bow for the second time in succession.

2.4 The rule of down-bow

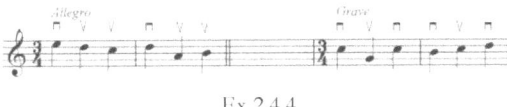

Ex 2.4.4

The double down-bow, shown above in the Grave example, feels and looks awkward at first. However, Muffat recommends the use of it only in slow tempos. When the tempo moves a little faster, Muffat allows the third beat to be taken on another up-bow, as the Allegro example shows above.

> More often, however, the second and third notes are played in the same up-bow stroke, divided distinctly in two. This is called *craquer*. It allows the measure to go a little faster with greater ease.

Adjustments are often needed to accommodate the rule of down-bow. Muffat's *craquer* (a broken up-bow with two notes):

Ex 2.4.5

This would be executed as a tucked in up-bow, or broken slur, without taking the bow off the string. Several writers, J. Rousseau amongst them, allow very fast (quaver or semiquaver) *craquer* pairs of up-bow notes to be slurred, if there is no time to stop the bow to break the pair. In the following example from L'Abbé le fils the two up-bows are played *craquer* in the manner described by Muffat nearly a century earlier, and bring the bow in the right direction for the down-beat. Even at this relatively late date, dance music still uses the strong and weak bowings. Note the marked 4th finger where notes continue to descend.

Ex. 2.4.6 *f*: L'Abbé le fils (1761), p. 4

The short note after the dotted note is usually tucked into an up-bow, and hardly ever on the down-bow. Muffat's example:

Ex. 2.4.7

For syncopations off strong beats Muffat provides the following bowing:

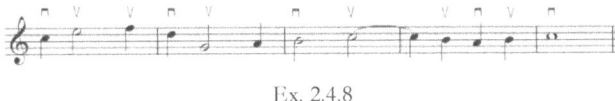

Ex. 2.4.8

The c in the middle of bar 3 might be better on a retake down-bow if there is a strong dissonance on the down-beat of bar 4.

♪ Tracks 5-6, 18-24, 34-36 for dances using the rule of down-bow.

Even bowing

Towards the end of the Baroque period, as the hierarchy of the bar broke down, and the strict application of the rule of down-bow was disappearing, Quantz (1752), Tartini (1770) and Geminiani (1751), all suggest practicing the 'wrong' direction of bow, to strengthen the up-bow and even out the differences between up- and down-bow.

2.4 The rule of down-bow

Quantz:
> To make your bow-strokes uniform, and to make yourself equally familiar with the up and down movements, practise a Gigue or Canarie in six-eight time which proceeds in quavers, and in which the first of each three of these quavers is dotted. Give each note its separate stroke, so that, without repeating strokes, the first and third notes of each figure first receive down-strokes, then up-strokes; and always play the note after the dot very short and sharply.
>
> Although certain notes must necessarily be taken with a down-stroke, an experienced violinist with the bow completely under control can also express them well with an up-stroke. This freedom of the bow must not be abused, however, since on certain occasions, that is, if one note requires considerably more sharpness than the others, the down-stroke remains superior to the up-stroke.
>
> (1752) XVII.II.11, tr. Reilly, pp. 222-3[24]

Tartini:
> ... you first play with the point of the bow; and when that becomes easy to you, that you use that part of it which is between the point and the middle; and when you are likewise mistress of this part of the bow, that you practise in the same manner in the middle of the bow; and above all, you must remember in these studies to begin the allegros or flights sometimes with an up-bow, and sometimes with a down-bow, carefully avoiding the habit of constantly practising one way.
>
> (1760) in (1771) tr. Jacobi

Geminiani:

Ex. 2.4.9 *f*: Geminiani (1751), Essempio XXIV, p. 33

The above exercise by Geminiani evens out the up and down-bow strokes. g stands for *giu* down-bow (above the stave), and s for *su*, up-bow (below the stave), for the repeat of the extract with the reverse bowing.

Dotted notes

Leopold Mozart says:
> In quick pieces the bow is lifted at each dot ... and performed in a springing style.
>
> (1756) I.III.10, tr. Knocker, p. 41

He gives bowings for dotted rhythms. When there are four notes in a group,
> ... if the first and third note be dotted, each note is played separately and with a special stroke, in such manner that the three-stroked notes [demi-semi-quavers in a dotted semi-quaver rhythm] are played very late and the following note played immediately after it with a swift change of bow.
>
> (1756) IV.13, tr. Knocker, p. 77

Quantz:
> The semi-quavers following the dots must always be played very short and sharply in slow and quick tempos; and since dotted notes generally express something of the majestic and sublime, each note, if no slur stands above it, requires a separate bow-stroke; for it is not possible to express the short note after the dot as sharply with the same stroke, by detaching the bow, as can be done with a new up-stroke.
>
> (1752) XVII.II.13, tr. Reilly, p. 224

---

[24] A suitable Gigue or Canarie may be found in part 2.5

CASE STUDIES

1. The rule of down-bow

Muffat's double down-bow (ex. 2.4.4, 'grave'), which is used in a slow tempo, need not be executed with a huge retake, but can be accomplished by using a slow bow-speed to limit the distance travelled down the bow, then hardly taking the bow off the string for the re-iterated down stroke. When the weak beat (3rd beat of a menuet, for example) is played down-bow, it should be played lightly with very little bow, and should not give the impression of being an up-beat. Muffat's method of bowing a slow minuet produces a wonderful lift at the bar-line, and gives more emphasis to the first beats of the bar. Sometimes it is necessary to play three down-bows consecutively:

Ex. 2.4.10: J. S. Bach, Orchestral Suite no. 2, Menuet

This bowing would be impractical beyond a certain speed.

Following bowing rules for emphasis can have some strange results. Here is another example of three down-bows in a row: a new down-bow for the theme in the third bar is desirable, followed by the anticipated strong down beat of the next bar (assuming that this bowing is adopted from the start of the movement).

Ex. 2.4.11: J. S. Bach, Brandenburg concerto no. 4, Presto

2. The loud rest

Where there is a rest on a strong beat, an up-bow would normally be taken immediately after it. In simple or duple time, this rule is easy to follow. However, here is a situation in compound time which defies that rule:

Ex. 2.4.12: J. S. Bach, St. John Passion, 'Erwäge'

2.4 The rule of down-bow

The phenomenon of the 'loud rest' occurs frequently in accompaniment figures. If the first part of the beat (i.e. strongest) is a rest, the subsidiary parts of that beat should diminuendo from the blank beat if the same harmony is maintained. A quaver rest followed by two or three repeated notes is a frequent figure in accompaniment, and this should fade away from the main (first) part of the beat. In the above example the violas d'amore might begin down-bow after the rest, in order that the figure will fade away until the next beat (this choice would only apply in compound time). The first beat is not in fact blank in the music, as the rest in the upper parts is filled by a bass note. The violas should bounce off this strong point. This way of thinking of the music as a whole rather than one part in isolation is a valuable one to cultivate, as the harmonic structure often over-rides melodic considerations observed in only one part.

3. Syncopation

Bowings are decided upon by the hierarchy of the bar, the first beat being the strongest, but this rule can sometimes be over-ridden by a strong harmonic feature not on the first beat, or an anticipated down-beat, in which case the strong harmony or rhythmic interruption may equal the first beat in importance (see p.3 ex 1.1.2).

Beware of accenting syncopated figures which bounce off a strong beat when both notes belong to the same harmony. If the second, syncopated note is higher, players are often tempted to play this note louder, or with an accented down-bow. If both belong to the same harmony, the second note should be considered to be a weak note, of the same or less importance than the first, and should be taken up-bow (e.g. viola part bar 1).

Ex. 2.4.13: Handel, Concerto Grosso op. 6 no. 7, Hornpipe

In the following example from the fugal section of the overture from J. S. Bach's Orchestral Suite no. 2, the syncopated minims (up-bows) should bounce off the strong first note (down-bow) which has the function of a written-out appoggiatura. The last crotchet in these bars should be taken with another up-bow to arrive on the strong down-beat quaver figure with a down-bow.

Ex. 2.4.14: J. S. Bach, Orchestral Suite no. 2, Overture

4. The dactyl

The common rhythmic figure consisting of a long + 2 short notes (the dactyl) occurs sometimes as an up-beat figure, and sometimes as a down-beat figure. The quaver note may be lifted on an up-bow or emphasised on a down-bow. The choice of bowing will depend on the function of the beat (lifted up-beat or emphasised down-beat). In the following example, from Handel's *Messiah*, both functions are shown. The down/down/up bowing might be used on a trumpet-like figure where the notes remain on the same pitch.

Ex. 2.4.15: Handel, Messiah, 'Blessing and honour, glory and power, be unto him'

5. Italian bowing style

Much Italian music is composed of longer, more singing phrases. Bowing style will be more 'bowed out' with less *craquer* used to correct before the bar-line. This agrees with the Italian concept of the 'stream of sound', described by Le Blanc, uninterrupted and flowing but with nuance within the continuous line.[25] The following three examples are from Corelli's *Concerto Grosso* op. 6 no. 3, and could all be bowed out without retakes or corrections to the direction of the bow. If this bowing method is used in the allegro and vivace movements, one bar starts down-bow, and the next one up-bow. The falling tessitura gives a subtle difference of inflection in the second bar of each pair without the need for pre- arranged dynamics:

Ex. 2.4.16: Corelli, Concerto Grosso op. 6 no. 3

6. Dotted rhythms

A major technical problem for the Baroque player often occurs in the execution of dotted rhythms. The unequal nature of the bowing, where hooked down-bows are generally avoided, creates a big problem unless an intelligent bowing strategy has been worked out. Lifting the bow frequently is the stock-in-trade technique of the Baroque string player to avoid using the same amount of bow for the dot and for the short note which follows it.

However, a big retake after every dot is unnecessary, as no two successive dotted notes will be equal in importance. In a French overture type of movement, the player may try to vary the amount of retake to avoid consecutive equal accents: smaller retakes before weak beats, and larger ones before strong beats.

---

[25] (1740) tr. Garvey Jackson (1973), p. 22 quoted p. 161

2.4 The rule of down-bow

The points for larger retakes are marked in the example below. The strongest points harmonically are the first beats of bars 1 and 3. Bar 2 leads through in dynamic to bar 3, the articulation at the point of the retake giving extra emphasis to the strong down-beat of bar 3, before fading to a weak bar 4 by staying on the string and moving further down the bow. When lifting the bow so frequently, the player soon learns to be more economical with the length of bow used in order to minimise the distance to be covered when returning to the heel for the next strong stroke. The strength in the stroke is obtained by using more pressure than length.

Ex. 2.4.17: Handel, Messiah, Overture

Much English music by Purcell and his contemporaries and followers consists of movements with continuous dotted rhythms in triple time. The dotted rhythm should not be too aggressively pronounced, but 'swung' in a light-hearted tripletised manner. With a lazy dot, this rhythm may be performed by working down the bow for two or three beats on each down bow, and retaking the bow by lifting just before the next strong beat, giving one accent per bar. By this method, the bow stays on the string until just before the next bar line, and a jerky accented up-bow in every beat is avoided. Sometimes, the triple dotted bars are more definitely in a 2 beats +1 beat pattern, with the 3rd beat an up-beat to the next pattern. In which case, only 3 notes are taken in one bow length, and the retake comes before the other 3 notes in the bar. In this case, the bow is lifted after the dotted 3rd beat note—'zigzag' bow technique:

Ex. 2.4.18: Purcell, King Arthur, Chaconne (♪ track 36)

Ex. 2.4.19: Purcell, Chacony

In triple time, two or three dotted notes may be played working down the bow without retaking until the up-beat to the next strong beat. A feeling for harmonic hierarchy is indispensable for achieving this effect sensibly, and giving overall shape to the phrase from first down-beat to final cadence. This technique prevents the jerky, equally accented effect often heard in dotted movements and also avoids having a gap after every note which eliminates any sense of direction or phrasing in the music. The weak dotted notes can be played with very little bow and the stronger ones can sing out, always using the weight and depth of the bow-stroke rather than length. Bringing the focus of the bow-stroke nearer to the heel is the main difference between the modern and Baroque bow technique, and mastery of this will aid the new way of thinking and articulating. The Tourte-style bow was designed to even out the power of the stroke throughout its length. The tapering Baroque bow fades in sound towards the point, with most power in the lower-middle area.

Getting stuck in the upper half of the bow when playing dotted rhythms will result in a feeling of frustration, and in heavy up-bow semiquavers as you try to return to the heel without lifting the bow.

Here are some hints for practising dotted bow technique, and strategies to consider when playing any dotted passages of music:

1. Retaking should be practised by playing repeated down-bows of minim-length notes in the lower half, with a slow bow-speed, minimising the length of bow used to make it easier to get back to your starting point.
2. Then, add an anticipatory short up-bow note crushed immediately before each long note.
3. To play faster dotted rhythms try and remain in nearly the same spot in the bow, lifting between each dotted note and the short note which follows it. Use very small hand and arm movements to minimise the amount of bow used.
4. Avoid using the same amount of bow for the dotted note and the little note.
5. Before a strong beat, lift the bow back to the lower half for the small note up-bow, which is connected to the next main note.
6. Before a weak beat, leave the bow on the string and use a short stroke for the semiquaver and the following (weak) dotted note in the middle or upper half of the bow.
7. Try to avoid playing two consecutive dotted notes with the same weight or bow-stroke. Play strong/weak-beat dotted rhythms to practise retaking on alternate beats.

Summary: bowing rules

The bowing rules of Muffat only make sense if the technique and appropriate train of thought is in place with which to implement them. This means: economy of length of bow used; a willingness to pick up the bow and return to the heel as often as is demanded by the musical context (mainly before the next strong beat); the technique of zigzagging with minimal retake up and down the bow length to avoid gaps and emphases in the music which are not required. Use zigzag bow technique in music where many consecutive pairs of notes are in long/short groups (dotted rhythms, or crotchet/quaver movement in compound time signatures). Care should be taken not to apply the rule of down-bow in an inappropriate context: slow movements in Italian sonatas, and contrapuntal music without bar-line hierarchy.

It is important, especially when commencing to play according to the rule of down-bow, not to manipulate the bowing direction for convenience. Try to adhere to the hierarchy in the bar (first beat strongest etc.), applying the discipline to every note. Only correct the direction of the bow immediately before the note which needs to be emphasised or weakened, not a bar or so in advance, which might result in other notes becoming bowed in the 'wrong' direction.

The Muffat/Lully rules are easiest to learn and appreciate in the context of dance music: the following part 2.5 gives analysis of dance characteristics and bowings.

2.5 The dance

> Most of the authorities hold that dancing is a kind of mute rhetoric by which the orator, without uttering a word, can make himself understood by his movements and persuade the spectators that he is gallant and worthy to be aclaimed, admired and loved.
>
> Arbeau (1589), p. 16

It is impossible to get away from the dance when playing Baroque music. Types of dance movement appear in the music even when not labelled as such. This section will help the performer to recognise and identify the characteristics of each dance, in order to select an appropriate tempo and the correct affect. Many dances have French and Italian forms with different rhythmic characteristics, and the style of performance most suitable to their country of origin and date of composition will be described. Most dances are in two sections known as binary form. Normally both sections are repeated, perhaps with some ornamentation added by the performer in a suitable national style. Many dance movements include, after the repeat of the second section, an extra repeat of the final (usually 4) bars. A sign or the indication 'p.r.' indicates from where the *petite reprise* is to be taken, for example in the *Canarie à deux* by Feuillet, (ex. 2.5.7). Muffat:

> The art of playing ballets on the violin in the manner of the most celebrated Jean-Baptiste Lully is so ingenious a study that one can scarcely imagine anything more agreeable or more beautiful. To reveal to you, gracious reader, its chief secrets, know that it has at one time two aims: namely, to appeal to the ear in the most agreeable way and to indicate properly the measure of the dance, so that one may recognize at once to what variety each piece belongs and may feel in one's affections and one's feet, as it were without noticing it at all, and inclination to dance.
>
> (1698) in Strunk (1998), p. 140

Muffat continues with five considerations for the successful performance of *airs de ballet* in the French manner according to the late Monsieur Lully's method:

> First, to play in tune. Second, for all the players in the band to observe the same manner of drawing the bow. Third, to keep constant the true tempo of each piece. Fourth, to heed certain practices concerned with repetitions, interpretation of certain notes, stylistic propriety and dance-character. Finally, to know how to use with judgement beautiful decorations and appropriate ornaments, which light up the piece, as it were, like precious stones.
>
> (1698) tr. Cooper & Zsako, p. 222

My aim in this chapter is to describe the factors which the performer needs to be aware of to fulfil Muffat's aims as described above, and to find out what the performer should do to make the affect of each dance immediately recognisable. The structure of the 17th- and 18th-century suite is described, with the differences in approach which should be taken into consideration by the performer as the dance forms evolve through the period. There follows a catalogue of the most commonly occuring dances and their characteristics, emotional affects and hints for performance, including some original bowings from Muffat, Corrette and L'Abbé le fils.

The 17th-century suite

The sequence starting with a freely composed movement (fantasia or ricercar) followed by a selection of dances, was a form well known to the viol consort, and was shared and integrated into the violin family repertoire during the 17th century. The English 'fantasia-suite' for upwards of two players, sometimes with a written out organ part mostly doubling the string parts, was a standard form in domestic use. North describes the English fantasy-suite:

> During this flourishing time, it became usuall to compose for instruments in setts; that is, after a fantazia, [came] an aiery lesson of two straines, and a tripla by way of galliard, which was stately, courant, or otherwise, not unsuitable to, or rather imitatory, of the dance. Instead of the fantazia, they often used a very grave kind of

> ayre, which they called a *padoana*, or pavan; this had three strains, and each being twice played went off heavyly, especially when a rich veine failed the master. These setts alltogether very much resembled the designe of our sonnata music, being all consistent in the same key.
>
> J. Wilson, p. 295

Some pairs of dances in the early suite may be performed segue with a related pulse, but with a change in pace and character. Morley said:

> After every pavan we usually set a galliard (that is a kind of music made out of the other), causing it to go by a measure which the learned call *trochaicum rationem*, consisting of a long and short stroke successively.
>
> (1597), p. 296
> (see below ex. 2.5.24 & 25)

17th-century dance forms are slightly different in character from their later versions. In the early minuet and saraband, for example, tempi should be much faster (♪ tracks 28 and 31 for fast sarabands). The time signatures of 6/4 or 3/4 often appear in the 17th-century saraband (ex. 2.5.51). The later sarabande grave is usually in the slower 3/2 time signature. Pairs of dances are found in related duple and triple metre, such as pavan and galliard, allemande and courante, and are frequently based on the same melodic and rhythmic motifs.

The movements in the 17th-century suite are more varied than the later type and sequences frequently contain two examples of one type of dance. The order of movements might be Fancy—Alman—Galliard or Ayre—Ayre of an Allemande type and Coranto—Saraband or Minuet.

The English theatre suite of the later part of the 17th century was assembled from incidental music from plays or semi-operas into a suite which consisted of an overture followed by a number of short dances which were played between the acts (in the Purcell suites mostly eight).

♪ tracks 33-36 for music from Purcell's theatre suites; tracks 25-28 Locke, *The Broken Consort*; 29-31 Jenkins *Fantasia suite*; and 21-22 a serious pavan and galliard by Morley.

Italian dance music before the 1660s was organised by type of dance or scoring (e.g. collections by Uccellini and Cazzati). Later, Corelli's pattern of the genre (op. 2, op. 4, op. 5 nos. 7-11 and op. 6 nos. 9-12) has slow preludios or allemandas followed by dances in the general pattern fast—slow—fast. The final sonatas in op. 2 and 5 are sets of variations over a dance type ground bass (ciaccona and follia, related to the sarabande). Where dances are short, as in Purcell theatre suites, look for consecutive movements which may be linked by a common pulse. Long gaps (especially for tuning) between movements can spoil the unity of this type of suite.

The 18th-century suite or overture

The later French overture or suite consists of a grand opening, often characterised by dotted rhythms, followed by a fugal allegro section, both of which are repeated. Sometimes dotted material is re-introduced after the fugue (e.g. J. S. Bach, Orchestral Suites). There follows a series of dances, the most common choice being allemande—courante—sarabande—gigue. Pairs of the same type of dance often appear together, the second one using contrasting material, before a recapitulation of the first (often marked *alternativo*). Dances occurring in pairs among others are minuets, bourées, gavottes and passepieds. The suite, *partie* or *partia* (J. S. Bach's own title for the suites for unaccompanied violin) or *partita* consists solely of dance-style movements.

The French type of Baroque dance suite was much favoured by German composers such as J. S. Bach, Handel and Telemann.

Mattheson gives us the shape of the German 'French' suite:

> The Allemanda, as a true German invention, precedes the courante, as the latter goes before the sarabande and gigue, the sequence of which one calls a Suite.
>
> (1739) II.13.128, tr. Harriss, p. 464

2.5 The dance

The pricipal affects are described:

Overture	Lively, uplifting
Allemande	Proud, grave, slow
Courante	Hopeful, graceful
Sarabande	Ambitious, languid, majestic
Gigue	Cheerful, gay, fast
Chaconne	Proud, majestic

Lully's instructions for playing dance music (written down by Muffat) might have been inspired by the rather casual customs already in use. It is probable that most bands would have played from memory, learning repertoire by imitation through an unbroken aural tradition. With the establishment of lavish musical events at the court of Louis XIV, the larger numbers of players per part would have made it necessary to codify bowing practices for the sake of uniformity and quality of execution. The violin band repertoire was played by professionals in the theatre and for the noble classes to dance to in the ball-room. The more refined chamber repertoire using the quiet instruments such as flute, lute and viol, was used by the music masters to teach their noble pupils in more private surroundings. Louis XIV was known to have chamber music accompany his every activity from getting dressed in the morning to going to bed at night.

Did they dance to it?

Baroque music is full of dance forms, and aristocratic people of that time spent much of their copious leisure time dancing. It was certainly one of the main opportunities for social interaction and one of the principal forms of exercise. Some writers give us clues about when dance music was used for dancing, and when it was purely aural entertainment:

Muffat describes his *Florilegium* suites as

> ... composed in Passau and performed with great applause at this illustrious court, both for dancing and at many instrumental concerts.
>
> (1698) in Strunk (1950), p. 85

and

> ... for the dancing practice of noble youths.
>
> (1698) tr. Cooper and Zsako, p. 222

but his concertos in the Italian style as

> ... suited neither to the church (because of the ballet airs and airs of other sorts which they include) nor for dancing (because of other interwoven conceits, now slow and serious, now gay and nimble, and composed only for the express refreshment of the ear, may be performed most appropriately in connection with entertainments given by great princes and lords, for receptions for distinguished guests, and at state banquets, serenades, and assemblies of musical amateurs and virtuosi.
>
> (1701) Strunk (1950), p. 89

Obviously, contrapuntal 'interwoven' music was unsuitable for dancing. Mattheson, seeking a 'proper, straightforward dancing' minuet, rejected keyboard versions, and sung types. He recommended looking to French composers and

> ... their skilled imitators in Germany, among whom Telemann is the most important: as is well known.
>
> (1739) II.13.86, tr. Harriss, p. 453

The solo prelude

Sometimes a solo instrumental suite will start with a prelude, which Mace says

> is commonly a *Piece of Confused-wild-shapeless-kind of Intricate-Play*, (as most use It) in which no perfect *Form*, *Shape*, or *Uniformity* can be perceived; but a *Random-Business*, *Pottering*, and *Grooping*, up and down, from one *Stop*, or *Key*, to another; And generally, so performed, to make *Tryal*, whether the *Instrument* be *well in Tune*, or not; by which

doing, after they have *Compleated Their Tuning*, They will (if They be *Masters*) fall into some kind of *Voluntary*, or *Fansical Play*, more *Intelligible*.

(1676), p. 128

Mattheson puts in one category: Fantasie, Capricii, Toccate, and Preludes, and says

although all of these strive to appear as if they were played extempore, yet they are frequently written down in an orderly manner; but they have so few limitations and so little order that one can hardly give them another general name than good ideas. Hence also their characteristic is fancy.

(1739) II.13.132, tr. Harriss, p. 465

The dances

Allemande

Literally: German, from its origins. Also (earlier) called Alman in English. Morley called it 'a more heavy dance than the galliard.'[26] Grassineau in his Musical Dictionary (1740) described it as 'a sort of grave, solemn music, whose measure is full and moving'. By this time, the dance had become a purely instrumental movement. However, Mace says that the '*Allmaines*, are *Lessons* very *Ayrey*, and *Lively*',[27] demonstrating the faster tempo that many of these dances exhibit during the late 17th century.

Ex. 2.5.1 *f*: J. S. Bach, Partita no. 2 in D minor for violin solo

Frequently the first movement of a suite in the 18th century, the allemande is in common time, starting in the true French forms with a quaver or semiquaver up-beat which should be connected to the down-beat (often the same note). It should have a free improvisatory character within the basic pulse, with a slow tempo, especially if marked *Grave*. Mattheson says:

... the allemande is a broken, serious, and well-constructed harmony, which is the image of a content or satisfied spirit, which enjoys good order and calm.

(1739) II.13.128, tr. Harriss, p. 464

The character is serious and the semiquavers should be melodically expressive. When occurring in step-wise motion in French-style movements, semiquavers should be performed *inégales*. Called *allemanda* in Italian, this movement is much livelier than the French version and may be taken quite fast, but watch out for a tempo instruction:

Ex. 2.5.2 *f*: Corelli, Sonata op. 2 no. 6

Ex. 2.5.3 *f*: Corelli, Sonata op. 2 no. 2

---

[26] (1597), p. 297
[27] (1676), p. 129

2.5 The dance

Largo, adagio and presto tempo markings all occur in allemandas in Corelli trio sonatas op. 2. In op. 5 we find an allegro:

Ex. 2.5.4 *f*: Corelli, Sonata op. 5 no. 10

Corelli also composed allemandas and calls them preludio as in the first movement of op. 5 no. 7, an allemanda in disguise marked vivace. These examples show the freedom of an instrumental form, not tied to dance steps. Each allemande should be judged on its own affect, and fitted into context—the preceding and following dances of the suite should be taken into consideration when selecting a tempo. There is no absolutely correct speed for any dance type, even when dancers are present.

Bourée

The character of the bourée is easy-going, relaxed and not at all serious. It has a time-signature of 2 which represents 2 minims, and the tempo should be medium fast.

Ex. 2.5.5: Muffat

Muffat's instructions above bow out quavers on weak beats, and the minim is played as a rebound up-bow off the strong first beat down-bow.[28] He gives possible alternative bowings (*craquer* up-bow quavers).

Quantz says

> A *bourrée* and a *rigaudon* are executed gaily, and with a short and light bow-stroke. A pulse beat falls on each bar.
>
> (1752) XVII.VII.58, tr. Reilly, p. 291

If there is a crotchet up-beat, it should be played exactly in time and lifted slightly. The rhythm crotchet—minim—crotchet is a common occurrence and should be played with strong emphasis on the *first* note of the bar, not on the syncopated note. This is a 'rebound' syncopated note, not to be heavily accented. If *notes inégales* are applied, the quaver will be the correct note value to use, but a fast tempo will exclude this possibility. At a fast tempo, one main beat per bar is enough, and the movement should run ahead lightly, stopping for breaths at cadences. Bar 5 in the Bach example below should be bowed out according to Muffat's example above.

Ex. 2.5.6: J. S. Bach, Orchestral Suite no. 1, Bourée

Canaries

A type of gigue in fast compound time (see also gigue entry). Quantz:

> The *gigue* and the *canarie* have the same tempo. If they are in six-eight time, there is a pulse beat on each bar. The gigue is played with a short and light bow-stroke, and the canarie, which is always in dotted notes, with a short and sharp one.
>
> (1752) XVII.VII.58, tr. Reilly, p. 291

Mattheson:

> ... must have great eagerness and swiftness.
>
> (1739) II.13.102, tr. Harriss, p. 457

---

[28] (1698) tr. Cooper and Zsako, p. 229

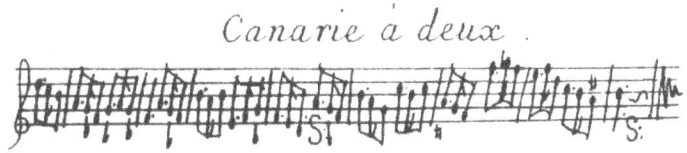

Ex. 2.5.7 *f*: Feuillet (1700)

The dotted rhythm should be bowed out, alternating up- and down-bow bars.

Ex. 2.5.8 *f*: Purcell, Dioclesian

Chaconne

Also chacona, ciaccona (Italy), chacony (England). Early forms consisted of a simple chord sequence, repeated many times with variations. Mattheson calls it

> ... the greatest among the dance melodies ... along with its brother, or its sister, the *Passagaglio*, or *Passecaille*.

He gives four characteristics to distinguish the two forms:

> ... that the *chaconne* proceeds more deliberately and slowly than the passecaille, not the other way round; that the former prefers the major keys, while the latter prefers the minor; that the *passecaille* is never used in singing, like the *chaconne*, but only for dancing, hence naturally has a quicker movement; and finally, that the *chaconne* has a constant bass theme, which, though one occasionally deviates from it for variations and from fatigue, soon reappears and maintains its position.

(1739) II.13.135, tr. Harriss, p. 465

Two examples of chaconnes which use the ground bass known as Folie d'Espagne:

Ex. 2.5.9 *f*: Playford, The Division-violin (1684)

Ex. 2.5.10 *f*: Feuillet (1700)

2.5 The dance

Quantz says it should be performed

> ... majestically. In it a pulse beat takes the time of two crotchets.
>
> (1752) XVII.VII.58, tr. Reilly, p. 291

In the following example from Corrette[29] the chaconne pattern starts again in bar 5 (the first three notes are the same.

Ex. 2.5.11 *f*: Corrette, l'École d'Orphée (1738), p. 24

Muffat gives all down-bows for one note per bar (1st example), and alternate up- and down-bows for sections of chaconnes which have only one note per bar on the off-beat (2nd example):[30]

Ex. 2.5.12: Muffat

This dance in triple metre has continuous variations over a repeated harmonic progression in similar style to the passacaglia, and sharing some of the characteristics of the sarabande (see below). It has a formula of changing bass phrases of four or eight bars in length, often with a minor section in the middle. In some earlier versions of the dance, each four-bar section is repeated (e.g. Muffat, concerto '*Armonico Tributo*' no. 5, 1682). The tempo was faster in the 17th century than the 18th, when it became grander and more dignified. It breaks the binary pattern of most dance forms, often being quite long with increasingly complex material reaching a climax before a subdued ending. If in a minor key, there is often a contrasting passage in the relative major (or a minor passage in a major key) towards the end.

The first and second beats are often of equal weight and importance, especially where the harmony changes on the second beat. If there is no significant harmonic change on the second beat, this should be played equal or weaker than the first:

Ex. 2.5.13 *f*: Purcell, King Arthur (♪ track 36)

---

[29] (1738), p. 24
[30] (1698) tr. Cooper and Zsako, pp. 226, 228

Some chaconnes begin on the second beat, some after a bass down-beat.

Ex. 2.5.14 *f*: Couperin, 3ième Concert Royal, Chaconne legere

Each subsequent phrase should mirror this shape, landing softly on the down-beat before the new phrase begins on the second beat, with direction to the following bar-line. Articulation here will be necessary, and it may also be necessary to take a new down-bow on the second beat, or try the Corrette bowing, above (up-down/down). Bach's monumental chaconne in the D minor Partita for solo violin has a second beat start, and must claim to be the high point for the genre. It may be distant from the danced form in tempo, in complexity and in its development of the basic chaconne structure, but in the performance of any chaconne, it is important to maintain the harmonic structure clearly, regardless of any fanciful variations, and keep a dance swing to the rhythm.

Coranto - Corrente - Courante

Meaning 'running', or more appropriately in the slower French version 'flowing', there are various types reflected in the different terms: coranto, corrente and courante.

Coranto

17th-century English corantos in the Italian style are according to Mace

> ... of a *Shorter Cut* [than galliards], and of a *Quicker Triple-Time*, commonly of 2 *Strains*, and full of *Sprightfulness*, and *Vigour*, *Lively*, *Brisk*, and *Cheerful*.
>
> (1676), p. 129

Corrente

Ex. 2.5.15 *f*: Corelli, Sonata op. 2 no. 6

The later Italian type of corrente (Corelli above, and Couperin below) is likely to be in 3/4 time and with more running quaver figures (also J. S. Bach, cello suite no. 1, Partita for solo violin no.1). It is principally an instrumental composition, not designed to be used for dancing, and can be a real 'show-off' piece especially if coupled with a 'double' (J. S. Bach, Partita no. 1). Couperin wrote French and Italian style courantes. The Italian type is similar to the corrente in style. Notice the time signatures, and the different type of note values used:

2.5 The dance

Ex. 2.5.16 f: Couperin, 4ième concert, Courantes Françoise and a L'italiéne

Courante

Matteson's opinion is that the basic affect is

> ... sweet hopefulness.
>
> (1739) II.13.123, tr. Harriss, p. 462

It was a favourite dance of Louis XIV of France and Charles II of England, and is described as noble, rather than pompous.[31] Quantz says that

> ... the bow is detached at every crotchet, whether it is dotted or not.
>
> (1752) XVII.VII.58, tr. Reilly, p. 291

Muffat's bowing for the courante[32] is generally bowed out, using a *craquer* double up-bow for the pair of quavers at the end of the section.

Ex. 2.5.17: Muffat

In the suite the courante normally follows the allemande, and in 17th-century music, may be connected to it by related tempos. Early courantes have crotchet up-beats which should be lifted. Later the up-beat was often shortened to a quaver. In the following example, the up-beat to bar 1 reflects the same rhythm in the middle of bar 2. In English dance music of the late 17th century, rhythms should often be played as written, not over-dotted. Later courantes have a quaver up-beat which should be connected to the down-beat (as in ex. 2.5.17 above).

Ex. 2.5.18: Locke, Suite no. 6 in A minor 'for several friends', Courante

The French courante is more restrained and elegant than the livelier Italian versions (coranto or corrente). The rhythmic characteristic is an ambiguous bar of 2 or 3 beats in a bar of 6 crotchets, usually marked 3/2 but occasionally 6/4. An up-beat note leading to the same down-beat note is a common feature. As in the bourée, the performer should try and avoid accenting more than one beat per bar, even at a slow tempo, thus achieving a tantalising ambiguity of cross-rhythms matching the dance steps which are often divided unequally in the bar and cross bar-lines.[33] The crotchets should be short, gently lifted and unaccented.

---

[31] Hilton (1977), p. 161
[32] (1698) tr. Cooper and Zsako, p. 228
[33] Hilton (1977), p. 171, Little, p. 115

Ex. 2.5.19: J.S. Bach, Orchestral suite no. 1, Courante

Long phrases composed of short sections of uneven length which run into one another are characteristic of the courante, sometimes making difficulties with phrasing and musical sense.

Little claims that the later courante is the slowest of the dances with three beats to a bar.[34] However, look out for tempo indications which might affect the mood as well: courante grave, or courante gaye.

Entrée

Literally French 'entrance'. See also Italian Intrada entry. The entrée is related in style to the introductory section of the French overture (without the fugue) and should be performed in a similar manner. It is found mainly in dance and theatre music. Mattheson describes the predominant characteristic of the entrée as austerity, and that its purpose is to arouse the attention of the audience to expect something new and strange.[35] It may set the mood for a type of grand processional entry. Mattheson also observes that the French call any dance melody by the general name entree, especially for processions in plays.[36] Quantz says that

> the *entrée*, the *loure*, and the *courante* are played majestically, and the bow is detached at every crotchet, whether it has a dot or not.
>
> (1752) XVII.VII.58, tr. Reilly, p. 291

Ex. 2.5.20 *f*: Corrette, l'École d'Orphée (1738), p. 18

The characteristic dotted rhythms and quavers *inégales* should portray an uplifting, proud affect, with the long notes lengthened, and the single short notes slightly shortened without being too aggressively loud or jerky. Corrette (ex. 2.5.20) gives a *craquer* up-bow for a pair of quavers on a weak beat. The tempo should not be too slow (think of a slow march tempo). In common time, there should be two beats to the bar. Observe the rules of hierarchy, in the bar and of the harmony, to give this movement the majesty suggested by Quantz.

Forlana

Closely related to the gigue (French type) and loure, the forlana is a wild gay dance in 6/4 with two beats to the bar. Dotted rhythms feature strongly, and phrases are usually in regular four-bar lengths.

---

[34] Little, p. 115
[35] (1739) II.13.98, tr. Harriss, p. 456
[36] ibid. II.13.100, p. 457

2.5 The dance

Ex. 2.5.21 *f*: Feuillet (1700)

Muffat's bowing for this dance requires a retake before each main beat, which gives a clue to the (slow) tempo:

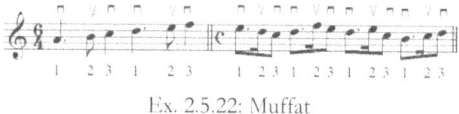

Ex. 2.5.22: Muffat

This bowing may be applied directly to the Forlane in J. S. Bach's orchestral suite no. 1:

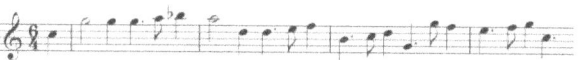

Ex. 2.5.23: J. S. Bach, Orchestral Suite no. 1, Forlana

Starting up-bow on the lifted up-beat, bow out bar 1, then retake the bow for a strong down stroke at bar 2 and 3. See also, loure and gigue. Muffat allows hooked down-bows when the same dotted compound rhythms appear in the faster gigue.

Galliard

Also known as gagliardo, gallarda, gaiarda meaning vigorous and robust, this dance was used to display agility. This dance is the companion of the pavan, and should follow it closely. In the early examples of this pair of dances, a related tempo may be adopted.

Ex. 2.5.24: Albarti

The pavan and galliard had their hey-day in the 16th and 17th centuries, and do not feature in the 18th-century suite. Morley:

> After every pavan we usually set a galliard. . . . This is a brighter and more stirring kind of dancing than the pavan.
>
> (1597), p. 296

Ex. 2.5.25: Morley, Southerne's Pavan and Galliard

However, Mace eighty years later says galliards

> . . . are perform'd in a *Slow, and Large Triple-Time*; and (commonly) *Grave, and Sober*.
>
> (1676), p. 129

His near contemporary Talbot disagrees:

> . . . a lofty Frolic Movement suitable to the gay temper of the Nation [France], is properly set in a pretty brisk Triple.
>
> (1690) in Donington (1963), p. 397

The pavan is written in duple time with slow note values, so that when the galliard commences, the effect should be lighter with more movement, which reflects the more agile leaping dance steps it has to accompany. The dance is in a steady quick triple time often with a hemiola at the conclusion of the phrase. Whether written in 3/4 or 3/2, the first few notes may often be treated as up-beats to the first strong beat, and when written in compound time, a certain ambiguity is desirable within the bar.

♫ tracks 1-2 and 8-9 for the above examples of the pavan and galliard.

Gavotte

Gavot, gavotta, gavat. The gavotte was an extremely popular form during the 17th and 18th centuries, appearing in dance suites, solo works, trios, choruses and cantatas. Mattheson writes that the gavotte should sound skipping or hopping, not running. He also describes the type of Italian gavotte specially written for the violin, probably containing variations:

> with its excesses this gavotte often fills no less than entire pages; these pieces, however, are not quite as they ought to be. But whenever an Italian can do something to show off his speed, he will make anything out of anything.
>
> (1739) II.13.88, tr. Harriss, p. 453

The English writer North in 1726 notes that the dance called the gavot is

> . . . not now used.
>
> J. Wilson, p. 99 fn. 6

One supposes him to mean actually danced, as many forms of this dance appeared in instrumental and orchestral overtures and suites throughout the first half of the 18th-century. Quantz likens it to a rigaudon

> . . . but is a little more moderate in tempo.
>
> (1752) XVII.VII.58, tr. Reilly, p. 291

Muffat points out the error of rushing the beat which often is

> . . . easily committed, especially in gavottes, on the second and fourth note in two-beat measures, and on even-numbered eighth notes in four-beat measures. Instead it is always better to hold back the said notes slightly than to rush them.
>
> (1698) tr. Cooper and Zsako, p. 232

The gavotte is in common time and starts with two up-beat crotchets before the bar. This pattern is repeated throughout the movement. It is important to show the structure of the gavotte, which is often composed of two short phrases followed by a long one. In the following example, articulation should take place between each two-bar phrase, and the second and fourth crotchets of the bar should be held back as recommended by Muffat. A written-out *tierce coulé* occurs in bar 4 on the weak second crotchet.

Ex. 2.5.26: J. S. Bach, Orchestral suite no. 1, Gavotte

Occasionally a movement with gavotte-like characteristics starts on the first beat:

Ex. 2.5.27 *f*: Corelli, Sonata op. 2 no. 5

2.5 The dance

The tempo should be moderate, and quavers performed *inégales* if appropriate. The affect should be fairly joyous and gay. (Bach chose a gavotte for the final movement of his 'wedding' Cantata 202 'Weichet nur, betrübte Schatten'). A great deal of poise and articulation between phrases is needed for the successful execution of this dance. Where phrases end on a minim, clear the sound before continuing, and avoid making a 'slurping' connection between phrases (the dancers are stationary whilst waiting for the next two up-beats). The gavotte form is often used as a vehicle for variations, or in the form of a gavotte en rondeau. A slight change in tempo may reinforce the affect of a specially grand or pathetic variation or *couplet*.

♪ track 21 for a gavott by Locke.

Gigue

This dance featured as a principal constituent of the standard French type of Baroque suite, often situated at the end of the suite and giving it an exciting conclusion. Forty-two gigues by J. S. Bach have survived in solo and orchestral works.[37] Bach also uses the title *gique* in the suites for unaccompanied cello. The mood should be essentially cheerful and happy. Mattheson says

> English *gigues* are characterised by an ardent and fleeting zeal.

He lists types of gigue as

> ... the common one, the *Loure*, the *Canarie*, the *Giga*.

He gives the gigue

> ... four principal affects: passion or zeal; pride; foolish ambition and the volatile spirit.

> (1739) II.13.102, tr. Harriss, pp. 457-8

Brossard says it should have

> ... a skipping quality.

> Little, p. 146

The French type:

Ex. 2.5.28 *f*: Feuillet (1700)

Ex. 2.5.29 *f*: l'Abbé le fils, Principes du Violon (1761)

In general, dotted rhythms are bowed out by l'Abbé le fils and Muffat (examples above and below).[38] Where two notes occur before the bar line in the fast dotted French form, a down-bow is permitted on the semiquaver. Contrast this bowing with the slower forlane example.

Ex. 2.5.30: Muffat

---

[37] Little, p. 143
[38] (1698) tr. Cooper and Zsako, p. 229

2.5 The dance

Little[39] advises that the tempo should be less fast when the gigue is not placed at the end of the suite, particularly when followed by the slower minuet, and should never be so fast that it generates frenzy or anxiety. The Italian type is more likely to contain frenzy and can be played fast and wild. Usually in compound time, with simple continuous groups of three quavers of irregular phrase lengths, rhythmic features vary.

Ex. 2.5.31 *f*: Corelli, Sonata op. 2 no. 7

Mattheson describes the

> Italian *Gige*, which are not used for dancing, but for fiddling (from which its name may also derive), force themselves to extreme speed or volatility; though frequently in a flowing and uninterrupted manner: perhaps like the smooth arrow-swift flow of a stream.
>
> (1739) II.13.102, tr. Harriss, p. 457

Slurring can be infinitely varied according to taste and speed, and can incorporate entertaining rhythmic devices. In the 17th century, gigs in 2/4 time may require tripletisation. Corelli, among others, sometimes uses a combined time-signature (op. 2 no. 6, op. 6 no. 4 ex. 3.3.2) giving common time and 12/8 time signatures. Where dotted rhythms appear in simple time in *gigue* movements these may be tripletised.[40] Closely related to the gigue by their use of compound dotted rhythms but with differing up-beat figures are the canaries and the loure (see separate entries). The English Jig is usually in simple time, and is a fast dance related to the hornpipe. Mace says

> *Toys*, or *Jiggs*, are *Light-Squibbish Things*, only fit for *Fantastical*, and *Easie-Light-Headed People*; and are any sort of *Time*.
>
> (1676), p. 129

Hornpipe

Essentially a British dance, it is also called 'maggot' by Playford in his *Dancing Master*, 1695. Mattheson puts hornpipes with country-dances and ballads[41] in a category of English dances and states

> ... hornpipes ... have something so extraordinary in their melodies that one might think that they originated from the court composers of the North or the South Pole.
>
> (1739) II.13.112, tr. Harriss, p. 460

The simple dance often appears in 2/4 or 4/4, but the type most familiar to us through the 17th-century music of Locke, Purcell and others is a country dance in 3/2 using cross- rhythms.

Ex. 2.5.32 *f*: Purcell, The Double Dealer

The Purcell hornpipe is a type of dance, which includes the courant and galliard, where the complexity of rhythms in each bar should be clearly articulated. The ambiguous nature of the rhythms can be suggested by one main accent, and then a cooling-off until the next down-beat. At other times, the strong cross rhythms will need to be stressed. This might result in frequent retakes to arrive on a down-bow on the first beat, but this

---

[39] p. 148
[40] see pp. 170-171 for examples
[41] (1739) II.13.109, tr. Harriss, p. 459

2.5 The dance

adds to the strong flavour of the hornpipe rhythm. This dance requires a very steady, poised tempo to realise its full effect.

♪ track 34 for a hornpipe by Purcell.

Intrada

The Italian form of 'entrance' dance. Mattheson says the affect

> ... should arouse longing for more.
>
> (1739) II.13.136. tr. Harriss, p. 466

Brossard's dictionary draws a comparison with the entrée in a ballet, and says that it is for regulating the paces.[42]

Loure

Mattheson describes the affect as

> ... slow and punctuated [dotted] ... [exhibiting] a proud and arrogant nature.
>
> (1739) II.13.102, tr. Harriss, p. 457

Brossard's dictionary gives us

> ... beat slowly and gravely and one marks the first beat of each bar more noticeably than the second.
>
> (1702), p. 293

Walther writes

> ... to be taken in a dignified and slow fashion. The first note of each half bar has a dot, which is to be well prolonged.
>
> (1732) in Donington (1963) p. 398

Little tells us that numerous French writers referred to the loure as a 'slow gigue', but warns us that it must be a French type of gigue not an Italian giga.[43] In other words, it has to have characteristic dotted rhythms, be notated in 6/4, and be taken at a much slower tempo than the gigue.

Ex. 2.5.33 *f*: Couperin, 8ième concert, Loure

There are two slow beats to a bar (Couperin writes pesament meaning heavy). Phrase lengths are unequal (often five or seven bars), which can be difficult to make sense of on the first reading. Applied to the above loure, Muffat's bowing for dances in 6/4 compound time (such as the forlane) would give a double down-bow for the two crotchets of the bar. Heavy accents should support the *pesament* instruction.

Ex. 2.5.34 *f*: J. S. Bach, Partita no. 3 in E major for solo violin

---

[42] (1702), p. 50
[43] p. 186

2.5 The dance

Minuet

Menuet (French), tempo di minuetto. A dance usually in 3/4 time, the minuet was the most popular and well known 18th-century dance. Mattheson states that a minuet should have

> ... moderate cheerfulness and sometimes may be quite noble, but it certainly is not a vehicle for violent passions.
>
> (1739) II.13.81, tr. Harriss, p. 451

Muffat pleads that the final note in a group of three in a bar

> ... should have its full value, rather than play it, as some do, shorter than it deserves, thereby rushing the beat imperceptibly.
>
> (1698) tr. Cooper and Zsako, p. 231

Muffat's minuet bowing mixes down-bow retakes with two up-bows (*craquer*):

Ex. 2.5.35: Muffat, (1698) tr. Cooper & Zsako, p. 230

Ex. 2.5.36 *f*: l'Abbé le fils, Principes du Violon (1761) p. 4

Ex. 2.5.37 *f*: Corrette, l'Ecole d'Orphée (1738) p. 15

The first two examples show *craquer* up-bows for quavers on weak beats above, and lifted double down-bows for bar-lines. The hemiola (Corrette bars 6-7) is bowed out. Muffat allows down/up/up bowing when the tempo is a little faster. Two and four bar phrase units should be clearly articulated, and it is unusual to find any up-beat figures. Poise across the bar line, and between phrases is very important to the affect of this dance. A very common formula for the phrasing is 2 + 2 + 4 bars, ending with a hemiola figure. Minuets in disguise often appear as movements in 3/4 such as arias, movements forming part of an overture etc. Sometimes the first bar may be thought of as a up-beat bar, leading to the second bar as in the above example by Corrette and shown in ex. 1.2.6. The musical emphasis is in opposition to the dance steps which come in patterns of six (i.e. two bars) with a strong emphasis on the first and third beat of the first bar.[44] Corelli did not write any minuets, demonstrating the essentially French character of this dance. In Purcell and Handel suites, quavers could be performed *inégales* in the French style:

Ex. 2.5.38 *f*: Purcell, Gordian Knott Unty'd

In the above minuet, each bar could start down-bow, to show the 2 + 2 + 4 bar structure. Minuets often appear just before the final gigue or at the very end of a very long suite or theatrical overture to achieve a calming 'return to earth, prepare for drama' effect. (e.g. Handel *Concerti Grossi*, Boyce trios). The minuet was so popular and versatile as a form that it lived on far into the 18th century as a major component in the classical symphony long after all other Baroque dances had disappeared from general use. See

---

[44] Hilton (1986), p. 52

2.5 The dance

ex. 2.4.10 for Muffat's menuet bowing and how it may be applied to the music of J. S. Bach, and ex. 1.2.6 for Mattheson's minuet example for phrasing and articulation.

♫ track 35 for a minuet by Purcell played in a French style.

Musette

A French pastoral movement, containing imitation of the small bagpipe of that name. Look for long drone notes in the middle and bass parts, with a melody in the treble. A fairly sustained bow-stroke gives the desired effect of imitating the sound of the musette instrument. The melody part should be bowed out in a lilting manner, and played on the string to match the drone underneath. Leaning slightly on the bar lines of the tied notes gives the drones a hurdy-gurdy effect.

Ex. 2.5.39: Handel, Concerto Grosso op. 6 no. 6, Musette

Ex. 2.5.39a ƒ: Couperin, 3ième concert, Musette

Passacaille

In Italian passacaglia. An extended movement in triple meter with variations over four-bar bass sequences. Similar in character and structure to the danced chaconne, there does not seem to be a consensus of opinion about the differences between these two dance forms: Brossard (1702) said that the melody of the passacaille was more expressive and tender than that of the chaconne. Quantz on the other hand, asserts that

> . . . a *passecaille* is like the preceding type [the *chaconne*], but is played just a little faster.
>
> (1752) XVII.VII.58, tr. Reilly, p. 291

See chaconne entry (above) for further information. Certain bass lines and their harmonic patterns have become associated with both forms. Bowing and phrasing rules for playing a passacaille are similar to the chaconne. The following two examples show a similar falling four-note bass line being used in a passagalia and a chaconne:

Ex. 2.5.40: Biber, 'Rosary' sonata no. 16, Passagalia

2.5 The dance

Ex. 2.5.41 *f*: Playford, The Division Violin, The Second Part

♫ track 36 for a chaconne by Purcell.

Passepied

A fast French court dance in triple time with the same dance steps as the minuet, but played faster.[45]

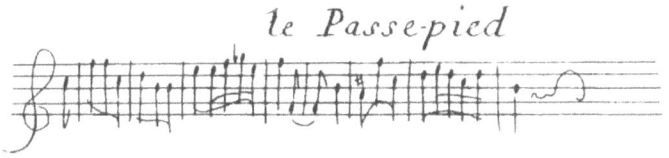

Ex. 2.5.42 *f*: Feuillet (1700)

Mattheson describes the passepied as a fast melody and its character as follows:

> Its nature is quite close to frivolity: for with all its disquiet and inconstancy, such a passepied has by no means the zeal, passion or ardour which one comes across with a volatile gigue. Meanwhile it is still a kind of frivolity which does not have anything detestable or unpleasant about it, but rather something pleasant: just as many a female who, though she is a little inconstant, nevertheless does not therewith lose her charm.

(1739) II.13.113, tr. Harriss, p. 460

Quantz instructs that the passepied must be played lightly and the tempo is faster than a minuet.[46] Often two bars are connected making hemiola patterns, and Little writes that the longer phrases of a passepied with fewer points of arrival, contain 'unusual rhythms and off-beat accents which occur at surprising times to delight (or possibly upset) the listener.'[47] In the following example, the anticipated down-beats tied over into bars 3 and 7 might be points of delight or upset.

Ex. 2.5.43: J. S. Bach, Orchestral Suite no. 1, Passepied

The passepied sometimes appears in pairs with a repeat of the first. The up-beat should be played as written, lifted and short.

---

[45] Little, p. 85
[46] (1752) XVII.VII.58, tr. Reilly, p. 291
[47] Little, p. 83

2.5 The dance

Pavane

Italian pavana, English pavan, German paduana. A court dance from the 16th and early 17th centuries in slow duple time. The spondaic rhythm of two equal pulses give a slow serious character. Mace described the dance as

> ... very *Grave*, and *Sober, Full of art, and Profundity*, but seldom us'd in These our *Light Days*.
>
> (1676), p. 129

Morley:

> ... a kind of staid music ordained for grave dancing.
>
> (1597), p. 296

Ex. 2.5.44: Locke, Suite no. 1 'for several friends', Pavan

Purcell was one of the last composers to use the form before it became obsolete, and it is not mentioned by writers such as Quantz (1752) or Mattheson (1739). There are usually two or three sections, each repeated. The pavan consisted of very simple steps and often fulfilled a processional role. It should be performed in a steady tempo with two beats to a bar. Be careful not to play this dance too slowly because it is notated in minims, which was the beat unit in music with the old-fashioned alla breve time signature. Beware of drawing out the ends of sections, especially before repeats. Head for the final cadence and then breathe before repeating or continuing. The bow should maintain a calm slow speed without sudden movements which would make notes stick out of the texture. Notice when all the parts move together or when the texture is more contrapuntal.

♪ tracks 2 and 8 for pavans.

Polonaise

Literally, Polish. Italian: alla Polacca, German: Polnischer Tanz. This dance is slower than a minuet and processional in character. Mattheson called it

> ... frank and free.
>
> (1739) II.13.108, tr. Harriss, p. 459

Stylized in the 18th century as a noble dance, it is in triple metre. Apart from that element, the polonaises that are best known (by J. S. Bach: Orchestral Suite no. 2, Brandenburg concerto no. 1) have few characteristics in common. Telemann was very fond of the polonaise, and his works contain many fine examples. In the polonaise from the Orchestral Suite no. 2 for flute and strings, J. S. Bach writes an elaborate 'double' for the flute and continuo alone, the cello repeating the melody first heard in the upper voice.

Ex. 2.5.45: J. S. Bach, Orchestral Suite no. 2, Polonaise

The upright, noble character of this melody may be characterised by playing the semiquaver in the first beat of the principal melody as written, and individual quavers short and lifted.

Rigaudon

Originally a French folk dance, the rigaudon became popular at courts all over Europe. A gay dance with a lifted up-beat, it is usually in duple time, and appears in compound and simple metre versions.

Ex. 2.5.46 *f*: Feuillet (1700)

Matheson claims its character to be

> ... trifling and joking ... [its origins are associated with water, as] *rigo* means a stream or river [which is why] it is in common use with sailors.

Matheson calls the rigaudon

> ... a mongrel, joined together from the gavotte and bourée.
>
> (1739) II.13.93-94, tr. Harriss, p. 455

Ex. 2.5.47 *f*: Corrette, L'Ecole d'Orphée (1738) p. 18

Corrette gives *craquer* up-bows for pairs of quavers occurring on weak beats of the bar. The tempo is quite fast, as indicated by the single figure time signature.[48]

Ex. 2.5.48 *f*: Couperin, 4ième concert, Rigaudon

The above example shows an Italianate Rigaudon with an instruction for equal quavers. An unusual slur (which could be taken on another down-bow) includes the two semiquavers onto a strong beat in bar 5. Rameau appears to have been very fond of the rigaudon, and often set this dance for piccolo and bassoon as if to emphasise its amusing nautical character.

Rondeau

Italian: rondo, English: round O. Literally: circular. Appears in duple or triple metre. The music alternates the main section (refrain, reprise) with contrasting episodes (couplets). Quantz says it should be played

> ... rather tranquilly.
>
> (1752) XVII.VII.58, tr. Reilly, p. 291

---

[48] see part 1.4 Tempo

2.5 The dance

Ex. 2.5.49: J. S. Bach, Orchestral Suite no. 2 for flute and strings
1st line: rondeau, 2nd line: beginning of 1st couplet

In France the form evolved from songs of courtly love, so the inherited character of the rondeau is one of serene longing and reminiscence for things past. The episodes between the rondeau statements are frequently more dramatic. In the famous rondeau by Purcell from the theatre suite *Abdelazar*, the rondeau theme (the first strain) is the strong element and the episodes either brighter or more pleading in character.

Ex. 2.5.50 *f*: Purcell, Abdelazar

1st line: rondeau theme (minor key), 2nd line: 1st episode (major key), 3rd line: 2nd episode,
4th line: end of 2nd episode showing the instruction to return to the rondeau theme to end.

Sarabande

Italian: sarabanda, English: saraband. A dance in triple metre, for most of the 17th century the sarabande was a fast dance, written in 6/4, accompanied by castanets and guitars, with a reputation for lasciviousness attributed to it by its opponents. Mace says that the saraband is

> ... more *Toyish*, and *Light*, than *Corantoes*.
>
> (1676), p. 129

Ex. 2.5.51: Locke, Broken Consort suite in C major, Saraband

Seventy years later, Mattheson, our 18th-century source, claims that the sarabande expresses

> ... no other emotion but ambition. [He calls it] bombastic [and claims that] it permits no running notes, because *grandezza* abhors such, and maintains its seriousness.
>
> (1739) II.13.118, tr, Harriss, p. 461

Other writers describe its character as majestic, with a serious intensity of expression, 'always melancholy, exuding a delicate yet serious tenderness'.[49]

Ex. 2.5.52 *f*: Feuillet (1700)

The later noble French court dance, the sarabande grave assumed a languid character with a slow tempo (now often in 3/2). Talbot (1690) describes it as

> . . . a soft passionate Movement, always set in a slow triple . . . apt to move the Passions and to disturb the tranquillity of the Mind.
>
> Donington (1963), p. 402

In the following example, a simple 3 time signature is qualified by the written instructions 'grave, et tendre', implying a slow tempo.

Ex. 2.5.53 *f*: Couperin, 8ième concert

Ex. 2.5.54 *f*: Corelli, Sonata op. 2 no. 8

The above example (2.5.54) shows a slow Italian sarabanda in simple 3/4 time marked adagio. An extremely popular form, the sarabande was one of the principal constituents of the suite: in the 17th century often appearing as a fast concluding number, and in the later Baroque suite taking a central position at the heart of the dance sequence, appearing before the more frivolous bourée or gigue movements.

The serious affect can be maintained by slight over-dotting (lengthening the dotted notes and slightly shortening the following short notes), and by a certain lingering on the dissonant harmonies (in ex. 2.5.53 above, bars 6 and 7 take a surprising harmonic turn). The character of the later French sarabande is indicated by a slight leaning on the second beat. In ex. 2.5.53 above, bars 2, 3 and 6 could all have leaning second beats. A double down-bow however, would give too much accent to the second beat, which needs to lead onwards to the next bar. A pushed up-bow on the second beats is quite effective in maintaining the line and leading forwards to the next bar line. Quavers in 3/4 and crotchets in 3/2 should be played *inégale*, especially in the sarabande grave. Ornaments in this type of French sarabande should be particularly expressive. Long *appoggiature*, *ports de voix* and accelerating trills should be added to taste.[50]

J. S. Bach wrote more sarabandes than any other dance.[51] He uses both French and Italian forms of the title word (see examples below). His Partita no.1 for violin solo includes a double in the Italian running style using continuous triplet quavers which can be played bowed out all the way through. Emphasise the tension and relaxation of the harmonies by placing more weight on the bottom of the arpeggio figures, (e.g. bar 6) and by relaxing the sound into end of section cadences.

---

[49] Little, p. 94
[50] see Ornamentation part 1.5
[51] Little, p. 102

2.5 The dance

Ex. 2.5.55 *f*: J. S. Bach, Partita in B minor for solo violin

A particular feature of the sarabande in the Partita in D minor for violin solo is the repeated quaver note at the end of the first and second bars. As the sarabande starts with a down-beat, it is a mistake to perform these notes as deliberate upbeats to the following bars. They should be connected to the previous note and played very lightly as exact quavers on an up-bow. Couperin marks an articulation after a similar repeated-note figure in the sarabande of the suite 'la Françoise'. It is very unusual for a dance to acquire an up-beat pattern within a section if there is no up-beat to the first bar. Two down-bows on the first and second notes of the first two bars will give equal weight to both chords.

Ex. 2.5.56 *f*: J. S. Bach, Partita in D minor for solo violin

Mattheson claims that

> . . . the familiar Folies d'Espagne appear in a certain way to belong among the sarabandes; they are however by no means trivialities, seriously speaking. For there is truly more good in such an ancient melody, whose compass is only a small fourth, than in all Moorish dances which may have ever been invented.
>
> (1739) II.13.120, tr. Harriss, p. 462

See chaconne entry for a musical example of the *Folies d'Espagne*. As in the chaconne, care must be taken in sarabandes not to play the second beat strongly if the harmony is the same. However, a certain holding back is appropriate during the second beat to reflect the sarabande dance affect. If the harmony changes, then lean a little on the second beat. If the second beat is the same harmony with a large chord, and is taken on another down-bow, it should be non-aggressive. (J. S. Bach, Suite no. 3 for solo cello, the final bars of both sections). This rule also applies to arpeggios which are, after all, only chords spaced out (cello suite no. 4, final bar of sarabande).

♪ tracks 23, 28 (Locke ex. 2.5.51) and 31 for fast 17th-century sarabands.

2.5 The dance

Siciliana

A movement in compound time in the style of an aria with lilting dotted rhythms. Mattheson linked it with the barcarolle,[52] and recommended that it be performed slowly and was best used to evoke melancholy passions.[53]

Ex. 2.5.57: Handel, Concerto Grosso op. 6 no 8, Siciliana

The siciliana has been used to evoke a pastoral world, as in Handel's *Messiah*: the pastoral symphony. A lilting rhythm, not too sharply dotted, with the bow-stroke on the dotted note and the third quaver of each group not too sustained, but lightened. Sicilianas often occur incognito. Here is an example:

Ex. 2.5.58: J. S. Bach, Sonata for violin and harpsichord no. 4

Further details of dance tempos, including Quantz's metronome marks, may be found in Donington, (1963), chapter XXXVII. Muffat's bowing rules (1698) are contained in *Musical Quarterly*, 1967, pp. 220-45, tr. Cooper & Zsako and in Muffat's writings on performance practice trans. D. K. Wilson. Olsson (chapter 18, in Carter, 1997) writes on 17th-century dance types with costume details and lists of music. Little (1991) is recommended for much useful information from many sources about Baroque dances and their performance, with emphasis on the works of J. S. Bach.

See also Judy Tarling, *The Baroque Dance 1660-1725. A performance study book for treble and bass instruments*, Corda Music Publications 496

---

[52] *Das neu-eroffnete Orchestre* (1713)
[53] *New Grove*, 'Siciliana'

2.6 The slow bow

The basic bow-strokes for use with an early bow divide broadly into two types: the soft edged stroke used for long notes, and the fast articulated stroke which bites the string. These two strokes are clearly described by Tartini (1760) in the famous letter written by him to his pupil Maddalena Lombardini. His instructions to her on how and what to practise form the basis of the following analysis of early bow technique. Infinite variety should be sought within these extremes for a bow-stroke repertoire to cover every possibility of nuance and expression.

The following sections of 2.6 describe the variety of uses for the slow bow on long notes, in using the *messa di voce* and bow vibrato, and part 2.7 describes the articulated stroke used in fast passages.

Long notes

The basic bow-stroke is described in great detail by several 18th-century writers. As the hair of the bow sits freely in the open frog, it is only natural that many writers describe a soft beginning to the long bow-stroke, even when playing loudly. A forced attack with bite at the beginning of a long note became easier with the invention of the ferrule which gives the hair near the frog the greater tension required for an explosive start to a note. Although this stroke *may* be applied with a Baroque bow, it is uncharacteristic, and stylistically anachronistic except as a special effect. The beauty of the long note and its nuance was an element looked for and admired by many writers. The sweetness and purity of sound made by a long smooth bow-stroke was especially admired in the Italian style of playing. Matteis (d.? 1707) was the first Italian virtuoso to make an impression in England and his playing astounded all who heard him. Corelli's music was a superb vehicle for showing off this technique, and encouraged a new rage for the Italian style in England.

Tartini:

> Your first study, therefore, should be the true manner of holding, balancing and pressing the bow lightly, but steadily, upon the strings; in such manner as that it shall seem to breathe the first tone it gives, which must proceed from the friction of the string, and not from percussion, as by a blow given with a hammer upon it.
>
> (1760) in (1771) tr. Jacobi, p. 133

Leopold Mozart:

> Every tone, even the strongest attack, has a small, even if barely audible, softness at the beginning of the stroke; for it would otherwise be no tone but only an unpleasant and unintelligible noise. This same softness must be heard also at the end of each stroke.
>
> (1756) V.3, tr. Knocker, p. 97

From these two statements, the shape of the long Baroque stroke is already clear: a soft beginning, and the soft ending before the change of bow. Tartini describes what happens next:

> ... laying the bow lightly upon the strings at the first contact, and on gently pressing it afterwards; which, if done gradually, can scarce have too much force given to it, because, if the tone is begun with delicacy, there is little danger of rendering it afterwards either coarse or harsh.
>
> (1760) in (1771) tr. Jacobi, p. 133

The importance of bow pressure and its control in every part of the bow makes up the basic vehicle of the Baroque string player's technique. Tartini again:

> Of this first contact, and delicate manner of beginning a tone, you should make yourself a perfect mistress in every situation and part of the bow, as well in the middle as at the extremities ... my advice is, that you first exercise yourself in a swell upon an open string, for example ... that you begin pianissimo, and increase the tone by slow degrees to its fortissimo ... beginning with the most minute softness, encreasing the

2.6 The slow bow

> tone to its loudest degree, and diminishing it to the same point of softness with which you began, and all this in the same stroke of the bow. Every degree of pressure upon the string which the expression of a note or passage shall require, will by this means be easy and certain; and you will be able to execute with your bow whatever you please.
>
> (1760) in (1771) tr. Jacobi, p. 133

In the above passage we find confirmation of the existence of that much-criticised effect: the swell or *messa di voce*. The inappropriate use of this effect has made many enemies of so-called 'historical style'. After examining written descriptions of Baroque techniques (the only evidence we have), players need to choose how to incorporate these into their playing to a greater or lesser extent. An effect can enhance the musical point or, when used indiscriminately, become an annoying mannerism. The degree to which these effects are exaggerated or merely hinted at is a question of that most elusive of things: good taste, which Geminiani calls 'a peculiar gift of nature'. Geminiani writes:

> One of the principal beauties of the violin is the swelling or encreasing and softening the sound; which is done by pressing the bow upon the strings with the fore-finger more or less. In playing all long notes the sound should be begun soft, and gradually swelled till the middle, and from thence gradually softened till the end.
>
> (1751), p. 2

From Tartini's description of the basic long note execution, a 'pear' shape is conjured up, with the fullest sound emerging directly after the soft start of the stroke. At the end of the note, particularly if it is a final one, an imperceptible diminishing of the sound should be observed, lightening the pressure until it disappears into thin air and silence. The swelled bow-stroke is not accomplished by speed. All the descriptions of the execution of this stroke discuss control of pressure. Bow speed is not mentioned. Leopold Mozart describes the combination of pressure and distance from the bridge, and also the pressure exerted by the fingers of the left hand:

> The finger of the left hand which is placed on the string should, in the soft tone, relax the pressure somewhat, and that the bow should be placed a little farther from the bridge; whereas in loud tone the fingers of the left hand should be pressed down strongly and the bow be placed nearer to the bridge.
>
> (1756) V.4, tr. Knocker, p. 97

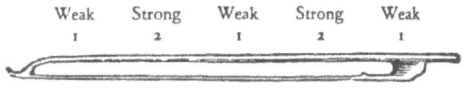

f: (1756) tr. Knocker, p. 99

Leopold Mozart shows in the diagram above how variations in nuance on long notes should be practised under one bow, mastering the subtlest degrees of pressure by swelling the sound up and down, the bow being divided into three or five sections increasing and lightening the pressure in turn. A description of a long bow-stroke by North:

> I would have them learn to fill, and soften a sound, as shades in needlework, *insensatim*, so as to be like a gust of wind, which begins with a soft air, and fills by degrees to a strength as makes all bend, and then softens away againe into a temper, and so vanish.
>
> J. Wilson, p. 18

Any amount of pressure can be exerted immediately after the 'softness' at the start. To develop the control of the bow, practise long notes with the pressure increasing and decreasing in various parts of the length. Many long notes need a soft start combined with a quick increase of pressure using weight for a solid, but not aggressive effect. If the stroke increases in speed suddenly after the soft beginning, a sudden bulge in the sound occurs, instead of a beautifully rounded note. Always be aware of the shape of the note, and avoid making sudden lunges with the bow as a substitute for shape by pressure and weight. Use a slow bow speed to concentrate the sound.

2.6 The slow bow

The combination of pressure and distance from bridge has a useful application in the playing of unequal rhythms in triple time, where the longer note can be played with more pressure nearer the bridge, and the shorter, lighter note slightly further away from the bridge with a faster stroke, even lifted slightly should the occasion demand it. This technique in combination with working down the bow on weak intermediate beats, only retaking for strong ones (described in ex. 2.4.18 & 19) is especially useful to avoid an accent on every beat. Down-bow hooking should be avoided wherever possible, except for quick notes in compound time in a fast tempo.

Some points to consider when practising long notes:

1. It is important to keep the bow speed constant. Watch the point of the bow to make sure it does not lurch in speed when pressure is increased.
2. Achieve the swelling effect by leaning more on the first finger as the down-bow progresses, with the weight transferred back to the other fingers during the up-bow.
3. As more pressure is exerted, keep the bow near the bridge.
4. Try on each stroke to make the speed of the bow slower than the last.
5. The bow arm should be kept low, giving weight to the stroke as it develops and releasing the weight towards the change in the direction of the bow.
6. The wrist should collapse upwards as the up-bow progresses as if a puppeteer's string were attached to it, and push downwards on the down-bow, as if squashing something into the floor with the heel of the hand.
7. Bring the elbow inwards on the up-bow and make it swing outwards on the down-bow. Imagine the elbow and the wrist describing opposing circles in the air.

The key difference between using the Baroque bow and the modern one is the use of the slow bow combined with fine control of pressure. Some modern violinists will have learned this use of the bow already and have it ingrained in their technique. The early bow has much less power towards the point than the Tourte model, with the result that most of the nuance and expression has to be executed with a stroke controlled in the lower half and middle. The use of the shorter lighter Baroque bow means that fast bow speeds, especially on long notes, will result in a weak tone. It is worth investing a great deal of time practising slow bow control, going to the extremes of pressure near the bridge to see how slowly you can control your bow without producing a nasty sound. It is said that Corelli's test of a good player was to require him to sustain, with a powerful tone, two notes double-stopped for ten seconds.[54]

The messa di voce

Messa di Voce is the Italian term used to describe the 'measuring out' of long notes. Many sources give detailed descriptions of how to execute the swelling of long notes and tell us about their application. Obviously, slow movements offer the most opportunities for the use of swelled long notes. Piani describes the shape of bow-strokes used on long notes, and specifies their uses in the violin part:[55]

---

[54] see Zaslaw (1979)
[55] *Avertissement* to sonatas (1712), p. 2

2.6 The slow bow

Ex. 2.6.1 *f*: Piani, Sonata IV

Veracini also gives performance instructions for the use of this effect:[56]

Ex. 2.6.2 *f*: Veracini, Sonata prima op. 2, Toccata

Quantz's advice is that

> ... long notes must be sustained in an elevated manner by swelling and diminishing the strength of the tone.
>
> (1752) XII.18, tr. Reilly, p. 132

Geminiani places 'swelling and softening of the sound' in his list of ornaments and indicates the effect by two triangular signs, left and right-facing (Essempio XVIII 7 and 8).[57]

(7*th* and 8*th*) Of Swelling and Softening the Sound.
These two Elements may be used after each other; they produce great Beauty and Variety in the Melody, and employ'd alternately, they are proper for any Expression or Measure.

Ex. 2.6.3 *f*: Geminiani (1751)

Ex. 2.6.4 *f*: Geminiani (1751)

---

[56] *Intenzione dell'Autore*, opus 2 *Sonate Accademiche* (London and Florence 1744)
[57] (1751), pp. 7, 26

2.6 The slow bow

Signs are found in his musical examples (extract from Composition 1a above[58]) over the notes he would like played with a swell. Geminiani uses the same sign for the swell as for the notes he calls buono (i.e. important and interesting notes), but it is fairly obvious which notes require a swell by the length of the note over which the sign is placed. Swell signs over smaller notes at the end of slurs probably mean 'do not make a diminuendo here'. The wavy line over the minim G indicates the use of vibrato in addition to the swelling of the sound.

Marais lists a swelling of the sound in his list of ornaments, the use of which are all precisely indicated in the music. The letter 'e' stands for both *enfler* to swell and *exprimer* to express; he places it exactly over the part of the note to be swelled. The wavy line indicates the use of vibrato.

Ex. 2.6.5 *f*: Marais, 3ième Livre, Sarabande

> ... you must express or swell the bow-stroke by putting more or less pressure on the string according to the demands of the piece and that can be sometimes on the beginning of the beat or on the value of the dot after the note according to where the mark is; in this way one gives feeling to pieces which would be too uniform without it.
>
> *Pièces de Violes Troisième Livre* tr. Gammie p. 5

Simpson says:

> Gracing of Notes is performed two wayes, viz. by the Bow, and by the Fingers. By the Bow, as when we play Loud or Soft, according to our fancy, or the humour of the Musick. Again, this Loud or Soft is sometime express'd in one and the same Note, as when we make it Soft at the *beginning*, and then (as it were) swell or grow louder towards the *middle* or *ending*.
>
> (1659), p. 10

Corrette recommends the use of the swell on long notes at the ends of phrases in the Italian style, for *un tres bel effet*:

Ex. 2.6.6 *f*: Corrette (1738), p. 34

> In sarabandes, Adagio, Largo; and other such pieces, one should play the semibreves, minims and crotchets with long bows swelling the sound towards the end, A, B. For the endings and cadences of melodies, the note should begin with a gentle bow strengthening in the middle and dying away at the end, CDE. This way of bowing makes a wonderful effect.
>
> (1738), p.34

---

[58] ibid., p. 33

2.6 The slow bow

If a sequence of long notes appears, they should be varied in effect. Quantz:

> If, however, several long notes are found in succession where, in strengthening the tone, the time does not permit you to swell each note individually, you can still swell, and diminish the tone during notes like this so that some sound louder and others softer.
>
> (1752) XIV.11, tr. Reilly, p. 166

If the performer possesses the necessary feeling and insight, the adagio affords him a great opportunity to show off his bow control on long notes. The aim of the player should be to vary the tone of each note, making a hierarchy within the chain of long note sound. Any long note ought to have some sort of shape, either growing to a harmonic tension, or diminishing away from one. The habit of changing the bow direction both for convenience and to maintain a note's even sound is to be avoided. There are very few occasions in Baroque music where the bow has to be changed on a long note. Examples might include a sustained pedal point, or a long note in accompanied recitative. At the start of a long note, the bow speed should be adjusted according to the duration of the note. Often the loudest part (i.e. the dissonance) is to be found at the end of a long note, in which case, the bow has to be 'parked' at a very slow speed until the moment comes for a swell, assuming an inch or two of bow still remains.

Endings

Long notes as pedal points are often prolonged dominants having a tendency to grow to the end in a build-up of tension to the point when the pedal finally resolves to the tonic. On the whole, a change of bow should be avoided on any long note as this destroys the shape which is inherent in it. This is especially true on long notes at the end of movements. A *messa di voce* on the final note can make an enormous difference to the overall effect, rounding off the whole movement and giving it a satisfying conclusion. Often in otherwise commendable performances, final notes of movements are considerably cut in length because without the development in sound given by the *messa di voce* the last note dies. Beware of making a big *messa di voce* on the resolution of 'amen' or plagal cadences where the last chord is weaker than the penultimate chord. A final cadence note should never have only a crescendo, especially with a change of bow and a jerk on the end to round it off folk- style. Quantz particularly mentions his disapproval of players who

> ... make a close, especially in arias, with a full chord where none should be. This they seem to have learned from tavern fiddlers.
>
> (1752) XVII.VII.15, tr. Reilly, p. 272

In music where harmony is not the over-riding structural factor, the use of the *messa di voce* may be inappropriate. In contrapuntal style, most long notes need to be sustained evenly to fit into a melodic line, which weaves against other parts. Continual swelling of long notes interrupts the lines of the voices, and makes the music difficult for the listener to understand. Avoid using the *messa di voce* on long notes in contrapuntal music with slow moving parts.

Summary

The *messa di voce* may by used in the following places:
1. Any suspension or tie onto a dissonance.
2. Dissonances on or during long notes in general.
3. A line of suspensions or other sequences incorporating long notes, which may be played alternately swelled and not swelled.
4. A long note at the end of a section or movement.
5. A long introductory note at the start of a movement.

2.6 The slow bow

CASE STUDY – LONG NOTES

Corelli's adagio from op. 5 no. 6 has a variety of shapes and harmonic functions on the long notes:

Ex. 2.6.7: Corelli, Sonata op. 5 no. 6

1. Bar 1 leads to 2, which may be played with a simple *messa di voce*.
2. Both players should lead from bar 3 onto 4 which is stronger than 2 because of the 4/2 dissonant harmony.
3. In bar 6 the long note should swell to the harmonic dissonance at the beginning of bar
6. The bass should make the two notes in bar 6 lead to bar 7.
4. Bar 8 is stronger than 9 shown by the seventh in the harmony.
5. The cadence at bar 9 should be a weak resolution, the long note fading.
6. In bar 9 the bass line should play the first note short and weak and start a new phrase on the second beat, and give direction towards the 4/2 on the following 4 bars, sustaining the ties notes across the bar-lines.
7. The cadence at the 1st beat of 16 should land softly. In the following bars, 16-19, each part should be strongest at the bar-line, making each 2 bar phrase start at a higher dynamic level as the violin part follows the tessitura.
8. Bar 22 leads to 23 for the 4/2 chord, perhaps with a slight articulation on the bar line to emphasise the dissonance.
9. In bars 27 and 29 the violin down-beat has the function of a written out appoggiatura, making the 2nd beat resolution weaker but these notes, although starting less, should be sustained because of the 7th harmony on the 1st beat of the following bars (28 and 30).
10. Bar 31 starts with a strong 4/2 and is the beginning of a hemiola bar (play a 6/2 or 3/1 bar without emphasis on the bar-line of 31-2). The bass line assumes the commonly smooth shape for the hemiola.
11. The movement finishes harmonically in bar 33, where it returns to the 'home' key of F$\sharp$ minor. The final 2 bars and a beat form the coda which leads into the next movement. The B in the penultimate bar should have a cadential trill added, and perhaps a flourish or roulade leading to the final note which should have a *messa di voce*.

Slow movements in Italian sonatas such as this one would have provided a vehicle to show off the free ornamentation of the performer. It is always a good idea to practise the movement first without any ornamentation, to assimilate the phrase shapes and the strong and weak points in the harmony, before deciding on the choice of ornament.[59]

Bow vibrato

One of the techniques which may be unfamiliar to the modern string player is that of vibrato with the bow. This bowing effect is often labelled in 17th-century music 'tremolo'. The word tremolo has been much misunderstood by later writers about Baroque string effects and techniques. It has become confused with the modern use of the term for fast unmeasured separate bows which create a shimmer of sound. Another complication is that in 17th-century music, the indication *tr* may mean tremolo (i.e. bow vibrato) or trill according to context.

The origins of bow vibrato

The first known printed use of the term *tremolo con l'arco* is by Marini in his opus 1 (1617), as an instruction to the string players in the group to imitate the tremulant stop of the organ. This is shown below by the various instructions to the players in the group:

---

[59] see ornamentation pp. 41-43 and Italian Style part 3.

2.6 The slow bow

The top two lines are violins (or cornetts) who should tremble *con l'arco*.

The third line is for trombone or bassoon whose players should tremble *col strumento*.

The bottom line is for organ who *metto il tremolo* (uses the tremulant organ stop).

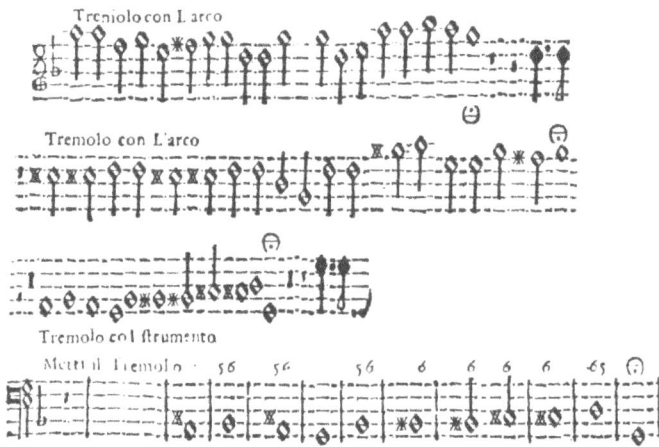

Ex. 2.6.8 *f*: Marini, Sonata 'La Foscarina' op. 1 (1617)

Numerous other uses of this word in early Italian music with a notated explanation would seem to rule out the modern interpretation of the term for repeated fast *unmeasured* re-iterations of the note. It is unlikely that this effect was used before the 19th century. Monteverdi uses a *measured* semiquaver figure in the battle scene in *Combattimento di Tancredo e Clorinda*. Carter points out that the tremulant stop of the organ and by analogy, bow vibrato was generally used for a gentle effect and not a violent one.[60] Farina (1627) reinforces this interpretation of bow vibrato telling us

> . . . the tremolo is done with a pulsating of the hand which has the bow, imitating the manner of the organ tremulant.
>
> Carter (1991) p. 44

An organist is depicted in Farina's *Capriccio Stravagante* (1627) by four string players in synchronised bow tremolo. The music gives the impression that Farina's simulated organist has dropped off to sleep and is experiencing a bad dream as he plays wilder and more remote chords full of 'wrong' notes. This organ tremulant type of bow vibrato should be played with a continuous bow movement, by varying the pressure, not by stopping the bow to detach the pulsations. The player should play a minim containing a slight quaver pulse within a continuous bow-stroke, keeping the bow speed constant, and making the pulsations with pressure from the arm and fingers. Leopold Mozart advises students to practise a similar stroke for the control of bow pressure, particularly at a slow speed on long notes.[61] Wind players accomplish this affect by varying the diaphragm pressure on a continuous note. Mattheson describes vibrato with the bow separately and immediately after discussion of the left-hand type:

> Whoever is acquainted with the tremolos in organ works will know that simply the wavering air itself performs the effect and no higher or lower keys are touched on the keyboard . . . on violins the same trembling can also be accomplished on one tone within one bowing; without another being necessary for it.
>
> (1739) II.3.28, tr. Harriss, p. 270

---

[60] Carter (1991) p. 44
[61] (1756) V.9, tr. Knocker, p. 99. For diagram see above p. 123

2.6 The slow bow

A tradition of a pulsating quaver bow-stroke originated in music of the early 17th-century Italian violinist composers such as Marini and Fontana, with the bow vibrato notated as groups of four quavers under a slur, and later in the century with dots under a slur. Sometimes, plain minims are accompanied by the word *affetti*, as in this extract from Marini's Sonata in d minor:

Ex. 2.6.9 *f*: Marini, Libro Terzo op. 22, Sonata in D minor

There is no firm evidence that the word *affetti* denotes the use of any specific 'affect' such as bow vibrato, although this would be appropriate at such places. The use of divisions or other Italian-style ornamentation (running or arpeggiated) should be tried.

In Castello's *Sonata seconda a soprano solo*,[62] the *affetti* are written in groups of linked quavers and marked *tremolo*:

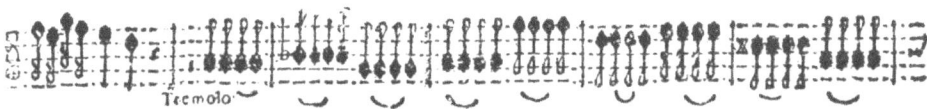

Ex. 2.6 10 *f*: Castello, Sonata secunda

Later in the 17th century, in addition to the slur over four quavers, a wavy line was often added as an additional clue to the performance of the bow vibrato effect. Vocal parts were treated in the same manner with wavy lines to indicate a vocal tremolo. Lully's opera *Isis* (1677) contains a trembling chorus which probably inspired Purcell's 'Frost Scene' in *King Arthur* (1691). Brossard's *Dictionnaire* (1703) refers to Lully's piece and confirms the execution of the tremble effect:

> One finds it used very often, either [written] in full or abbreviated 'trem', to advise those who play string instruments to make many notes on the same degree in a single stroke of the bow, as in imitating the organ tremulant. This is notated very often for the voice. We have an excellent example of both in the [scene of the] 'tremblers' in the opera *Isis* by Monsieur de Lully.
>
> Carter (1991), p. 54

The tremolo was essentially Italian in its use and origin. North writing in London at the beginning of the 18th century complains about misinterpretation of the bow vibrato indication by players when they play the quavers with too much separation (the editor points out that North's 'trembling hand' is the right hand, as he refers to vibrato as 'wrist-shake').

> There is another mode of the *Grave* that frequently occurs in our Itallianezed sonnatas, which I have known intituled *Tremolo*, and is now comonly performed with a tempered *stoccata*. And that [method] I take to be an abuse, and contrary to the genius of that mode, which is to hold out long notes inriched with the flowers of harmony and with a trembling hand, which of all parts together resembles the shaking stop of an organ.
>
> J. Wilson, p. 186

Long notes marked *affetti* may be performed with a quaver pulse (as written above) by altering the pressure on the bow with the hand. This affect often occurs in a well-defined section of the music where the special bow effects are presented to achieve maximum impact, frequently in a passage of strong chromatic harmony. The chords through which the music passes should be played with ebb and flow of dynamic and flexibility of tempo. Rising sequences could crescendo and accelerate while descending ones die away. Often more than one part has the *affetti* at once (e.g. violin and violone), in which case the

---

[62] *Sonate concertate in stilo moderno* (1629)

2.6 The slow bow

pulsations should be well co-ordinated between the players. The use of left-hand vibrato combined with the pulsed bow vibrato would be superfluous and, in my opinion, detract from the effect. Corelli's adagio movements are full of pulsating harmonic passages:

Ex. 2.6.11: Corelli, Concerto Grosso op. 6 no. 4

It would seem to be perfectly legitimate, from the above evidence, to use bow vibrato in groups of fours or twos in line with the harmonic movement in any Corellian adagio. Indeed this practice reflects the Italian style and may have been assumed by the composer. A calm, serene effect is thus obtained instantly revealing North's 'flowers of harmony'. Bow vibrato is obviously required in this passage from Handel's *Messiah*, setting up a calm smooth pulse in half-bar units for the words 'Comfort ye!' which follow:

Ex. 2.6.12: Handel, Messiah, 'Comfort ye'

J. S. Bach's works have many instances where bow vibrato might be used, even if not specifically indicated. Wherever repeated quavers are found in groups in accompanying passages, it is worth trying this type of bowing. Bach often writes groups of four repeated quavers within a slur with and without dots. The degree of separation is a matter for the performer and the context, but remember that if the pulsations become too separated, the effect of the bow vibrato is lost, as each note becomes more accented and then player might as well use separate bows. The effect of bow vibrato should be like a harmonic cushion, giving minim pulses, with each group slightly defined, but not the quavers within the group. Sometimes Bach writes quavers in groups on the same note interspersed with quavers moving onto different pitches. The repeated notes may be played as bow vibrato, and the same stroke continued through the passage with the moving notes. It is usually obvious where the effect should stop and start, by some indication of change of affect by harmony, rhythm or word stress. In the following example, groups of three notes in a bow may be started in the first bar in the second violin and viola parts and continued until dots are marked in the ninth bar. What is the purpose of the dots, apart from a signal to make a new kind of articulation? The whole passage, in my view, is suitable for bow vibrato as it contains groups of repeated notes.

2.6 The slow bow

Ex. 2.6.13: J. S. Bach, Christmas Oratorio 1st chorus, bars 17-27 (string parts only)

Dots or spiked dagger signs over repeated notes without a slur may be there to confirm that separate bows are definitely required, and the pulsating stroke should cease.

Although the rhythmic pulse of bow vibrato is usually in quavers, a faster rhythm may be demanded by the composer. For example, in *Hortus Chelicus* by Walther (1688), the affect is written as semiquavers with a wavy line over them, and the rubric *organo tremolante* describes the expected method of performance.

2.7 Quick notes

The basic bow-stroke

In his letter to Lombardini, Tartini describes how to practise fast notes using one of the three allegros written in continuous semiquavers from Corelli's opus 5 sonatas:[63]

Ex. 2.7.1: Tartini (1760)

He advises that the passages should be first practised slowly, and then a little faster each time through, until the maximum possible speed is achieved, and that these allegros are to be practised in all parts of the bow, both starting up-bow and down-bow for versatility, for the practice to have maximum effectiveness. In the same source, presumably to be practised in the same manner resting between each note, Tartini gives us an exercise for agile string crossing at speed:

Ex. 2.7.2: Tartini (1760)

The two terms staccato and spiccato have similar meanings in the 17th and early 18th centuries. Corrette's definition of 'staccato or spiccato' gives:

> ... should be played dry [sec], without drawing the bow, and well detached, as often found in largos and adagios of concertos.
>
> (1738), p. 43

Brossard defines spiccato as

> *separer, disjoindre*: detach or separate the sounds from the others. A special term for stringed instruments, a bit like staccato.
>
> (1702)

Articulation in allegro movements

Tartini advises in his 'rules for bowing' to distinguish between cantabile and allegro passages by means of articulation. In the former the bow-strokes should be so smooth that no silence is heard between the notes, and in the latter they should be separated. In order to decide which should apply, he instructs the player to play step-wise melodies cantabile and legato (with separate bows or with slurs added). If the melody moves by leaps, the passage is allegro and should be played detached.[64] Quantz agrees with this principle saying

> ... sustained and flattering notes must be slurred to one another, but gay and leaping notes must be detached and separated from one another.
>
> (1752) XI.11, tr. Reilly, p. 123

---

[63] (1760) in (1771) tr. Jacobi, p. 135
[64] (1771) tr. Jacobi, p. 55

Selecting a tempo for movements with continuous fast notes

Mace is against playing very fast and says

> *Many Drudge*, and take much *Pains* to Play their *Lessons very Perfectly*, (as they call It that is, *Fast*) which when they can do, you will perceive *Little Life, or Spirit in Them, meerly for want of the Knowledge of This last Thing, I now mention, viz.* They do not labour to find out the *Humour, Life* or *Spirit* of their *Lessons*.
>
> (1676), p. 147

C. P. E. Bach also advises us that the use of excessive speed is likely to wipe out the expressiveness of a piece:

> More often than not, one meets technicians, nimble keyboardists by profession, ... who astound us with their prowess without ever touching our sensibilities. They overwhelm our hearing without satisfying it and stun the mind without moving it.
>
> (1753) tr. Mitchell, p. 147

Matteis, the virtuoso violinist, writes in his 'good advice to play well' that

> ... you dont play your tune to fast, because your quick playing is apt to confuse you, so that you ought too play clearly and easily.
>
> (1682), p. 79

Rushing

Quantz warns against rushing and says each note must be distinct, played with liveliness and articulation and have its proper value. He advises:

> Everything that is hurriedly played causes your listeners anxiety rather than satisfaction. Pains must be taken to play each note with its proper value, and to avoid carefully either hurrying or dragging. To this end, the player should keep the tempo in mind at each crotchet, and should not believe it sufficient to be in accord with the other parts only at the beginning and end of the bar. Hurrying of passage work may occur, particularly in ascending notes ... To avoid this, the first note of quick figures must be stressed and held slightly.
>
> (1752) XII.11, XII.5, tr. Reilly, pp. 131, 130

Many writers in the 17th and 18th centuries encouraged the musician to imitate the ancient orators. The advice of the ancient classical rhetorician Quintilian is:

> It is only he who learns to speak correctly before he can speak with rapidity who will reach the heights that are our goal.
>
> II. iv. 17

North suggests two solutions to the hurrying of 'devisions':

> The allegro devisions, they are either *correnti* or *arpeggianti*. The former is when a part takes a carriere thro' a whole strain without ceasing, and the other parts favour the action, by short touches in the accords. It must be observed, that who ever hath this part, never thinks he runs fast enough, and comonly being warm in his pratise, he mends his pace. But if one may profer a temper to this extravagance, it should consist in two means. The one is some abatement of the hurry, so as to take along a middle part by way of andante, or some other melody by the attendants, which would have a reasonable agreement and effect, by being reduced to a state of being understood. The other means is a powerfull application of emphases, which, falling upon the accord places, would produce a shape of a consort; and the gross measures of the proper times would be seen (as it were) thro' the tinsell devision; as if there were a kind of pause upon the first of every 4, 6, or 3 (notes), whereof the notion is obvious, and the effect manifest.
>
> J. Wilson, p. 191

On the subject of divisions in a lively acoustic and fast playing in general, North remarks:

2.7 Quick notes

> This kind of agillity is pleasing to many, but to none so much as to the performers, who all the while are wrapt in the joy of their owne excellence; and in order to partake of those joys, few persons that practice faile to strain their facultys in the exercise of acceleration . . . and the fatall defect of such usage is the confusion that at a moderate distance will happen; because the sound spreading in the air, the swift notes run into one and another, and are not distinguisht, but dye in a meer hum- drum.
>
> J. Wilson, p. 235

Leopold Mozart on rushing in dotted rhythms:

> The dot should in fact be held at all times somewhat longer than its value. Not only is the performance thereby enlivened, but hurrying—that almost universal fault—is thereby checked; for otherwise, owing to the shortening of the dot, the music easily tends to increase in speed.
>
> (1756) I.III.11, tr. Knocker, p. 41-42

PRACTICAL APPLICATION

My interpretation of Tartini's short bow-stroke, followed by a rest, is a staccato stroke which is dug into the string with a little bite, and then released. After using this method to practise fast passages in slow motion with press—bite—release technique, the result when played at speed is a brilliant articulation which would be lacking in a more superficial stroke. It is important to use very little bow for the 'bite', ensuring that pressure is used from the hand (mainly first finger), and that the bow comes to rest between strokes, before tensing and pressing for the next 'bite'. The clearest articulation comes in the middle of the bow, a little further up from the point of balance, where the bow is strongest and the press—release mechanism feels easy. Tartini's instruction to practise in all parts of the bow may still be useful. However the player will notice that nearer the point, the stroke becomes weak and lacks sparkle as the Baroque bow curves away and a disproportionate amount of force must be used to overcome the tapering of the stick. Any amount of time spent practising fast passages with this technique is well worth the effort. The slow motion bite-release method may also be used to secure the co-ordination of left and right hand where string crossings are involved, as in *bariolage* passages and arpeggiated chord sequences crossing more than two strings.

The Baroque bow should remain near the string at all times when playing fast passages, and should not be allowed to bounce on to the string. If the bow wants to rebound away from the string, this is good as long as the basic stroke starts on or near the string and is not splashed or crashed on to it. The right hand should keep the pressure on throughout the fast note passage to maintain the bow's closeness to the string. After mastering this stroke, the modern player used to a longer, heavier bow will be amazed at the speed with which separate strokes can be played with the lighter Baroque bow with a slight flick of the hand. This is a necessary technique for playing early 17th-century music where fast passages and many ornaments are played with separate bows.

All the early definitions of the word spiccato imply space between the notes. Brossard (1702): 'Dry, without drawing the bow': in other words, a short, individually controlled bow-stroke well defined from its neighbours. The use of the word for a fast thrown stroke does not apply until after the invention of the Tourte bow, with its ability to ricochet and its greater bounce.

The word 'detached' is often misinterpreted as an instruction to use a *martelé* or *détaché* type of bow-stroke in the upper half of the bow. This is not a stroke suitable for the design of a Baroque bow, as the upper half of the bow is very weak due to the tapering of the stick. The word 'detached' in a Baroque context only means separate bows, not a particular bow-stroke. A lifted stroke in the middle to lower half (according to tempo and affect) is more appropriate for detached (i.e. separated) notes. This stroke can then be brought on to the string and made longer by degrees for more conjunct notes. When writing about bowing, modern writers who are not themselves string players often use this word which gives the wrong impression to a string player, to whom the word 'detached' means a particular stroke associated with the Tourte model bow.

Articulation and emphasis in passages of continuous fast notes

When playing continuous fast passages, the performer should avoid creating a seamless monotonous feeling with equal emphasis to each note. Starting with the strongest notes at the bar-line position, look at the harmonic structure to see if and when this pattern is broken. Groups of notes needing special emphasis (where interesting harmony is present) may have selected notes lengthened or accented a little. Rushing through as fast as possible should be avoided, as the affect of the passage will be lost. Strong points should be approached with a pulling back of the tempo, or an articulation made before the point for emphasis. Another device to direct the shape of the performance is the geographical shape of the notes. Patterns and sequences should be noted, and the places where the patterns start, or are broken should be articulated. A small articulation emphasises the structure of sequences or patterns, which often occur in the form of two short phrases followed by a longer, differently shaped one. This effect may also be achieved by dynamic means, with the weakest note at the low point in the sequence, followed by a crescendo to the highest.

The length of notes in passages of continuous quavers should be varied, giving interest and life to the music. However, this may be ruled out by the word andante when a walking bass in quavers might be performed with equal length notes. The harmonic interest should still be shown, perhaps with weight rather than length. In passages of very fast notes, the bow may not have much time to register differences in the length of individual notes (in an Italian style coranto, for example), so emphasis and nuance may be achieved by dynamic. In long sequences of fast notes, cadences should generally be weak, especially where the notes continue onwards without a break. Leaning on the important harmonies, and bending the tempo round interesting harmonic progressions can lead the listener through all the salient points, even when the written notes are all of the same note value. A variety of dynamics should be used, perhaps dropping down before a rising sequence, or making a diminuendo as the music descends into a lower register. Sometimes, a crescendo downwards is called for if the harmony at the bottom is strong. Look for two-voice patterns with higher and lower answering phrases.

Selecting a tempo for movements with many fast notes

It is often better to adopt a slightly slower tempo and play every note clearly (not necessarily equally), as it is frequently the case that a fast passage played at moderate speed with brilliant, varied articulation and interesting phrasing is more exciting than when it is played as fast as possible without time for the musical points to register with the listener. This is particularly true in a room with a lively acoustic. When selecting a tempo for a movement containing continuous fast notes, the first factor to consider is the rate of harmony change: one change per bar probably means a faster tempo than where there are lots of interesting harmonic points to be expressed and negotiated within a bar's length. Extremely fast tempi are rarely appropriate in movements which consist of continuous semiquavers, particularly for movements marked only allegro, meaning gay as well as quick. Short bursts of runs or tiradas featured as written-out ornamentation should be very fast and brilliant, but for movements where the fast notes are continuous in a regular way (as in Corelli's opus 5 semiquaver allegros) and contain many turns of expression and harmonic points, a moderate tempo is usually more telling. Written reports of virtuoso players throughout the 17th and 18th centuries tend to emphasise beauty of tone, and tasteful ornamentation, rather than speed of execution, which is often regarded as vulgar and tasteless (North's 'tinsel division'). For the string player, it is advisable to think of breathing points when playing fast passages, as a continuous breathless rush makes no sense of the music. When breaths are incorporated into the movement, as would be necessary for a wind player, the music is more easily understood, and the player avoids the risk of rushing from one phrase to the next. This is a particularly useful technique at the ends of sections and before making repeats or da capos. Take a deep breath before returning to the beginning of the section. Imagine the orator pacing his delivery with full stops and colons: each phrase needs proper

2.7 Quick notes

punctuation whatever the speed adopted. Silence while a breath is taken can be more compelling than a gabbled sentence which falls over itself. The addition of accents can make a passage of continuous notes seem faster and more exciting while the elimination of accents can make it seem slower.

Presto and allegro di molto might indicate faster speeds than merely allegro or vivace (meaning only 'lively').[65] Care should be taken not to rush continuous fast notes, and practising with the metronome cannot be too highly recommended.

If dynamics are included for special effects, articulation is recommended before the sudden change for emphasis. Both Mattheson and Quantz recommend making an articulation between two affects in order to distinguish clearly for the listener one from the other.[66]

CASE STUDIES

Care should be taken to identify the functions of the fast notes by examining the harmonic progressions underneath. The changing harmonic rate can give you a clue as to the best speed to adopt. Examine the bass line to find out what type of harmonic pattern is being shown. Places where there is a slow-moving change in the bass (1st example) should be given emphasis. If the bass stays still on the same note or chord, a fantasy-like effect may be produced, similar to a cadenza in flexibilty and rubato (2nd example).

Ex. 2.7.3: Biber, Sonata 2 (1681)

The above example is from the 1st variation of an Aria ground bass movement, of a type often found in the sonatas of Biber and Schmelzer. Small variations in the length of the fast notes are permissible as long as the half-bar harmony changes are regular.

Ex. 2.7.4: Biber, Sonata 1 (1681) opening of the Finale

This finale follows a long Aria with variations, and breaks the pattern of the previous triple, one-in-a-bar pulse with a cadenza-like outburst. Rhythmic freedom is possible, and probably intended, in situations such as this where the bass line is stationary or has a long pedal note held over several bars. If the bass moves slowly (as in the first example) but regularly the fast notes may only be flexible within the main beats.

The following movement by J. S. Bach from the sonata in G minor for violin solo should be played quite fast as the time signature and tempo marking indicate (3/8 Presto). However, the effect of the slurring detail marked by Bach would be lost beyond a certain velocity. Even at speed, this sort of detail should be emphasised and brought out to provide variety and interest. The first four bars maintain the same harmony and need very little bar-line accentuation. The harmony then moves in two, two-bar units with a slur in the first of the pairs of bars, followed by a falling sequence of single-bar harmonic changes, before moving into a new more complex figure with slurs. It is interesting to note that every other bar-line is only partially marked, as if Bach wants to imply double length bars.

---

[65] See also tempo selection part 1.4
[66] See Articulation pp. 9-10

Ex. 2.7.5 *f*: J. S. Bach, Sonata in G minor for violin solo

The Giga from the Partita in D minor displays the same sort of variety of detail in the marked slurs.

Emphasis of the harmonic changes will give half-bar or even bar accentuation, making the whole movement lighter and more dance-like. Avoid an emphasis on every beat, or a continuous monochrome stream of notes with no emphasis at all. The strongest notes where the changes of harmony occur are the lowest (on the first beats of bars 1 and 2). The cadence in the fifth complete bar (end of second line) should arrive weakly, bouncing off the bar-line and dominant (bottom A) which precedes it. The resolution note (dotted quaver D) is the conclusion of the first phrase, still in the home key. This point should feel like a minor resting point before introducing the new material which follows, leading the music into new harmonic territory.

Ex. 2.7.6 *f*: J. S. Bach, Partita in D minor for violin solo

2.7 Quick notes

In the following extract from Corelli op. 5 no. 1 a performance based on emphasising the strong harmonic points (information given by the figured bass) and pointing out the sequences is suggested:

1. The movement starts strongly, brightly rather than aggressively, dipping into the middle of bar 1 and making towards bar 2.
2. Bar 2 is weak in the middle.
3. A sequence of 2 short phrases and a long phrase starts at the end of bar 2 eventually leading to the strong middle of bar 4.
4. The dynamic should drop down at the beginning of bar 5 for the rising sequence which has 2 short and 1 longer fragment.
5. A falling sequence of stresses at the half-bar points leads to a low point at 10 where a series of short crescendos starts building on the rising figures to the half-bar points and away to the bar-lines. Etc.
6. Try to lead to the strong points, and shade away to the weak ones, so that the emphatic points are not merely accented, but the whole movement ebbs and flows, leading us and directing us through the main points of the harmonic plan. Try leaning on or lengthening the important notes as suggested above by Quantz and North. This plan is only a suggestion, and the reader should experiment with similar movements using the same principles. There are three movements with continuous semiquavers in Corelli's opus 5 sonatas.

Ex.2.7.7: Corelli, Sonata op. 5 no. 1, Allegro

Up- and down-bow staccato

The up-bow staccato (many up-bows separated within one stroke) was first used for brilliant effect by the virtuoso violinists of the 17th century: Walther, Biber and Schmelzer. Later, in the 18th century, J. S. Bach used this bowing in his *Mass* in B minor 'et in unum' for a lighter effect:

Ex. 2.7.8: J. S. Bach, Mass in B minor, Credo: 'Et in unum'

G. F. Handel used a similar bowing in the opening of Concerto Grosso op. 6 no. 1:

Ex. 2.7.9: Handel, Concerto Grosso op. 6 no. 1

Biber's music contains an unusual bowing for the 17th century which is often called the 'Biber bowing'. Two notes are played in one down-bow creating a virtuoso show when played at speed.

Ex. 2.7.10 *f*: Biber, 'Rosary' sonata no. 4, Ciacona

It should be practised in a slow deliberate way, at first using one movement for the double down-bow, then gradually speeded up until the appropriate tempo is reached. It can be played strongly and quite violently, or gently as the context demands.

Summary for playing fast notes:

1. Practise the biting articulated bow-stroke.
2. Note points of emphasis from harmonic information.
3. Choose phrasing, articulation or breathing spaces from melodic contours.
4. Use the function and rate of movement of the bass part to help select a suitable tempo.

2.8 The slur (lié, liaison, coulement, binding or legatura)

The bowed slur has been in use from the 16th century. Ganassi (1542) indicates a divided articulated slur similar to the tucked-in bow-stroke. Ortiz (1553) suggests slurring in his manual of divisions:

> When there are two or three crotchets in a bar, only the first is articulated, the rest pass under the same bow stroke as I have already said, and as this can be demonstrated (in practice) rather than in theory I leave it to the good judgement of the musician.
>
> (1553) tr. Gammie, p. 4

Tosi gives a good general definition of the slur in 18th-century music:

> The first Note is a Guide to all that follow, closely united, gradual, and with such Evenness of Motion, that in Singing it imitates a certain Gliding, by the Masters called a Slur.
>
> (1723) tr. Galliard (1743), p. 53

The slur is a line which connects a selection of notes together. For string players it is primarily a bowing instruction but it is also used by composers to indicate phrasing and general points of emphasis or articulation. The writer with the most to say about the use of slurs is Leopold Mozart:

> Not only must the written and prescribed slurs be observed with the greatest exactitude but when, as in many a composition, nothing at all is indicated, the player must himself know how to apply the slurring and detaching tastefully and in the right place ... which however must be in keeping with the character of the piece.
>
> (1756) XII.11, tr. Knocker, p. 220

During the 18th century the slur was also regarded as a diminuendo. When only two notes are slurred, the second of a pair of quavers is to be played softer than the first. Quantz:

> The second note in the bar, which is slurred to the first, may be expressed a bit more softly than the others.
>
> (1752) XVII.II.8, tr. Reilly, p. 218

Ex. 2.8.1: Quantz (1752)

Leopold Mozart emphasises the use of the slur as a diminuendo:

> Often three, four, and even more notes are bound together by such a slur and half-circle. In such a case the first thereof must be somewhat more strongly accented and sustained longer; the others, on the contrary, being slurred on to it in the same stroke with a diminishing of the tone, even more and more quietly and without the slightest accent.
>
> (1756) VI.17, tr. Knocker, p. 220

However, where many quick notes are slurred in large groups, Leopold Mozart advises the following example to be

> ... played so that the first note of each bar is strongly marked by an accent from the bow.
>
> (1756) tr. Knocker, p. 112

Ex. 2.8.2: Leopold Mozart (1756)

The slur essentially implies 'joined'. Quantz emphasises its uninterrupted, smooth nature:

> In slurring notes in the Adagio, you must be careful not to make them seem detached, unless there are dots beneath the slur that is above the notes. Likewise *pincemens* must

2.8 The slur (lié, liaison, coulement, binding or legatura)

not be introduced, especially if they are not indicated, lest the sentiment that the slurred notes are to express be in any way impeded.

(1752) XVII.II.12 tr. Reilly, p. 223

When playing smooth and joined notes in a slur, several writers remind the player not to 'mark' the rhythm with the bow. This instruction seems to contradict the instruction above, where the beats are marked in the long slur containing many notes, but Leopold Mozart intends this instruction to apply to single notes which cross beats, as in syncopation:

> ... in such a case one must not only avoid letting the middle note be heard in two parts by means of an after-pressure of the bow, but must also bind the third note on to the second quite smoothly, and without any particular accent.

(1756) IV.22, tr. Knocker, p. 81

Ex. 2.8.3: Leopold Mozart (1756)

If the player decides to add slurs, Leopold Mozart gives some guidelines:

> If, and when they should be slurred or detached? Both depend on the cantilena of the piece and on the good taste and sound judgement of the performer, if the composer has forgotten to mark the slurs, or has himself not understood how to do so. Still, the following rule can serve to some extent: Notes at close intervals should usually be slurred, but notes far apart should be played with separate strokes and in particular be arranged to give a pleasant variety.

(1756) IV.29, tr. Knocker, p. 83

This advice agrees with Tartini (to whom Leopold Mozart is indebted for many of the ideas in his treatise). Tartini's advice on slurring and articulation follows the same principles:

> Notes ascending or descending by semitones should always be played in a single bow. In a slurred passage, if the first note does not have the same value as the following ones, it should be played in a separate bow.
>
> If a passage consists partly of leaps and partly of stepwise movements, bow the former in one way and the latter in another.

(1771) tr. Jacobi, p. 57

Geminiani gives examples of many different slurred patterns to practise:

Ex. 2.8.4 *f*: Geminiani

> This example shews in how many different Manners of bowing you may play 2, 3, 4, 5 and 6 notes.

(1751), p. 23

If slurred notes are to be performed smoothly, this implies that any changing of position or string crossing should be avoided if at all possible. However a string crossing is often preferable to a position change which would more seriously interrupt the smooth effect of the slurred notes.

Many writers in the late 17th and 18th centuries list the slur as an ornament. When regarded as such, it may be added to the music at the whim of the player in the same spirit in which a trill is added. Some composers such as Couperin and J. S. Bach use the slur in a very precise way. In the music of these composers additional slurs should be

2.8 The slur (lié, liaison, coulement, binding or legatura)

added with caution. Other composers leave their music practically slur-free, expecting the player to add the conventional slurs to taste.

Sometimes, a slur occurs over the first of a group in a repeated pattern of notes. It may be assumed that the pattern should be continued, until the musical idea changes. From Handel's Israel in Egypt, the plague of flies and lice only has the first three groups slurred, but the slurs should continue through the whole passage.

Ex. 2.8.5: Handel, Israel in Egypt

When observing the slurs written in by the composer, it should be assumed that the rule of down-bow is still in operation. Long slurs where the slur is regarded as a diminuendo are probably more comfortable on a down-bow. Sometimes it is unavoidable to have up-bows where there are several consecutive long slurs.

Breaking slurs for the convenience of what happens next in the music is not good practice. Try to keep the slurs intact for their effect, and re-arrange the bowing by taking an extra tuck in the up-bow, or retake another down-bow as close as possible before the most important point for the bow direction. If a slur is split, the phrasing and articulation will automatically be changed. Often the effort involved in maintaining a slow bow to execute the marked slur is part of the effect required: it should sound held back. If the bowing is too free and easy, aspects of the music demanding long slurs with a slow bow speed are inevitably lost. When long phrases (i.e. slurs) are split up into shorter ones there is inevitably a loss of the intended articulation.

CASE STUDY

Ex. 2.8.6 *f*: J. S. Bach, Partita in D minor for violin solo, Corrente.

Here is an example of a slur being changed to obtain a convenient bowing. The 1 + 8 notes slur in bars 5, 7, 8, and 9 (above) has been read as 9 notes in the slur (below), with quite a different effect. The cumulative tension of the long, slow, slurred up-bows leading to the first notes of the next bar followed by the next long slur is much more exciting than the 'easy' version of 9 notes to a bow, played with an even bow speed. The affect of the 1 + 8 notes may be compared to the effort made by the acceleration of a car changing up through the gears, against a bland, easy 9 notes in top gear.

Note that Bach uses the Italian dance title 'corrente' to match the style of writing. The editor of the *Bach Gesellschaft* edition (ex. 2.8.7) has used the inappropriate French form.

2.8 The slur (lié, liaison, coulement, binding or legatura)

Ex. 2.8.7: J. S. Bach, Partita in D minor for violin solo, Corrente.

Early slurs

The treatise by Ortiz (1553) contains no slurs in the music, although he commends their use, confirming his trust in the good judgement of the musician (see p. 142). With the development of the early Italian violin repertoire, the slur appears in Farina's works (1620s) as a special imitative effect, and bow vibrato was first used by Marini.[67] As the 17th century progressed, short slurs joining notes of different pitch became more common, mainly on pairs of quick notes.

Ex. 2.8.8 ƒ: Playford, The Division-violin (1684)

The Italian style

Ex. 2.8.9 ƒ: Castello, Sonate Concertate, Libro Secondo (1627)

In early 17th-century Italian music, slurs appear only on groups of a maximum of 4 notes as decoration, on tied notes or in bow vibrato figures. The primitive state of 17th-century Italian printing technology may have influenced the limited use of slurs in printed editions.

Ex. 2.8.10 ƒ: Matteis, Ayrs for the Violin, Second Part, Sonata p. 58

Long ornamental flourishes appear slurred in the engraved works of the Italian violinist Matteis (1680s). Matteis used the slur in a very advanced and imaginative way, in longer phrases, notes with leaping intervals, and across strong beats.

Corelli and Veracini use the slur combined with dynamic contrast as an ornament and to vary repeated passages:

---
[67] see pp. 129-130

2.8 The slur (lié, liaison, coulement, binding or legatura)

Ex. 2.8.11 *f*: Corelli, Sonata op. 5 no. 11, Gavotta, Allegro

Ex. 2.8.12 *f*: Veracini, Sonata op. 2 no. 3, Allegro

Note that in ex. 2.8.12 the bow-stroke at piano would have to be re-iterated where the same note is repeated.

The French style

Ex. 2.8.13 *f*: Marais, Pièces en Trio, Chaconne (1er dessus)

Most slurs are purely ornamental, and rarely include more than 2 or 3 notes.

Ex. 2.8.14 *f*: Couperin, 2ième Concert Royal, Echos

A rare long slur over a whole bar. Couperin was meticulous in marking the articulation and slurring. Note that the viol part deliberately has a different slurring/phrasing.

Slurs in ornamentation

All of the 'small graces' should be played slurred (trill, appoggiatura etc). A slur and a trill should often be added to a dotted note with a written-out ending, particularly in later 18th-century music (see ex. 1.5.29). The ending of the ornament is slurred to the trill and leads to the next beat.

2.8 The slur (lié, liaison, coulement, binding or legatura)

Ex. 2.8.15 *f*: Marais, Pièces en trio, Menuet (1er dessus)

Most ornaments of the division type should be played with separate bows. However, Simpson gives divisions for rising and falling intervals with slurs (ex. 1.5.8a)

Slurs with words

It is tempting to add slurs to match vocal melismas, especially when instruments double the voice parts. However, it may be more appropriate and is often more flexible to keep separate bows in these situations. The subtleties of articulation in the voice part may be reflected in the bow-stroke, sometimes pairing, and varying the smooth or detached syllables with matching bow articulation. Committing yourself to playing exactly the same slurs as the voice is, in practice, a more inflexible approach. The occasional paired slur on adjacent notes may then be allowed to match a syllable.

Ex. 2.8.16 : Purcell, three examples from A Song for St. Cecilia's Day (1692)

Purcell's own instrumental slurring does not always match the vocal slurs, but it is possible to imply the varying lengths of note with separate bows, either smooth and long, or shorter and lifted where appropriate.

Summary

Throughout the Baroque period, where slurs appear they should be clearly defined. How much articulation is required and how clearly defined the slur becomes will depend on the context. Where a sequence of slurred pairs occurs, the usual rule of bar and harmonic hierarchy should be applied to prevent the repetition of the slurred figure becoming monotonous, by varying the weight on the first of the paired notes in accordance with its importance within the bar, or within the beat. Some pairs will then become weak, and some strong.

Unless a comic effect is required, the player should avoid the clipped hiccup which often makes its appearance through an over-zealous wish to point out the slurs. On the other hand, completely legato playing between slurs is definitely un-stylistic. A lightening of the bow-stroke is sometimes enough to point the existence of the slur, without a complete cessation of sound (in a slow affettuoso, for example). Practise keeping a thread of sound going between bow-strokes, to assist the line of melody to flow where many short slurs are present. On other occasions, a clear gap will be necessary to point the slur at both ends. The amount of weight and articulation applied to the slur at either end will depend on the affect of the movement. It is hard work articulating at both ends of the slurs in the following lively gig, but gives a brilliant effect:

2.8 The slur (lié, liaison, coulement, binding or legatura)

Ex. 2.8.17 *f*: Corelli, Sonata op. 5 no. 7, Giga

Performance considerations:

1. The first note may be emphasised or lengthened a little ('the first note is a guide to all that follow').
2. Articulation should occur at both ends of the slur to a greater or lesser degree.
3. Most slurs are diminuendos.
4. The bow-stroke should be as smooth as possible.
5. Avoid string-crossing or position-changing under a slur.
6. Slurs may be added in certain circumstances, such as pairs of conjunct notes.

2.9 Chords and double stopping

The way of playing chords in the modern conventional way is the '2 + 2' method, where the lower two notes are played together before the beat, closely followed on the beat by the top two notes which are sustained evenly. A similar method is used to play chords of three notes, with the middle note held through the split. This method of realising a chord supposes that the most interesting and important feature of the music is the top part, i.e. the melody line. In Baroque music, where harmonic considerations rule, the player's priorities should be focused on the bass line, with the bottom note as the strongest point in the chord, usually played on the beat. The other notes of the chord may be spread in a variety of ways according to the context, speed of the music, or consideration of other parts which may be moving or static. Where there is time, as for example at the end of an adagio movement, a chord may be spread slowly, lingering on the effect of each note, but if there is not much time, a quick spread will have to be made.

Simpson's description of chordal playing on the viol is very clear:

> When two, three, or more notes stand over one another they must be played as one, by sliding the bow over those strings which express the sound of the said notes . . . be sure always to hitt the lowest string first; and let the bow slide from it to the highest, touching the middle notes in its Passage betwixt them.
>
> (1659), p. 9 para 13

Mace says:

> *Therefore I Advise ever when you come to a Full Stop, be sure to give the Lowest String a Good Full Share of your Bow (Singly, by It self, before you Slide it upon the Rest) and Leave It likewise with a little Eminency of Smartness, by Swelling the Bow a little, when you part with That String. This will make your Play very Lovely.*
>
> (1676), p. 249

Although the above instructions are found in viol tutors, it may be taken for granted that this method was observed by all stringed instruments. By 'full stop' Mace means a chord stopped, i.e. fully fingered. The Italian immigrant violinist Matteis called the second part of his *Ayrs for the Violin*

> Other Ayrs Preludes Allmands Sarabands &c with Full stops for the Violin.

This contains more elaborate and difficult music than the first part, including the use of double stopping and chords. In the following example, the notation of the last chord implies a quick spread and only the top note to be held long:

Ex. 2.9.1 *f*: Matteis, Ayrs for the Violin, Second Part, Ricercata

Occasionally, there may be an indication to spread downwards from the principal top note for dramatic effect, or even down and immediately upwards in a free manner. Avoid doing this if it is not specified, especially in counterpoint (Bach).

Ex. 2.9.2: Leclair, Sonata V, Book III

There is no rule as to which notes should be sounded together; the above writers describe how the bow should slide across the strings from the lowest to the highest. The imagination of the player should be brought to bear on the possibilities for an effective chord performance. How long to dwell on the bass note, how quickly to slide the bow

2.9 Chords and double stopping

across, and how long to sustain the top note or notes? There is no set formula. Sometimes it may be appropriate to sustain two notes at the top, leaving a single top note for the final thread of sound. It would be inappropriate to sustain the top two notes of the chord if this produces an interval of a fourth or fifth. The intervals of third, sixth or octave produce a more pleasant and harmonious result. Another method is to roll the chord from the bottom up and down, delaying the arrival on the top note until the last minute. The general effect of this way of playing chords is much less aggressive, and gives rise to a more expressive way of including chords in the music, sometimes using an up-bow, which is impossible when the '2 + 2' technique is employed. Chords should not automatically be played loudly or aggressively, but follow the expressive basis of the movement in question, varying the speed of spread according to the affect required. Sometimes languid as in the following example:

Ex. 2.9.3 *f*: Bonporti, Invenzione VI.

and sometimes quick and lively:

Ex. 2.9.4 *f*: Veracini, Sonata opus 2

As the opening three-note chords are marked staccato, it may be assumed that they are also loud, and that all three notes may be made to sound simultaneously. The four-note chords which follow will need a quick spread. The staccato instruction probably still applies in bar 3 despite the lack of dots. It is easier to make three notes sound simultaneously when playing loudly with an instrument fitted with a Baroque-style bridge, which has less curvature than the modern model.[68] In the above example, down/up/down/up bowing for bar one might only be possible with an old-style bridge. If being played on a modern violin, the player may have to use all down-bows to create the desired effect.

Occasionally a two-note chord or double stop may be split to imitate a fuller chord by emphasising the bottom note alone before playing the two together.

In orchestral music, the usual modern practice of dividing the chord between the players to make all the notes sound simultaneously should be ignored in favour of the earlier method of spreading the chord slightly. In Baroque string music a chord is usually written for a certain affect, not just for the purpose of filling in the harmony. To synchronise the notes would deny the affect of a grand flourish at the end of a movement or the first bar of an Italian overture. Chords usually employ open strings contributing to the 'ring'.

Sometimes chords are written with more than one note on one string, in which case, the player should just play the written notes consecutively upwards, without sustaining anything, in an arpeggiated manner. It is not necessary to move to an outlandish position in order to continue with the 2 + 2 formula with only one note per string.

---

[68] see drawings p. 237

2.9 Chords and double stopping

Contrapuntal playing

North is not impressed with double stops on the violin:

> The use of double notes is too much affected, and done as if a consort of 3 or 4 parts might be obtained that way; but at best it proves hard and uncouth, and is not worth the paines and difficulty that belongs to it. But masters must doe (seeming) wonders, as tumblers shew tricks which none else can performe, to obtain esteem by pleasing the ignorant.
>
> J. Wilson, p. 234

Where continuous music is written with triple and quadruple stops, the player should not try to realise in sound literally what he sees on the page. J. S. Bach in particular is meticulous in writing the parts strictly, with the direction of the tails of the notes indicating a continuous line in the music. He often includes rests where parts stop and before they start, to indicate the counterpoint. The lowest part may be differentiated in tone colour to give a bass-line character.

Ex. 2.9.5 *f*: J. S. Bach, Sonata in G minor for solo violin, Siciliana

Players should not expect to play or hear every note as written. It is impossible to sustain more than two notes at once, and the player should aim at a general impression of the several parts. The most important line should be identified and emphasised without aggression and by various subtle means. Sometimes it is sufficient merely to touch a lower note to give the impression of the harmonic movement whilst continuing to keep the other part(s) going. In this Walther sonata (1676) minims only need be lightly registered while concentrating on the moving part. In some bars it would be impossible to sustain the minims through their true value. The bowing should not be literal either: slurs may be added (e.g. quavers bar 2) to help the continuity of part writing.

Ex. 2.9.6 *f*: Walther, Sonata in G major, 1676

Choice of fingering can assist the contrapuntal effect if one part is kept on a lower string using 4th finger, and the other on a higher one using the open string (the e^2 minim at the end of line 2, use 4th finger, then open $e2$ on the next beat).

Many composers notated two tails on an open string note to indicate that both the stopped and open string should be played to enhance the resonance of that note. Often this occurs on strong beats where it is worth the effort of trying to play both notes, but just as frequently, it occurs on a weak part of the beat, in which case, it might be better to ignore the instruction. Sometimes, the double tail might only indicate a unison to satisfy the counterpoint where two parts meet, and so playing one note should be sufficient (Walther sonata: the double d^2 on the pause).

2.9 Chords and double stopping

Arpeggio and bariolage

Written chords are often accompanied by the instruction *arpeggio*, as in Corelli op. 5 no. 1. Where the instruction to arpeggiate is given, rhythmic patterns should be adopted to fit in with the moving bass line:

Ex. 2.9.7 *f*: Corelli, Sonata op. 5 no. 1, Allegro

Bach demonstrates a method of arpeggiating in the first chord before merely indicating the harmonies with the word *arpeggio*.

Ex. 2.9.8 *f*: J. S. Bach, Partita in D minor for solo violin, Chaconne

Sometimes the arpeggio instruction is a vertical wavy line:

Ex. 2.9.9: J. S. Bach, Sonata no. 2 in A major for violin and harpsichord

Geminiani also supplies us with a selection of arpeggiated figures from which to choose

> ... by which the learner will see in what the art of executing the arpeggio consists.
>
> (1751), p. 28

Ex. 2.9.10 *f*: Geminiani

2.9 Chords and double stopping

The later violin tutors give arpeggio patterns with fingerings:

Ex. 2.9.11 ƒ: L'Abbé le fils, Principes du Violon (1761)

Where the top note of an arpeggiated figure is E, Leopold Mozart says it should always be played open.[69]

Ex. 2.9.12: Leopold Mozart (1756)

If there is a moving lower part, as in the J. S. Bach sonata no. 2 (ex. 2.9.9), the arpeggios should be played in a strict rhythmic pattern to fit with the moving middle part, even though there is a static pedal note in the bass.

The word arpeggio (originating according to Leopold Mozart from the word harp) gives the player freedom to split the chord into a rhythmic pattern which should last as long as the written note. In a sequence of these chords the pattern may be varied, perhaps starting in triplets and accelerating to semiquavers as the sequence progresses, and three note chords change to four-note chords. The notes may be played slurred, separate, or a mixture of the two according to context. It is usually more satisfying harmonically to commence with the lowest note of the written chord.

Any arpeggiated figure, no matter how brief, should use open strings as the bright ringing of the E or other open string enhances the brilliant quality of such writing:

Ex. 2.9.13 ƒ: Corrette, L'Ecole d' Orphée (1738)

---

[69] (1756) VIII.III.18, tr. Knocker, p. 163

2.9 Chords and double stopping

In this example, an Italian style corrente, open strings should be used in bars 3-4 and 13-14 to increase the brilliance and sonority of these passages.

Chordal or harmonic *bariolage* figures which cross the string should make full use of open strings to enhance the sonority and give the passage increased resonance. Use of the 4th finger instead of open strings only serves to deaden this effect. For this reason, low positions should be used wherever possible, as the longest possible string length should be maintained to give the greatest resonance. Fingers of the left hand should be kept down for the duration of the harmonic point. The importance of holding the fingers of the left hand in place for as long as possible (the *teniie*) should not be under-estimated. The contrapuntal effect is enhanced by the lingering resonance of the note after the bow has left the string on which that note is played.[70] As vibrato and position changing are much less commonly used in Baroque playing, this habit is easy to acquire.

Another effect similar to *bariolage*, but slurred across two strings is *ondeggiando*. This device is indicated by a horizontal wavy line. A shimmering effect is achieved in a type of bow vibrato which crosses two strings, breaking the double stop and alternating the two notes in a slurred bow. This may be what Bach intended at the end of the prelude of the A minor sonata:

Ex. 2.9.14 *f*: J. S. Bach, Sonata in A minor for solo violin, Grave

It is important to realise when broken chords appear written out in the music. Chords often appear written out in *bariolage* form. Interesting high points such as dissonances, often in the form of 7ths, as in the next example (on the bar-lines) should be emphasised, and less important chords (resolutions in the form of 6ths) glossed over. Use low positions wherever possible and play across the strings for increased resonance.

Ex. 2.9.15: Handel, Concerto Grosso op. 3 no. 1

Overall direction in a continuous chordal passage should be apparent and exaggerated by the performer. Often the arpeggiated figure over a pedal point commences quietly and works itself up into a frenzy with a final flourish.

Ex. 2.9.16: J. S. Bach, Brandenburg concerto no. 4, Presto

The very fast speed means that the *bariolage* effect is heard almost as tremolo double stopping, contributing to the excitement of the affect.

The heavy downward spread chords often heard on modern interpretations of the unaccompanied sonatas for violin by Bach are needlessly aggressive and instead of enhancing the contrapuntal line, only serve to obscure it in a series of accents which disturb the affect of the music. The ear picks up the expected notes from elaborate double stops where a thematic line is threaded through the phrase, without the player having to use tricks to emphasise certain notes in an unnatural and confusing way.

---

[70] see p. 73 for more on this subject

2.9 Chords and double stopping

Ex. 2.9.17 *f*: J. S. Bach, Partita in D minor for solo violin, Chaconne

In bars 9-11 the line in the lower voice can be heard without sustaining these notes in the chord. The intermediate beats without chords carry the line through so that the ear understands the part writing.

It is a commonly held misconception that playing contrapuntal music in sustained lines in more than two parts is possible on the earlier violin with its lower and less curved bridge. The fact is, that if it were possible to sustain the sound on more than two strings at once, it would be impossible to play on a single string at all, as the angle of the bridge would be so shallow that the bow would unavoidably touch the adjacent strings. The lower curvature of the bridge does make chords and arpeggiated figures easier to play, but, as with the highly curved modern bridge, three notes are only possible in loud passages where quite heavy pressure with the bow can force the middle string to be depressed sufficiently to allow the two adjacent strings to be heard. The Baroque bow has no particular features which enable it to sustain three strings simultaneously. Only hurdy-gurdies with their circular bow hair surrounding the instrument can play on more than two strings at once in a sustained manner.

Double stopping and national style

Bohemia

The Italian violinists of the late 17th and early 18th centuries were very fond of full chords in their sonatas, and used them copiously for dramatic effect. The South German violin school of the late 17th century was under the Italian influence and very advanced contrapuntal and chordal writing is to be found in the works of Biber, Schmelzer, Walther and Westhoff.

Ex. 2.9.18 *f* and modern edition: Westhoff, Suite III

In the above extract, the original notation appears first, with a modern version of the first two bars below. The use of the great stave with various clefs makes the contrapuntal writing easier to see, but for modern players rather difficult to read.

The peak of the art of contrapuntal writing for the violin, evolving from the compositions of his predecessors Westhoff and Biber, must be the works for unaccompanied violin by Bach, where the fugues offer no concessions to the limitations

2.9 Chords and double stopping

of the instrument, with full three-part writing. The Chaconne from the D minor Partita shows us the limits to which every chord and arpeggio might be taken.

French

Although French viol composers such as Marais and Forqueray were using double stopping for melodic enhancement in the solo repertoire in the 17th century, the use of full-blown chords in violin music is not evident until the later works of Leclair, which combine the best of both French and Italian styles.

English

English violinists were using chords and double stopping in the solo division form from the 1680s. Under the influence of virtuoso immigrant violinists such as Baltzar (described by North as 'using the double notes very much') and the Italian Matteis, English players started to incorporate chords and multiple stopping into their compositions. North describes the playing of Matteis:

> I know no master fitt to be named with Corelli but him. His manner of using his violin was much out of the common road of handling, but out of it he made the utmost of sound double, single, swift, and all manners of touch which made such impressions that his Audience was not onely pleased, but full of wonder at him and his way of performing.
>
> J. Wilson, p. 309

Conclusion

As with all the musical elements in Baroque music, the player needs to seek out the main expressive purpose of the movement when playing chords and double stops. Applying a rigid formula when confronted with four-note chords results in predictable and monotonous playing. The Baroque bridge with its shallow curvature makes double stopping easier, and gives scope for more variety in expression when playing chords.

PART THREE
NATIONAL STYLE

The concept of 'Baroque' as a period of time, approximately 1600-1750, is a modern one. The first known published use of this word to describe music, meaning bizarre and grotesque, was applied in 1734 to Rameau's *Hippolyte et Aricie* in an anonymous letter published in *Le Mercure de France*:

> ... no thought, no expression at all. It ran through every trick with speed, unsparing of dissonances without end; sometimes two notes were persistently repeated for a quarter of an hour. There was much noise, force, humming; and when, by chance, two measures were encountered that could have made a pleasing melody, there was a quick change of key, of mode, and of meter. Continually it was sadness instead of tenderness. The uncommon had the character of the baroque, the fury of din.
>
> Claude V. Palisca, '*Baroque* as a Music-Critical Term', chap. 1 in Cowart, p. 8

The meaning of the word 'Baroque' has changed gradually since that time, arriving at today's use applied to a period of time in architecture, art, and music. If we are looking for a single 'Baroque' style, we shall be disappointed. The variety of styles found within this period (150 years is a long time in musical development) cross temporal and geographical boundaries. Various styles of composition, and therefore performance, may occur even within the same city for music being performed in church, theatre, or court.

In order to perform in the correct style, the player should be able to identify which style is the most suitable. If 'style' means 'choice',[1] then the player should be aware of the choices available to him. The most frequently played and popular style of Baroque music heard today is by a small group of composers: Vivaldi, Bach, Telemann and Handel. These composers tend to receive performances in an all-purpose Italianate Baroque style which has become the accepted norm. However, if the player's repertoire is extended sideways to France and backwards into the 17th century, more unfamiliar Baroque styles appear. Couperin, Purcell, Bach and Telemann all composed in the French and Italian style, and unless we are familiar with these, the music of composers who were influenced by these two styles may be misunderstood.

The two principal models of style in musical composition at the opening of the 18th century were Corelli (Italian) and Lully (French). These two composers were acknowledged by their contemporaries and immediate successors as being the acme of the two national styles. It is difficult to over-emphasise the influence they had on subsequent musical composition. I shall concentrate on these two styles and their characteristics in order that players may become familiar with and can identify characteristics of these two types of music. First, I will give some clues to help identify which style is being used, and then practical advice to apply the style in performance.

Much ink has been spilled discussing the length of the dot in Baroque music. Dotted rhythms are a feature of French style, particularly in the overture. A brief survey of views on the length of the dot and style of playing this movement is contained in part 3.4.

The emancipation of the violin in the early 17th century led to it acquiring a repertoire of its own. Italian violin sonatas of this period written in the *stylus phantasticus* bear little formal resemblance to the better-known sonatas of the 18th century. This area may still be undiscovered by some violinists and may be thought difficult to approach by others, so a short review of performance considerations in this repertoire follows in part 3.5.

---

[1] see Baillot quote (p. v)

3.1 Identifying national style

Much Italian violin music shares a bowing style with the contrapuntal consort repertoire of the 17th century. Based on vocal lines, examples of this type of music are described in part 3.6.

3.1 Identifying national style

	ITALIAN (Corelli, Vivaldi, Muffat concertos)	FRENCH (Lully, Couperin, Muffat *Florilegium* suites)
	Music is 'pure' sound for its own sake. Sudden silences.	Music often represents something, either emotion or event.
Form	Canzona, sonata, concerto, sinfonia, da capo aria.	Overture, suite, dances in binary form.
Key use	Adventurous, chromatic, shocking.	Conservative, subtle use of affect.
Figuration	Arpeggios, *bariolage*, jumping intervals in melodies, and passages in continuous fast notes.	Smooth lines without many leaps. Only continuous fast notes found in storm scenes.
Double-stop/chords	Frequent use.	Hardly ever used.
Range	From the lowest to the highest.	Moderate, keeping within one octave per part. Never very high.
Method of composition	Contrapuntal, all parts contributing to the musical argument.	Melody and bass with middle parts as harmonic filling.
Ornaments	Free, running, extravagent. Written out (J. S. Bach) or left to the performer when plain notes written. Cadential trills expected.	Small graces and trills only, which may or may not be indicated by specific signs. Cadential trills expected.
Pauses	Cadenzas added *extempore* at pauses.	Do not occur.
Dances	Not many. Composed in instrumental style unsuitable for dancing e.g. Corrente continuous fast notes.	Many different types used for dancing. Courante flowing, gentle, elegant.
Part-writing	Two violin parts in same range.	String parts descend in range (often only one violin part).
Tempo	Italian word instructions.	In French. Time signature often a single number.

In England, North describes Purcell as being 'warm in persuit' of the Italian style when he sadly died.[2] He describes Italian music as being full of 'stabbs and stoccatas' and acquired a taste for the dissonant Italian style

> ... dashing upon the harsh notes which makes their consorts more saporite than the musick was when the parts did but hunt one another, from concord to concord.
>
> J. Wilson, p. 297

North used to attend weekly meetings in London to play music with friends from the 1670s onwards:

> And it was my fortune to be in that company which introduc't the Italian composed entertainments of musick which they call Sonnata's, and in old time more imitated by our masters in what they call Fancys. The Court, about this time, entertained onely the theatricall musick and French air in song; ... the Italian had no sort of relish. But wee found most satisfaction in the Italian, for their measures were just and quick, set off with wonderfull solemne *Grave's*, and full of variety.
>
> J. Wilson, p. 25

---

[2] Purcell describes his sonatas (1683) in the preface as 'a just imitation of the most fam'd Italian Masters'

3.1 Identifying national style

The Frenchman Raguenet describes the two styles of composition:

> It is not to be wonder'd that the Italians think our musick dull and stupifying, that, according to their taste, it appears flat and insipid, if we consider the nature of the French airs compar'd to those of the Italian. The French in their airs aim at the soft, the easie, the flowing, and coherent; the whole air is of the same tone, or if sometimes they venture to vary it, they do it with so many preparations, they so qualifie it, that still the air seems to be as natural and consistent as if they had attempted no change at all; there is nothing bold and adventurous in it; it's all equal and of a piece. But the Italians pass boldly, and in an instant from sharps to flats and from flats to sharps; they venture the boldest cadences, and the most irregular dissonances; and their airs are so out of the way that they resemble the compositions of no other nation in the world.
>
> (1702) in Strunk (1998), p. 167

The Bonnet-Bourdelet family writings of mid-18th-century France contain many criticisms of the Italian style:

> One can say also that Italian music resembles an amiable coquette, although somewhat painted, full of vivacity, always rushing about, seeking to sparkle everywhere without reason, and not knowing why; like a scatterbrain who shows her passions in everything she does; when it is a question of tender affection she makes it dance the gavotte or gigue . . . in Italian music all the passions appear alike: joy, anger, sorrow, happy love, the lover who fears or hopes - all seem to be painted with the same features and the same character; it is a continual gigue, always sparkling or leaping.
>
> Can one not say without offending the partisans of Italian music that their too frequent and misplaced ornaments stifle expression, that they do not sufficiently distinguish their works, being in that like Gothic architecture, which, too heavily adorned with ornaments, is obscured by them, so that one can no longer distinguish the body of the work?
>
> In MacClintock, pp. 241-9

Another Frenchman, Hubert Le Blanc, identifies Italian style with harmony and the French with melody. He describes the listener's reaction in Italy:

> Ah! how touching the music is

and in France:

> Ah! how witty the musician is
>
> (1740) tr. Garvey Jackson (1973), p. 17

thereby crediting the French performer and the Italian composer with the more convincing powers.

Performing the style

North related how the playing of the Italian virtuoso violinist Matteis who used 'a very long bow' astounded all who heard him, particularly his bow-stroke which was 'as from the clouds'. His style of playing is described by North as 'querolous expostulary' with a 'conference of extreams, whereof the like I never heard before or since'.[3]

Raguenet noticed the difference in volume between the orchestras of the two countries:

> The Italians have . . . the same advantage over us in respect of the instruments and the performers as they have in regard of the singers and their voices. Their violins are mounted with strings much larger than ours; their bows are longer, and they can make their instruments sound as loud again as we do ours. The first time I heard our band in the Opera after my return out of Italy, my ears had been so used to the loudness of the Italian violins that I thought ours had all been bridled.
>
> (1702) in Strunk (1950), p. 126

---

[3] J. Wilson, p. 309

3.1 Identifying national style

	ITALIAN	FRENCH
General impression	Assaults the ear.	Tickles and refreshes the ear.
Tempo	Arbitrary (Quantz).	Prescribed by dance.
Dynamics	Extremes of loud and soft.	Moderate, nothing too extreme.
Fast movements	Dazzle and show off virtuousity and technical brilliance.	Either dance, or represent storms, battles etc.
Bowing style	Singing style needs continuous stream of sound with nuance. 'Long and dragging' bow stroke.	Dances use rule of down-bow with many lifted bow strokes.
Ornaments	To be liberally added by the performer in the florid style.	Small graces at specific points in the music as marked by the composer.
Equipment	Long bows, thicker strings.	Short bows, thinner strings.
Quavers	Played equally (although still subject to hierarchy of beat and harmony).	Played unequally.[4]
Pitch[5]	Generally higher, (N. Italy).	Generally lower, (opera/chamber).
Suggested seating	1 & 2 violin sections opposite.	Violin and bass sections opposite.

Raguenet's comparison of French and Italian music gives another account of the differences between the styles of playing:

> As to the instruments, our masters touch the violin much finer, and with a greater nicety than they do in Italy. All the Italians' bow strokes sound harsh, when they detach them from each other, and when they want to connect tones, they fiddle in a most disagreeable manner.
>
> The French would think themselves undone, if they offended in the least against the rules; they flatter, tickle, and court the ear, and are still doubtful of success, tho' ev'ry thing be done with an exact regularity. The more daring Italian changes the tone and the mode without any awe or hesitation. . . . He'll make a swelling of so prodigious length, that they who are unacquainted with it can't chuse but be offended at first to see him so adventurous. . . . He'll . . . instill a terror as well as surprize into the listener, who will immediately conclude, that the whole concert in degenerating into a dreadful dissonance; and betraying 'em by that means into a concern for the musick, which seems to be upon the brink of ruin, he immediately reconciles 'em by such regular cadences that everyone is surpriz'd to see harmony rising again in a manner out of discord itself, and owing its greatest beauties to those irregularities which seem'd to threaten it with destruction.
>
> As the Italians are naturally much more lively than the French, so are they more sensible of the passions, and consequently express 'em more lively in all their productions.
>
> (1702) in Strunk (1998), pp. 165-168

French orchestral style is described by Muffat:

> The greatest dexterity of the true Lullistes consists of this, that among so many repeated down-bows one never hears anything disagreeable or coarse, but, on the contrary, one finds a marvelous joining of great speed and long bow strokes, an admirable evenness of beat with diversity of rhythm, and a tender sweetness with lively playing.
>
> (1698) in Strunk (1998), pp. 145-6

---

[4] for detail see part 3.2
[5] for detail see part 4.1

3.1 Identifying national style

In his tract *Defense de la basse de viole contre les entreprises du violon et les prétensions du violoncel*, Le Blanc makes a vicious attack on the violin, identifying it with Italian style, and the viol with the French. The cello is associated with the violin, being described as

> . . . a miserable dunce . . . and flattered himself that he would receive many caresses instead of the viol.
>
> (1740) tr. Garvey Jackson (1973), p. 26

Double stopping and chords form part of the 'show-off' Italian style which is described by Le Blanc, comparing the national styles with famous orators:

> The chords in music and the beauty of the violin excite the admiration of the Italians - like Demosthenes they go right to the heart, while the French seek, in the manner of Cicero, to admire the composer for his method of treating the subject; his approach appeals to the intellect.
>
> The violin with its sound dragged out and not lifted up, is unable to be tender with chords in the sonata, or stamps its boots brutally in concerts to transport the opposites which it seduces in its whirlwind, and to extort, to steal approval rather than to attract it.
>
> (1740) tr. Garvey Jackson (1974), p. 25

He describes the bowing style of the Italian sonata as

> . . . drawing forth a continuous sound, which like the voice, is masterfully shaped in motion, like clay on the potter's wheel.
>
> (1740) tr. Garvey Jackson (1973), p. 21

> The bow, by down-bows and up-bows, uniform and connected, without their succession being perceptible, produces cascades of notes, multiplied infinitely, which only appear as a continuity . . . the bow pressing on the string produces a column of pliable sound, like the stream of water flowing from a fountain on whose outlet the hand is held, controlling the release of as much or as little water as is wanted or stopping it completely if desired.
>
> (1740) tr. Garvey Jackson (1973), p. 22

Le Blanc relates how, when the Italian violinist Somis (1686-1763) visited Paris, his playing was admired at first, but eventually the ladies got bored with his elaborate ornamentation. Somis's playing and compositions are credited with considerable influence in Italianising the French style of composition for the violin.[6]

> Somis appeared on the stage. He displayed the majesty of the most beautiful bow-stroke in Europe. He conquers the limitations where one often comes to grief, surmounts the dangers where one runs aground - in a word he reached the peak of a great endeavor on the violin, *the holding of a whole note*. A single down-bow lasts so long that the memory of it makes one breathless to think of it.
>
> (1740) tr. Garvey Jackson (1973), p.31

The mixed style

As the styles of France and Italy overlapped, a new mixed style became popular. German composers in particular took elements from both styles to create new forms. Kusser was the first German to acknowledge French influence, entitling his collection: *Composition de musique suivant la méthode françoise, contenant 6 ouvertures de théatre accompagnées de plusieurs airs.*[7] Muffat visited both France and Italy and wrote his *Florilegium* orchestral suites (1695, 1698) using the French style of writing and orchestration of one violin part, three viola parts and bass-line. Later he described the manner of his new concertos in the mixed style:

> This first collection of my instrumental concertos, blending the serious and the gay, entitled 'of a more select harmony' because they contain (in the ballet airs) not only the liveliness and grace drawn intact from the Lullian well, but also certain profound and unusual affects of the Italian manner, various capricious and artful conceits, and alternations of many sorts, interspersed with special diligence between the great choir

---

[6] *New Grove*, 'Somis'
[7] pub. Paris (1682) quoted in le Huray, p. 70

3.1 Identifying national style

> and trio of soloists. These concertos, suited neither to the church (because of the ballet airs and airs of other sorts which they include) nor for dancing (because of the interwoven conceits, now slow and serious, now gay and nimble, and composed only for the express refreshment of the ear) may be performed most appropriately in connection with entertainments given by great princes and lords, for receptions of distinguished guests, and at state banquets, serenades, and assemblies of musical amateurs and virtuosi.
>
> (1701) in Strunk (1950), p. 89

Muffat goes on to acknowledge that Corelli was the inspiration for these compositions. It is interesting to note that he declares that the dance movements in these concertos are not composed for dancing, but 'only for the express refreshment of the ear'.

Telemann wrote a large number of orchestral suites called *Ouvertures*, many of which include movements which are typically French in style. J. S. Bach wrote extensively in the new mixed style, and also composed keyboard pieces in both styles (e.g. The Italian Concerto and The French Overture, *Clavierübung II*). Couperin was the first composer to formally bring the opposing factions together in a series of *concerts* which were called *Les Gouts-Réunis*. This set of suites contains a wide variety of different movements, overtures and dances, attempting to cover the gamut of both styles, although the prevailing musical language is French. Some movements are marked to be played *égale* and are more Italian in character. In the *Apothèoses de Lully* and *Corelli*, which describe the great composers' journey to Parnassus, tributes are paid to both by various means, such as using French violin clef for Lully's music when the two play a duet (see ex. 3.2.2). Following the merging of the two styles, many composers adopted the mixed way of composing: in France, the virtuoso violinist Leclair uses Italianate features such as chords, double stopping and moto perpetuo movements to create his own style of violin writing.

The ultimate examples of the mixed style are contained in the works of J. S. Bach. He composed suites and concertos using the French and Italian styles, combining these with Polish and Bohemian elements on occasion.

Alteration of written rhythms

Unwritten conventions abound in the performance of Baroque music. One of the most tantalising of these and an important feature of 'playing the style' is the alteration of written rhythms in performance. However many descriptions are read and instructions carried out, it is impossible to know exactly how much performances of the 17th and 18th centuries differed from the written notes. The amount of rhythmic alteration in the performances of any era is a matter of degree governed by the performer's taste.

The following three sections describe the main areas of possible rhythmic alteration:

- The use of *notes inégales* in music written in the French style (part 3.2)
- The alignment of mixed note values found mostly in Italian style music (part 3.3)
- Dotted notes (part 3.4)

3.2 French style - inequality

The principle of inequality pervades many aspects of Baroque music: tuning and temperaments, good and bad rhythmic stresses and harmonic progressions, up- and down- bows, right hand fingering for plucked stringed instruments and different types of tonguing for wind instruments. The idea of uniformity in minor rhythmic details did not appeal or perhaps even occur to musicians of the 17th and 18th centuries. Natural strong/weak emphasis was acknowledged to be part of a performer's good taste and musicianship, and this is reflected in the slight lengthening and shortening of strong and weak parts of the beat. The lengthening of the first of a pair of notes, known in France in the 17th century as *notes inégales*, may have been applied in much earlier times, and was also advocated later by Quantz.

Which notes?

St. Lambert:
> The equality of movement that we require in notes of the same value is not observed with eighth notes when there are several in a row. The practice is to make them alternately long and short, because this inequality gives them more grace.
>
> (1702) tr. Harris-Warrick, p. 46

Vague, in *L'art d'apprendre la musique* thinks it worth mentioning the circumstances when notes are to be played equally:
> One may observe that notes in disjunct intervals are ordinarily equal in whatever the measure may be.
>
> (1733) in Hefling, p. 165

Couperin:
> We write differently from the way we play, which is the reason why foreigners play our music less well than we play theirs. On the contrary, the Italians write their music in the true note values in which it is to be played. For example, we dot several eighth notes in succession moving by conjunct degree; however, we write them in equal time values. Our custom has enslaved us, and we continue in it.
>
> (1717) tr. Halford, p. 49

The application of inequality to notes 'several in a row' and 'eighth notes in succession moving by conjunct degree' is now made clear: notes which leap or arpeggiate (disjunct intervals) are to be played equally, and notes which move in stepwise motion are to be played unequally.

Which note values?

Corrette gives specific instructions as to which note values should be played *inégales*, according to the time signature:

2	Quavers unequal. Rigaudons, bourées, galliards, gavottes.
3	Quavers unequal. Menuets, sarabandes, courantes, passacailles, chaconnes.
₵	Quavers unequal. Fugues, entrées and beginnings of overtures.
C	Quavers equal, semiquavers unequal. Often found in church music, and often used in Italian music as in allemandes, adagio, allegro, andante and presto of sonatas and concertos.
2/4	Quavers equal, semiquavers unequal. Often found in reprises of overtures and Italian music such as vivace, allegro, presto. Andante and adagio.
3/4	Quavers equal, semiquavers unequal. Courantes in sonatas.

3.2 French style - inequality

3/8	Quavers equal, semiquavers unequal. Passepieds, and sometimes reprises of overtures. The Italians use it in allegro, adagio, affetuoso.
6/4	Quavers unequal. Loures, forlanes. Hardly found in Italian music.
3/2	Crotchets unequal. Very little used in French music. Italian sarabandas and adagios.[8]

Written instructions

In order to clarify the position for the performer, composers often use word instructions either to prevent the use of inequality, or to encourage it:

croches égales	quavers to be played equally
lourer	mild inequality (often found in minuets, can also be applied to slurred pairs)
marqué	equal and with equal stress
mesuré	equal and in a measured fashion
notes égales	equal
piqué	strong inequality—almost dotted (can also mean detached and equal when staccato daggers are used)
pointé	dotted, and various degrees of lengthening the 1st note of a pair

Good taste

There are many descriptions of alterations to written rhythms which were expected of a good performer. The Burwell Lute Tutor compiled *c*.1660-72:

> The humour and fyne ayre of a lesson which cannot be taught but is stolen better by the eare in hearing those that play well. Yet we will give some Rules for it with a Demonstration. You may gett that art by breaking the stroakes that is dividing of them by stealing halfe a note from one note and bestowing of it upon the next note that will make the playing of the Lute more light and skipping. The hearing of Violins and singing is a great helpe to learn this liveliness and sweetness.

ch. 12 f. 4v

This extract demonstrates the common 17th-century practice of performing pairs of equal notes in an unequal 'skipping' manner by violinists, singers and lutenists. Quantz's ideas about playing in good taste describe the playing of unequal rhythms:

> You must know how to make a distinction in execution between the principal notes, ordinarily called accented or in the Italian manner, good notes, and those that pass, which some foreigners call bad notes. Where it is possible, the principal notes must always be emphasized more than the passing. In consequence of this rule, the quickest notes in every piece of moderate tempo, or even in adagio, though they seem to have the same value, must be played a little unequally, so that the stressed notes of each figure, namely the first, third, fifth, and seventh, are held slightly longer than the passing, namely the second, fourth, sixth, and eighth, although this lengthening must not be as much as if the notes were dotted. Among these quickest notes I include the crotchet in 3/2 time, the quaver in 3/4 and the semiquaver in 3/8 time, the quaver in alla breve, and the semiquaver or demisemiquaver in 2/4 or common duple time.

(1752) XI.12, tr. Reilly, p. 123

The precise amount of inequality is left to the discretion of the performer. St Lambert:

> It is a matter of taste to decide if they should be more or less unequal. There are some pieces in which it is appropriate to make them very unequal, and others in which they should be less so. Taste is the judge of this, as of tempo.

(1702) tr. Harris-Warrick, p. 46

---

[8] (1738), pp. 4-5

3.2 French style - inequality

The amount of inequality is determined by a number of factors: tempo, mood, affect, and whatever else is happening in the music at the same time. The most usual note value to which this convention is applied is the quaver (in French *croche*). Inequality is usually applied to the smallest note values (semiquavers in a slow allemande in 4/4, or quavers in a minuet in 3/4). This custom of playing pairs of notes unequally should not be applied to written-out ornaments or other *fast* note values found in music written in the Italian style. However, lengthening of selected important notes would fit in with the Italian manner of performance, and should be encouraged. It is interesting that Corrette includes Italian music in the list of time signature uses included in the inequality application, implying that inequality should continue to be used in Italian music (see above in 3/2 and ₵ in 4). Perhaps inequality in this instance does not just mean just pairing, but lengthening the first of a group of four semiquavers in 4/4 and 2/4, as also recommended by Quantz. The faster the note values, the less opportunity there is for altering the rhythm, and as fast notes are a feature of Italian style, this would preclude the use of paired inequality in continuous fast passages. Corrette lists the time signatures 6/8, 9/8 and 12/8 without any inequality instructions, as might be expected in compound time.

CASE STUDIES – NO WRITTEN INSTRUCTION

Ex. 3.2.1 *f*: Couperin, 8ième concert, Ouverture

In the above example, the lines of conjunct quavers should be played unequally. Dotted rhythms appear immediately afterwards for the cadence and provide a contrast to the smooth quavers. In the 5th bar, the quaver should be shortened in imitation of the bass motif which immediately precedes it.

The rule of inequality applies to pairs of notes in conjunct motion: scales and linear movement qualify (i.e. where notes are adjacent on the stave), single-note up-beats, and single quavers (as bar 6 above) but repeated notes, leaps and arpeggios do not.

In the following example, the bass arpeggio in bar 1 should, strictly speaking, be played with equal semiquavers. Inequality starts from the 6th semiquaver where the bass joins the upper two parts (time signature ₵ in 4 means semiquavers unequal, see Corrette above).

Ex. 3.2.2 *f*: Couperin, Apothéose de Lully

3.2 French style - inequality

Sometimes it is appropriate to pair intervals of a third by lengthening the first note, especially where these appear in ascending or descending patterns in a movement which languishes and is not too lively in character. If an interval of a third appears in the middle of a group of conjunct notes, this may also be played unequal, as the second note in the interval of the third may be thought of as belonging to the following notes which are played unequal. Evidence of this way of playing comes from various sources: mechanical instruments which have been programmed to play music which is also written down, and from written descriptions and instructions from various writers.

The tempo to be adopted when playing music which includes *notes inégales* is critical to the success of the piece. If the tempo is too fast, inequality is difficult or out of the question. *Notes inégales* should never sound aggressive, but always elegant and sophisticatedly nonchalant.

CASE STUDIES – WRITTEN INSTRUCTION

Sometimes instructions are written at the beginning of a composition as a descriptive message: *pointé* or *piqué* over a dotted passage, or *lourer* at the head of a movement marked with slurred pairs of notes, emphasising the character of the movement.

Dots placed over the notes mean play equally.

Ex. 3.2.3 *f*: Piani, instruction from the avertissement and example from sonata V (Paris 1712)

Dots can indicate equal stress. In the next example, the crotchets should be played with a lifted equal stroke with direction towards the bar-line. The commas show articulation points, and the slurred pairs of quavers make a contrast to those in thirds, which should be played unequally. The dot over the first note in the bar indicates equal stress with the previous two notes, even though there is a slur. The slur falls unbroken onto the second note forming a written-out appoggiatura.

Ex. 3.2.4 *f*: Couperin, 8ième concert, Air Tendre (lentement)

In the next example, dots occur in the bass emphasising the equal performance of notes with both large and small intervals. In the second extract from later in the same movement, notes without dots means normal inequality applies on conjunct quavers.

Ex. 3.2.5 *f*: Couperin, Apothéose de Lully, Saillie-Rondement

There are more indications of when not to play *inégale* than positive instructions, suggesting a practice that was commonplace. Playing *inégale* was taken for granted under certain conditions, and a positive instruction to play unequally was unnecessary.

Ex. 3.2.6 *f*: Couperin, 1ier concert, Gavotte

In the above example, conjunct notes would normally be performed unequally, but the written instructions counteract this convention and indicate 'equal and smooth'. Contraindications for inequality might include *notes égales, marqué, mesuré* according to context and, thanks to the influence of Corelli, the word andante. The walking bass (*andare* meaning 'to go') arrived in France and England with Corelli's compositions and several writers note the first appearance of this instruction. Brossard (1702) defines *andante: pour les Basses Continues, qu'il faut faire toutes les Nottes égales, & bien separer les Sons* (equal and well-detached notes). North describes the andante as 'an imitation of walking *equis passibus*' (with equal steps).[9]

Where dotted rhythms and *inégales* style quavers are mixed in simultaneous movement, the performer is left in a difficult dilemma. Are the dots there to encourage strong inequality? The different written rhythms might be there for contrasting purposes, and not meant to be aligned. There is no clear-cut answer to this question, but two possible solutions in performance are:

a) to play up the differences by making the dotted rhythms quite sharply dotted, and the inequality quite smooth and mild or

b) to align the dots and unequal quavers in a lazy triplet-type rhythm.

---

[9] J. Wilson, p. 194

3.2 French style - inequality

When this dilemma occurs in music by a composer who was very precise in his notation, such as Couperin, the performer would need very good reasons for not sticking to the *inégale* in one part and dotted rhythm in the other. Differences would be very difficult to maintain in parts moving in 3rds or 6ths, however. If the parts seem to be independent yet not imitative, the differences between the rhythms should be exaggerated. Loulié and Vague say that where inequality is intended to be sharper than mild, one should write a dot, confirming the rule that there is no rule about the amount of dotting or inequality demanded, except by the affect of the phrase.[10] Occasionally, large intervals occur in inner parts (in the multiple viola parts in French music, for example) accompanying smooth treble or bass parts, in which case a certain amount of licence with the rules may be taken, and the inner parts should match the rhythm of the principal part.

When surveying a piece of music for possible inequality, watch out for clues. French composers such as Couperin when writing in a deliberately Italian (equal) style will indicate this by an instruction. German composers such as Muffat and Fischer (both of whom studied with Lully) often used the French style and key words such as rondeau, menuet, or allemande indicate that unequal rules may apply.

During the 18th century the language of educated society in Germany and at the courts of Europe was French. According to C. P. E. Bach, his father 'acquired a thorough grounding in the French taste' during his Lüneburg years from a French dancing master.[11] J. S. Bach, Telemann and other German composers undoubtedly considered the mixed style to be the height of good taste, and J. S. Bach's music reflects elements of both styles in a miraculous amalgam. However, whether inequality should be used in J. S. Bach's music at all is a vexed question, and opinions differ. It is possible to use inequality in various degrees, and it's use should not be thought of as an 'on' or 'off' effect. Some pairing of conjunct notes might give a flavour of French rhythmic freedom, without giving the notes the full unequal treatment.

Notes inégales and dotted rhythms in England

During the reign of Charles II, musicians were sent from England to France to absorb the French style. In 1666 a 'Frenchified' Catalan called Louis Grabu became Master of the Music and director of the King's string band of twenty-four violins.[12] English post-restoration composers such as Purcell and Blow absorbed what had become known as the French style, (although violin bands had already been in the habit of playing unequally in England, as we have seen in the Burwell Lute Tutor extract) and the practice of playing *inégales* should be observed when performing their music. In the next two examples, the conjunct quavers may be 'swung', or played *inégales*.

Ex. 3.2.7 *f*: Purcell, The Double Dealer

---

[10] (1696) in Hefling, p. 16
[11] Obituary of Bach by C. P. E. Bach and Agricola (1754) in David & Mendel, p. 217
[12] Holman (1993), p. 293

3.2 French style - inequality

Ex. 3.2.8: Purcell, Chacony

It may be that when such music is written dotted, that a lilting inequality is more appropriate than a sharply dotted style. As usual, varying degrees of dotted and unequal rhythms may be selected according to context. Hefling argues that when composers such as Blow and Croft write dotted rhythms they mean them to be played in an unequal manner (as recommended by Loulié), not sharply dotted, and that equally notated rhythms should therefore be played as written.[13]

PRACTICAL APPLICATION

Inégale technique

To practise playing *inégale*, play pairs of quavers in scale-like formations starting with a minimum amount of inequality by emphasising the weight of the down-bow and lightening the up-bow, keeping the bow on the string all the time, producing a paired effect without much alteration of the rhythm. Gradually increase the length and weight of the down-bow and shorten and lighten the up-bow note. Passing through a triplet ratio 2:1, work towards making the rhythm almost dotted: ratio 3:1, with the second note of each pair nearly as short as a semiquaver. Try this bow exercise at different tempos from a gay frisky allegro to a serious largo. Keep the bow returning to the same place for the start of every down-bow. The bow must be kept glued to the string all the time, and not lifted off as it might be when playing a written dotted rhythm.

The most important technical consideration when performing *notes inégales* is the weight of the arm bringing the bow down into the string on the stronger longer note, and lifting the weight on the up-bow. Bow pressure must be applied alternately strong and weak to each pair of notes to achieve the desired effect. The bow speed on the down-bow should be kept slow and the whole effect is achieved by the down-bow weight and pressure being relieved on the up-bow. Try to make circular, well-oiled movements with your elbow and wrist.

---

[13] Hefling, p. 54

3.3 Italian style - alignment of mixed note values

Italian music also demands rhythmic alteration on occasion. A common rhythmic device in Italian-style music is the use of triplets coinciding with dotted rhythms in time signatures 2/4, 3/4, 4/4. It should not be assumed that these mixed rhythms should always be aligned: Quantz instructs the performer to keep the two rhythms accurate and distinct:

> You must not strike the short note after the dot with the third note of the triplet, but after it. Otherwise it will sound like six-eight or twelve-eight time.
>
> (1752) V.22, tr. Reilly, p. 68

He emphasises the different affects the two possible renditions would have: the tripletized version 'very lame and insipid' and the preserved dotted version 'brilliant and majestic'. However, earlier in the century it is apparent from Brossard's dictionary entry 'Giga' and from the Corelli musical example following, that combined time signatures in Italian compound time dances were performed uniformly:

> The Italians usually indicate the movement of the gigue in 6/8 or 9/8 time for the violins and sometimes with the sign of C or quadruple measure for the bass. The bass is played then as though it were dotted.
>
> (1702) tr. in Little, p. 176[14]

PRACTICAL APPLICATION

In mixed simple/compound time signatures, pairs of equal notes are usually tripletised.

Ex. 3.3.1: Corelli, Concerto Grosso op. 6 no. 3, Allegro

In the final allegro of Corelli's *Concerto Grosso* op. 6 no. 3, the concertino group are marked with the time signature 12/8, and the ripieno C. Where the 2nd violin parts are in unison (bar 3 of the above example), the rhythm is shown tripletised in one and even quavers in the other. The obvious solution in performance is for the ripieno player to tripletise the pair of quavers.

If the following movement had been written in 6/8 it might be played at a faster speed than Corelli intended:

---

[14] See also Little, pp. 175-184 'Gigues notated in duple meter'

3.3 Italian style - alignment of mixed note values

Ex. 3.3.2: Corelli, Concerto Grosso op. 6 no. 4

Several writers (including Neumann, 1978) have pointed out that no notation was available in the 18th century to accommodate the required triplet rhythm in simple binary time signatures. The dilemma forced upon the performer when confronted with this problem seems to have been solved in modern times by the habit of automatically aligning the two differently notated rhythms.

Ex. 3.3.3: J. S. Bach, Brandenburg concerto no. 5, Allegro

Normally it is assumed that the semiquaver will line up with the third note of the triplet, but the dotted figure, if consistently using a leaping interval (as in ex. 3.3.3) may be given a more sprightly character than the more linear triplets, making a contrast between the two figures which does not offend, and may result in the two figures being not 100% aligned. The dotted figure should not sound 'lame and insipid' even if it is aligned.

Differences in the two rhythmic elements are easier to preserve at a slower tempo; at a faster tempo, compression of the rhythms becomes inevitable. The overall affect and tempo of the movement are major factors when deciding on degrees of alignment. A lilting happy allegro movement with gig-like tendencies calls for complete tripletisation, while a more serious contrapuntal movement with distinct themes containing the two rhythmic elements might ask for the integrity of the two separate ideas to be maintained, as in the following movement:

3.3 Italian style - alignment of mixed note values

Ex. 3.3.4: J. S. Bach, Sonata for violin and harpsichord in E major, Allegro

Ex. 3.3.5: J. S. Bach, Sonata for violin and harpsichord in C minor

In ex. 3.3.5, it might be assumed that the semiquavers are tripletised. However, there is a case for altering the length of the little note slightly according to the affect and harmonic implications. As the movement progresses, the harmony becomes more tortured, and altering the length of the semiquaver is an effective tool of expression. Towards the end of the movement, the harmony becomes more peaceful, and the semiquaver may resume its triplet character.

It is important that any written 3-note triplet figures are preserved accurately when used as a foil to the duple element. If these two elements appear in separate passages in the same movement, and are never aligned it may be more convincing to retain the written rhythmic characteristics, and in doing so the triplets will be heard in contrast to the dotted material. Quantz suggests stressing the first of triplet groupings:

> You must take care to make the triplets quite round and equal, and must not hurry the first two notes in them, lest they sound as though they have yet another crook; for in this fashion they would no longer remain triplets. Thus the first note of a triplet, since it is a principal note in the chord, may be held slightly, so that the tempo is not forced, and the execution in consequence distorted.
>
> (1752) XII.10, tr. Reilly, p. 131

Two-against-three written rhythms must be preserved, and can be found throughout Bach's works often giving an underlying excitement and life to the accompaniment. A mixed time signature (C 12/8) is a sure sign for tripletisation and appears often in the works of J. S. Bach and Handel.

In the opening bars of J. S. Bach's Brandenburg Concerto no.1, it is part of the essential character and special effect of the horn calls that they maintain the triplets as a foil against the semiquaver and quaver patterns in the rest of the orchestra.

It could be argued that the triplets in ex. 3.3.6 are merely decorating the basic duple movement, but this would be very difficult to maintain in practice, and it is inevitable that the single quavers will become tripletised.

There is no rule or formula to solve the problem of mixed rhythms and if, after consideration of the above points a solution does not appear to be obvious, then it probably does not matter which route is chosen. Experiment with tempo and articulation to guide you to a workable solution.

3.3 Italian style - alignment of mixed note values

Ex. 3.3.6: Handel, Concerto Grosso op. 3 no. 2 [Gavotte]

3.4 Dotted notes

This section discusses the problem of how long dotted notes are to be played, and the consequent length of the note(s) which follow them. The bow technique required for playing dotted notes using the rule of down-bow is described in part 2.4, pp. 95-96.

The length of the dotted note in Baroque music has generated much hot air. Attempts by theorists from the 18th to the 20th centuries to reduce the discussion to a mathematical formula seem irrelevant to players with bows in their hands. Whatever the length of the dotted notes, there are two critical elements in the debate: tempo and affect. In my experience, the tempo adopted for the first section of a typical dotted French overture (of the 17th or 18th centuries) is frequently too slow for the desired affect, making difficulties of ensemble when aligning rhythms (if indeed they are to be aligned) which disappear when a slightly more lively tempo is taken. Descriptions of this type of movement from the 18th century include: 'lively' and 'uplifting'. A slow tempo with a relaxed lethargic stroke does not achieve this. The proud majestic affect required can be obtained with a firmer, faster bow-stroke.

The extremes of interpretation of the dotted notes and their associated rhythms are: to play every note literally as written, and, to over-dot every dotted note and consequently shorten the little note that follows it. It is my opinion that the tension required by this type of movement is lost when long up-beats do not coincide with shorter notes in other parts. However, this only applies when all parts are moving together in harmonic blocks, not where parts are independent of each other. In between these two views, various compromises depending on the situation are used by players and directors in performance. There is no 'correct' solution to this problem, and it is to be expected that players will have strong views to support a variety of solutions in practice.

The 'French' overture - 17th and 18th centuries compared

The dotted style is assumed by all 18th-century writers to be synonymous with French style: Mattheson tells us that

> If the French, whom I regard as great masters in instrumental style, had to forgo the dots beside the notes, they would be like cooks without salt.
>
> (1739) II.12.21, tr. Harriss, p. 422

Most of the written evidence about the practice of over-dotting comes from the mid-18th century. The affect of the dotted section of a French overture is variously described by Quantz, Leopold Mozart and Mattheson as proud, majestic or sublime, and lively rather than sleepy. Overtures may have been performed faster in the 17th century than in the 18th. This is shown by time-signatures, earlier ₵ meaning in 2, and later, as in the next example, plain C without any word tempo indication (ex. 3.4.1). Although some theorists of the early 18th century maintained that C was twice as slow as ₵, there was some disagreement, and some used ₵ as only slightly faster than C.[15] Word instructions began to be added in the late 17th century to modify the tempo indicated by the time-signature, mostly grave in the case of the French overture.

In ex. 3.4.1, Bach writes the correct number of rests to give a semiquaver at the middle and end of bar 1. Quite an effort is required to play the quaver in bar 2 as written and one's natural instinct is to shorten it in order to match the semiquaver in the other parts, continuing the lively effect.

---

[15] Houle, p. 57

3.4 Dotted notes

Ex. 3.4.1: J. S. Bach, Suite no. 2 for flute and strings, Overture

The little notes are frequently shown in faster note-values in later music, as in ex. 3.4.3 below, to maintain the 'fizz' uplift affect at a slower tempo. This may not only be a development of more accurate notation, but an indication of the manner of performance. If a relatively fast tempo is adopted giving two in a bar, the little notes in ex. 3.4.2 may be played exactly as written. The later, slower tempo should still feel in two large beats to a bar, but with the little notes played quickly giving the lively affect.

Ex. 3.4.2: Purcell, Abdelazar, Overture

Ex. 3.4.3: Handel, Concerto Grosso op. 6 no. 10

At a slower tempo, the application of playing strictly as written results in a loss of the liveliness described by several writers. The single quavers in ex. 3.4.3, if played exactly as written, would be played before the three fast notes in the other parts, surely not the intended execution or affect. In 17th-century music, it is more likely that dotted notes and their accompanying short notes may be played precisely as written without contracting the little notes, if the music does not move together in harmonic blocks (i.e. they overlap in a linear contrapuntal way).

In the French overture, the player should be aware of the difference between earlier writing, where parts using quaver up-beat figures which overlap can be played as written, and the type of writing where blocks of harmony need to be performed in a more triumphal, grand style, with a slight shortening of the little note to give the feeling of uplifting the spirit. Mattheson describes 'a special elevation of the soul' when listening to the first part of a good overture. Literal interpretation of the written notes, especially the single quaver up-beats, is often applied to 18th-century music. Unless a lively tempo is adopted, this practice can make the music heavy and Mattheson's 'elevation of the soul' is lost.

3.4 Dotted notes

The feeling of grandeur and resonance from the released dotted note in places where all the parts move together is described by North as

> ... the stop, striking after a quaver rest all together. ... Harmony cannot be had with more advantage than by these stopps, being of the whole consort at once, and (as ought to be) of the richest notes. For at every stopp there will be a kind of rattle [i.e. reverberation], which aided by the memory is softened, and so made purer, than [the sound] taken from the gross strokes, as the eccho is always sweeter than the voice.
>
> J. Wilson, pp. 185-6

It is important that string players enjoy the resonance caused by the energetic lifting of the bow, without damping the string with the fingers of the left hand.

Crotchets in the overture and entrée

Single crotchets, or pairs of crotchets should be played short and lifted. Quantz:

> The *entrée*, the *loure*, and the *courante* are played majestically, and the bow is detached at each crotchet, whether it is dotted or not.
>
> (1752) XVII.VII.58, tr. Reilly, p. 291

Summary for style in French overtures

This summary inevitably reflects my own views on this subject, based on my experience of many different types of performance.

- Tempo: it is likely that tempo in overtures started fast and became slower during the Baroque period. However, always feel two, not four beats.
- In 18th-century French overtures the little notes may be shortened in all tempos.
- The main dotted note gets longer in later slower tempos, with the fast notes more compressed, and shorter in earlier fast ones, enabling the performer to play the little notes as written.
- Affect: dotted overture figures are variously described as detached, jerky, lively not sleepy, and majestic.
- Movement in other parts: does the group play one jerky affect in unison, or is the writing smooth and vocal, with parts overlapping? If the parts imitate and answer each other, the single quavers may often be played as written.
- The length of the dot is regulated by what follows—i.e. when there are several notes to fit in before the next down beat, the long note may be cut off sooner than when there is only one note. The fast notes may not add up to a definite part of a beat (5 or 7 little notes written with 3 beams but only a single dot on the preceding note).
- Where the predominant rhythm is a dotted crotchet followed by two semiquavers, the bowing may be taken mostly as it comes without retakes, as long as strong harmonies occur on down-bows. As the lines are generally smoother in this case, the result will be longer dotted notes.
- If the main pulse is kept strong and regular, small alterations to the lengths of the little notes are possible according to the harmonic context and the affect required (for example, slightly lengthening some upbeats before particularly strong harmonies, or chromatic movement).
- All crotchets should be short and lifted.

♪ tracks 27 and 32 for 17th-century overtures by Corbett and Purcell, which both contain examples of unaltered up-beat rhythms.

Dotted notes in other situations

Shortening of dotted notes is a feature of the mid-18th-century *style galant*. Quantz tells us:

> ... the time of the short notes after the dots cannot actually be fixed with complete exactness.
>
> (1752) V.21, tr. Reilly, p. 67

C. P. E. Bach states:

> Short notes which follow dotted ones are always shorter in execution than their notated length
>
> Part 1 (1753) tr. Mitchell, p. 157

He also pleads for a variety of ways to perform dotted notes, not always according to 'a general rule':

> Because proper exactness is often lacking in the notation of dotted notes, a general rule of performance has been established which, however, suffers many exceptions. According to this rule, the notes which follow the dots are to be played in the most rapid manner; and often they should be. But sometimes notes in other parts, with which these must enter, are so divided that a modification of the rule is required. Again, a suave affect, which will not survive the essentially defiant character of dotted notes, obliges the performer slightly to shorten the dotted note. Hence, if only one kind of execution is adopted as the basic principle of performance, the other kinds will be lost.
>
> (1762) tr. Mitchell, p. 372

Quantz recommends a slight lengthening of the dotted note:

> ... the notes after the dot in (c) and (d) must be played just as short as those in (e) whether the tempo is slow or fast.
>
> (1752) V.21, tr. Reilly, p. 67

Ex. 3.4.4: Quantz (1752)

> Care must be taken not to begin prematurely the notes following short rests that occur in the place of the principal notes on the downbeat. For example, if there is a rest in the place of the first of four semiquavers, you must wait half as long again as the rest appears to last, since the following note must be shorter than the first one [i.e. the note that the rest represents].
>
> All dotted notes are treated in the same manner if time allows; and if three or more demisemiquavers follow a dot or a rest, they are not always played with their literal value, especially in slow pieces, but are executed at the extreme end of the time allotted to them, and with the greatest possible speed, as is frequently the case in overtures, entrees and furies. Each of these quick notes must receive its separate bow-stroke, and slurring is rarely used.
>
> (1752) XIII.VII.58, XII.12, tr. Reilly, pp. 131, 290

Quantz states that one elongates the dot as much as possible

> ... because of the animation that these notes must express.
>
> (1752) V.21, tr. Reilly, p. 67

Leopold Mozart agrees even in *adagio*:

> There are certain passages in slow pieces where the dot must be held rather longer ... if the performance is not to sound too sleepy. For example, if here [ex. 3.4.5(a), below] the dot were held its usual length it would sound very languid and sleepy. In such cases dotted notes must be held somewhat longer, but the time taken up by the extended value must be, so to speak, stolen from the note standing after the dot.
>
> The dot should in fact be held at all times somewhat longer than its value. Not only is the performance thereby enlivened, but hurrying—that almost universal fault—is

3.4 Dotted notes

thereby checked; for otherwise, owing to the shortening of the dot, the music easily tends to increase in speed. It would be a good thing if this long retention of the dot were insisted on, and set down as a rule. I, at least, have often done so, and I have made clear my opinion of the right manner of performance by setting down two dots followed by a shortened note: [ex. 3.4.5(b), below]

Ex. 3.4.5: Leopold Mozart

It is true that at first it looks strange to the eye. But what matters this? The point has its reason and musical taste is promoted thereby.

(1756) I.III.11, tr. Knocker, pp. 41-2.[16]

Notice his assumption that dotted notes are used to animate slow movements. Quantz describes how to perform music representing majesty, again with 'liveliness' on the dotted notes:

Majesty is represented both with long notes during which the other parts have quick motion, and with dotted notes. The dotted notes must be attacked sharply and must be executed in a lively fashion. The dots are held long, and the following notes are made very short.

(1752) XII.24, tr. Reilly, p. 133

CASE STUDIES – ALTERATION OF WRITTEN RHYTHMS

Ex. 3.4.6 *f*: Couperin, 8ième concert

Before reading on, play or sing both lines of the extract to yourself, and notice how you read the written rhythms. Several issues of rhythmic alteration should be considered:

- Should the first note in the treble and bass be shortened?
- Should the treble part imitate the dotted rhythm in the bass in bar 2?
- How long are the quavers in bar 3?
- Should the intervals between notes influence your decision to alter the rhythm? All the dotted notes in the extract are between notes which are conjunct, or the same note. Does this mean that those on a rising fourth should be played as written, as in *inégale* rules? In bars 1 and 3, the falling line is in conjunct notes, so a case for quavers to be *inégales* could be made.
- How dotted is dotted? Would you play the dotted quavers very dotted, or just tripletise the dots?
- Is intended *inégale* rhythm sometimes written dotted?

This is not a test, and there are no 'correct' answers. A consistent approach throughout the movement between all the players is the most important consideration, and achievement of the correct affect(s) should be the main aim.

---

[16] Notes with double dots had in fact already been used in the 17th century by keyboard player-composers 1650-1700 (Hefling, p. 70)

3.4 Dotted notes

My own approach to this piece would be to consider first the interval of the rising fourth between the first two notes, which needs to feel triumphant and heroic, without being massive and heavy (this *concert* is subtitled *dans le goût théatral*). Whether the first note is shortened or not, it should be played lightly and unaccented. The dotted quaver rhythms should sound noble rather than aggressive, in other words, not too sharply dotted, except perhaps for the repeated notes which need to sound more lively, like trumpet calls. The descending lines in bars 1 and 3 need to sound melodically smooth, perhaps *inégales* (longer than a semiquaver) or nearly full-length.

Ex. 3.4.7: Purcell, Dido and Aeneas, Overture

This 17th-century overture demonstrates the various choices to be made when deciding whether to shorten the little note or play it as written. Factors which could influence the decision are:

I. The intervals between the notes, and whether they rise or fall.

II. Whether parts move together or independently. My reading of this overture follows:

The first five bars use a contrapuntal weaving style over a pedal bass note, so are played as written.

1. The top three parts answer each other in bars 2, 3 and 4 with lines made up of close intervals which should be played in a sustained manner, without gaps between the dotted notes and the quavers. The tension builds through the pedal note, until it moves away at the peak of the 1st violin's first phrase. The sustained writing in the upper three parts milk the dramatic harmony in the opening bars of this story of love and fate.

2. After falling down onto the first note of bar 6, the mood and structure change dramatically. Suddenly, all parts move together for one bar. The rising interval of a 5th in the 1st violin part is like a hero's call to arms, and to achieve this tension a shorter quaver can be played, but immediately the mood changes back. In bar 8 smooth, falling or chromatic figures resume (the fates will have their way!), played with quavers of full value.

3. Experiment with various ways of playing this passage, first over-dotting everything, and then playing as written to discover the various affects which are available in the music with each method. It is up to the players to make all these informed choices from the information given in the parts. If they are convinced, the audience will be too.

Stephen E. Hefling, *Rhythmic Alteration in Seventeenth- and Eighteenth-Century Music* (New York, 1993) is an indispensable and thorough study of dotted notes and *notes inégales* in Baroque music.

3.5 The 17th-century Italian sonata

The sonata (literally 'sounding' as opposed to cantata 'singing') was born in Italy. The sonata was a purely instrumental composition, similar to the canzona. Merula demonstrated how these terms had become interchangeable when he wrote his *Canzoni, overo Sonate* in 1637. As a contrapuntal ensemble work, the form appeared for larger groups of players (for example Gabrieli's multi-part compositions). Cima is generally thought to have written the first sonata specifically for the solo violin (1610), although this sonata is, strictly speaking, a sonata *a due* for violin, bass and continuo.

The early sonata was pure instrumental music emancipated from words, text or dance forms. Unlimited now in its form and expression, the violin was able to develop its own voice and idiosyncrasies. It became a vehicle for players to show off their technique and imagination using Monteverdi's new *stile concitato* (excited style), combined with a rhapsodical fantasy type of writing described by Kircher in 1650 as *stylus phantasticus*.[17]

Pulse

The early Italian sonata consists of a series of short contrasted sections strung together. The more lively sections play with short canzona-like motives, the slow sections are often dreamy or grotesque dramatic fantasies, and the triple sections dance-like. To perform this type of sonata the player should look for tempo relationships between the different sections. The parts of the sonata should not be regarded in the same way as movements in a classical sonata, with a lengthy pause between movements. In many works of this type, a related pulse may be used throughout. Slowing up at cadences should be avoided-there are sometimes many of them. A small easing of the tempo at the end of a very long section may be permitted to point out the larger elements of the overall structure, but where the phrase of one part overlaps into another section (across a double bar, for example) the music should remain fluent. If there is a new time signature, try to relate the pulse between the two sections. Avoid accenting the first note of the new time signature where it is also the resolution or last note of the previous section: a new idea or motive is often preceded by a weak cadence. Frequently, duple time precedes triple time. In most cases, the triple time should sound faster and lighter than the duple as serious duple polyphony or canzona moves into lighter dance music.

Much music in the early 17th century is written in large note values. A 3/2 or 3/1 triple section written in minims or semibreves looks like slow music to the modern eye, but should be played with one beat per bar, and at a fair pace. Sometimes, helpful editors double the note values to assist modern performers to achieve a brisker tempo: look for information about changed note values in the editorial commentary. A section in 3/4 may look like a minuet-unlikely in this type of composition-when the original notation was 3/1, implying a faster one-to-a-bar pulse.

♪ tracks 3-4, 11, 12, 13-17 for music with related tempo changes between sections.

Rubato

In the solo sonata more rhythmic freedom is possible than in larger ensembles, especially where the bass line consists of slow-moving harmonies. However, where the bass takes an active role in the music with faster-moving notes, the solo violinist should maintain strict time. If the bass line is sitting on a long held pedal, this gives the soloist licence to pull the rhythm around until the bass line moves off again (see ex. 2.7.3, 2.7.4).

---

[17] quoted in Bianconi tr. Bryant, p. 50

3.5 The 17th-century Italian sonata

Ornamentation

In early violin sonatas, elaborate ornamentation is often written out by the composer (for example sonatas by Fontana and Castello). The most obvious places for added embellishments are at cadences: the Italian word *cadenza* implies freedom to elaborate at these points. The performer may elaborate in similar ways to anything already written, or improvise a cadential ornament of his own. Beware of elaboration which holds up other movement (in the bass-line, for example).

Italian affect

The flair and imagination found in the early Italian sonatas gives the player endless possibilities for showing off, both technically and with emotional affects. When so many short sections are strung together, the player should identify and set the emotional character of each as quickly as possible in order to exploit the full potential of each phrase. 'Act' the music, and exaggerate each feeling in order to portray the emotion of each section. The Italian character (then as now) is flamboyant, capricious, volatile and full of gesture.

Performing early Italian sonatas

- In the early multi-sectional sonatas, look for sections which require a related pulse.
- Adagio or allegro instructions may mean keeping the same pulse, as the larger or smaller note values take care of the change of tempo.
- Go for affect: extremes of emotion or dynamics.
- Play freely in written out cadential passages where the bass is stationary.
- Add florid ornamentation to slow-moving passages.
- Identify singing (canzona) or dancing (triple) passages.

Italian influence moves north

The Italian influence spread north in the mid-17th century as composers such as Schütz (a pupil of Monteverdi) returned from working and studying in Italy. The Bohemian composers Biber, Schmelzer and the Lübeck composer Buxtehude, among others, reflect the Italian style of composition. The same tactics should be used in the performance of sonatas by these composers: look for continuity between sections, and find a pulse suitable for any consecutive sections that could be related.

In the sonatas of Biber (1644-1704), there is frequently a free fantasy-like prelude section, often with many fast notes. A single pedal note may last for pages. There usually follows an aria (theme) with variations, which should adopt a tempo suitable for the whole section. Even if there are word tempo indications, they may already be catered for by the way the music is written. At a cadence, for example, the note values might suddenly enlarge where adagio is marked to give the effect of slowing down without changing the pulse. There are often short transitional passages that bring about a modulation between the main sections, which may be played with more freedom, and if written in large note-values, elaborated with flourishes. Biber and Schmelzer both include a coda-like finale in some sonatas: a free cadenza-like form over a pedal note.

♪ tracks 13-17, a sonata by Finger illustrates many of these points.

The ground bass sonata

Italian-style sonatas are often constructed over a ground bass. Biber 'Rosary' no.16, Schmelzer sonata no.4, Lonati sonata no.12 Ciaccona and Cavalli canzona a 3 all use the popular descending four-note 'lament' theme. Stradella sonata no.12 is a set of variations over a 13-bar bass. Corelli op. 5 no.12 uses the well-known 'Follia' ground for a set of variations. Many sections of Biber's sonatas use the Aria (theme) and variation over a ground bass form. Try to maintain a reasonably constant tempo for the ground, even though the sonata may be composed in sections which differ in character.

♪ track 10 for a set of Italian variations on a ground bass and track 11 (final section) for a descending 4-note ground bass.

Later 17th-century Italian violin sonatas

Violinists could be forgiven for thinking that there is a large gap in the solo repertoire after the period of the *phantasticus* sonatas. However, there is a rich repertoire of little-known sonatas which have remained in the shadow through being unavailable in useful modern editions or even facsimile. From the mid-17th century, the old-fashioned printing techniques being used by the Italians were largely unsuitable for the more complex double-stopping of the virtuoso violinist-composers such as Lonati and Colombi, and so the works of these composers did not receive the wide circulation they deserved.[18] The sonatas of Lonati in particular are most interesting, as the only source known to have survived World War II is in photo-copied form. These sonatas are available in a score published in 1982. Of the set of twelve sonatas, four use scordatura, and all exhibit characteristics we would recognise as strongly 'Corellian' (Corelli's solo violin sonatas were published in 1700 and Lonati's in 1701). Lonati was a member of Stradella's circle and was Capellmeister to Queen Christina of Sweden. His writing surpasses that of Corelli in technical difficulty (ascending to a^3). Geminiani is known to have taken lessons from Lonati in Milan.[19]

♪ track 12 for a large ensemble sonata by Stradella

Da chiesa - da camera

The later 17th-century Italian sonata was composed in two types which have become commonly known as da chiesa and da camera. The first type has preludes, fugal movements, allegros and adagios and is composed in a serious style. The second is more light-hearted and consists of dance movements in the Italian style: allemanda, corrente, sarabanda, and giga.[20] By the 1670s, the sonata had developed separated movements in a slow—fast—slow—fast pattern. Often the initial slow prelude is followed by a fugal movement. There follows a slow adagio, often simply notated in minims. This movement is a vehicle for the famous Italian free ornamentation, some examples of which exist written down as models by contemporary musicians. North comments:

> The most skillfull of the elder Italians leave all those (gracing) matters to the performers, and write their music plain. . . . but (with all that) they had the soul of musick in their compositions, which the modernes, with their many motive and slurring ornaments have corrupted.
>
> J. Wilson, p. 263

The last movement of an Italian sonata is normally a lively allegro or giga.

---

[18] an idea put forward by Peter Allsop at the IMS Congress, 1997
[19] Lonati *Violinsonaten* (1701) foreword, p. 7
[20] see Allsop (1998)

Italian style in England

The fashionable Italian style swept through Europe, in England replacing the vogue for the French music of Mr. Lully (who, incidentally, was born in Italy). Purcell was caught up by this trend when he composed his *Sonnata's of III Parts* (1683). The preface to this set of sonatas states that they are 'faithfully endeavour'd a just imitation of the most fam'd Italian masters'. Contrary to most string players' expectations, these Italian masters probably did not include Corelli, as it is uncertain whether Corelli's opus I trios (published in Rome in 1681) had reached London by 1683. The Italian masters most likely to have been imitated by Purcell include Vitali, Cazzati and Legrenzi.[21] After Purcell's trios were published, Lonati (see above) lived in England 1685-89 and is likely to have met leading English composers. Matteis, an Italian immigrant, helped to spread the Italian taste in violin playing which was much more advanced technically than anything previously heard in England. Early in the new 18th century North describes the effect 'the great Master' Corelli's trio sonatas had on English music-making:

> . . . the onely musick relished for a long time, and there seemed to be no satiety of them, nor is the vertue of them yet exhaled, and it is a question whether it will ever be spent, for if musick can be imortall, Corelli's consorts will be so. Add to this, that most of the yong Nobility and Gentry that have travelled into Italy affected to learne of Corelli, and brought home with them such favour for the Itallian musick, as hath given it possession of our Pernassus. And the best utensill of Apollo, the violin, is so universally courted, and sought after to be had of the best sort, that some say England hath dispeopled Italy of viollins. And no wonder after the great Master made that instrument speak as it were with humane voice, saying to his scollars - *Non udite lo parlare?*
>
> J. Wilson, pp. 358-9

The great Italian violinist/composer tradition continued unabated into the 18th century with Vivaldi, Veracini, Tartini and Geminiani. These last two became teachers of great influence (Geminiani settled in London), and their treatises are among some of the most valuable records of contemporary violin playing. Paganini, a maverick whose virtuoso technique and legendary performances astounded the public all over Europe, represented the peak in the Italian 18th-century violinist tradition.

For more information about the repertoire and history of the early Italian sonata see Newman, Allsop (1992) and Apel.

---

[21] Holman (1994), pp. 87-8

3.6 The consort style

I have referred to the style of performance used for playing contrapuntal music as 'consort style'. In the violin and viol consort repertoire, parts (voices) interweave in a more flowing style. Phrases overlap and answer each other in a conversational manner. Bowing choices should be applied to whole musical phrase units rather than by the bar as in dance music. With the vocal, linear way of playing, heavy accentuation of individual notes is not necessary, and because most consort music of the early 17th century was written without bar-lines, the players would not have imposed any emphasis registering strong down-beats at any regular fixed points in the music. The time signature in this type of music suggests a beat, and may indicate whether this should be divided into three or two notes.

Factors which should help the player identify the consort style:

- The parts overlap all the time.
- The parts look and feel like vocal lines.
- Imitation is a major component.
- The phrases go across bar-lines without regard for main beats.
- The writing is similar to the fantasy found in viol music, without definite form, but freely inventing and introducing new themes in different sections, each one with a new character.

Ex. 3.6.1: Locke, Broken Consort suite in C major

In the above extract (♪ part of track 25), look for places where the parts play together, and where they overlap, answering each other. Notice how the mood fluctuates, even though no change of tempo is marked: slow note values automatically give the impression of an adagio, and quicker ones more flowing movement. Look for new motifs: sometimes only two or three notes set off the development of a new idea. Any of these clues should make the player play in a much more vocal style, forgetting the rules of down-bow and going with the rise and fall of the line, and the interplay of ideas.

Ex. 3.6.2: Purcell, Sonnata of III parts no. 7

In the above trio sonata, all parts can bow out from the first note making long overlapping phrases. Purcell frequently uses this style of writing for one section of a trio sonata, surrounding it on either side by dance forms. The music might suddenly dissolve from being in a strictly harmonic vein, to a fugue-like working out of points. Look from bar to bar to see how the music works. If harmonic considerations dominate, and the parts move in a parallel way, use the rule of down-bow, but if the parts overlap and intermingle in a contrapuntal way, immediately be on the alert for bowing out according to melodic shapes and emphases.

Clarity of the voices

Projecting and characterising the lines of the music as they weave together is essential for clarity. In order for each part to be clearly heard by the listener, the parts should retain the integrity of the phrasing within themselves, no matter what other parts may be doing at the same time. North warns against taking too fast a speed for contrapuntal movements:

> If fuges require a conformity in swifter action, I must say that such a fuge will appear indistinct, or no better than a confused hudle, which is one of the worst qualitys of a consort. For the audience ought to be sensible what each part is doing.
>
> J. Wilson, p. 193

Particular care must be taken, in the consort style of playing, to avoid bulges on long notes in the middle of phrases. Sustained lines are more appropriate, and long notes often need to be fitted into the melody line rather than be used as a function of harmony. Harmonic tensions still exist, but only as a result of the crossing and merging lines, and not as the prime consideration. Longer lines mean fewer re-takes with the bow, and more bowed-out phrases.

Stilo antico

Look out for this type of writing in works by later composers such as Handel and J. S. Bach, who often write fugues in an old-fashioned style (*stilo antico*) using large note values in long vocal lines where the more bowed-out way of performance might be applied. The technique of this linear way of playing is distinguished by an ability to maintain a constant bow speed, no matter how much the note-values vary, so that individual notes do not stick out from the line. This is in contrast to the different bow speeds necessary to execute the rule of down-bow. Shapes of themes should be maintained, and entries imitate each other, regardless of the position of the bar-line. This method should be applied to contrapuntal music of any period, which is characteristic of Italian style.

♫ consort music by Gibbons (tracks 3, 4), Morley (tracks 8, 9), Cavalli (track 11), Locke (track 25), and Jenkins (track 29).

PART FOUR
TUNING AND PITCH

4.1 Tuning and pitch

Historical attitudes towards unequal and 'pure' intonation are examined in the part, and the string player is given instructions on how to tune the open strings to fit with the prevailing temperament. Mersenne[1] wrote that he loved the violin particularly because it is able to vary the intonation at will, as voices do. The problem of mixing the violin family instruments with fixed instruments such as harpsichords will be considered.

Equal versus unequal tuning

Modern tuning divides the octave into twelve equal semitones, a tuning system known as equal temperament. The perception that players of Baroque instruments play 'out of tune' stems from the fact that most players of historic instruments adopt an unequal tuning system. Tuning a perfect fifth and another above it until the 'circle of fifths' is completed and the starting point is reached results in a gap, or comma, between the starting note and the finishing note. This gap has to be lost or distributed between the twelve semitones of the scale. Where the gap is evenly distributed, this is called equal temperament. In equal temperament, all the intervals are slightly 'out of tune' and have a fluctuation in the sound called beating. The speed of the beating indicates how far away the two notes are from the perfect interval. There are no perfectly in tune intervals in equal tuning, except unisons and octaves. The benefit of equal temperament is that every key matches every other one whether in C major or C♯ major.

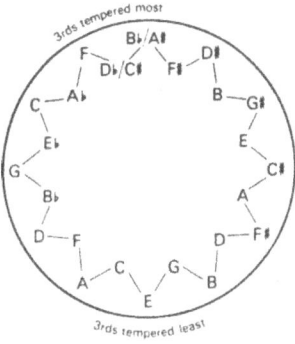

Ex. 4.1.1

The above diagram[2] shows how in historic tuning systems, the gap, or comma is distributed unequally, giving some perfectly in tune keys and intervals, and others which are more out of tune than in equal temperament. The most important intervals to have in tune when playing in historic temperaments are the third and the sixth. One of the earliest systems used was called 'mean-tone' and gives pure thirds and sixths by tempering or narrowing the fifths in selected keys. In mean-tone tuning the comma is lost by

---

[1] (1636) *Livre Quatriesme*, p. 177
[2] *New Grove*, 'Temperaments'

4.1 Tuning and pitch

splitting it over fewer intervals, so the more remote intervals are very out of tune, but these are hardly ever encountered in the music, or if they are, are used for special effect by the composer. In mean-tone temperaments the diatonic semitones are larger than the chromatic giving D♯ lower than E♭. One result of this was the appearance of keyboard instruments with split keys, where a choice of sharp or flat was available (e.g. D♯ and E♭).

Crome describes this system of enharmonic tones:

> A flat is a very little higher than G sharp. The difference is what is generally call'd a quarter note but you never use G sharp and A flat at the same time. There is about the same difference in the rest of the semi-tones and as it would be perplexity to treat much about quarter notes, the best way will be to lay them quite aside and trust to the ear for if your ear is good you will play them though you don't know it, as it is impossible to measure the distances.
>
> *c.*1740 The Fiddle New Model'd, or a Useful Introduction for the Violin quoted in Riley (1954), p. 203

In other words, the sensitive violinist who has a choice of altering his intonation on the stopped notes will automatically select the most appropriate solution. Later in the 18th century tuning systems began to move towards equal tempering, giving a wider choice of more in tune intervals as music developed more complex harmonic patterns, and used a greater range of keys. J. S. Bach would still have been using an unequal temperament in the Well-Tempered clavier, (*well*-tempered, not *equally*-tempered) but in more remote keys he composed music which avoided the most out of tune intervals.[3] However, it was not until the 19th century that equal temperament became generally used. The shift in style towards melodically as opposed to harmonically based compositions also had the effect of pushing leading notes and thirds higher, with the result that D♯ became higher than E♭.[4]

Different types of tunings were employed in different situations, depending on the instruments used and the music played. Neidhart gives four temperaments from the very unequal to almost equal:

> I believe in general that the first is suited to a village, the next to a town, the third to a city, and the fourth to a court.
>
> (1724) quoted in Haynes (1995), p. 200

North complained about the problem of tunings that

> ... to reconcile them in practise there is a great puzle.
>
> J. Wilson, p. 205

Composers were aware of the different affects of keys, and the choice of key for a particular composition was critical, and key colour really existed.[5] Baroque wind instruments with no or few keys had limited tuning capabilities, and key colours formed an integral part of the choice of key for flute or oboe music, with 'good' or 'covered' tonalities giving extra expressive significance to a piece. Many shades of key colour were possible and composers used this fact consciously. 'Home' keys would in general be more in tune than remote keys with more accidentals. The term 'home key' could apply to the key of the instrument (stringed instruments better in D and G) or the key of the composition. Ozanam wrote:

> Whatever precaution we might take in tuning our instruments to render all the chords equal, there is always left therein some inequality that causes us to notice a je-ne-sais-quoi of sadness or gaiety, of the melodious or the harsh, which (in turn) makes us distinguish one key from another by ear.
>
> (1691) quoted in *New Grove*, 'Temperaments'

---

[3] Barnes, pp. 236-249
[4] ibid.
[5] see p. 7 for a table of key characteristics.

The 'buzzing' or beating of a harsh, out of tune interval was exploited by composers so that the perfectly tuned resolution gave a sense of relief. Mace describes, in his section on tunings for the lute, the concept of the expressive variety of the keys:

> *'Tis well known to all Masters in This Art, That in Nature, Naturally there are but 7 Keys Distinct, and Proper; by which we Express All Things, in Musick; for when we come to the Eight from any one Key, we have but (as it were) Rounded the Circumference, and come again to the same Point, where we first began;*
>
> (1676), p. 191

Mace describes his feelings for the affects of several commonly used keys on the lute: C major is the most noble, heroic and majestic key in the whole scale; D is stately and noble; E is handsome free and pleasant; F is brisk, lofty and sparkling. These feelings arise from his choice of unequal tunings for the instrument. Rameau also endorsed the affective benefit derived from unequal tuning:

> For it is good to note that we receive different impressions from intervals in keeping with their different [degree of] alteration. For example the major 3rd, which [in its] natural [state] excites us to joy, as we know from experience, impresses upon us ideas even of fury when it is too large; and the minor third, which [in its] natural [state] transports us to sweetness and tenderness, saddens us when it is too small. Knowledgeable musicians know how to exploit these different effects of the intervals, and give value, by the expression they draw therefrom, to the alteration which one might [otherwise] condemn.
>
> (1726) *New Grove*, 'Temperaments'

Most 18th-century tunings aim for close to pure thirds and sixths (i.e. smaller and lower than in equal temperament), and arrange the rest of the intervals around these. String players should note that the result of this is narrow fifths. As the century progressed, and use of tonality became more complex, tunings moved towards equal temperament. Rameau, eleven years after his previous views were recorded retracted his ideas and became positively in favour of more equal temperament:

> He who believes that the different impressions which he receives from the differences caused in each transposed mode by the temperament [now] in use heighten its character and draw greater variety from it, will permit me to tell him that he is mistaken. The sense of variety arises from the intertwining of the keys and not at all from the alteration of the intervals, which can only displease the ear and consequently distract it from its functions.
>
> (1737) *New Grove*, 'Temperaments'

Thus, the increased use of all the keys by composers pushed the old tuning systems out of use.

Mattheson gives us general guidance about playing in unequal temperament:

> The most common type of temperament... rests on the following three statements:
> 1. Octaves, minor sixths and minor thirds must everywhere be pure.
> 2. One must raise major sixths and fourths somewhat.
> 3. One must however lower fifths and major thirds somewhat.
>
> How much or how little this somewhat should be is another question...
>
> (1739) I.7.88, tr. Harriss, p. 168

Tuning the open strings

Sorge lamented:

> Oh! When so many fiddlers begin to play their parts without having even properly tuned their instruments, how will pure tuning ever be achieved?... Oh blindness! Oh ignorance! How great you remain in so many parts of the world of music.
>
> (1748) quoted in Haynes (1991), p. 373

4.1 Tuning and pitch

PRACTICAL APPLICATION

What does inequality of tuning mean in practice for the early string player? A few basic conventions will suffice to make us feel comfortable with the early tuning systems: if the player has a fixed tuning source, e.g. a harpsichord or organ which has been carefully tuned, the open strings should be tuned separately to this source. As open strings will be frequently used while playing, compatibility with the continuo instrument is essential.

When tuning a string group, the keyboard player should be persuaded to offer three chords: D, G and c. These three chords cover all the open strings of the group. Players must be persuaded not to alter the resulting (narrow) fifths. At first the E will seem low, and the D- A and G-D intervals will be narrower than the player is used to when tuning perfect fifths. When the group has tuned thus, the interval from the c of the violas and cellos should be checked with the E of the violins. A perfectly pure third should be the result. The Gs of the violins should be well in tune with their Es. It is worth spending some time getting used to this tuning method, as it will make a noticeable difference to the sonority of the string section, and make the use of open strings more acceptable. If this method of tuning from chords is used in a concert, a pause should be left for the ears of the audience to empty themselves of the tonalities set-up by the tuning process, which becomes a type of orchestral prelude, otherwise an unexpected modulation might be the result of hearing the first chord of the piece. Fingering adjustments which should be noticed with the new, low E string include a higher first finger for the violins on the note F, and a low second finger on open strings where this note is the third of the chord.

This method of tuning is endorsed and suggested by various sources:

Werckmeister:
> If the 5ths are tuned purely [on a violin], the result will be impure intonation.
>
> (1691) quoted in Haynes (1991), p. 367

Rameau:
> . . . the best masters [on the violin] . . . as I have been told by Guignon, one of his Majesty's musicians, narrow the fifths slightly, in order to sweeten the overlarge 6th . . . [between] the bottom and top strings.
>
> (1737) quoted in Haynes (1991), p. 369

Many writers (see Mersenne above) comment on the ability of 'free' instruments, i.e. those without fixed tuning, to alter selected notes to become 'pure' intervals. String players without frets, and singers are most able to do this:

Telemann:
> My system is not based on any keyboard temperament; rather, it displays the sounds found on unrestricted instruments like the cello, violin etc, that can play purely (if not always entirely so), as day-to-day experience teaches.
>
> (1742/3) quoted in Haynes (1991), p. 372

J-J. Rousseau:
> In modulations, the mechanisms of temperament cause such unpleasant notes, for example D and G♯, that they are impossible to listen to. . . . . Singers never conform to them . . . except where forced to do so at points where they are in unison with the instruments.
>
> (1743) quoted in Haynes (1991), p. 372

Problems may occur when playing in unequal temperaments with a keyboard instrument doubling notes played by the strings. Sometimes the extreme effect of unequal intonation is intolerable, in which case, the keyboard player should be persuaded to omit the offending note. This problem is more apparent when playing with an organ, as the sustaining nature of the instrument is merciless at showing up the differences in the string-keyboard tuning. Quantz recommends:

> Since, then, these notes cannot always be avoided, especially in those keys in which many flats or sharps appear, the accompanist would do well to seek as much as possible either to hide them in a middle or lower part, or, if one of them forms a minor third, to leave it out entirely.
>
> (1752) XVII.VI.20, tr. Reilly, p. 261

With regard to extreme intervals in ensemble tuning he states:

> It is true that you cannot perceive this difference as distinctly if you play alone on the harpsichord, or if you accompany a large ensemble, but if these notes are found in unison with another instrument, the difference is all too clearly heard, since other instruments give them in their true ratios, while upon the keyboard they are tempered; for this reason it is better to omit them entirely than to offend the ear ... the poor intonation is not as apparent to the ear in the low register as in the high.
>
> (1752) XVII.VI.20, tr. Reilly, p. 261

Quantz observed that when tuning takes place in a large group, everyone will have tuned slightly differently from one other:

> If each instrument in a large accompanying body were tested separately, it not only would be found that almost every instrument is untrue in itself, but also that frequently not even two or three would be in tune with one another. considerable damage is done as a result to the good effect of the ensemble.
>
> (1752) XVII.VII.2, tr. Reilly, p. 266

The difficulties arising from the fact that string players can alter the pitch of most of the notes they play as they go along, and keyboard players cannot, is a source of much heartache and argument. Quantz recognises this:

> It is true that each of the string players follows the judgement of his ear when he plays, and can shift his fingers up or down accordingly; but untrue tuning can still be detected on each instrument from time to time through the open strings, especially the low ones, which cannot always be avoided ... To tune the violin quite accurately, I think you will not do badly to follow the rule that must be observed in tuning the keyboard, namely, that the fifths must be tuned a little on the flat side rather than quite truly or a little sharp, as is usually the case, so that the open strings will all agree with the keyboard. For if all the fifths are tuned sharp and truly, it naturally follows that only one of the four strings will be in tune with the keyboard. If the A is tuned truly with the keyboard, the E a little flat in relation to the A, the D a little sharp to the A and the G likewise to the D, the two instruments will agree with each other.
>
> (1752) XVII.VII.3, tr. Reilly, pp. 266-7

North complains about the inconveniences of science in revealing the inequality of the scale:

> The harmonious oeconomy [sic] of sounds hath bin accused of divers defects and imperfections, to all of which I shall securely plead Not Guilty; for nothing can be more perfect in accord, than the common musical scale is. And if the sounding part had bin left to the voice, which conforms to all truth of accords, whereof the ear is judge, there never had bin any suspicion of such majors, minors, dieses, commas, and I know not what imaginary devisions of tones, as some clumsye mechanick devises called Instruments have given occasion to speculate. And even of them, such as have not the tones fixed, but give liberty to obey the ear's determinations, as the violon and violin (mostly), are not incumbred with any irregularitys that disturb the perfection of accords.
>
> J. Wilson, p. 204

If the string player is without a fixed tuning source (such as an exactly tuned keyboard instrument), the above method described by Quantz should still be observed. The problem presented to viola and cello players by tuning only to an A is that the error is compounded if the usual pure fifths are tuned from the top string downwards. Falck in his *Idea Boni Cantoris* of 1688 observes that if tuning is started with the D string on the violin, the E string when reached will be higher in pitch than the same note on the keyboard to which it is being tuned. A tuning source near the middle of the instrument (A for the violin, D for the viola) is less likely to lead to errors in tuning.

4.1 Tuning and pitch

A common cause of complaint from string players is that after tuning only to an A, when play commences the D string seems flat, and has to be raised to suit the prevailing intonation. It would be better if players adopted the habit of tuning narrow fifths to start with, whatever the circumstances.

Gut strings are more susceptible to fluctuations in temperature and humidity than covered strings, absorbing moisture rapidly and going flat in a warm or candle-lit room. A dryer atmosphere means a generally more stable tuning. Unfortunately, woodwind instruments (including organs) tend to alter in the opposite direction, with the pitch rising as the wood becomes warm.

The usual method of tuning stringed instruments seems to have been by lightly plucking the strings while holding the body of the instrument under the right arm, guitar-style. Merck[6] describes this method in his *Compendium Musicae Instrumentalis Chelicae*, and in his treatise *Musicus Avtodidaktos*, Eisel[7] advises using the bow to tune rather than striking the strings with the thumb, which was presumably common practice. Mattheson realised that the plucking method was not very reliable when a visiting director from Hannover

> . . . had the praiseworthy custom that he, before the beginning for example of an overture, accurately tuned one violin himself, and indeed with the bow, not pizzicato; when that was done, he played it for the first violinist, one string after another, until both were absolutely in tune. Afterwards, the first violinist made the rounds and did the same for each of the others. Here we tune them all simultaneously and they hold the instrument under their arm. That never yields true purity.
>
> (1739) III.26.22, tr. Harriss, p. 868

Playing in tune is the first of Muffat's observations:

> With regard to correct intonation, there is no difference among the best masters, no matter what their nations be, whose precepts only weak pupils or unprofessional ignoramuses fail to observe . . . nothing is more helpful than frequent practice with players of exquisite taste and to avoid playing with those who would corrupt more ears and fingers than they would improve.
>
> (1698) quoted in Strunk (1998), p. 140

Several tutors recommended the use of frets or marks on the fingerboard to accustom the novice player to the distances between the notes. Playford[8] advocated the use of frets for beginners and included a system of tablature for the violin (ex. 4.2.1). Although frets were no longer used in the 18th century, the system of marking the position of the notes on the fingerboard continued and is still used by some teachers today. The use of frets must have resulted in very inaccurate intonation, and the transitional period when the frets were removed must have been very upsetting for the pupil, as he would have to start using his ears for the first time.

See also Ross W. Duffin, *How Equal Temperament Ruined Harmony (and Why You Should Care)*, Norton (2007).

Pitch

Until recently, information about historical pitches has only been available piecemeal, often emanating from factions with axes to grind in favour of one view or another. We now have a survey of the subject unprecedented in the amount of detail and hard information which it contains. This work – Bruce Haynes, *Pitch Standards in the Baroque and Classical Periods*, (unpub. diss.) Montreal, 1995 (published as *A History of Performing Pitch: The Story of 'A'*, 2002) – is the result of many years' research in which all the known surviving fixed pitched instruments have been recorded. The historical, social and musical backdrop to this information is extremely complex and the analysis in this study examines all the variables of place and time, alterations to instruments through the centuries, and

---

[6] (1695) quoted in Riley (1954), p. 261
[7] (1738) ibid., p. 267
[8] (1674) *Introduction to the Skill of Musick & lessons for the treble-violin*

conditions under which the musicians worked which influenced the variety of pitches in use.

The term 'pitch' to a modern musician usually means one thing: $a^1=440$. This pitch has been used by the majority of performers since it was standardised earlier this century by the British Standards Institution conference, May 1938. This pitch is known as 'modern pitch', although it was in use throughout the 17th and 18th centuries in certain locations. In fact, there were two dozen pitch standards in use at various times from the mid-16th to the mid-19th centuries in Italy, France, Germany, England and Austria, which covered a range of 6 semitones.[9] In the Renaissance and Baroque periods pitches were usually identified by names according to their location and usage (e.g. *Chorton* for church pitch, and *Cammerthon* for chamber pitch).

The concept of using different pitches for different musical contexts may seem strange for musicians accustomed to playing at only one pitch. The phenomenon of 'perfect pitch' can be a severe disadvantage if the player or singer does not understand that this is a learned association connecting a sound with a particular note on the stave. Problems experienced by people with 'perfect pitch' can be overcome when the learned pitch recognition is erased through experience with other pitches. The most common early pitch used today to play Baroque music is $a^1=415$ which is conveniently a semitone lower than $a^1=440$. If a player has pitch recognition fixed at $a^1=440$ this shouldn't create a problem with tuning if they are playing exactly a semitone lower than the pitch they are used to, although the visual/ aural connection at a semitone might be more disturbing than a larger interval. The concept of associating a written note with a particular sound is a considerable handicap when starting to play a Baroque instrument as the player might be expected to play at different pitches (including $a^1=440$) for various types of music.

When playing in a lower pitch than that to which they are accustomed, players tend to play sharp until their ears adjust to the new pitch centre. In practice, this might mean adapting to only one new pitch, $a^1=415$, if one is to play Baroque music in normal circumstances. Many period instrument players now have $a^1=415$ fixed in their pitch memories, and string players find it difficult to adapt to even lower pitches when required. However in earlier times, pitches did not occur at convenient semitone steps. For various reasons musicians settled into other pitch zones such as those in the region of $a^1=405-410$, which was a common Baroque chamber pitch. Other factors such as fluctuations of materials and temperature can alter fixed-pitch instruments up or down by a few cents from day to day.

How do we know which pitch was used where? There is much information to be learned from studying fixed-pitch instruments: organs, pitch pipes and wind instruments. The trouble is that many of these sources have been altered by lengthening or shortening the pipes. Other factors such as drying out with age, and temperature and humidity fluctuations have to be taken into account when measuring the pitches of these instruments. It is not easy to generalise, but broad bands of pitches can be identified for various situations: the pitch at the Paris opera was always lower than other local establishments, and as late as 1780 was still only $a^1=404$.[10] The commonly held belief that pitch rose continuously from a low level to the heights of today must be put aside when faced with the historical evidence. Very high pitch ($a^1=465-70$) was used from early in the 17th century in northern Italy, whilst at the same period in Rome, church pitch was approximately $a^1=392$ and remained at this level until the time of corelli. Very low and very high pitches were often used side- by-side using transposition as an aid to compatibility. As a general rule, chamber pitch was lower than church (i.e. organ) pitch, and as a result the two elements were often at odds with each other. Instrumental music in church was not encouraged where the difficulties were too great to be overcome, but where there was a favourable attitude, organs were lowered in pitch to facilitate instrumental collaboration. For example, in Dresden at the end of the 17th century the old Renaissance instruments such as the cornett which played at high pitch were being replaced with lower pitched French oboes. From 1730 church organs were built at the

---

[9] Haynes (1995), p. 35
[10] ibid., pp. 104-142

4.1 Tuning and pitch

lower *cammerthon* to match these new instruments. Where church councils were ignorant of the technicalities of organ building, organ makers were in a position to make extra profit by recommending high pitch, enabling them to make shorter sets of pipes, thereby saving money on expensive materials.[11] In 1764 Halle wrote:

> . . . other church organs commonly observe chorton, in order to save tin; for that reason organists using Musick have always, for the sake of the fiddles, to transpose.
>
> Haynes (1995), p. 251.

'Using music' meant using instrumental additions to the organ.

Pitch and sonority

The quality of sound of stringed instruments is dependent on various factors:

- the thickness and material of the strings used
- the angle of the fingerboard to the table of the instrument
- the height of the bridge
- the type of bow being used
- the acoustic

In general, for a short string length and higher pitch, thinner strings should be used, and for a longer string length and lower pitch, thicker strings. The overall tension resulting from the sum of all these factors is an important element in the resulting sonority, and crucial to the overall effect of the music. When all these factors meet in perfect balance, the instrument will speak at its best.

The violin family offers various sizes of instrument adapted for different situations, the smallest model being used for the higher pitches. Small (roughly 3/4 size) Italian violins pre-1600 came from the workshops of makers such as Linarol and the brothers Amati, and these instruments resonate and speak at their best at the higher range of pitches (a^1=465-70). The stringing and the angle at which the neck and bridge are set obviously matter when considering the pitch at which to play a particular instrument. Most violins of the 16th and early 17th century had a short neck with the result that a small violin would have a very short string length, (29.7 cm.) facilitating tuning up to the higher pitch. Several writers (not only for the violin) covering a period of 200 years specify that the pitch was to be set by tuning the top string to its tightest (just before it breaks).

Agricola:

> The treble of the fiddle family is tuned as high as it can stand. Tune the highest string so high that it cannot stand one more turn.
>
> (1529) tr. Hettrick, pp. 45, 47

Playford:

> . . . wind up his first or *Treble string* as high as it will bear.
>
> (1674), p. 112

Prelleur:

> Screw up ye treble string to as high a pitch, as it can moderately bear.
>
> (1731), p. 2

Transposition and sonority

Because of the use of so many different pitches, sometimes in the same locations, transposition played an important role. In church, for example, a situation which demanded woodwind instruments to play with a very high pitched organ might result in the wind instruments transposing a tone or a minor third away from the written key to coincide with the organ pitch. As the oboe (originating in France) replaced the cornett in

---

[11] ibid., pp. 205-6

church, organs began to be made at lower pitches. Stringed instruments would have re-tuned if the distance was reasonably small. Semitone transpositions were not very comfortable for wind instruments because in unequal tuning they would be playing in unsuitable outlandish keys (from c a semitone down gives the key of B, and upwards C♯ or D♭ both of which would be unacceptable for an instrument designed to be played in unequal temperament). Playing in an uncomfortable key is often the unfortunate result when 20th-century editors confuse pitch and sonority. Transposing string parts up a semitone makes the advantages of using old instruments with their free resonating sonorities redundant (for example, F major into G♭ major, giving a forest of flats unheard-of in Baroque music). If this adjustment is necessary for any reason, re-tuning is a much better solution, giving the option of using open strings and increasing the resonance of the instruments. The relative position of the fingers on the strings should remain as close as possible to the composer's original directions. Both J. S. Bach and Kuhnau on occasion asked the string band to tune up or down to suit the organ writing.[12] Ill-founded transposition often takes instruments out of their natural range, creating technical difficulties out of all proportion to the musical ones, and affecting the result with poor tuning and muffled sound. Agricola wrote:

> If such arias are transposed (that is, set in a higher or lower tonality), the result will be generally less satisfying than in the tonality in which they were actually composed, often with careful consideration, not to mention the discomfort such changes often cause the instrumentalists.
>
> (1757) quoted in Haynes (1995), p. 244

Baroque musicians were much more accustomed to transposing than their modern counterparts, but only between 'comfortable' keys and most organists would have thought nothing of transposing at sight. Where pitches were completely incompatible, players from separate establishments who needed to play together used different sets of instruments. Such was the case in mid-17th century Paris, for example, where the *écurie* (the stables, i.e. outdoor music) pitch was high and the opera pitch was low.[13]

The popularity of using $a^1=415$ for Baroque performances in modern times arose from the easy transition for transposing keyboard instruments during the period when historical instruments and their techniques were coming back into use. Music from the mid-18th century up to Beethoven is now usually played at $a^1=430$, although this is also an arbitrary 'convenience' pitch and was chosen to meet modern standards rather than as a historically accurate pitch, as many fixed pitch instruments of the classical period are at $a^1=425$.

More adventurous musicians are beginning to experiment with using a greater variety of pitches, where the wind players and their instruments permit. The greater variety and richness of sonorities which result from the use of different pitches to match the music and the instruments being used, is well worth the effort involved. The use of the correct historical pitch also opens up possibilities for learning about the different functions of the various models of stringed instruments that were in use from the mid-16th through to the end of the 18th centuries.

---

[12] ibid., p. 294
[13] ibid., pp. 104-142

4.2 Scordatura

Literally meaning 'mis-tuned', this device was used to obtain special effects and sonorities on instruments of the violin family, and reached its zenith in the works of Heinrich Biber.

Tablature

The use of a variety of tunings was common in the lute and viol repertoire and players of these fretted instruments were accustomed to reading music from tablature. Violin tutors used this notation for a short time in the 17th century, but it was restricted to elementary use, and was clearly a stepping stone to reading staff notation.

Ex. 4.2.1 *f*: Playford (1674)

In the type of tablature used by Zannetti, the use of the fourth finger is only indicated for notes a semitone lower than the next open string, or on the top string.

Ex. 4.2.2 *f*: Zannetti (1645)

The first line shows the normal printed notation, and the line below the tablature version of the same music. In the original publication the two versions were printed on opposite sides of the same page opening. The top line represents the G string, and the bottom line, the E string (Italian violin tablature placed the highest sounding string at the bottom, a convention shared with Italian tablature for lute and guitar). The numbers in Zannetti's system indicate the fingers to be used, as opposed to the position at which the string is stopped as in the Playford example, which follows the fretted instrument system. The rhythm appears on the top of the stave (continue with the same note-value until a different one is shown).

Unorthodox tunings

Factors which influenced the use of various tunings were mainly key and sonority. In some tunings notes, chords or unisons normally impossible to play became possible. When tablature was used to notate the music, the player could easily play in different tunings without the effort of re-thinking the position of the notes.

Bach used scordatura in his fifth suite for unaccompanied cello, which he wrote in hand-grip notation (see below). The top string is tuned down one tone to g, allowing the use of chords which would otherwise only be available with difficulty. This tuning for the cello was commonly used in solo repertoire, the two Gs giving a good resonant sonority.

Ex. 4.2.3 *f*: J. S. Bach, Suite 5 for solo cello

Practical Application

Violin tablature and hand-grip notation

Although tablature for the violin (as shown above) made a brief appearance in the publications for beginners by Zannetti and Playford, it did not catch on. A different system of notation for music written in scordatura was developed called 'hand-grip' notation. This system maintained the visual connection between finger and the position of the written note, but because of the altered tuning, the resulting sound on the re-tuned strings was different to the written pitch. In other words, what you see is not what you hear. There is no provision in hand-grip notation for indicating the use of the fourth finger when an open string is available for the same note. This can be confusing when a composer wishes to have a higher note than the next open string played on a lower one, as often happens in bariolage passages, for example. One rule which must be observed when playing from hand-grip notation is that the player has to play in first position and use open strings whenever these are indicated by the written pitch. The new tuning might result in a different pitch if a fingered note representing an open string is played. If the normal tuning is altered by a tone, the player should expect sounding unisons in hand-grip notation, played with the open string and a stopped string together, to be written as seconds. Occasionally, the player needs to be aware that the rule of always playing an open string when that note occurs breaks down, and a choice will have to be made between open string and fourth finger to achieve the desired notes. If the top string is tuned down, and a higher note is needed on the second string, the only way to write it is the note which is normally the open string. composers rely on the player's common sense at these points. The frequent occurrence of unisons is one of the features of music written for scordatura violin, as composers exploited all the novel effects in the new tunings.

Understanding handgrip notation:

Ex. 4.2.4 *f* and modern edition: Biber, sonata XII, (The Ascension)
from the 'Rosary' or 'Mystery' sonatas

- The new tuning is usually notated at the start of the piece, before the clef sign.
- The first line above (with the bass part) shows the handgrip notation as it appears in Biber's original. Note the alto clef in this example.
- The second line shows the sounding violin part. Notes in brackets normally indicate notes that are not possible without the new tuning.
- The third line shows the modern edition with handgrip notation. The resulting 'key signature' for placing the fingers is shown, even though some of these notes are not used.

Tuning the violin

When re-tuning the violin, it is advisable to allow some time for the new tuning to settle, as the strings tend to revert to their original pitch. When performing in scordatura, I have found that within the space of a 20-minute interval or a fairly long item performed by another player programmed immediately before the scordatura item, the violin will adjust sufficiently to play with fairly accurate intonation. If you are fortunate enough to own more than one violin, it is useful to keep one in a different tuning when learning music in scordatura.

Intonation is very difficult when first using a new tuning as the relative distances of the semitones on the fingerboard change. When the E string is tuned down a tone, first finger on the E string, f^2, is now the note $e^{\flat 2}$. When playing in unequal temperament, the effect this can have on the placing of the fingers is considerable. The best way to learn to adjust to the new tuning is to play with a sustained accompanying instrument such as an organ which is also tuned to unequal temperament. The adjustments will become obvious. Practising with double-stopped intonation checks across the strings whenever possible is also useful when learning to play in new tunings. Remember that every new tuning will require different adjustments to intonation in the left hand.

The wonderful new sonorities available on the violin from using different tunings are also a limitation, as the range of keys easily available in any particular tuning became reduced. The tuning a-e^1-a^1-e^2 for example (used by Biber in *Harmonia Artificiosa* sonata no. 3) is wonderful in A major, but not compatible with flat keys. The result of this is to make some keys extremely sonorous at the expense of others. This may be why scordatura is not used at all in Bach's works for unaccompanied violin, as the harmonic limitations which it imposed became a barrier to the free use of all the keys.

Scordatura and national style

Italy

The first known use of scordatura for the violin is the sonata seconda from opus 8 by Marini called *d'Inventione*. The player has seven bars' rest to re-tune the E string down to c^2. The music continues in thirds which would be impossible to play with normal tuning. There is no aid offered in the form of hand-grip notation, and the player has to work out for himself the new fingering resulting from the re-tuned E string. It is not as easy as it looks as the written thirds (fingered as fifths) are not perfect intervals and use two different fingers.

Bohemia

Biber wrote many sonatas using scordatura and raised the technique to unsurpassed heights. The set of sixteen sonatas known as the 'Rosary' or 'Mystery' sonatas are untitled, but each is prefixed with an illustration representing the holy mysteries of the Rosary (see ex. 4.2.4 and 4.2.5). The set contains two sonatas with normal tuning (the first 'The Annunciation' and the last 'The Guardian Angel'). Each of the fourteen other sonatas has a different tuning. The most extreme tuning reverses the pitch of the middle two strings so that the D string becomes higher than the A string, a possible reference to the 'impossibility' of the resurrection, and involving the symbol of the cross.

Ex. 4.2.5 *f*: Tuning from Biber, sonata XI 'The Resurrection'

Other tunings enhance the keys in which the sonatas are written. The simplest re-tuning occurs in the tenth sonata 'The crucifixion' which tunes the E string down to d^2. This would be a good sonata for a first attempt at playing in scordatura. The top d^2 string of the violin resonates with the lower d^1, and the player new to scordatura will immediately sense the benefits of the device.

Biber also wrote non-programmatic sonatas using scordatura. In one of these the player is required to re-tune in the middle of a movement during a few bars' rest (as in the Marini sonata). The E string is tuned down to d^2. There follows an arpeggio using the newly tuned string for several bars, just to make sure the new pitch is correct—the player's last chance to adjust the string before continuing with the rest of the piece:

4.2 Scordatura

Ex. 4.2.6: Biber, 8 sonatas, sonata VI

Walther, in the preface to his *Hortulus Chelicus* pours scorn on violinist-composers who use 'false' tunings. The violinist must

> ... equip his violin with four true strings, from quint to quint. ... It is no better to touch a lot of strings in alternately rapid variation without restraint or form, producing false tones so that even listeners in far corners become of necessity nauseated.
>
> (1694) tr. Riley (1954), p. 395

England

In England, variations or sets of divisions on ground basses written in scordatura appear in Playford's *The Division-violin*:

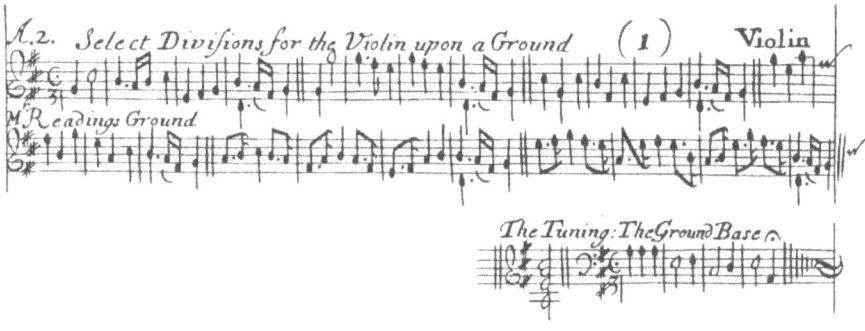

Ex. 4.2.7 *f*: Playford

France

Corrette includes a selection of *Pieces a Cordes Ravallées* in his *L'Ecole d'Orphée*[14] for violin. The first piece, a Menuet, makes the consecutive thirds easier to play as with the new tuning they are now fingered in fourths, and includes a unison d^2 at the *fin*, which would be impossible to play with normal tuning:

---

[14] (1738), p. 39

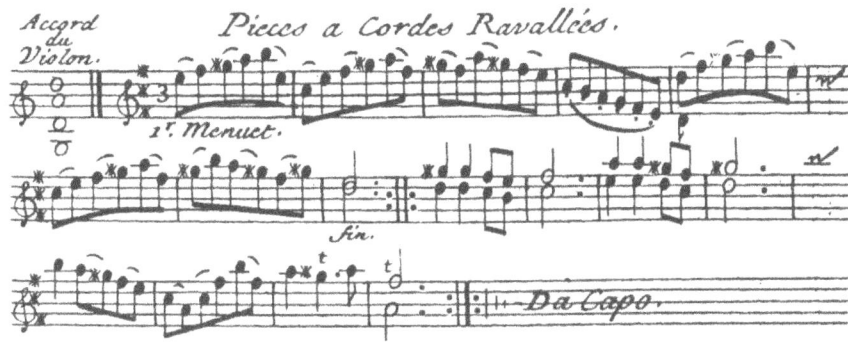

Ex. 4.2.8 f: Corrette (1738)

There follows a piece in fanfare style using thirds and fifths in imitation of trumpet music. The next piece is *Concerto à Violon Seul* with the D string (d^1) tuned down to b which contains some elaborate arpeggiated figures using the re-tuned D string as the bass note.

Scotland

Scottish music in the 18th century used scordatura in many beautiful laments and lively reels. The pentatonic basis of many Scottish tunes is well suited to the use of tunings of more limited key application. From Johnson, *Scottish Fiddle Music in the 18th Century* (handgrip notation):

Ex. 4.2.9: Mackintosh's Lament[15]

The written thirds in the above example sound as unisons, and the four-note open-string chord sounds as A major. The use of scordatura died out in domestic Scottish music making from 1800 onwards, and Johnson attributes this to the inability of pianists to cope with reading the hand-grip notation. It continued in use for the unaccompanied fiddle and is still commonly used in folk and blue-grass music. Folk music usually has limited harmonic range, and is well suited to the use of different tunings. The most common tuning is to tune the G string up by one tone, giving a sonorous a-d^1-a^1 on the bottom of the instrument, with the possibility of playing easy resonant chords. The next most popular tuning is a-e^1- a^1-e^2, producing a very brilliant effect.

The Violino piccolo

The violino piccolo is, as its name suggests, a small violin. It was used for special effect with varied tunings by many composers including J. S. Bach and Fux. During the early part of the violin family history, violins of various sizes were made, principally to suit high pitches, and to play very high parts using a tuning a fourth higher to avoid using the upper positions (this tuning would fit the pattern of fifths already set up in the violin family in the 'French' tuning, given by Mersenne (1636) and corrette (ex. 6.1.2) among others, starting with bottom B♭ in the bass violin). Music written for the violino piccolo

---

[15] Johnson, p. 134

4.2 Scordatura

in later Baroque works is usually written in hand-grip notation, for an instrument tuned up a minor third.

Ex. 4.2.10: J. S. Bach, Brandenburg concerto no.1, 1st movement

Handgrip notation (above) and the normal violin part (below) are written differently but sound the same. The usual difficulties of intonation in scordatura must be overcome, as the left-hand adjusts to the distances between the notes in the new tuning, in addition to the problems presented by a much shorter string length. As the piccolo violin has to play in unison with the normally tuned ripieno violin some of the time, there are even more difficulties than usual. A ¾ sized violin (in modern terminology) is often used today as a violino piccolo, although a ½ size would be more appropriate and works well in the higher tuning.[16]

---

[16] For further detailed information, including pictures of unaltered instruments in the Shrine to Music Museum, South Dakota, showing the different forms and uses of the violino piccolo, see Banks (1990)

PART FIVE
THE BASS DEPARTMENT

Baroque music has a special use for bass instruments. The practice of using the bass line as a fundamental support for harmony, indicated in the part by figures, is one of the main features which distinguishes the language of Baroque music from the earlier Renaissance and later Classical musical languages. The structure of the music based on these principles should be understood by all players, not just those who play bass instruments, in order to fulfil their roles in acknowledgement of the supremacy of harmony in Baroque music.

Brossard's dictionary (1703) defines *basso-continuo* as one of the most essential elements of modern music. Early in the 17th century players of chordal instruments, organ, harpsichord and lute, tried to fill in the parts as best they could above the bass line reading from the score. Eventually, a shorthand version of the other parts was written in the bass line in the form of figures.[1]

This chapter will identify the special knowledge players of bass instruments should bring to the performance of Baroque music. The system of writing figures with the bass line will be explained, and how the player should realise the information provided by the figures in performance. There follows guidance about the choice of bowed stringed instrument(s) for playing continuo in different areas of the repertoire. The performance of recitative will be examined, and finally the roles and functions of the viola and double bass will be briefly surveyed.

5.1 Playing from a figured bass part

The structure of Baroque music is built on the foundation of harmony. The ebb and flow of the music depends on friction between strong dissonances and weak resolutions. The tension created by surprising harmonic progressions contrasts with the feeling of security engendered by expected harmonic cliches such as cadences.

Cadences

Music is composed in sentences which end in cadences. These do not only occur at the end of a movement or section, but sometimes occur fleetingly in the middle of a phrase. It is desirable that the performer recognises cadential harmonic patterns in order to understand the structure and language of the music. When a perfect cadence is reached (dominant—tonic or V—I), this indicates the end of a phrase or sentence, similar to a full-stop; imperfect cadences or half closes (tonic—dominant or I—V) may be compared with a semi-colon or comma; the interrupted cadence, just as the name implies, creates a continuation in the music with a surprising twist when the listener is expecting the final closing of a phrase (dominant—supermediant or V—VI). The short-hand language of figured bass does not use the names of the home key or its relative chords named above (dominant, subdominant etc): the figures are used to indicate intervals above the bass note.

---

[1] For a clear explanation of how figured bass evolved see *Music and Society: The Early Baroque Era*, ed. Curtis Price, pp. 9-12

5.1 Playing from a figured bass part

Unfigured basses

In most 18th-century Baroque music harmonies are indicated by figures written above or below the bass line. Earlier music is often unfigured and the player has to use his ears and eyes to assimilate the important harmonic points as they pass by. If a keyboard player is involved in the performance, he will probably write the figures into his own score, but a cellist playing from an unfigured part will need to notice and mark in the important dissonances.

Expressing the figures

If the bass part has figures written in by the composer, the cellist should know how to interpret these to make the bass line come alive and deliver all the nuances of the harmonic language. The recognition of dissonant chords represented by the figures is particularly important. Quantz describes dissonances as

> ... the means to vary the expression of the different passions.
>
> (1752) XVII.VI.10, tr. Reilly, p. 254

The other players in the ensemble will be listening to the bass department to give a lead in this respect, and an uncommitted bass line in a group can make the performance sound bland and insipid.

Quantz lays great responsibility in the hands of the cellist:

> If the violoncellist understands composition, or at least something of harmony, he will find it easy to help the soloist bring out and make apparent the different passions expressed in a piece by its composer ... The violoncellist can contribute much to the perfection of a good ensemble if he does not lack feeling, and if he directs the proper attention to the whole, and not just to his own part.
>
> (1752) XVII.IV.7, tr. Reilly, p. 244

Quantz instructs:

> In ligatures or tied notes the cellist may allow the second note, above which the interval of the second or fourth is usually found, to swell by strengthening the tone, but he must not detach the bow.
>
> (1752) XVII.IV.8, tr. Reilly, p. 245

Quantz gives us a list of notes which must be stressed and brought out more than others which includes those that are raised irregularly by a sharp or natural sign, or lowered by a natural or a flat. Quantz also lists those dissonances which require more emphasis than others, combined with a hierarchy of the dissonances and how loudly they should be played.

1st class: mezzoforte	the 2nd with the 4th
	the 5th with the major 6th
	the major 6th with the minor 3rd
	the major 7th
2nd class: forte	the 2nd with the augmented 4th
	the diminished fifth with the minor 6th
3rd class: fortissimo	the augmented 2nd with the augmented 4th
	the minor 3rd with the augmented 4th
	the diminished 5th with the major 6th
	the augmented 6th
	the diminished 7th
	the major 7th with the 2nd and the 4th

Table extracted from information in (1752) XVII.VI.14 Table XXIV, tr. Reilly, p. 256

5.1 Playing from a figured bass part

Ex. 5.1.1: Quantz (1752) Table XXIV, tr. Reilly p. 257
showing dynamic importance of various harmonics

He then likens different dissonances with salt and spice at meals, since the tongue always feels more effect from one kind than from the others.[2] Stressed and unstressed harmonies are merely the combination of different intervals clashing or resolving continuously, providing means for expressing different *affekts*.

Mace describes how intervals between notes provoke various emotions:

> Let any 2 *Voices*, endeavour to *Sing* (strongly) together, *Gam-ut* and *A-re*, *A-re* and *B-mi*, or any other 2 of the *Scale*, (next adjoyning) and there will quickly be perceiv'd *That Tormenting Unsufferable Horrour* before mentioned; even such, as a *True Harmonical Ear*, is no more able to endure the noise of, than the cutting of his own *Flesh*.
>
> And This is that we call a *Discord* in *Musick*; and is a most *Exact*, and *Lively Simile* of the *Bad Nature*, viz. *Perplexity*, *Vexation*, *Anxiety*, *Horrour*, *Torture*, *Hell*, *Devilishness*; yea, of the *Devil* It self; so *Abominably Hateful*, and *Contrary* is It, to *Perfect Unity*, or *Goodness*: And is the *True Nature* of *Those 2 Distances* in *Musick*, viz. the *2d*. and the *7th*. so that although they be (of all other *Distances*) the nearest to *Unity*; yet are They the *Most Remote* in their *Nature*, *Contrary*, and *Hateful*; so that *That Old Common known Proverb*, (*The Nearer the Church, the further from God*) may Here be said, to find its *Original*; and It may as Aptly be said of *This Experiment*, viz. *The Nearer to Unity, the farther from Agreement*.
>
> There is yet another *Distance*, called a *Discord*, viz. the *4th*. but nothing of the *Nature*, or *Kind* with Those other Two; But (as I use to say) a very *Favourable Discord*; Its *Hurts* not like to the other. . . . It is a *Hard-Staring-Note*.
>
> (1676), p. 266

The fundamental principle of strong dissonance and weak consonance, or resolution of that dissonance, is the basis of the expression of emotional *affekts* through harmony. Quantz sums up:

> To excite the different passions the dissonances must be struck more strongly than the consonances. Consonances make the spirit peaceful and tranquil; dissonances, on the other hand, disturb it. Just as an uninterrupted pleasure, of whatever kind it might be, would weaken and exhaust our capacities for remaining sensitive to it until the pleasure finally ceased, so a long series of pure consonances would eventually cause the ear distaste and displeasure, if they were not mingled now and then with disagreeable sounds such as those produced by dissonances.
>
> (1752) XVII.VI.12, tr. Reilly, p. 254

Here are a few basic guidelines for reading figured bass:

1. In a bass part with figures, an unfigured note probably has a third above it.

2. A single figure such as 6 (an abbreviation of 6 3) or 7 (abbreviation of 7 5 3) means the notes upwards from the bass rise in thirds or fourths until the number indicated makes such an interval with the bass. E.g. 6 above a note means 1st inversion (a concord) which is a third with a fourth on top, and 7 is a 7th (a dissonance) which is a series of thirds the top note of which is a 7th away from the bass note. However, in practice, the keyboard player will probably re-arrange the notes of the chord according to convenience, and may not play all the notes to make a complete chord, particularly at speed.

3. Suspensions should be leaned on, and these often occur at the end of a tied or long note. The main suspensions occur on intervals of 4ths, 7ths and 9ths from the bass and resolve downward.

---

[2] (1752) tr. Reilly, p. 258

5.1 Playing from a figured bass part

4. Some ornaments are used to form dissonances deliberately to add interest to the melodic line: an appoggiatura (meaning to lean) usually forms a dissonance with the bass before resolving downwards. A *port de voix* forms a dissonance and resolves upwards.

CASE STUDIES

Ex. 5.1.2 *f*: Corelli, Sonata op. 5 no. 11, Gavotta

In the above extract, the chromatic movement on the second crotchets in the first two bars should be stressed, even though on weak beats. The tension is released by the cadence in the last bar. Any movement of a chromatic nature will be of some importance, as it will lead the harmony away from safe home keys. If you can, play the intervals listed by Quantz above on a keyboard instrument so that you learn to recognise the different types of dissonance (e.g. the 7th, and the 4/2).

Ex. 5.1.3: Corelli, Concerto Grosso op. 6 no. 2

In the above example, strong dissonances occur in the middle of the bar, and at the end of the tie. The bass line should lean into the tie before relaxing on the resolution d^1 (tenor clef), before beginning to swell again through the minim to the next bar. As two equally dissonant chords occur close together, some priority should be decided upon. The upper parts could assist the direction towards the bar-line, which becomes stronger than the middle of the bar. Another way of playing this passage would be to emphasise the middle of the bar, and drop away to the bar-line. However, I would prefer the first option, as the next dissonance occurs where the pattern is broken in the middle of the third bar. Here, as so often in Baroque phrasing, the repetition of an idea is contradicted by different emphasis where the ear expects a third similar pattern.

Surprising harmonic turns are not always emphasised by being played louder, as recommended by Quantz. In the following example, Bach marks a chromatic turn into the coda *piano*, which also serves to highlight the cello's more important role at this point.

5.1 Playing from a figured bass part

Ex. 5.1.4: J. S. Bach, Brandenburg Concerto no. 6, Adagio ma non tanto

5.2 Choice of continuo instrument(s)

The chamber sonata: 17th century

The *basso continuo*, *basse chiffré*, general bass or figured bass may be played by a single instrument or by a group of instruments. Many audiences are confused when four people sit down to play a trio sonata. This is because there are three parts, but the bass part is sometimes played by two players, one a melodic bowed instrument and one realising the harmony in chords as well as playing the bass line.

The true trio sonata *a 3* should have three equally contributing contrapuntal parts. In 17th-century sonatas with two trebles, there is often only a chordal accompaniment, as in the following example, and this is known as a sonata *a 2* (even though there may be three players).[3] A simple bass line which does not contribute equally to the musical argument does not need a bowed *and* a chordal instrument. In this case, a theorbo, organ or spinet would be sufficient (see section on Italy below).

Ex. 5.2.1: Rossi, Sonata sopra la Bergamasca

Purcell wrote: *Sonnatas of III Parts: Two Viollins And Basse: To the Organ or Harpsecord*, (1683), and *Ten Sonnata's in Four Parts*, (1697). In spite of the difference in their titles, both sets of sonatas have two treble parts and a divided bass part, the string bass (probably a viol) playing a more elaborate version of the slightly simpler keyboard part. Compare the two parts in bass clef in ex. 5.2.3.

Ex. 5.2.2 *f*: Purcell, Sonata VII of III parts

---

[3] Allsop (1992)

5.2 Choice of continuo instrument(s)

Ex. 5.2.3: Purcell, Sonata VII of III Parts

The choice of melodic and/or chordal instrument for the continuo role is quite complicated and may depend on several factors: the country or even city of origin (in the 17th century, Venice had different pitch standards compared with the rest of northern Italy), the size of the ensemble, the purpose and location (e.g. church or chamber), and date of composition.

The chamber sonata: 18th century

Unfortunately, many performers regard the authority of C. P. E. Bach as inviolable and apply his instruction universally to all music from the Baroque period:

> The best accompaniment, one which is free of criticism, is a keyboard instrument and a cello.
>
> (1753) tr. Mitchell, p. 173

His choice applies to a specific period and type of music composed in his *style galant*, not to a period of one hundred and fifty years throughout Europe. How do we know which instrument or instruments to use? Many clues are to be found on title pages, in archives, diaries, and contemporary descriptions, paintings and reports of performances. However, the terminology used in many cases poses more questions than are answered by the information supplied.

On the title page of the Corelli solo violin sonatas opus 5, we find *a violino e violone o cimbalo*. These sonatas are usually played with organ or harpsichord and cello, but 'o' meaning 'or' suggests that it is possible that only one of these continuo instruments is expected to play. The continuo team would probably have been playing from the same copy, with the bowed bass player looking over the shoulder of the keyboard player, thus blurring their roles from the point of view of analysis of the written instruction.

Violone

The word *violone* in particular has caused much scratching of heads, and frequent misguided use of an unsuitable instrument. In modern times, players have assumed that this word refers to a double bass, or fretted great bass viol at 16-foot pitch. It is now generally recognised that this word may indicate the use of any large bass instrument of the viol or violin family, at 8-foot pitch. However, it has been established by Bonta that the word means a bass violin or large cello in Corelli, and by Snyder that in North Germany (for example in the music of Buxtehude) it means a great bass viol playing at 8-foot pitch.

Da braccio or da gamba?

An important choice which has to be made for the bowed continuo instrument will be that of *da braccio* (i.e. cello, the bass member of the violin family) or *da gamba* (bass viol). There are some occasions where the choice is not important, as either instrument will do. However, there are large areas of the Baroque repertoire where there is a definite first choice of bowed continuo instrument. If a good edition or facsimile is being used, the use of particular clefs might indicate which instrument is more suitable: if the alto and bass

5.2 Choice of continuo instrument(s)

clefs are used, the work was probably written with the viol in mind; if tenor and bass clefs are used, the cello is likely to be more suitable. However, modern editions tend to use the tenor clef for much bass viol music, presumably to make it more accessible to cellists. No rule is without its exceptions and in this case, J. S. Bach's use of the alto clef in the suites for unaccompanied cello (as copied out by his wife Anna Magdalena) demonstrates that this 'rule' is to be treated with caution.

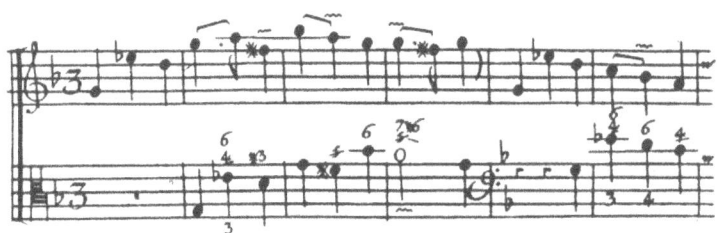

Ex. 5.2.4 *f*: Couperin, 7ième concert, sarabande grave

Ex. 5.2.5 *f*: Corelli, Sonata 'La Follia' op. 5 no. 12

Couperin's music is generally more suitable for viol (in the French style), and Corelli's (in the Italian style) for cello.

Italy

In the 16th and early 17th century the viol was much used in contrapuntal ensembles in Italy, but not as a continuo instrument. Towards the middle of the century it fell out of favour, being superseded by bass instruments of the violin family. Writing about Italian music making in 1639, Maugars commented:

> As for the viol, there is no one in Italy now who excels at it, and indeed it is very little played in Rome.
>
> (1639) tr. Wiley Hitchcock, p. 66

Twenty years later, Hill wrote from Lucca:

> The organ and the violin they are masters of, but the bass-viol they have not at all in use, and to supply its place they have the bass violin with four strings, and use it as we use the bass viol.
>
> Walls (1989), p. 67

The cello or violoncino is first mentioned about 1641 in Italy, the word serving as the diminutive for violone. A bowed bass instrument is sometimes suggested as an *alternative* to the chordal choice (organ, theorbo or harpsichord), especially where violins play. The melodic bass instruments trombone and bassoon are often suggested without a chordal instrument. There is frequent mention of a single chordal accompanying instrument without bowed bass. Often, a title page may indicate more than one suitable instrument or combination of instruments for the upper parts (for example, *per ogni sorte d'stromento* - Marini, Libro Terzo, op. XXII). This was, in addition to being guidance for the performer, in order to appeal to a wider range of players and thereby sell more copies. Even when this occurs, the basso continuo instrument is often specified, such as organ, but mention of a bowed instrument doubling the bass line is conspicuously absent. Here are some examples of 17th-century Italian title pages of instrumental music:

5.2 Choice of continuo instrument(s)

Note: *o, od* and *overo* mean 'or'; *e* means 'and', *se piace* or *a beneplacito* means 'optional'. Instrumental part books are in normal type. Title page or *tavola* (table of contents) information is in Italics.

1610	Cima, Concerti Ecclesiastici *sonata a 2: violino & violone, sonata a 3: violino, cornetto, & violono*
1622	Rossi trios *due violini, et un chittarrone o altro stromento simile*
1626	Buonamente trios *due violini, & un basso di viola*
1641	Fontana, sonate *Sonate a 1. 2. 3. per il Violino, o cornetto, Fagotto, Chitarone, Violoncino o simile altro Istromento* Note: The first mention of *violoncino* (previously viola, basso di viola, violone)
1642	Cazzati, *canzoni* *a 3. Doi violini, e Violone, col suo Basso continuo* Note: The first trio sonata for 4 players: 2 types of bass specified
1645	Uccellini, *opera quarta* all sonatas *a violino* (1, 2 or 3) *e Basso; a 3* is *doi violini e Basso*
1656	Cavalli, *Messa a 8 Voci* *Concertata con due Violini, e Violoncino, Ripieni, & altri Istrumenti, se piace*
1656	Cazzati, *Suonate opera Decima Ottava* *A due Violini Col suo Basso Continuo per l'Organo, & un altro a beneplacito per Tiorba, o Violone* Note: choice of one or two continuo instruments: organ & either plucked or bowed
1666	Gio. B. Vitali described as *Sonatore di Violone da Brazzo in S.Petronio di Bologna*, (Bass violinist in St. Petronio of Bologna) *Correnti, e Balletti da Camera a due Violini, col suo Basso continuo per Spinetta, o Violone*
1667	Cazzati, *Correnti e Balletti a Cinque, alla Francese, et all'Italiana* V.I, V.II, Alto Viola, Tenore Viola, Basso Violone da Brazzo, Bc.
1667	Bononcini, *Sonate da Camera, e da Ballo a 1. 2. 3. e 4* V.I, V.II, Spinetta o Violone
1673	Penna, *op. 7 Correnti Francesi* *due Violini, Violetta, e Violone, con il basso continuo per il clavicembalo, o Tiorba*
1674	Vitali, *op. 3 Balletti, Correnti alla Francese* V.I, V.II, Alto Viola, Spinetta o Violone
1676	Valther [Walther] *Scherzi da Violino Solo Con il Basso Continuo per l'Organo o Cimbalo, accompagnabile anche con una Viola o Leuto*
1678	Sanvitali, *Arie, e Correnti a tre, due Violini, e Violone* Note: no chordal continuo
1680	Pauli, *Suonate A due Violini, con il Basso Continuo per l'Organo*
1682	Corelli *op.1 Sonate a tre, due Violini, e Violone, o Tiorba, col Basso per L'Organo*
1684	Vitali, *Sonate Alla Francese, & all'Itagliana a sei Stromenti.* V.I, V.II, V.III, Alto Viola, Tenore Viola, Spinetta o Violone
1687	Albergati, *Sonate da Camera op. 5 a due Violini, e basso con Violoncello obligato.* V.I, V.II, Violoncello, Cimbalo

Source: Claudio Sartori, *Bibliografica della Musica Strumentale Italiana* (Florence, 1952 & 1968)

The above list is presented as a compendium of possibilities when playing 17th-century Italian chamber music, and as evidence of the importance of getting the right balance between the contrapuntal and the chordal instruments. Also note that the doubling of the bass line of the chordal instrument was unusual. An extra bass instrument is specified mainly where there is an independent or obligato part. The use of the double bass in such ensembles is extremely unsuitable, and the designation violone has led many players to include a 16-foot sonority when it is clearly not required. Sometimes, selected notes or phrases on the great bass viol, the chittarone and theorbo can be played at 16-foot pitch if the notes at the lower octave are available in the tuning being used. Compare this list with the 17th-century *sonata a tre/due* details at the beginning of this section.

5.2 Choice of continuo instrument(s)

The list also serves as a warning about the potential confusion in nomenclature. The word viola is used in all its senses, as a stem for all sorts of prefixes and suffixes, as well as on its own. It can mean large cello, viola, bass viola da gamba, or vihuela *d'arco* or *da mano* (not used after the 16th century). The term *violone* is also used to indicate a bass member of the violin family (e.g. a cello), and could be large or small, with various tuning possibilities. Bonta thinks that *basso di viola* probably refers to the bass member of the gamba family and was not much used in church, as this indication is found mainly in collections of dance music.[4] This is supported by evidence from Brossard's dictionary, which implies that *basso di viola* is viola da gamba, and *violone* a member of the violin family. Bonta also points out that *violetta* may be a small version of the bass or tenor (i.e. viola) size of violin family instrument, suitable for playing concertante parts.

Ex. 5.2.6 *f*: Cima, Sonata (1610), Partitura book,
thought to be the first sonata written specifically indicating the violin.

When playing 17th- and early 18th-century Italian chamber music, ensembles should be wary of using more than one continuo instrument. Where the bass part is divided with an ornamented version in addition to the slower-moving basso continuo part, the use of a plucked and a bowed instrument would make sense. However, where a single bass line appears, the above evidence suggests that caution should be exercised when adding extra players to the continuo line in small instrumental groups. The term *basso* or *basso continuo* in this context probably means only one instrument.

In early 17th-century Italian opera, groups of chordal instruments are specified for the continuo. In *Orfeo*, for example, Monteverdi specifies harpsichord, organ and regal in addition to other plucked instruments, but no bowed bass except in the string band ritornelli.

Remember, that Corelli writing at the tail end of the 17th century specified harpsichord *or* violone as continuo for his *Sonatas* opus 5. Vivaldi's *Sonatas* opus 2, are described as being for *violino e basso per il cembalo* (Roger edition, Amsterdam). However, the bass parts of both these sets of sonatas contain much imitation and elaborate figuration, and the presence of a cellist in this type of writing would free the chordal instrument from playing all the notes, in order to play the harmonic structure only, not all the semiquavers (see ex. 5.2.5). Another possibility where the bass-line is simple would be to dispense with the chordal continuo instrument altogether, a practice known to have been widespread. The cellist would fill in harmonies at appropriate points, either with added figuration or chords where the implied harmonic effect of the two parts was too thin. Many trio sonatas where the bass has an equal role can survive perfectly well with three bowed parts without a chordal filling.

More detailed information about the choice and use of bowed continuo instruments in Italy may be found in the following articles:

Ashworth/O'Dette (1997), Baines (1977), Bonta (1977 and 1978), Burnett (1970), Dixon (1981 and 1986), and Watkin (1996).

♪ track 11: Cavalli, *canzona a tre* played by two violins, bass violin and organ.

---

[4] (1978), p. 40

5.2 Choice of continuo instrument(s)

France

Chamber

The viol came into its own in mid-17th-century France as a courtly solo and continuo instrument. Most of the solo French Baroque repertoire up until the 1680s is written in an idiom unsuitable for playing on the cello, which was not used at that time as a solo instrument in France.[5] Double stopping and figures which lie under the hand on the viol with its tuning in fourths with a third in the middle are impossible or very difficult to play on the cello.

Couperin in the preface to his *Concerts Royaux* describes the instrumentation as *au clavecin; mais aussy au violon, a la flute, au hautbois, a la viole, et au basson*. This list reflects the practice of mixed wind and stringed instruments doubling treble and bass lines *en symphonie* in chamber works. Continuo groups using a mixture of chordal and bowed instruments are a feature of French style, in contrast to the sparse instrumentation of the Italians at this period. However, the practice of using a single bowed instrument realising the harmony also applied in France: the Brossard dictionary of 1703 suggests that the basso continuo was often played

> ... simply, without figures on the bass viol or cello, which the Italians also call Basso Viola, Violone &c.[6]

Instruments may be added or subtracted for individual movements, or chosen for particular affect: a flute and viol for a *sarabande tendre* for example. In the *Avertissement* to his *Leçons de Ténèbres*, Couperin wrote that

> ... if one can join a Bass Viol or a Bass Violin to the accompaniment of the Organ or the Harpsichord, that will be good.
>
> (1714) tr. Donnington (1963), p. 362

Couperin used the term *basse d'archet* to indicate bass viol *or* cello.[7]

The viol was predominant in small ensembles and the solo repertoire, although some composers such as Charpentier used the *basse de violon* in a solo role in its four- and five-string forms. His *Sonate* (c.1686) is scored for *2 flutes allemandes, 2 dessus de violon, une basse de viole, une basse de violon a 5 cordes, un clavecin et un teorbe*.[8] In his chamber works, Rameau used the idiom of the bass viol to its full capacity, notably in the *Pieces de Clavecin en Concerts*, which would be impossible to perform on the cello. However, he supplies an alternative part for the pieces to be performed with a second violin instead of the bass viol.

Orchestral

Orchestras or string bands such as the *Vingt-quatre Violons* of Louis XIV[9] used the large four- or sometimes five-stringed *basse de violon*, playing in sections of six or more players, sometimes with bass viols playing the same part. In England during the early Restoration period, the French model was imitated, with the bass violin in Bb tuning being used in orchestral groups. The '24' was later enlarged to include oboes and more players on the outer parts.

In the Paris opera orchestra in the 18th century, it has been argued that where large violin family bands play dance music, the continuo group should remain silent where the figuring stops, playing to accompany solo singers where the figures re-appear.[10] This idea is still under discussion and may not apply until after the period of Rameau. Rameau's operatic works use the full string band: two violin parts, divided violas, cellos and basses.

---

[5] Sadie, p. 332
[6] '*simplement, & sans chiffres sur la Basse de Viole, ou de violon &c ... d'ou les Italiens la nomment aussi Basso Viola, Violone &c.*'
[7] Sadie, p. 331
[8] ibid., p. 331
[9] 24 instruments of the violin family: probably 6 violins, 3 viola parts of 4 players each, and 6 *basses de violon*
[10] Sadler, pp. 148-157

5.2 Choice of continuo instrument(s)

The *petit choeur* contains cello and double bass which plays in the accompanied recitatives only.[11]

♪ tracks 5-6, 18-24, 32-36 for orchestral music using bass violins.

Germany/Austria

Early dance bands comprised of professional players would have been made up of instruments from the violin family after the French model (see above), using a bass instrument such as a large or small violone of the cello type, tuned either in C in the Italian custom, or B♭ in the French. Hamburg's theatres probably retained the old-style French orchestra format using basse de violons into the early 18th century.

The bass viol is important as a solo instrument in the mid- to late 17th century, and is frequently found in chamber ensembles with the violin. As in France, the bass viol developed a solo role in the hands of composers such as Buxtehude, and subsequently J. S. Bach. The bass instruments most often called for by Buxtehude are the violone and the fagotto (bassoon). The violone of the violin family plays with the large tutti ensemble only, not as a soloist, and doubles the general continuo line. Violone is specified by Buxtehude in only one chamber work where the other bass instrument is viola da gamba, and Snyder advises us that in this case it would have been an 8-foot pitched large viol.[12] This author also informs us that there is no mention of violoncello in any of Buxtehude's works. The violone at 16-foot pitch may double the continuo throughout in large choral works through figured and unfigured passages, especially when performing in large buildings.[13]

The violin was an increasingly popular solo instrument around the turn of the 18th century, and with it came the ascendancy of the cello as the complementary accompanying instrument. The viol's more delicate and reedy sonority became reserved for special uses (as in J. S. Bach St. Matthew and St. John passions, and Handel's early oratorio *La Resurrezione*), and solo roles (Telemann 'Paris' quartets, and concertos for small groups of soloists which include the viola da gamba). As the 18th century progressed, the cello took over from the viol as the bowed continuo instrument in general use in small and large ensembles, resulting in C. P. E. Bach's recommendation of the cello with the harpsichord as 'the best accompaniment'.

In Austria the bass viol maintained an important position in the solo field and in chamber repertoire up until the end of the 17th century, and as a companion to the violin in trios with concertante bass lines. However, many of the virtuoso 'church' sonatas for violin and continuo by Biber, Schmelzer and their Bohemian contemporaries follow the Italian custom of using one continuo instrument, either plucked or bowed. An organ of reasonable size and strength provides sufficient support for the violinist's technical fireworks and sonorous arias in these works. The slow-moving bass lines are somewhat unsatisfactory when played on the non-sustaining harpsichord, and the bowed bass viol or bass violin player may feel slightly uncomfortable with such a static line to play in the free improvisatory passages. It was probably for these reasons that the early Italian composers specified only one continuo instrument for the early Italian solo sonata repertoire. However, if a small portable chamber organ is used for convenience, the bass registers may not provide enough support, in which case a bowed string bass may be added. The decision whether to add additional bowed support to the organ depends on the acoustic and other variable factors such as the size of the performing space.

---

[11] Cyr, p. 166
[12] Snyder, pp. 371-2
[13] ibid., p. 379

England

In Restoration England, instrumentation practices were similar to the French customs. String dance and theatre bands used the basse de violon in what became known as French tuning (B♭ F c g) for the bass section, either with single players or in large sections. A look at the ranges of bass lines in the theatre music of Purcell and his contemporaries indicates, by the presence of the occasional bottom B♭, that this was the tuning used by the bass violins. Solo singers in Purcell's music would be accompanied by the bass viol, or organ and theorbo (in the verse anthems, for example), with the violin family bass instruments being reserved for the tutti sections, as in the French usage. Similarly, song accompaniments and chamber music (♪ e.g. Locke *Broken Consort* tracks 25-28) require the viol, but dance bands and ensembles with more than one player per part use the bass violin (♪ e.g. Locke suite of brawles tracks 18-24). In the French-style orchestra, bass viols or small violones (great bass viols playing at 8-foot pitch and tuned in G) would sometimes have been mixed in with the bass violins in larger groups.

Late Baroque

In the 18th century, the old-style large cello known as the 'bass violin' gradually disappeared from use, but the term violone went on being used far into the century all over Europe. However, by this time, the term was generally used to mean the cello as we know it today. In orchestral situations, a 'violone' or double bass at 16-foot pitch would have been used as well. The practice of using a cello and harpsichord as the continuo team in chamber music was still not as widespread as some of today's performers assume it to be. Quantz shows this with the use of the words *whether or not* and *if*:

> In a trio the keyboard player must adjust himself to the instruments that he has to accompany, noting whether they are loud or soft, whether or not there is a violoncello with the keyboard, whether the harpsichord is loud, soft, open or closed, and whether the listeners are close by or at a distance. If the keyboard player has a violoncellist with him, and accompanies soft instruments, he may use some moderation with the right hand, especially in a *galant* composition.
>
> (1752) XVII.VI.6, tr. Reilly, p. 252

The Double Bass

The use of the double bass in orchestras from the beginning of the 18th century is not in doubt, but the irregular situation which existed up until that time is still the subject of much debate. First of all, what is a double bass? The original use of the terms *double*, *grande*, *contra-*, *grosso*, *doppio* nearly always indicate an instrument playing at 16-foot pitch, an octave below the written note (8-foot pitch). The use of 16-foot pitch combined with instruments playing at 8-foot pitch should be carefully monitored in 17th-century music. Where large bass violins are used tuned in B♭ (France and England), it is very likely that the musical requirements will exclude the use of a double bass. As the smaller violoncello came into use in the second half of the 17th century, the loss of bass sonority required the extra support the double bass provided, allowing composers to write elaborate high concertante parts for the cello. Composers first used the double bass for special effects, for example thunder, storms and God-like wrath.[14] The fretted instrument known today as the violone comes in several sizes, at 8- and 16-foot pitch, so the specification violone may not necessary mean double bass, or double bass viol, as we have seen in the discussion above.

The term violone may be applied to any large bass instrument (bass violin, great bass viol, double bass). Some fretted violones were tuned in G and could play as high as middle C, permitting playing at pitch where the line did not rise too high. A lower octave could be

---

[14] Cyr, p. 156

5.2 Choice of continuo instrument(s)

selected if desired. It is important when jumping up and down the octave to select an appropriate point in order to preserve the line and to make musical sense.

Some composers approve of the addition of a 16-foot instrument in certain circumstances: Buxtehude in large choral works in a cathedral setting, for example,[15] or Muffat where the number of players in the concerto grosso ripieno section is large.[16] The double bass is more likely to be used in large ensembles in Italian 17th-century music than French or English music, where large bass violins use B♭ tuning.

The instrument designated by Bach for his Brandenburg concertos, is described by him as *violono grosso*, and is obviously a large bass instrument, although a suitable tuning has yet to be decided upon.[17] Praetorius writes that the great bass viol (Italian *violono*, or *contrabasso da gamba*) is usually tuned in fourths, and reminds us that

> ... how a player tunes his violin or viol is unimportant if his technique and intonation are in order.
>
> (1618) tr. Crookes, p. 53

Baines describes the violone known in Germany as 'Bassgeige' and its use and tunings:

> It was the advent of the continuo bass which made the violone so important, particularly in churches, because the lower pipes of the organ *Gedakt* are rather ineffectual by themselves, especially if the bass moves fast. They are to be seen in profusion in pictures, mostly by Dutch and German painters, and mostly dating from the first half of the 17th century.
>
> They have either five, six or seven strings. The German name, surprisingly enough, was *Gross Bassgeige*, but it was commonly referred to by the Italian *violone* tuned FF-C-G-d-a. Strictly speaking, if five-stringed, it was tuned in fifths only this is the '*Gross Bassgeige*'. According to Zacconi, those with six or seven strings are tuned GG-C-F-A-d-g-d¹. Schutz writes at the end of his *Musicalische Exequiem*: The *violone* or *Gross Bassgeige* is the most convenient, agreeable and best instrument to go with the concertato voice when sung to the sole accompaniment of a quiet organ ... not only shown by its effect but confirmed by the example of the most famous musicians of Europe who use them. We trust those who play this instrument to treat it with a sharpe ear and a keen understanding, but for the sake of the inexperienced I have included three short reminders. (1) If there is an alto or tenor clef marked, the *violone* can play through though always in the low register, i.e. octaves below. (2) If the parts are introduced successively the *violone* should play when the bass enters. (3) It must be especially observed that if one or more concertato basses are singing, the *violone* should not play since the vocal bass line is enough, and the *violone* with identical chords or unisons mars the effect.
>
> (1977) Baines, pp. 173-4

The 16-foot bass instrument is frequently used as a 'shadow' for more elaborate or fast moving bass lines. Where the cellist plays many notes, the double bass player should sketch the main harmonic structure, without filling in all the beats, in the manner of a rhythm section: the first note only in groups of four semiquavers, for example. Quantz gives an example of this technique:[18]

---

[15] Snyder, p. 371
[16] Strunk (1950), p. 90
[17] Finson
[18] (1752) XVII.IV.7 Table XXIII, tr. Reilly, p. 249

5.2 Choice of continuo instrument(s)

Ex. 5.2.7: Quantz (1752) Table XXIII

This selective note technique is also demonstrated in the Purcell trio sonata (ex. 5.2.2), and shows the kind of shadowing the chordal continuo instrument should carry out while the bowed bass instrument plays all the notes. The double bass is frequently omitted from solo sections where there are larger instrumental forces (concertos, arias and recitatives), re- joining the group for the tutti ritornelli. When the C clef (often appearing in the continuo part as the tenor clef) appears in the higher range, the string double bass player may be silent, contradicting the advice of Schutz above, given for a different context. In Corelli *concerti grossi*, this practice is assumed, and may be seen by comparing the concertino cello part with the general basso continuo part (see ex. 6.2.18).

5.3 Performing recitative

One of the most important roles of the continuo section in Baroque music is the performance of recitative. Derived from *recitare* to recite, recitative is a type of music which imitates speech, with chordal accompaniment and cadences for punctuation. There are two types of recitative in the Baroque period:

1. Recitative accompanied by short chords which punctuate the words played by the continuo section alone, known in Italian as *secco* or *semplice* and in French as *simple*.
2. Recitative accompanied continuously by the orchestra known in Italian as *recitativo accompagnato* and in French as *récitatif accompagné*.

Quantz describes the freedom of the singer in secco recitative and the necessity for stricter rhythm in the accompanied version:

> In an Italian *recitative* the singer does not always adhere to the tempo, and has the freedom to express what he is to execute quickly or slowly, as he considers best, and as the words require. If, then, the accompanying parts have held notes to execute, they must accompany the singer rather by ear, using their discretion, than by the beat. If the accompaniment is in notes that must be performed in tempo, however, the singer is obliged to regulate himself by the accompanying parts.
>
> (1752) XVII.VII.59, tr. Reilly, p. 292

Pasquali expresses the principles of accompanying the sung speech:

> Care must be taken not to strike abruptly, but in the harpeggio way . . . for common speech a quick harpeggio; for the tender a slow one; and, for any thing of passion, where anger, surprise, etc., is expressed, little or no harpeggio, but rather dry strokes, playing with both hands almost at once. The abrupt way is also used at a *punctum* or full stop, where the sense is at an end.
>
> (1757) *Thorough-Bass Made Easy*, p.47

Telemann tells us that a delay at the cadence was usual in cantatas, but in opera it coincided with the singer's final syllable.[19]

Quantz also recommends this:

> . . . when the singer has completed a phrase . . . the accompanists must not wait till the singer has uttered the final syllable, but must enter at the penultimate or preceding note [an appoggiatura may be meant], in order to maintain constant animation.
>
> In general the bass in all cadences of theatrical recitatives, whether accompanied with violins or plain, must begin its two notes, usually forming a descending leap of a fifth, during the last syllable; these notes must be performed in a lively manner, and must not be too slow . . . the cellist and double bass player [executes them] with a short accent with the lowest part of the bow; they repeat the stroke, and take both notes with down-strokes.
>
> (1752) XVII.VII.59, tr. Reilly, p. 292

Heinichen is the earliest German source for short accompaniment, complaining that

> . . . one's ear becomes irked by the constant monotony of the humming organ pipes.
>
> (1711) in Dreyfus, p. 76

Niedt's treatise published in Hamburg in 1717 requires the organist to play short accompaniment in church recitatives:

> I must insist that, *nota bene*, when they encounter a recitative with two or three measures set in sustained values, they do no more than play the beginning of each new note that appears and then pause until a new note follows in turn.
>
> Dreyfus, p. 77-8

The comments of a Frenchman after hearing performances of Handel operas in London in 1728 confirms the practice of using short chords (presumably played on the harpsichord) in Italian style recitative:

---

[19] *New Grove*, 'Recitative' p. 644

5.3 Performing recitative

> As you are not a devotee of Italian music, I do not mind telling you, Monsieur, that, except for the recitatives and the bad manner of accompanying them, cutting off the sound of each chord, there are some magnificent airs for the winds accompanied by the violins which leave nothing to be desired.
>
> Dreyfus, p. 78

In late 17th- and 18th-century Italian-style vocal music, static arias are linked by passages of recitative, which contain most of the action and dialogue and also serve as modulatory links. As will be seen below, composers write long notes in the continuo part even though the convention of the later Baroque period, as described above, was to play short notes.

Why short?

The 18th-century convention of playing short notes when they are written long came about so that the words could be heard clearly. As the plot often advanced dramatically in the recitative, it was particularly important to hear all the narrative detail. J. S. Bach made sure the players played short in some of the recitatives of his cantatas by writing crotchets in the part books, even though the score was written in long notes. The bassoon part particularly was marked in this way, as the string players of the bass line would have been more used to the custom of playing short.[20]

How short?

How long is short? A sensitive keyboard player will vary the spread of the chords according to the *affekt* of the words. The bowed continuo player should follow the keyboard player's lead, and play shorter with a quick bow-stroke for more agitated words, and slightly longer and slower for more reflective and languid phrases.

Most short recitative is written in crotchets, but there is no exact length to the note, as long as the longer notes do not drag on obscuring the words. The job of the accompanist is to enhance the affect of the words by sensitively reflecting the emotion of the singer. The cellist should listen to the fading of the sound of the harpsichord, and imitate the shape of the decaying sound in the bow-stroke.

Ex. 5.3.1: J. S. Bach, St. John Passion, secco recitative

By an unwritten convention (assumed to be known by continuo players) the notes in the bass should be played short (as crotchets) even though written long.

---

[20] Dreyfus, p.124

Accompanied recitative

Ex 5.3.2: J. S. Bach, St Matthew Passion, accompanied recitative

In this example, Bach shows where the bass is to play short when the rest of the strings are silent, but long where they join in, to emphasise the different methods of performance of secco and accompanied recitative.

French recitative

French recitative is composed in a different way, more song-like, and is accompanied with a continuous bass line in a melodious flow. The rhythm and emphasis of speech is re- produced by bars of different lengths:

Ex. 5.3.3: Lully, Le Bourgeois Gentilhomme

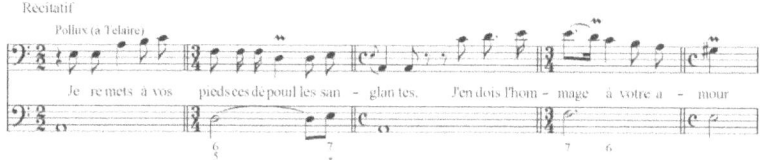

Ex. 5.3.4: Rameau, Castor et Pollux

5.3 Performing recitative

PRACTICAL APPLICATION

Cadences

In late Baroque opera the cadence should overlap with the singer's final note, to provide a continuous flow between the recitative and the aria which follows.

Ex. 5.3.5 & 5.3.6: Handel, Messiah,
'And lo! the angel of the Lord' and 'And suddenly there was with the angel'
two examples where cadences are written to overlap with the singer's final syllable

Down/up bowing for the two cadence notes enables the action to continue without coming to a full stop on a heavy down-bow. Quantz's down/down bowing suggested above is effective if kept short.

5.3 Performing recitative

Ex. 5.3.7: J. S. Bach, St. Matthew Passion

Here, the cadence is written after the singer's final word, making a fuller conclusion before the next movement. However, the emphasis of the language may preclude this practice, as stresses on the penultimate syllable are more commonly found in Italian than English, for example.

5.4 The viola

I have placed the viola in the bass section because of the principal function of the viola part in most Baroque music which is that of a written out realisation of the harmony. The viola was known as *alto* in Italy and tennor or *mean* in England; in France also, the viola parts were known by their equivalent vocal titles: *haute-contre* for the high viola role, *taille* for the next lowest part, and when there were three viola parts, the lowest was called *quinte*, literally the fifth part. In Italian music with two viola parts, they were normally called *alto* and *tenor*.

Ex. 5.4.1 *f*: Purcell Ayres for the Theatre, The Double Dealer
(the mezzo-soprano clef was often used for a tenor viola part)

Quantz:

> He [the violist] must not only have an execution equal to that of the violinists, but must likewise understand something of harmony, so that if at times he must take the place of the bass player and play the high bass, as is usual in concertos, he may know how to play with discretion, and the soloist need not be more concerned about the accompanying part than about his own.

> The violist must be able to judge which notes in his part must be played in a singing manner or dryly, loudly or softly, with a long or short bow . . . He must adjust his performance of the high bass to each sentiment, and accommodate it to the upper part.

> (1752) XVII.III.2-3, tr. Reilly, p. 237

The high bass parts mentioned are the passages when the bass is silent, and the viola has to take over the role of the bass line. This type of writing exposes the viola player to sudden unaccustomed attention. In the preface to the sonatas for viola by Flackton published in the mid-18th century, the position and function of the viola is admirably described:

> The Solos for a Tenor Violin are intended to shew that Instrument in a more conspicuous Manner, than it has hitherto been accustomed; the Part generally allotted to it being little more than a dull Ripiano, an Accessory or Auxiliary, to fill up or compleat the Harmony in Full Pieces of MUSIC; though it must be allowed, that at some particular Times, it has been permitted to accompany a Song and likewise to lead in a Fugue; yet even then, it is afflicted by one, or more Instruments in the Unisons or Octaves, to prevent, if possible, its being distinguished from any other Instrument; or, if it happens to be heard but in so small a Space as a Bar or two, 'tis quickly over-powered again with a Crowd of Instruments, and lost in Chorus.

> Riley (1980), p. 89

A footnote to this preface states that 'The greatest Masters allow the Tenor Violin to have a particular Delicacy of Tone'. Forkel writes that J. S. Bach is known to have played both the violin and viola:

> In musical parties where quartets or fuller pieces of instrumental music were performed and he was not otherwise employed, he took pleasure in playing the viola. With this instrument, he was, as it were, in the middle of the harmony, whence he could best hear and enjoy it, on both sides.

> (1802) quoted in David & Mendel, p. 334

C. P. E. Bach wrote of his father:

> As the greatest expert and judge of harmony, he liked best to play the viola, with appropriate loudness and softness.

> quoted in David & Mendel, p. 277

5.4 The viola

Quantz points out that it is not the importance of the part which gives pleasure to the player, but the whole musical effect of the performance:

> The accompanist actually experiences more pleasure from the music than the player of a concertante part; and anyone who is a true musician takes an interest in the entire ensemble, without troubling himself about whether he plays the first or the last part.
>
> (1752) XVII.III.5, tr. Reilly, p. 238

Mattheson agrees:

> One should not be ashamed to take up a viola, as most people are, and thus reveal more foolish ambition than desire for learning.
>
> (1739) II.2.48, tr. Harriss, p. 259

Corrette was the first to write specific instructions for the viola (*La quinte ou alto*), in combination with a double bass tutor.[21] He points out that accompaniment is more difficult in playing viola parts than bass parts as the viola rarely plays the root, but instead the third or fifth of the harmony.

In this chapter the function of the viola part in the Baroque ensemble of various types from the late 16th century will be examined. There follows a search for the specialist viola player in the Baroque ensemble. Did viola soloists exist in the period? Some comments about the viola player's role and demeanour are examined. Finally, an examination of the practice of arranging music for the viola.

The viola part in the structure of the music

It is important for the viola player to realise the musical function of the part he is playing in order to fulfil the role appropriately: to merge into the texture, give harmonic emphasis, or project an independent part.

The viola part(s) may sometimes be equal voices in a contrapuntal structure:

Ex. 5.4.2: J. S. Bach, Brandenburg Concerto no. 4, Presto

---

[21] (1755) in Riley (1954), pp. 133-4

The viola part may be allied to the bass line:

Ex 5.4.3: Handel, Concerto Grosso op. 3 no. 3, Allegro

At other times the violas team up with the second violins in accompanying harmonic padding (with the violins) and rhythmic impetus (with the bass):

Ex. 5.4.4: J. S. Bach, St. Matthew Passion, 'Gebt mir meinen Jesum wieder'

5.4 The viola

The violas may join the rest of the strings in unison:

Ex. 5.4.5: J. S. Bach, St. Matthew Passion, 'So ist mein Jesus nun gefangen'

The five-part ensemble

There is a huge repertoire of early consort music with multiple viola parts from Italy, Germany, Austria and England. Some of it, such as Dowland's *Lachrymae* in five parts is suitable for families of viols or violins (one violin, three violas and bass violin). This is the standard scoring for the French dance orchestra or *bande* in *ballets* and *divertissements*. The basic constituents of the *Vingt-quatre Violons* of Louis XIV (as described by Mersenne) and the Twenty-Four Violins of the English court of Charles II were: six violinists, four violas on each of the three parts, and six bass violin players (no 16-foot instruments). The basic group was later enlarged in the outer parts as we have seen above. The 'economy' *Petite Bande* was 16 players distributed: 62224. In French music the three viola parts maintain a different function, fulfilling the role of continuo in a written out harmonic padding, with very little imitative contrapuntal texture or voice leading, except in the fugal sections of overtures. This type of orchestra often played without a chordal continuo instrument.[22] The three middle parts, which realised the harmonic structure, were known as *parties de remplissage* and were often composed by an assistant of the principal composer of the opera, ballet or divertissement.[23] Composers such as Charpentier wrote in a similar style using four parts, in which case, the two middle parts are both played by violas fulfilling the *parties de remplissage*. This practice was much in use in England during the 17th century. The range of each part was limited, and this suited the variety of different sizes of viola, with the smallest playing the first viola part mainly on the top two strings, the second viola on the middle two, and the third viola keeping to the bottom range of the instrument. Thus, the best sonority was achieved through having a wide range of sizes of instrument, each size suited to their role in the band. The large tenor violas made by Gasparo da Salo and the Amati brothers were designed for playing low parts in the string consort, and the smaller instruments higher parts. The names of the three viola parts (*haute-contre*, *taille* and *quinte*) were descriptions of the range, corresponding to vocal titles, and not purely instrumental designations. Georg Muffat:

> As to the instruments, the *haute-contre* (to the Italians, *violetta*) part sounds better when played on a medium-sized viola, built some-what smaller than the *taille*, than on a violin.

(1698) tr. Cooper and Zsako, p. 233

In 17th-century French four- and five-part string music with only one violin part, the 1st viola part is frequently written in the treble clef in modern editions, giving rise to a misunderstanding about the instrument intended to be used.

---

[22] Sadler
[23] Holman (1993), p. 193

5.4 The viola

Ex. 5.4.6 *f*: Ballet des Festes de Bacchus

Three viola parts are shown in the above score of a typical 17th-century French ballet.[24] The viola parts use the C clef on the bottom (first viola) and next two lines up (second and third violas).

Ex. 5.4.7: Charpentier, David et Jonathan

The above example is a model of clear scoring in a modern edition. It shows the original clefs of the two viola parts.

---

[24] in Buch, p. 92

5.4 The viola

Ex. 5.4.8: Lully (misleading short score)

This short score of a Lully overture deceives us into thinking the scoring is two violin and two viola parts or even worse, two bass viols. The original clefs give us a clue that the second part down should be a viola part, making three viola parts as preferred by Muffat (p. 226 above).

Ex. 5.4.9: Charpentier, Te Deum (showing the wrong disposition of parts)

A similar deception is carried out in ex. 5.4.9, but with no indication of the original clefs (the four-part scoring in Charpentier's string section should be one violin, two violas and bass). As a general rule, in French-style ensemble music, if the range of the second part down is no higher than f^2 and the original clef is a C clef, it is likely that it is intended for viola. If the top two parts are of more similar range, and the second part rises to g^2 or above, and is written originally in the G clef, then it is very likely to be a second violin part. Some German music such as Biber's *Mensa Sonora* may also have used a viola on the second part. In most 17th-century French music, when a solo second violin is occasionally required, the music should be included in the single treble part (usually called *dessus*), giving the two players sitting together on the front desk the solo roles.

In later French music, by Rameau for example, the five part string section is divided into two violin, two viola (*haute-contre* and *taille*) and one bass parts. Rameau's two violin sections frequently play together in unison, and the violas also sometimes play in unison, giving a variety of four- and five-part textures, with a choice of two violin, or two viola part sonority. Muffat's concertos (1701) have a concertino group of two violins and bass, with ripieno consisting of two violin, two viola and bass parts. The layout of two violins, two violas and bass is normal in 17th-century German and Italian chamber sonatas.

The Baroque viola soloist

From the birth of the violin family in the 16th century until the end of the 17th century, the role of the viola was often equal in value and musical contribution to the violin and bass. In contrapuntal music, the middle parts contributed to a democratic musical structure. When harmonic influence dominated, as in much dance band music, the viola became sidelined as a mere tool for supporting the violin and bass lines. The predominant 18th- century chamber form, the trio sonata, excluded the viola and encouraged the popularity of the violin. This was reflected in the concertino group of the concerto grosso form, until the middle of the century when Geminiani allowed a small solo contribution from the viola (called here 'tenor') in the concertino group.

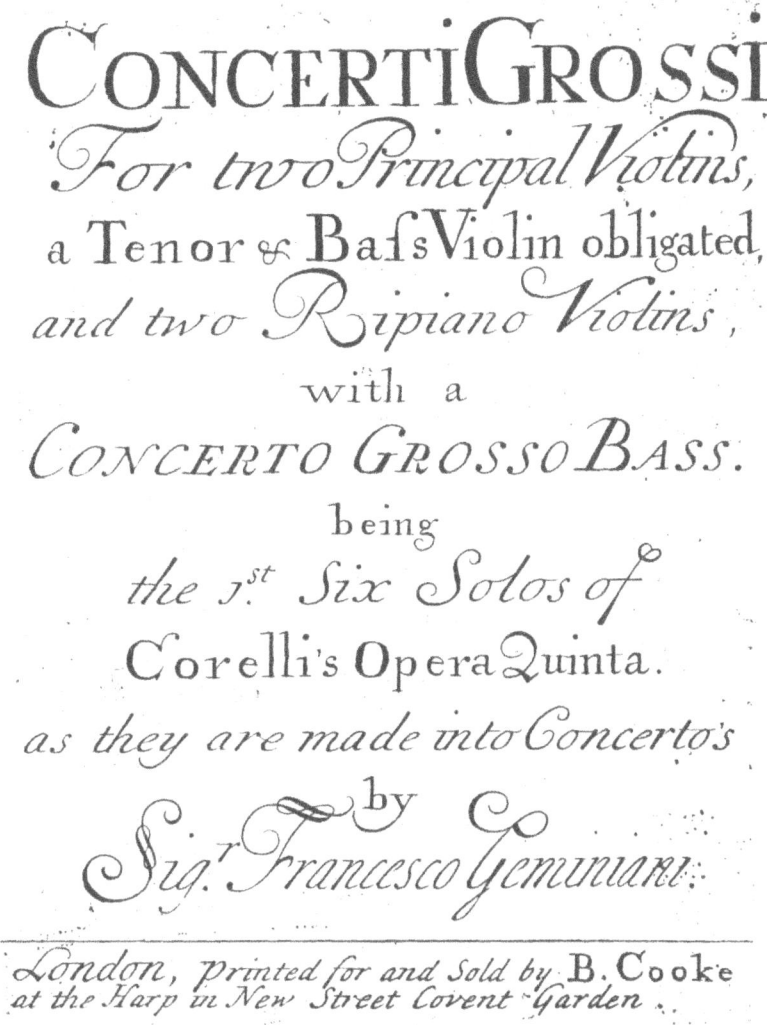

Ex. 5.4.10 *f*: Geminiani

The title page of Geminiani's arrangement of Corelli opus 5 for concerto grosso, above, shows the promotion of the viola to an obligato role with the cello. The role of the instrument remained essentially a supporting one until the end of the 18th century when the development of the Classical string quartet provided more independent musical interest in the life of viola players. Freed from a life of subservience to the harmonic structure, the viola came into its own again, helped by the solo works written for it by the viola-playing composers Mozart, Hummel, Dittersdorf and Stamitz.

It is probable that the viola specialist hardly existed during the Baroque period. Quantz describes the situation:

> The viola is commonly regarded as of little importance in the musical establishment. The reason may well be that it is often played by persons who are either still beginners in the ensemble or have no particular gifts with which to distinguish themselves on the violin, or that the instrument yields all too few advantages to its players, so that able people are not easily persuaded to take it up.

(1752) XVII.III.1, tr. Reilly, p. 237

As the viola may be regarded only as a large violin, played with basically the same technique, it is likely that most violinists would have played the viola as a matter of course, as and when they were required to do so. In most musical establishments, the number of available players would not have been so great that people would have minded playing violin or viola according to requirements.

5.4 The viola

Quantz again:

> It would not be too much to say that a good violist should be able to play even a concertante part just as well as a violinist, as, for example, in a concertante trio or quartet. Perhaps the reasons why this beautiful form of music has declined in popularity is simply that so few violists devote as much industry to their work as they should ... If they employed the necessary industry, they could easily improve their lot in a large establishment, and gradually advance their position, instead of remaining chained to the viola to the end of their lives, as is usually the case. There are many instances of people who, after playing the viola in their youth, achieved great eminence in the musical world. And later, when already qualified for something better, they were not ashamed to resume the instrument in case of need.
>
> (1752) XVII.III.5, tr. Reilly, p. 238

The repertoire

> Upon Enquiry at all the Music Shops in London for Tenor Solos, none were to be found, neither was it known by them that any were ever published.
>
> quoted in Riley (1980), p. 89

This footnote to the preface of the Flackton sonatas describes the sorry state of the viola solo repertoire in the mid-18th century. It is no wonder that in this milieu J. S. Bach's sixth and, to a lesser extent, third Brandenburg concertos stand out as pinnacles of desire for the viola player to perform. For modern viola players who love to play Baroque music, there is only one other important solo work: Telemann's G major viola concerto. There is also the slighter concerto for two violas by Telemann. It is for this reason that the practice of playing works composed for other instruments appears so attractive to today's specialist violists.

Baroque composers themselves arranged instrumental concertos for solo keyboard, solo concertos for orchestras, and so on. A number of compositions by Bach exist in more than one version, reworked by him with different instrumentation. Modern viola specialists should experiment with music written for violin, viola da gamba or cello, and then plunder music from other instruments in search of new repertoire for the Baroque viola.

The Viola d'amore

The viola d'amore is a flat-backed instrument with a viol-like shape, but without frets, and played on the shoulder. The most commonly used model has 6 or 7 strings which are bowed, and the same number of wire strings which run underneath the bowed strings and through the bridge, known as sympathetic strings, as they are tuned to vibrate sympathetically with the bowed strings. Descriptions of the instrument from the 17th and 18th centuries range from 4 to 7 strings. Early instruments may have been wire-strung without sympathetic strings. Leopold Mozart[25] describes an instrument with 6 strings and 6 sympathetic strings. He also mentions another, which he calls 'English violet', which has 7 strings and 14 sympathetic strings.

J. S. Bach used the viola d'amore at least four times, the most well known occasion probably being the St. John Passion (nos. 31 and 32, 2 violas d'amore). The other known occasions are cantatas 36, 152 and 205. The instrument is used in a melodic role by J. S. Bach, exploring the ghostly, other-worldly sonority of the instrument, rather than the chordal possibilities presented by the extra strings and various tunings which are exploited by Biber (*Harmonia Artificiosa* no. 7) and Vivaldi (many concertos). If violas d'amore are unobtainable, the St. John Passion music works well with muted violins, but is quite out of the range of the Baroque viola.

---

[25] (1756) tr. Knocker, p. 12

Methods

The first complete instruction book, the *Méthode Facile pour La Viole d'amour*, was published in Paris by Milandre in 1782 (available in facsimile from Minkoff). Various tunings are suggested according to the repertoire. Milandre gives a D major tuning: (a 7th string) d a^1 d^1 $f\sharp^1$ a^2 d^2 with the sympathetic strings tuned a^1-g^1 in a D major scale, and an equivalent D minor version. The St. John Passion music is suitable for a six-stringed instrument, and the tuning can be D minor d f a^1 d^1 f^1 a^2 d^2 or C minor c g c^1 $e\flat^1$ g^1 c^2, or mixed tunings c g d^1 f^1 a^1 d^2 or c g c^1 f^1 a^2 d^2. It does not seem to make a difference to the overall effect of the performance if the two players play in different tunings; in fact it might be better, as some of the open strings will be different, reducing difficulties of intonation.

Further information about the repertoire and history of this instrument is contained in Danks (1976).

PART SIX
EQUIPMENT

6.1 The instrument and bow

> I Write It also, for to *Vindicate*
> The Glory 'f *Instruments*, now out of Date,
> And out of *Fashion* Grown
>
> Thomas Mace (1676), Epistle to the Reader

'On original instruments'

Instruments of the violin family may be fitted with various types of neck, fingerboard, bass bar and bridge. The use of historically appropriate fittings gives rise to the term 'on original instruments'. Many players of modern instruments look sceptically at the use of this label for new copies of violins set up in the old way. If you own and play a valuable old instrument, it is rather galling to have a modern copy called 'an original instrument'. The whole question of what constitutes an 'original' instrument for commercial purposes is a matter of degree: a Classical string quartet plays on instruments with a modern set-up but with gut strings. Is this 'on original instruments'? A Baroque group plays Monteverdi and Gabrieli on 'Baroque' violins. Are these 'original'? If the players are using any covered strings for this early 17th-century repertoire, they have already made a compromise in the face of the knowledge available about the equipment in use at that time, as covered strings were not developed until after the mid-17th century. Modern musical performances are (fortunately) not restricted to one historical time zone, and the demands upon the players to play music from any period since the invention of the violin until the 19th century on the correct equipment with the appropriate style are escalating as the pace of research into all areas of performance intensifies. Inevitably, compromises are made with regard to the equipment being used.

If you have made the decision to buy a Baroque instrument, the problem of how to go about selecting the right instrument for your own financial requirements and musical needs is a complicated one. Where should you start? The first question to be considered is whether to buy an old instrument, or a new one. If an old instrument is being sought, the possibilities are either to buy an old instrument in modern set-up and have it converted to its original state, or to look for an old instrument which still has some of its original fittings.

Sources for old instruments are many, and players are often seen at auction rooms looking for instruments which might not have been altered or modernised. Dealers may be contacted and commissioned to seek a particular type of instrument. Since the number of players of Baroque instruments has increased over the last twenty years, more old instruments set up in historical style are being bought and sold amongst the players. It is still possible to buy a relatively cheap 18th-century instrument at auction and get it fitted up with appropriate neck and fingerboard, although the cost of this work may be a high proportion of the instrument's value.

If the player decides that the effort and risks involved in purchasing an old instrument are too great, the easiest way to obtain an instrument of the desired model and set-up is to commission one from a maker. Instruments may be tried at exhibitions held in conjunction with early music festivals, or borrowed for trial from players who already

6.1 The instrument and bow

own such instruments. The best makers have waiting lists of several years, and do not need to attend exhibitions to obtain commissions, but it is likely that good, younger and possibly cheaper makers will be found here. Choices have to be made about which model to order and how it is to be set up.

Many players try to get as close as the latest research and knowledge will allow in their search for a certain sonority. These players own several different instruments which are kept at different pitches and are set up according to the period of the music which they expect to play using these instruments. Many professional players have become daunted by the prospect of having to own so many instruments in order to fulfil the requirements of the many styles and periods of music which they are expected to perform. The economic implications involved in keeping an array of different instruments for use in various repertoires are rather serious, which is why the average professional 'period' player probably owns two instruments at the most to cater for earlier (Baroque) and later (Classical) music. Many players play all music from Gabrieli to Beethoven on a mid-18th-century style violin. Most string players have a selection of bows of various models which give them a greater range of stylistic possibilities.

Unfortunately, many period instrument players lack the interest to develop appropriate techniques to match their equipment. In this case, even if all the 'correct' criteria for the equipment have been fulfilled, the music sounds unstylish and unconvincing. If the player continues to use his modern bow technique with a Baroque bow, his money has been wasted, and he is merely currying favour with those elements which count the 'on original instruments' label to be of some value. In labelling recordings with the 'original instrument' sticker, the implication is that the players are also using old techniques, when this is often far from the truth.

In order to understand the various factors which count towards the 'original' label, I shall explain the elements which contribute to the style and sonority of instruments of the violin family in the 17th and 18th centuries.

The set-up

The principal elements of construction in instruments of the violin family which vary from their invention in the early 16th century are as follows:

> Angle, weight, length and thickness of the neck
> Angle, weight and length of the fingerboard
> Curvature of fingerboard (hollow or straight)
> Design and height of the bridge, and position on the belly
> Length and thickness of bass-bar
> Internal construction method (use of blocks or linings)
> Length, position and thickness of sound-post
> Arching and thickness of design of violin body
> Materials and gauges of strings used, and number of strings
> Size of instrument in relation to pitch used

The changes in the violin's fittings from the earliest times to present day have taken place by a process of gradual evolution as players and makers have altered the construction to suit the changing demands of players and the music, in a chicken-and-egg-like process. Musical demands on the instruments were always pushing forward. The amount and quality of sound changed as conditions and performances altered to suit the prevailing circumstances. In general, new developments resulted in increased tension on the whole instrument with a steeper angle of the neck to the body, higher bridge and larger bass bar. Some players were always ahead, developing new ideas and techniques, and others who felt no need to play the most modern music languished in the old-fashioned way, retaining old set-ups long after they became outmoded. The need to modernise was influenced by the repertoire in hand, so that even beyond 1660, theatre and dance band music which was restricted in range (up to c^3 on the violin or f^2 on the viola) was comfortably managed on the older model of instrument, with a shorter thicker neck. The more adventurous solo player who needed to play higher and move around the instrument with the left hand had a more streamlined neck, thinner and slightly longer, making the ascent into third position and beyond much easier.

The gradual evolution in the construction of instruments of the violin family may be roughly divided into the following periods, with developments overlapping at each end of the period, depending on musical function and geographical location:

*c.*1540 - 1660   The Renaissance violin and viola in various sizes, the bass violin in various sizes (also known as violone) and the double bass from *circa* 1580.

c. 1660 - 1760   The Baroque violin now more standard in size, violas in various sizes, bass violin, cello, and double bass. The term violone still used for any bass instrument. Invention and use of covered strings for the lowest registers.

c. 1760 - 1820   The transitional or Classical violin, viola, cello and double bass.

6.1 The instrument and bow

Instruments of the late Renaissance period

Ex. 6.1.1 *f*: Praetorius, Sciagraphia, the violin family 1620

In this guide to the violin family, Praetorius describes Italian practices of the time:

1 and 2: Small pochettes, or 'kits'[1] used by dancing masters for the convenience of putting them in their pockets when demonstrating dance steps. Sounds one octave higher. Number 1 is shaped like a rebec, as also illustrated and described by Ganassi (1542/3 Venice).

3: Descant violin tuned a fourth higher used for transposition.[2]

4: Standard size violin.

5: Tenor violin, or viola.

6: Bass violin with 5 strings.

(7: Tromba marina and 8: Psaltery are not included in our violin family discussion)

---

[1] See *New Grove*, 'Kits'

[2] For an explanation and details of this practice called *chiavette*, including Praetorius on the subject, see Parrot (1984) and Holman (1999), pp. 20-22. The Ricercate from *Il Dolcimelo* (circa 1590 published by London Pro Musica) illustrate the range of the violin at this time (top note c^2 extension from 1st position) and how transposition was used to avoid going higher.

6.1 The instrument and bow

The drawings below show typical features of the instruments of the period and illustrate general points. They do not represent any one particular instrument.

	Renaissance (c.1570, small model) a)	Renaissance (Maggini type, large model)	Baroque (c. 1680) b)	Transitional (c. 1780) c)	Modern (c. 1900) d)
Length of back	346 mm	367 mm	353 mm	355 mm	355 mm
Neck stop	105 mm	115 mm	125 mm	128 mm	130 mm
Body stop	190 mm	200 mm	195 mm	195 mm	195 mm
Bridge height	25 mm	28 mm	29 mm	32 mm	34 mm
Angle of neck	1		2	4	7
String length	298 mm	323 mm	321 mm	326 mm	330 mm
		(not illustrated)			

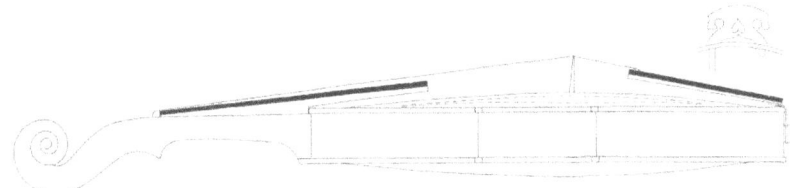

a) Renaissance violin

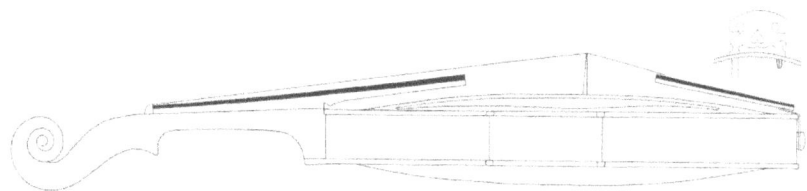

b) Baroque violin

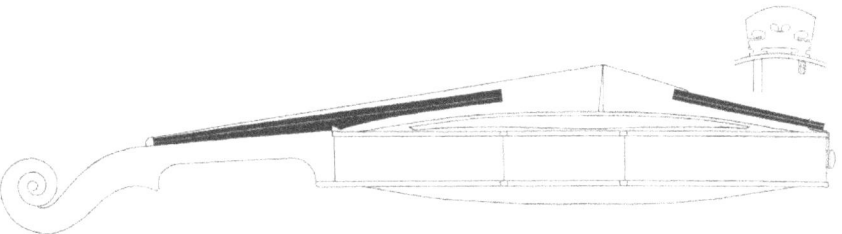

c) Transitional violin

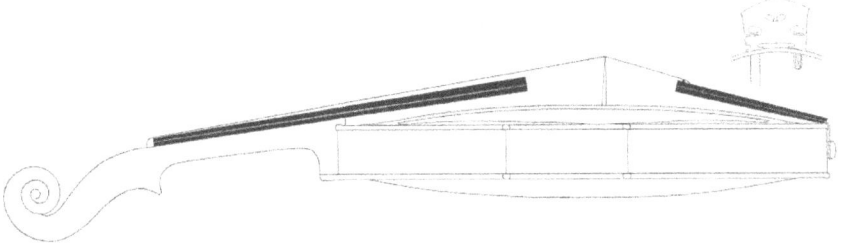

d) Modern violin

6.1 The instrument and bow

A short history of the violin family and its makers

The earliest instruments of the violin family were probably made in northern Italy. The famous Amati dynasty carried on a school of violin making from the birth of the violin in the first half of the 16th century nearly into the 18th century. Little is known about Andrea Amati who worked in Cremona: the earliest surviving instrument by him is dated 1564. His sons Antonio (b. Cremona c.1540) and Girolamo Hieronymus (b. Cremona 1561) known as 'the brothers Amati' carried on the tradition of violin making, and with other makers such as Linarol (active in Venice 1570-90), Gasparo da Salo (Brescia) and Maggini (Brescia c.1580-1632) set the high standard of craftmanship for the best instruments of this early period.

There were no standard patterns, although the outline of the violin shape was already quite distinct by the mid-16th century. Instruments by the Amati brothers had rather higher arching than those by makers of the Brescian school, such as Maggini, who favoured a generally flatter body and double purfling. All the instruments of the violin family came in a variety of sizes from the small model violin to the largest of violas. The bass violin (or basse de violon) is the large precursor of the cello, and the largest member of the violin family. A smaller bass instrument came into use around 1660 in order to play higher faster solo parts, and became known as the violoncello. At first, the bass violin used a tuning which extends the fifths downwards from the violin giving from the top g c F B♭, a tone below normal cello tuning. This tuning is known as 'French' tuning and given by Mersenne (1636) in his tuning for the complete violin family (example (a) below) and Merck (1695). The inconvenience of this tuning was changed in Italy from before 1600 to a d G C, but the 'ancient' tuning was retained in France, England and Germany throughout the 17th century. Tunings on the right (b) are from Corrette's cello tutor, giving the archaic and the normal cello tuning of his time (Paris, 1741).

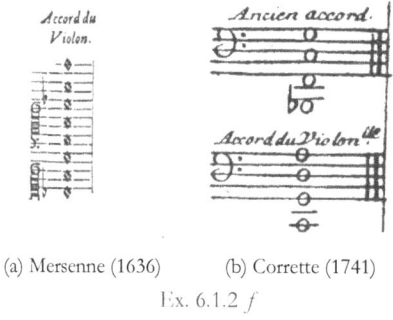

(a) Mersenne (1636)   (b) Corrette (1741)
Ex. 6.1.2 *f*

Kircher in *Musurgia Universalis* (Rome, 1650) shows a 'violone' which looks like a small cello with the tuning G d a e^1 (i.e. an octave below normal violin tuning). Five- and three-stringed instruments also existed early on in the bass instrument's history. Five-stringed cello-type instruments were still being used extensively in the second half of the 17th century, and are seen in many paintings of the period (also in Praetorius 1620, above). The double bass at this time existed in various forms combining features of the viol and violin families: flat backs, frets, C or F shaped sound-holes, occasional roses, sloping or violin- type shoulders, giving a wide diversity of shapes. The word *violone* at this time can mean any bass member of the violin family.

The choice of which size of instrument to use depended to a certain extent on its function. The small violin models were most used when at very high pitch (e.g. a^1=470 in northern Italy), for high parts when tuned up a fourth,[3] and for playing highly decorated music with many fast *passaggi*. The choice of instrument in the viola section would have depended on the range of the part to be played, so that the largest violas were used for the lowest (i.e. third) viola line, and the smallest for the highest line or to play music containing faster notes. The bass instrument of the violin family would have generally been the bass violin (also known as violone) as described above, playing at written pitch.

---

[3] Banks, p. 590

6.1 The instrument and bow

The earliest members of the violin family had a very short and thick neck, set straight onto the body of the instrument. The bridge is low and flat, sometimes without much carving, and frequently set low on the body of the instrument, below the F holes, as is seen in many paintings of the period. It is likely that very early violins were made without sound-posts or bass-bars, but there is no evidence to support the existence or absence of these two features. There may have been a small integral bass-bar. By the end of the 16th century the fitment of sound-post was well enough known to be used by Shakespeare in his play *Romeo and Juliet* as the name of one of the trio of characters Simon Catling, James Soundpost and Hugh Rebeck. At first the sound-post was positioned in the middle of the instrument and must have made a striking improvement in its resonance. Sometimes no corner blocks were used, which is why some very early models have long pointed corners to give greater strength to the instrument.

♪ See CD for tracks using 'Renaissance' instruments.

Instruments of the Baroque period

Nicolo Amati (1596-1684), the son of Girolamo, became the best known maker of his day, and was the teacher of Antonio Stradivari (?Cremona 1644-1737). Other pupils include Andrea Guarneri, Rugeri and Rogeri. In the Tyrol, Jacob Stainer (?1617-1683) was making violins that were in demand throughout Europe during the Baroque period. The Bohemian virtuoso vioinist Biber is known to have owned a violin by Stainer, as did J. S. Bach. Stainer developed high arching for a more powerful penetrating sound, producing a model that was much copied throughout the 18th century. Antonio Stradivari and Giuseppe Guarneri ('del Gesu' 1698-1744) established a different style of violin making using a flatter arching for projection and sonority, resulting in the fine-toned instruments favoured by Paganini as well as by many modern players.

During the Baroque period the neck was made thinner and longer to facilitate playing higher than third position. The bridge became more curved and higher to line up with the slightly steeper angle of the neck. The bass-bar became longer and thicker in order to reinforce the instrument and increase the treble response.

Corrette[4] credits Bononcini with the invention of the cello.[5] This was facilitated by the improvement in string technology which occurred in the second half of the century. The cello took over from the larger deeper and smaller higher-pitched bass violins in order to play faster and higher parts without loss of the bass register. In order to compensate for the lack of bass sonority, a large bass viol (six strings tuned in fourths or fourths with a third in the middle, and using frets) or double bass of violin family form (three, four or five strings, various tunings, sometimes with frets) was introduced to the string band, an octave lower than the cello where the range permitted.

Many of the instruments now in use which date from the 17th century have been altered to suit modern requirements (mostly cut down to make smaller instruments for playing a different type of music from that for which they were made). Very early examples in museums are now increasingly under suspicion, with the study of dendrochronology (dating of the wood using tree ring measurement) now revealing secrets hidden for centuries from unsuspecting violin collectors.[6] Collectors in the 19th century are known to have 'manufactured' instruments using old parts to piece together ancient-looking models of various sorts.

The term *violone* may indicate the use of any large bass instrument (cello of large model, bass violin, great bass viol, double bass).[7] Some fretted violones are tuned in G and play at 8-foot pitch, transposing down the octave at suitable moments.

♪ for tracks using 'Baroque' instruments.

---

[4] Preface of cello tutor (1741)
[5] He is probably referring to Giovanni Maria Bononcini 1642-1678 father of the famous cellist Giovanni b. Modena 1670
[6] for an introduction to dendrochronology see John Topham, 'Tree Ring Analysis Applied to English Instruments'
[7] see also part 5.2

6.1 The instrument and bow

Transitional instruments

The mid-18th century produced an accelerated rate of development in the violin family as performing spaces became bigger and violin technique developed. The technical developments in construction already under way continued, resulting in a highly-strung Classical instrument with a penetrating sound suitable for the demands of the large concert room, and the virtuosi who performed there.

Many of the earlier models continued to be used and altered to suit the new conditions. Large instruments were cut down and the internal structure re-set to accommodate different musical demands. When restoring an old instrument, it is satisfying to restore it to the appropriate set-up for its date of manufacture. It is perfectly acceptable, however, for earlier models to be set up with more advanced fittings, as good instruments were continually being altered to suit the prevailing tastes and demands of the players. Putting early fittings on an instrument of a later vintage is a dubious practice and unlikely to meet with much success or satisfaction for the player.

The double bass is by now well established as reinforcement of the bass line at a lower octave, but often simplifying running passages to reinforce rhythmic or harmonic features (see ex. 5.2.7). The use of frets on all sorts of large bass instruments seems likely, and was even a feature of the five-stringed instruments favoured by the Viennese soloists in the late 18th century though not, it seems, of the three and four string basses used at the same time and in the same place.

The double bass - general history and tuning

The history of large bass instruments is extremely diverse and the situation found in one place may not be reproduced in any other. The size, tuning and musical function vary so much that offering a practical course is to invite criticism: whatever is suggested, there will be a situation somewhere where this was correct, but in general, players made do with whatever instrument was found in any particular location.

Large bass instruments were made from the late 16th century in Italy, and subsequently elsewhere in Europe. It wasn't until the end of the 17th century that they were made in England. Whether these instruments belonged to the violin or viol family, it is hard to say, and probably an irrelevant consideration, as the pattern of construction and use of frets varied, giving no overall standard pattern. The number of strings varied from three to seven. Some early basses survive with evidence of the use of six strings, but by the time basses were used in concerted music, fewer strings were likely.

In surviving sources many tunings are suggested. Some very large instruments may have had low tunings, sounding as low as D, but contemporary strings required extremely long sounding length for such notes: such instruments could only have played a few notes in loud passages without being a considerable intrusion into the ensemble. Generally speaking, double basses played very little lower than their 8-foot counterparts, but added great strength to the bass line. GG would be a useful guide for the lowest note and the three-string tunings GG or AA-D-G and GG-D-A were probably common in the period when such basses came into use in concerted music, although five-string basses may have been preferred in the area we now know as southern Germany and Austria. The tuning in fifths requires a great deal of awkward position changing, and was ultimately discarded.

The 16-foot instrument might have been used at first for special effects (terror, thunder etc), but with the invention of the cello, became a normal part of the general bass department. Quantz[8] recommends that if two double basses are used in an ensemble, one should be larger than the other, to balance distinctness with gravity. Quantz[9] also suggests that the use of frets was desirable because the greater amplitude of vibration of the thinner strings often led them to rattle unpleasantly against the fingerboard unless they were held well away by a thick fret. He also recommends frets for the improvement of intonation. In a footnote to the French text, Quantz gives the double bass tuning

---
[8] (1752) XVII.V, tr. Reilly, pp. 246-50 'Of the double bass player in particular'
[9] ibid., p. 248

EE-AA-D-G. A commonly used tuning today is DD-AA-D-G, which is close to Quantz's advice.

For conventions of using the double bass in playing continuo see pp. 215-217.

The bow

The development of the bow throughout the Baroque period runs parallel to the development of the instruments of the violin family. New models were continually evolving. Tourte developed his revolutionary design during the latter part of the 18th century, which provided the basic model for the modern bow. Selecting a single bow for Baroque playing is difficult as there is a wide variety of shapes and lengths, each with its own best musical function. There are very few old bows still in existence, and not many of these are in circulation amongst players. Most old bows are in museums and bow makers use them as models. It is still possible to buy bows made at the end of the 18th century, suitable for Classical playing, by makers such as Edward Dodd and his contemporaries.

The earliest bows had clip-in frogs, which are of limited appeal today as they leave the bow susceptible to changes in temperature and humidity and have a limited range of adjustment to the tension of the hair. A ratchet mechanism was used in an attempt to provide more control over the bow tension until the invention of the screw mechanism (by 1694[10]) made fine adjustment of the tension possible in any climatic condition. The Bryant bow illustrated overleaf was made as a treble viol bow, but has been in use for many years as a Baroque violin bow. I have been unable to identify any significant differences between viol and violin family bows, which appear to be interchangeable according to their playing qualities.

Short bows

The shortest, lightest bows were used for dance music throughout the period, and for early 17th-century music where many fast notes may be played with separate bows for a brilliant effect (♪ tracks 7 and 10). The 'thumb under' grip is easier to manage with a shorter lighter bow and would have been used by French dancing masters (see p. 85).

Long bows

The Italian style of bowing was famous for its use of the long *arcata*. Consequently, the longer bow is thought to be more suitable for Italian music such as Vitali and Corelli. The soft beginning to the stroke described by many writers (see p. 122) is more apparent when using the longer bow where the hair is not so far from the hand at the frog, and the stick straighter and less out-curved than in the earlier dance bow. Many people imagine the Baroque bow to be extremely out-curved, but in most models, the main length of the stick when under tension is more likely to appear straight than curved.

---

[10] *New Grove*, 'Bow' (also contains a diagram of the ratchet mechanism)

6.1 The instrument and bow

	Bouman	Bryant	Doe	Waterhouse	Latour	E. Dodd
Length of hair to exit from frog	54.3 cm	58.5 cm	58 cm	61 cm	63 cm	64 cm
Width of hair	0.6 cm	0.6 cm	0.7 cm	0.7 cm	0.8 cm	0.9 cm
Overall length	63 cm	69.5 cm	70 cm	72.5 cm	71.5 cm	72.4 cm
Weight	40g	52g	50g	57g	50g	65g

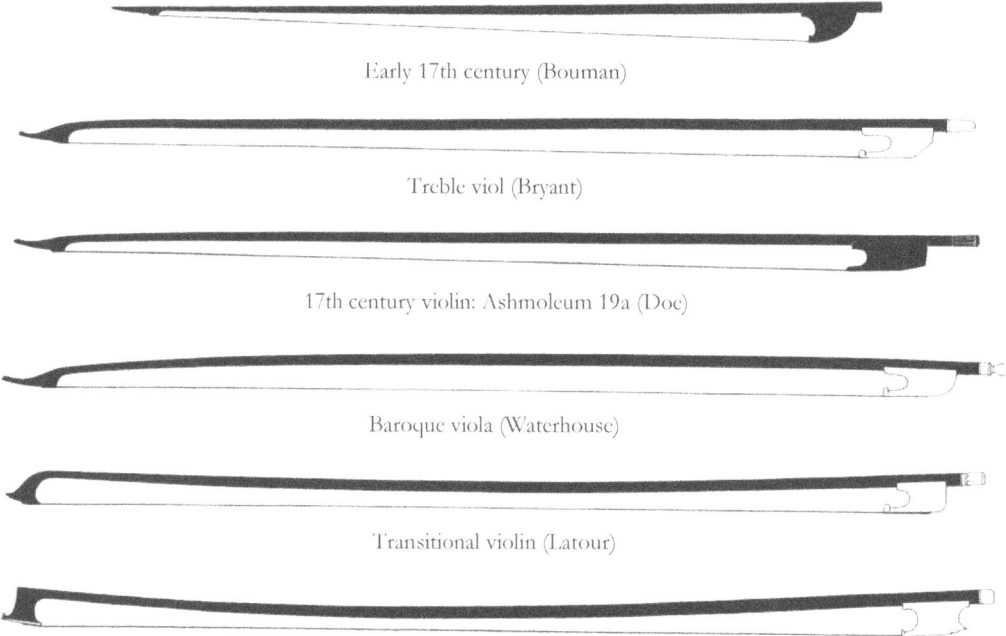

Early 17th century (Bouman)

Treble viol (Bryant)

17th century violin: Ashmoleum 19a (Doe)

Baroque viola (Waterhouse)

Transitional violin (Latour)

Late 18th century viola (E. Dodd)

The transitional bow

During the second half of the 18th century, the bow developed an inward curve giving more height and, as a result of this, more power in the upper half. This inward curve was the result of a fundamentally new technique of heating the straight stick to make it curve inwards without distorting the grain lines of the wood. A transitional bow of this type is very useful for early Classical music, combined with an alteration in technique and use of the bow. The basic bow-stroke used with this type of bow is less lifted but more linear and on the string. The upper half of the bow is used more for passage work in a *detaché* stroke. The elasticity of the area in the middle of the bow gives more spring and lightness to fast notes, with the bow bouncing naturally, using its own weight. The legato stroke maintains an even tone through to the point, with the ability to play longer slurred passages.

It is important to realise the variety of shapes, lengths, and therefore functions of different Baroque bows. When combined with other factors, such as thicker stringing for the earlier repertoire, a different sound-picture is built up which goes hand in hand with the musical requirements. The player should allow plenty of time when trying a new bow to discover its strengths and weaknesses, and should not impose an inappropriate technique upon it.

Further reading:

David D. Boyden, *Catalogue of The Hill Collection in the Ashmolean Museum, Oxford* (Oxford 1979).

David D. Boyden, 'The Violin Bow in the 18th Century', *Early music*, vol. 8 (April 1980), pp. 199-212.

John Dilworth, 'The Violin and Bow - origins and development' in *Cambridge Companion to the Violin*, ed. Robin Stowell (Cambridge 1995).

Margaret Downie Banks, 'The violino piccolo and other small violins', *Early music*, vol. 18 (November 1990), pp. 588-596.

Jaap Schröder and Christopher Hogwood, 'The Developing Violin', *Early music*, vol. 7 (April 1979), pp. 155-165.

Robert E. Seletsky, 'New Light on the Old Bow', *Early Music*, vol. 32/2 (May 2004) pp. 286-301 and vol. 32/3 (August 2004) pp. 415-426.

John C. Topham, 'A Dendrochronological Survey of Musical Instruments from the Hill Collection at the Ashmoleum Museum in Oxford', *Galpin Society Journal*, vol. 55 (April 2002) pp. 244-268.

John C. Topham, 'A Dendrochronological Survey of Musical Instruments from Three Collections in Edinburgh, London and Paris', *Galpin Society Journal*, vol. 56 (June 2003) pp. 132-146.

Peter Trevelyan, 'A Quartet of String Instruments by William Baker of Oxford (circa 1645-1685)', *Galpin Society Journal*, vol. 49 (March 1996) pp. 65-76.

Peter Walls, 'Mozart and the Violin', *Early music*, vol. 20 (February 1992), pp. 7-29.

Neal Zaslaw, 'The Italian Violin School in the 17th Century', *Early music*, vol. 18 (November 1990), pp. 515-518.

Strad magazine often contains articles on the early violin family. See in particular:

> Paul Bowers, 'F-hole positioning in Brescia', September 1995.
>
> John Dilworth, 'Mr. Baker the fidell maker' and other articles, May 1995.
>
> John Dilworth on the mysteries of the viola's evolution, 'Unfinished Journey', May 1996.
>
> Sorab Modi listens to complete quartets by Stradivarius and Stainer, June 1995.
>
> A special issue on Nicolo Amati, December 1996.

Rosin

Normal rosin is used on the bow. Gerle in his viol tutor *Musica Teusch* recommends:

> Take pains to see that the bow is not too greasy. If the hair gets too smooth, it will not draw; [if this happens] scrape the hair with a clean knife, and then rub it with colophane or with English rosin, which can be procured at the apothecary's.
>
> (1532) quoted in Riley (1954), p. 25

Tartini left us a recipe for rosin which he prepared for himself, using re-cycled kitchen waste for containers:

> Put resin and water in equal proportions into a glazed earthenware or silver vessel. Let it boil over a strong fire and skim with a spoon all impurities that are thrown up in the boiling. When no more impurities appear on the surface, boil down the residue, and pour it into prepared boxes or into egg shells, which can be afterwards chipped off as the use will demand.
>
> quoted in Riley (1954), p. 313

6.1 The instrument and bow

Strings[11]

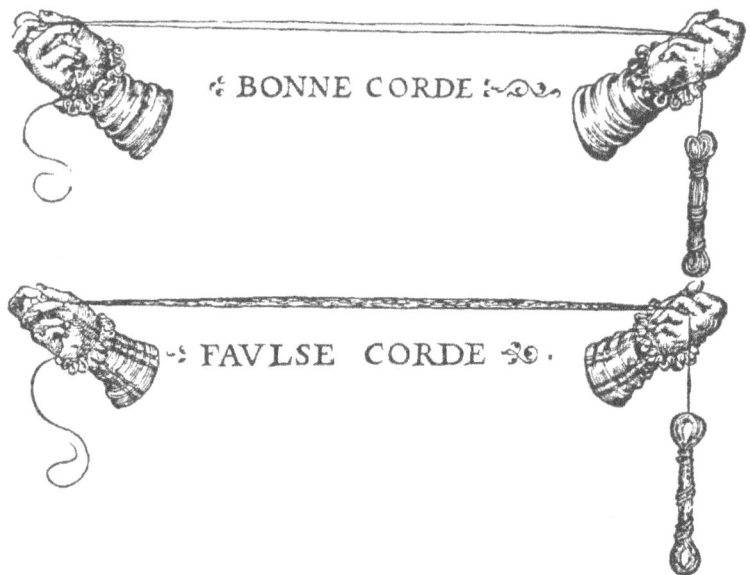

Ex. 6.1.3 *f*: Testing a string from Mersenne, Harmonie Universelle (1636)

Praetorius describes the use of wire strings on bowed instruments of the violin family:

> . . . they give a much more gentle, pleasant sound when strung with brass and steel strings than they do when gut strings are used.
>
> (1620), p. 56

However, the normal stringing material at that time was plain sheep's gut. Covered strings were introduced on the lower strings in Italy in the middle of the 17th century and may have been invented in England:

> Advertisement
> There is a late Invention of Strings for the Basses of Viols and Violins, or Lutes, which sound much better and lowder than the common Gut String, either under the Bow or Finger. It is a Small Wire twisted or gimp'd upon a gut string or upon Silk. I have made tryal of both, but those upon Silk do hold best and give as good a sound.
>
> Playford (1664)

However, as Mace describes below, and as reported in the Talbot manuscript, English players continued to use all plain gut from the violin down to the bass violin. Before the invention of covered strings, one possibility was a rope made of several strands of gut but there is no firm evidence to establish the use or manufacture of these. Nowadays, this type of string is often known by the old name of 'catline'. Research into, and the recreation of, early string manufacturing techniques is still at an experimental stage, with the effects of bleaching and polishing gut strings still being debated. A string made from gut loaded with metal salts has been manufactured since the 1980s and has become very popular with players seeking an alternative to the thick roped type of string, but it appears that there is very little positive evidence to support this method of giving thin strings more density, thus enabling the used of very thick gut to be avoided. As with the roped string, this is not to say that they did not exist, but that there is no surviving evidence to support their existence.

From the latter part of the 17th century when covered strings were invented, violas and cellos began to use these on the bottom string only. Early on in the development of covered strings (plain gut or silk wound with a layer of silver or copper wire) a half, or open wound string was popular. However, the use of this type of string may have been discontinued because the wire prevented the comfortable sliding of the finger. Brossard (c.1712) describes the use of an open wound D and fully wound G in his violin treatise, only parts of which survive.

---

[11] I am indebted to Oliver Webber for supplying the references from Playford, Brossard, Hartlib and Riccati.

Hartlib reports in 1659 that:

> Strings of Guts done about with Silver-wyre makes a very sweet Musick, being of Goretsky's Invention.

Hartlib was a member of the Oxford circle of inventors, which included Boyle, who engaged in 'ingenious pursuits'.[12]

Mace gives a catalogue of the various types of string available, and tips for caring for them to prevent moisture affecting their playing qualities:

> ... your best way is, to *wrap them up close*, either in an *Oyl'd Paper*, a *Bladder*, or a *piece of Sear-cloath*, such as often comes over with *Them*
>
> ... Which, when you have thus done, keep them in *some close Box*, or *Cupboard*; but not amongst *Linen*, (for that gives *moisture*;) and let them be in a *Room* where there is, or useth to be, a *Fire often* ... For *moisture* is the *worst Enemy to your Strings*.
>
> (1676), p. 66

He lists minikins, Venice-catlins, Lyons (for basses), and 'pistoy basses' which he describes as

> ... *Thick Venice-Catlins*, which are commonly *Dyed*, with a *deep dark red colour*.
>
> They are indeed the *very Best*, for the *Basses*, being *smooth* and *well-twisted Strings*, but are hard to come by.
>
> (1676), p. 66

On the choice of string, Mace advises equal tension:

> ... you must *so suit your Strings*, as (in the *Tuning* you intend to *set it at*) the *Strings* may all stand, at a *Proportionable, and even Stiffness*, otherwise, there will arise *Two Great Inconveniences*; the *one* to the *Performer*, the *other* to the *Auditor*.
>
> And here Note, that when we say, a *Lute* is not *equally Strung*, it is, when some Strings are *stiff*, and some *slack*.
>
> ... For it will be, as if a man were to shew *Nimble Footmanship*, and were confined to *Run over a piece of uneven Ground*, with *hard, and soft Places mix'd together*.
>
> Sure, he must needs *Run unequally*, in *Those places*, or *slack* his *Pace*, or else *stumble and fall*. Even so is it with such an *unequal Strung Instrument*.
>
> (1676), p. 65

Mace is instructing the lute player, but similar principles apply to the stringing of violin family instruments. Note his mention of the smooth thick Venice catlines, which suited the louder Italian way of playing.

The principle of equal tension advocated by Leopold Mozart and commonly adopted throughout the 17th and 18th centuries was established by Mersenne:

> As to the thickness and length of the strings, they ought to follow ... the ratios of harmony ... It is necessary that the four strings [of the lower instruments] be sesquialters ... both in length and thickness, and if the thickest of those of the alto descend lower by an octave than that of the treble, they ought to have all dimensions double those of the treble.
>
> Mersenne (1636), *4ième livre*, p. 180

A strong response when making the string speak is especially important on the lower strings, with the extra weight needed to make these thick strings speak compensating for the loss of the lower frequencies in performance. Quantz[13] recommends larger instruments with thicker strings for cellists playing in tuttis, and thinner strings on smaller instruments for solo playing. As has been noted (p. 159), the Italian style of string playing was reported by Raguenet to be louder than the French and was aided by their use of thicker strings. The idea of having less tension on the lower strings was first recorded by Riccati (Venice 1767), but it may have been already in use, evolving with the use of the covered G string.

---

[12] Jardine (1999), p. 325
[13] (1752) XVII.IV.1, tr. Reilly, p. 241

6.1 The instrument and bow

It is probable that thicker strings of gut, at higher tension than is customary today, were commonly used during the high Baroque period: gut for the upper three strings on the violin, viola and cello (perhaps using half-wound string on the viola and cello G). To obtain equal tension using Mersenne's sesquialtera principle, which is in proportion 2:3, a violin E string of 12 would require an A string of 18 and D string of 27. If a plain gut G is used, this would be 40.5 to continue the same tension downwards, but a covered string might be preferred. It should be born in mind that most 17th-century ensemble and contrapuntal music would rarely use the bottom string (except for the basses), the 'voices' being best in the upper/middle range, assuming that correct instrumentation is being used.

Gut violin D strings continued to be used into the 20th century, and Kreisler was one of the last well-known virtuosi to prefer a gut E string. In the last century Bachman's *Encyclopedia of the Violin* states that 'the fourth or G string is the only covered string used on the violin'.[14] The three-stringed double bass also used uncovered thick gut strings well into the 20th century.[15] It may be that the quality of covered gut strings was never good enough for universal acceptance and use until the high-tech methods of production of the 20th century produced a more uniform and reliable string.

The thickness of the strings to be used may be varied according to pitch and string length. High pitch on an instrument with a short string length will require thinner strings than a low pitch on a large instrument. String makers (but not necessarily suppliers) will assist you in selecting an appropriate thickness for the string length (the distance from the nut to the bridge) and pitch being used. String makers might also advise on matching the strings to give equal tension, particularly if the instrument is strung with a mixture of plain gut and other materials, but costly experimentation is likely to be the only way to achieve a satisfactory result.

Plain gut is not as durable as metal or covered strings, and is more susceptible to changes in temperature and humidity. If the player's hand sweats on to the string, the life of the string is shortened, as moisture is 'the worst enemy to your strings', as Mace observes above. Almond oil may be lightly rubbed on the string to help preserve the gut from attack by moisture and other elements. Varnishing strings may protect them temporarily, but does shorten their life.

Further reading

Djilda Abbott and Ephraim Segerman, 'Gut Strings', *Early music*, October 1976.

Ephraim Segerman's three articles in *Strad* magazine (January, March and April 1988) give a good introduction to the history of strings.

Play the Viol by Alison Crum (Oxford 1989, p. 146) contains an excellent photograph and explanation of the many different types of string available to the historic instrument player.

The total process of making gut strings from sheep to shop is described by Daniel Larson in the *Newsletter of the British Violin Making Association*, Spring 1998.

Oliver Webber, 'Real Gut Strings: Some New Experiments in Historical Stringing', *The Consort* vol. 55, 1999, pp. 3-29.

Oliver Webber, *Rethinking Gut Strings: a Guide for Players of Baroque Instruments*, (King's Music 2006).

---

[14] (1925), p. 150
[15] Segerman, p. 53

Suppliers and makers of historic strings

Aquila String Makers, 16 via Constantini, 36100 Vicenza, Italy. (www.aquilacorde.com)

Boston Catlines, Olav Chris Henriksen, 34 Newberry Street, Somerville, MA. 02144, U.S.A. (catlines@aol.com)

Bridgewood and Neitzert, 146 Stoke Newington Church Street, Stoke Newington, London N16 0UH. (www.londonviolins.com)

Damian Dlugolecki, 520 SE 40th Street, Troutdale, OR 97060, U.S.A. (www.damianstrings.com)

Gamut. Daniel Larson, 26N 28th Avenue E., Duluth, MN 55812, U.S.A. (www.gamutstrings.com)

Northern Renaissance Instruments, 6 Needham Avenue, Chorlton-cum-Hardy, Manchester M21 2AA. (www.nrinstruments.demon.co.uk)

Real Guts. George Stoppani, 6 Needham Avenue, Chorlton-cum-Hardy, Manchester M21 2AA. (www.stoppani.co.uk)

You may meet and talk to instrument and string makers at early music exhibitions held periodically at music festivals in London, Bruges, Utrecht, Boston and Paris.

6.2 Playing from facsimile editions

Most players interested in historic playing techniques are naturally attracted to play from, or at least examine, facsimiles of original editions of the music they are performing and there is now a wide range of these on the market, some lavishly produced, others more realistically priced. Many are clear enough for use on the concert platform. The reasons why a player may want to refer to or use these facsimiles are varied. One of the principal feelings the performer experiences whilst playing from facsimile is that by this means he is somehow closer to the composer and performers of the period. Another reason for playing from facsimile is to find out the extent of a modern editor's influence. It is important to discover for oneself the exact contribution the editor has made to the performance by way of adding or removing slurs, other articulation markings, fingerings or even such basic things as bar-lines. Many details become clear when seen in an unadulterated 18th-century edition, which may have become obscured through the intervening centuries by editorial accretions which have themselves become accepted practice.

However, the player should be on his guard if he thinks he is seeing 'the truth' in any particular old edition. Sometimes the edition chosen to be re-printed may not be the best one available, but rather the most convenient one to hand. Spurious claims or alterations may creep into early editions published soon after the original date of publication. Old prints are often full of mistakes. If the composer did not supervise the engraving closely, a non-musical printing apprentice could easily introduce errors which are perpetuated through subsequent printings. Wrong clefs, a group of notes a third out on the stave, inconsistent or ambiguous marking of accidentals and other errors are very common.

Here are some of the most common differences between editions of the same music published in the Baroque and modern periods:

	BAROQUE	MODERN
Format	Most solo 18th-century sonatas appear in score with solo and figured bass parts on double stave. Keyboard player needs to be able to play from figured bass.	Score will contain keyboard realization and un-edited solo part. Solo and continuo part-books have editorial markings.
Tempo markings	Frequently absent. Time signature contains relevant information about tempo. Tempo words, when used, modify time-signature instructions.	Word tempo instructions may be added to assist modern player unfamiliar with old tempo conventions. May be misleading, according to the experience of the player.
Dynamics	Very sparse, and used for special effects only (echos or storms). 18th-century music often marks swells (Geminiani, Piani).	Detailed editorial dynamics added for the player who may assume that because there are no printed dynamics, everything should be played at the same level. Repeats often marked piano. Swells or vibrato wavy lines nearly always omitted. May reflect unsuitable mode of performance.
1st/2nd time bars	Casually indicated, often by a wavy bracket, or pause mark over the two endings. Inconsistency between parts possible.	Usually clearly notated.
Key signatures	The final ♯ or ♭ is omitted (giving 2 sharps for A major, or 2 flats for E♭ major). The last accidental appears in front of the relevant notes. Flats and sharps may appear (or not) at higher or lower octaves, according to the range of the piece.	Modern key signatures show the flats and sharps in the familiar formation.

6.2 Playing from facsimile editions

	BAROQUE	MODERN
Accidentals	Apply only to the note immediately adjacent, but this is a rather loosely applied rule. Musical common sense often needs to be applied. Naturals seldom appear before 1730 and before this are shown as flats when applied to notes being lowered and sharps to those being raised.	Apply throughout the bar. In 17th-century music, accidentals need to be added sometimes when editors have been conservative in raising notes in rising scales and lowering falling ones.
Rests	Players need to become familiar with the 'building block' rest system, particularly in alla breve time, and in music without bar-lines.	Standard rest marks can be relied upon.
Double bars	Double lines without dots may indicate a section should be repeated. Notation of lengths of final notes is often inaccurate and time needs to be taken out for up-beats on the repeat.	Double bars with dots indicate repeated sections. Accurate final notes.
Repeat schemes	Common rondeau scheme AA B A C AA (given by Charpentier and Purcell).	Modern editors often omit these structural niceties.
Bar-lines	May not exist in the original music.	Added to facilitate rehearsal and reading.
Hanging dot	Only the dot is marked in the new bar to extend the value of the note by half.	Another note and a tie is printed.
Hemiolas	Long 3/2 bars often present in simple triple time (Corelli, Couperin).	Two 3/4 bars made out of one long 3/2 bar.
Beams	Irregular groups of fast notes common in 16th- and early 17th-century music. Beaming absent in early 17th-century printed music.	Beams rationalised to fit main beats sometimes destroying subtleties of phrasing and cross-rhythms.
Clefs	A variety used to avoid printing notes off the stave with leger lines. Clefs can move around freely on the stave. A change of clef may indicate change of scoring (Corelli *concerto grosso*). French violin clef (G on bottom line) used for violin, flute and oboe parts. Viola parts use clefs to indicate which part in the ensemble.	Standard clefs used (Italian G clef for violin, G and alto for viola, tenor and bass for cello).
White/black notation	*Croches blanches* and black note notation relics from earlier practices.	Modern notation substituted.
Inconsistencies	Degree of accuracy of all elements always suspect.	Editors have corrected 'mistakes' but may at the same time have deleted valuable information.
Naming of parts	Original nomenclature may confuse or mislead the unwary.	Instrumentation may be standardised for ease of modern performance, or mis-interpreted by editor.

6.2 Playing from facsimile editions

MUSICAL EXAMPLES

1. Double bars and repeats:

Ex. 6.2.1 *f*: Couperin, 3ième concert, Courante

Ex. 6.2.2 *f*: Couperin, 1ier concert, Menuet

Ex. 6.2.3 *f*: Couperin, 1ier concert, Gavotte (top) and Menuet

The above examples show different signs used by one composer to indicate the half-way double bar, and the end, all with 1st and 2nd time endings.

Double bars in dance music usually indicate that a repeat is expected even though two dots do not appear. In Purcell's *Ayres for the Theatre*, two lines indicate the end of the first part, and three lines the end. Both sections should be repeated.

Ex. 6.2.4 *f*: Purcell, Ayres for the Theatre, The Double Dealer, Minuett

The printer or engraver's repertoire of signs may have only included a double bar with repeat signs going both ways. It may be that the forward section is not repeated, and reference should be made to the end of the section following to discover the probable repeat scheme.

Ex. 6.2.5 *f*: Piani, Sonata IV for violin and continuo (Paris 1702), Allemanda, allegro ma non presto

The final note in a repeated section may not take into account the up-beat to which it returns, so the player should stop the note early in order to leave room for the up-beat portion of the bar.

2. Key signature

Accidentals are shown at more than one octave if they are to be used for these notes:

Ex. 6.2.6 *f*: Couperin, 5ième concert

Ex. 6.2.7 *f*: Couperin, 4ième concert

3. Rests

Building block rests are piled up to represent beats or bars rest:

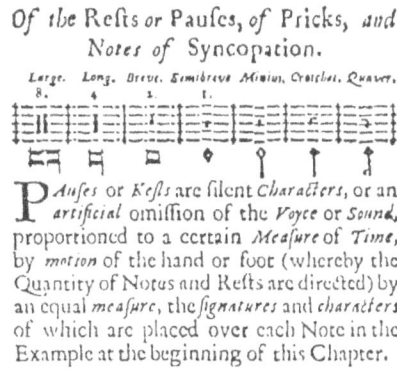

Ex. 6.2.8 *f*: Playford (1674)

6.2 Playing from facsimile editions

This is a particular problem in contrapuntal music without bar-lines where beats must be counted, not bars.

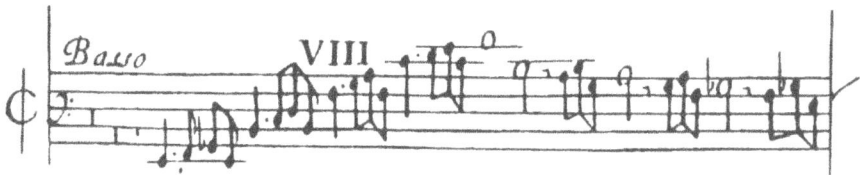

Ex. 6.2.9 *f*: Gibbons, Fantasia in 3 parts no. 8

The rests before the bass enters represent ten minim beats' worth of rests: a block which fills the space between the lines is four beats, and half a block is two (♪ track 4, try to count the rests for the bass player).

Ex. 6.2.10 *f*: Corrette (1738)

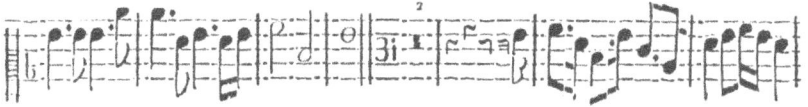

Ex. 6.2.11 *f*: Purcell, The Double Dealer, Overture (viola part) [♪ track 35]
Where there is one beat per bar, a whole block represents two bars' rest.

4. Bar-lines

Bar-lines can be added or moved by the modern editor. Bar-lines may be added by the editor for convenience in early contrapuntal music, to assist rehearsal. However, the player's perception of the music and phrasing may be completely distorted by the presence of a bar- line where it was not originally intended.

6.2 Playing from facsimile editions

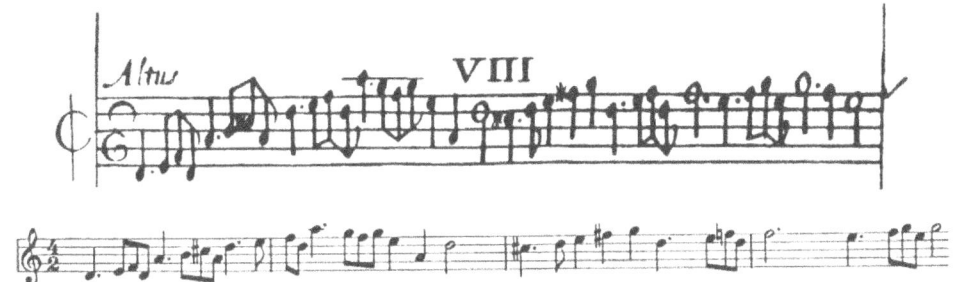

Ex. 6.2.12 *f* and modern edition: Gibbons, Fantasia no. 8 (♫ track 4)
Facsimile of the original part, and modern edited version. The first bar line occurs in the middle of the figure, giving the wrong impression if the player does not realise that the bar lines are placed for convenience, not musical effect.

The following extract from the same Gibbons fantasia shows how a modern editor deals with time changes inserted into the middle of sections:

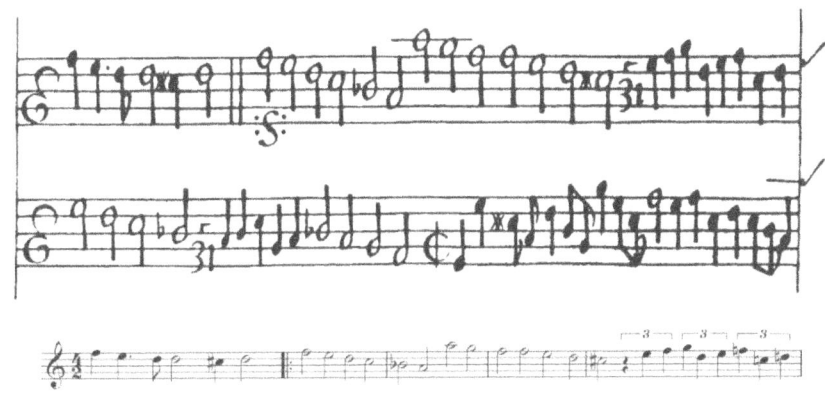

Ex. 6.2.13 *f* and modern edition: Gibbons, Fantasia no. 8 (♫ track 4)

5. The hanging dot

This is a practice inherited from music written without bar-lines, where the dot is placed after the bar-line instead of writing a tie. Ex. 1.5.26 shows a modern version.

Ex. 6.2.14 *f*: Purcell, Sonata of three parts no. VII

253

6. Long bars

Long 3/2 bars (2 bars' length in 3/4 time) which comprise 'hemiola' figures in music by Corelli and Handel are often regularised by editors into two bars of 3/4, with the possibility of tempting the player into unwanted accentuation of three beats. Long bars commonly occur before cadences, and can have the effect of slowing down the music by eliminating accents.

Ex. 6.2.15 *f* and 6.2.16 *f*: Corelli, Sonata op. 5 no. 1. Adagio

These two examples from the same work show the 1st edition (Rome 1700), and the 3rd edition (Roger, Amsterdam 1710), where the bar lines have been regularised to fit the 3/2 time signature. The ornamentation is attributed on the title page to Corelli, '*comme ils les joue*'.

7. Fast notes

Groups of fast notes are often originally arranged in groups which do not fit into regular beat patterns, but have important phrasing implications. The variety of fast note groupings found in much 17th-century block-printed music is often regularised by modern editors implying another phrasing and denying the performer access to the composer's original intentions. Here is an example where the original grouping has obviously been maintained:

Ex. 6.2.17: Bartolomeo de Selma, Canzona quarta

Groups of fast notes in runs and tirades in highly decorated Italian style *adagios* may not add up to whole beats, but the multiple beams are there to supply an impression of speed or acceleration, without necessarily containing the correct number of notes in a group.

8. Clefs

The variety of clefs used in 17th- and 18th-century music is confusing to the modern player, especially violinists who are used to only one clef. Sometimes valuable information may be gained by noticing when the clef changes. Corelli often uses the tenor clef for concertino sections, as these tend to occur higher in the register. The tutti entry is clearly defined in the following example by the re-appearance of the bass clef:

Ex. 6.2.18 *f*: Corelli, Concerto Grosso op. 6 no. 8, Pastorale

The use of a particular clef may indicate which voice or instrument should be playing that part (two or three violas see part 5.4).

French violin music is written in the French violin clef (G on the bottom line).

Ex. 6.2.19 *f*: Couperin, Apothéose de Lully

Couperin plays with the idea of national styles by writing the French violin clef for the character of Lully, and the Italian style clef for Corelli.

Reading strange clefs is easier if the player reads by interval and not by note name. The accidentals are then thought of as notes raised or lowered, not by their titles. Clefs indicate the positions of C, G or F. Sometimes an elegant squiggle is difficult to identify as any particular clef. The following examples show the F (i.e. bass) clef, and how, like the C clef it can move around the stave:

Ex. 6.2.20 *f*: Castello, Sonata seconda (1644)

Ex. 6.2.21 *f*

9. Articulation and bowing

The French in particular were very exact in their notation of articulation and bowing marks. Some composers devised their own system of markings: Marais indicates vibrato by a horizontal wavy line, and swelling with the bow (*enfler*) by the letter 'e'.

10. White and black note notation

White note notation (*croches blanches*) is often used for movements of a particularly tender nature, usually in triple time. Normal crotchet or quaver note values are left blank. However, the use of this form of notation is not consistent with any one affect, and examples can be found where there is no apparent emotional message implied by its use (see ex. 3.2.5).

Ex. 6.2.22 *f*: Couperin, 8ième concert, Grande Ritournele

Black note notation where black notes appear without stems, is a relic of older notation found in fast triple movements in Italian music of the 17th century.[16]

11. 17th-century part books

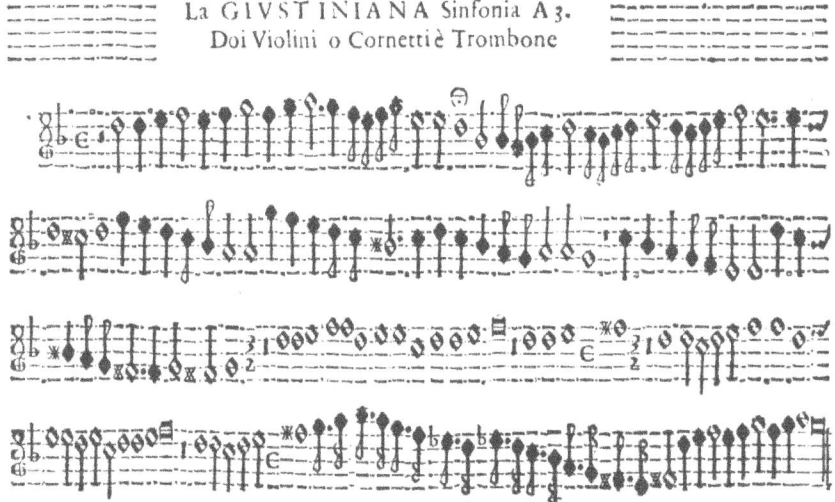

Ex. 6.2.23 *f*: Castello

A page from a mid-17th-century block-printed part book. Notice the following points:

Absence of bar-lines; block rests; the custos sign at the end of a line indicating the pitch of the next note; new time signatures appear without double bars to indicate the end of a section; large note values for the fast triple section: breves and longues; no beams to join groups of fast notes; sharp sign to raise flattened note to natural (line 3).

---

[16] For both white and black notation, see *New Grove*, 'Notation'

12. Instruction books

Each tutor or treatise had its own system of notating instructions for articulation, ornamentation and fingering. Prefaces of some books of sonatas (such as Veracini's *Sonate Accedemiche* opus 2) list detailed signs used in that particular composer's work (see ex. 2.6.2). In the following example information is given about fingering octaves. The number of dots indicates whether to use the second or third string, a device also used by violists such as Marais in the 17th century.

Ex. 6.2.24 *f*: Corrette (1738), L'Art De se perfectionner dans le Violon, p. 2

Inconsistencies

When playing from 17th- or 18th-century part books, inaccuracies in the text make playing in parts difficult where the part books disagree. Slurs and rhythms are inconsistently notated, even when it may be obvious that they are supposed to match. To enable a sensible musical performance to take place, players will have to make decisions themselves if no editorial advice is given. Beware of automatically tidying up motifs which appear to be the same. There are often deliberate reasons for small differences in articulation and written rhythms.

Rehearsal

An inconvenient feature of playing from facsimile parts is the absence of bar numbers and rehearsal reference figures. In short dance movements this is not a serious problem, but when rehearsing concerti grossi or other works with extended movements, it is essential to number the bars before starting to rehearse. This exercise is more demanding than it first appears because many lines of music finish with only part of a bar, the other part being on the following line. It is often more convenient to number the bars in a continuous sequence through a whole piece, as the occurrence of several allegro movements can make rehearsal confusing.

Choosing a good modern edition

When looking at facsimile editions it is a useful exercise to compare these with modern editions of the same works. By this means, the player is better able to judge the usefulness or otherwise of certain modern (or 19th-century) editorial practices. A good modern critical edition should provide editorial information which enhances the text, with clear explanations of any added tempo markings, slurs, articulation marks, etc. If it is difficult or impossible to tell where the editor has intervened, be suspicious and treat all markings with caution. However, the expertise of a good editor should not be underestimated when decisions on dubious slur ends have to be made, or when deciding on the accidentals which fit in with a difficult harmonic progression. Use facsimiles by all means, but do not be deceived into thinking that they are automatically 'better' then a good modern edition. Look for facsimile editions which have editorial notes supplied with them, as these provide valuable lessons in how to approach the use of facsimiles.

An example of editorial intervention clearly marked:

Ex. 6.2.25: J. S. Bach Sonata for viola da gamba in G minor (arr. Duncan Druce)

A slur made up of dots or broken by a line does not indicate a special type of bow-stroke.

6.2 Playing from facsimile editions

Many modern editions of Baroque works have editorial markings only in the parts, and a 'clean' text may often be found in the score. One big advantage of buying modern editions is that in most case separate parts are published along with a score. Certain scholarly editions are published only in score format (*Denkmäler der Tonkunst in Österreich*, for example), and the player may need to make up his own parts, or buy an inferior edition and refer to a master score. Parts for some *Musica Britannica* volumes are available from Stainer and Bell.

Obtaining facsimile editions and copies of original scores

Since this book was first published in 2000, there has been a dramatic increase in the quantity of music and associated literature that is available for download from the web, in many instances at no cost. As well as original 17th- and 18th-century publications it will often be possible to obtain later editions for comparison.

The International Music Score Library Project (also known as The Petrucci Music Library and accessible at imslp.org) contains hundreds of thousands of items of public domain material and is a good place to start searching, although other sites hold music that is not found here. New sites are appearing regularly and an internet search for a specific publication will often produce several options from which to choose.

For those who prefer to use a printed book (or for those items that are not readily available online) the following list is comprised of publishers whose editions are widely quoted in this book. One or two of these publishers are no longer in existence but some of their publications are still available, and it is recommended that players refer to the websites given:

S.P.E.S. Studio Per Edizioni Scelte (www.spes-editore.com).

> Beautifully produced, facsimile editions of mainly Italian music including works by Castello, Marini and Cima. Specially recommended: Bach works for unaccompanied violin, beautifully hard-bound; Corelli opus 5 violin sonatas containing 1st (Rome 1700) and 3rd (Amsterdam 1710) editions bound together.

Anne Fuzeau Productions (www.editions-classique.com).

> Smartened-up facsimiles of mainly French music, with tri-lingual prefaces and editorials. Compendia of French viol and cello treatises, a violin volume promised. Specially recommended: the chamber works of François Couperin, Leclair sonatas opus 1, 2, 3, 4 and the sonatas for two violins without bass, Rameau *Pièces de Clavecin en Concerts*, Buxtehude sonatas for violin, viola da gamba and b.c., Geminiani opus 1 and 4 violin sonatas, Pachelbel *Partien* for two violins and b.c. (some in scordatura), Vivaldi cello sonatas.

Editions Minkoff is no longer in existence but some volumes are still available from www.omifacsimiles.com.

> The hard-backed volumes are beautifully bound, although a commentary is not always included. Publications include Corrette and L'Abbé le fils violin tutors.

King's Music (www.earlymusicco.co.uk/clifford.bartlett)

> A practically produced range of facsimile editions covering a wide repertoire. Of particular string interest is the concerto/concerto grosso repertoire including works by Handel, Corelli and Vivaldi. Also Biber's 'Rosary' sonatas, Geminiani's *The Art of Playing on the Violin*, many trio sonatas and works for three violins and continuo.

Jacks, Pipes & Hammers (www.groovycart.co.uk/jackspipesandhammers)

> 17th- and 18th-century English music in facsimile. Series includes works by Matteis, Finger, Gibbs, Festing, Croft, Cervetto, Lanzetti and Cosimi.

Performers' Facsimiles, Broude Brothers, available from www.omifacsimiles.com.

> Very clean editions produced on thick quality paper. Large catalogue including of particular string interest: Gibbons, Fantasies of three parts, Purcell, Pergolesi (attrib. Gallo), and Handel trio sonatas, violin sonatas by Tartini, D. Purcell, and Finger, *The Division-violin; and Select Preludes and Vollentarys for the Violin* which includes unaccompanied preludes from Albinoni to Ziani; cello sonatas by Geminiani and Boccherini; part books for Purcell's *Ayres for the Theatre* (warning: viola part in mezzo-soprano clef!).

Other publishers offering good reliable modern editions of unusual repertoire:

London Pro Musica (www.londonpromusica.com).

> A large early Baroque and Renaissance catalogue of solo and ensemble repertoire. Clear and well-produced with good critical comment and editorial input. Early violin consort music by Thomas Simpson and Dowland, early divisions by Della Casa, Virgiliano and Rognoni.

Corda Music (www.cordamusic.co.uk)

> Publishes Duncan Druce's conjectural Brandenburg concerto no. 7 (arrangement of J. S. Bach's gamba sonata in G minor using the same scoring as concerto no. 6). Also series of orchestral music edited by Peter Holman (English 17th-century theatre suites, and an arrangement for French orchestral forces of Couperin's *8ième concert*).

Fretwork Editions (www.publishing.fretwork.co.uk)

> A small company specialising in viol consort repertoire. Of violin interest: William Lawes, The Royall Consort ('new' version specifically for violins); Jenkins Division Suites for 2 trebles, bass & organ; other consort music suitable for violins by Lupo.

A-R Editions (www.areditions.com)

> Impeccably researched and produced series. String interest: Leclair sonatas for violin and b.c. opus 1, 2, 5, 9 and 15. Albinoni opus 8 for two violins, cello and b.c.; Castello ensemble sonatas; string music from the library at Kromeriz.

Musica Repartita, available from www.groovycart.co.uk/jackspipesandhammers

> Produces 'semi-facsimile' in which sparse editorial marks are defined in the cleaned-up facsimile text, the most interesting volumes for the string player are by J. J. Walther (*c*.1650-1717) MR 58, *Scherzi Musicali* and MR59, *Hortulus Chelicus*.

Ut Orpheus (www.utorpheus.com)

> Publishes a wide range including Geminiani opus 5, Boccherini quintets, Albinoni concertos and Biber 'Mystery' sonatas.

Musedita Edizioni Musicali (www.musedita.it)

> Reasonably priced editions including Muffat concertos and chamber works by Becker, Bertali, Castello, Cavalli, Farina, Legrenzi, Marini and Rosenmüller.

Primalamusica (www.primalamusica.com)

> Publishes unusual repertoire from England, Germany and Italy.

Baroque Music Italy (www.baroquemusic.it) aims to make available modern urtext transcriptions of original printed and manuscript sources for free download.

Recommended modern editions:

- Bach concerto for two violins in D minor and 6 sonatas for violin with obligato harpsichord, violin parts bowed and fingered by Andrew Manze. (Bärenreiter).
- Corelli op. 5 sonatas (Schott/Universal Wiener Urtext edition).
- Biber 'Mystery' sonatas in 3 volumes. (Diletto Musicale).

6.3 Reading the treatises

An historical approach to string playing is bound sooner or later to lead the player to the writings of the period under examination. Unfortunately the selection of available sources is dependent on the whims of publishers as books go in and out of print. Facsimiles and reprints appear at random, often giving little guidance to the reader as to the importance of the various texts and how they fit into the picture of Baroque string playing from a modern perspective. If the string player-reader expects to find all the answers by reading the instruction books and treatises, he will be disappointed. What is left unsaid is almost as important as the positive instructions. Unwritten conventions should assume as important a role as written instructions. The violin was predominantly an instrument played by professionals in its early history, and there are very few instruction books from the first part of the 17th century. Traditions and schools of playing would have been passed on by example and 'word of ear'. Violinist dance masters and their bands would have played from memory, and private musical instruction for the nobility would not have included the violin. Jambe de Fer wrote in his *Epitome musical*:

> We call viols those [instruments] with which gentlemen, merchants, and other virtuous people pass their time . . . The other type [of instrument] is called violin; it is commonly used for dancing.
>
> (1556) tr. Boyden (1965), p. 32

The *Epitome musical* contains the few brief references to the violin, its uses and technique in the 16th century. Simple tutors appeared in the middle of the 17th century (Zannetti 1645, Playford 1651) for the growing band of amateur players, and it is not until the mid-18th century that detailed technical manuals appear, written by virtuoso professionals for their more advanced pupils. Many of these books (Corrette 1738, L'Abbé le fils 1761) contain duets for the pupil to play with the master, a tradition carried on through Louis Spohr in his tutor of 1832 until today.

In this book I have attempted to set out the conventions of the period which encapsulate the basic language and technique of playing Baroque music. Although the player may have absorbed an understanding of the basic language of Baroque music, his reading of the printed evidence should not thereafter be over-ridden by a slavish adherence to written rules, about which the writers themselves have plenty to say, as nowhere are 'the methods of practitioners' more different from each other than in their writings. Awareness of the style of the period and the unwritten conventions of performance are two important basic requirements for an understanding of the details of the treatises. This can be acquired by knowing and playing as much music of the period as possible, and applying basic principles in a spirit of experimentation. Most successful performances evolve through this system of trial and error. Reading the treatises should be a continuous activity linked to practical music making. As the player gains experience in various areas of the repertoire, new light will be spread on the detailed instructions and general comments offered by the treatise writers. The player will find that even after many years, understanding and awareness of details not previously understood will emerge. As the player's practical experience in applying the written instructions to specific repertoire grows, his perception of how each writer fits into the general picture will become clearer.

The treatise writer assumes a certain knowledge of style and musicianship in his reader. The treatise is being written for the novice instrumentalist, not the novice 18th-century musician. When starting to learn an instrument, the 18th-century novice will have been listening to music composed in his life-time for many years and be familiar with the sound of cadences and harmonic cliches, ornamentation in good (and bad) taste, *messa di voce* and other conventional compositional devices.

Most of the tutors for the violin which are readily available today are from the latter part of the period under examination (Corrette 1738, Geminiani 1751, Leopold Mozart 1756, Tartini written 1760s, L'Abbé le fils 1761). These are directed at the advanced player, although Leopold Mozart claims his book is directed towards beginners, and states his intention to write a further book 'for platform artists'. The elementary instructions found at the beginning of these tutors give way very quickly to exercises and examples to test

6.3 Reading the treatises

and develop an advanced technique. Earlier tutors such as those published by Playford (numerous editions from 1651) and Prelleur (1731) in England are very much of the 'do-it-yourself' variety, giving only basic technical information followed by many simple tunes and dances. Playford advocates the use of frets and tablature for beginners. These tutors would have been aimed at the mass of amateur players who picked up the violin from the late part of the 17th century onwards. In Italy Gasparo Zannetti published his violin method *Il Scolaro per imparar a suonare di violino* in 1645, which is an early source of information for basic bowing rules. Like Playford, he gives music written in tablature for use in the early stages of learning the instrument. Staff notation of each piece in tablature is printed on the opposite page, a convenient reference as the player gains confidence. It is dangerous to extrapolate universal rules and technical information from these basic tutors. From the very simple music provided, it is obvious, as Riley points out, that Zannetti's tutor was used by children and beginners only.[17] An advanced violin technique already existed taking the player into the high positions with complex written out ornamentation. Examples of the technical demands of the violin repertoire during the 1630s and 40s may be found in the works by Italian violinist composers such as Farina, Uccellini, Marini and Fontana. Here the range and complexity of decorated passage work shows that the limited technical information found in such tutors as Zannetti should be treated only as elementary advice for beginners.

It is apparent that some treatises were written to vindicate and promote a certain eccentric style of playing. The subject of vibrato, for example, touched a raw nerve with several writers, with insults being levelled at its overuse,[18] or encouragement to use it 'as often as possible'.[19]

Players today should not only look at tutors written for their own instrument. Matters of style can be applied across the instrumental spectrum and often, specific technical know-how takes up only a small proportion of the whole volume. Quantz (1752) is famous for his treatise *On Playing the Flute*, but only eight of the eighteen chapters of the book are about flute matters. He started his professional life as a violinist, so he is able to provide much helpful advice to string players, including a commentary on bowing rules (XVII. 8 & 9). The bulk of the text is concerned with matters of general musicianship and *galant* taste, which may be usefully studied by any musician. However, his approach to ornamentation, and particularly the execution of appoggiaturas, was criticised only a few years later as being old-fashioned by Burney among others.[20] String players should also direct their quest for knowledge of musical style and execution towards writers on the harpsichord such as St. Lambert (1702), Couperin (1716) and C. P. E. Bach (1753), and the viol: Ortiz (1553), Simpson (1659), J. Rousseau (1687), and Marais' introduction to Book IV (1717).

Information about how music was performed is contained in descriptions of performances, and reported by 18th-century travellers and commentators such as Burney and North. Descriptions of performances also reflect changing fashions, remarking on such matters as good taste in ornamentation and methods of holding the instrument.

Some treatises were written by teachers at the end of their careers, or to counter new fashions in playing styles. Corrette (1738) divided his violin treatise into the Italian and French styles of playing, giving two ways of bowing and of holding the bow. Quantz wrote his book long after he had returned from a grand tour, which included lengthy stays in England, France and Italy where he would have been exposed to the current styles. The tour ended in 1727, but his book was not published in Berlin until 1752, by which time the ideas he brought back with him had been moulded into a new mixed style of his own. Certainly, his compositions show a wide range of national techniques and influences, which must have been absorbed during the 1720s. However, the general musicianship lessons written by Quantz overcome stylistic and national boundaries in

---

[17] (1954), p. 294
[18] Leopold Mozart (1756) XI.3, tr. Knocker, p. 203
[19] (1751) Geminiani, p. 8
[20] (1752) tr. Reilly, p. xxxiii

6.3 Reading the treatises

their humour and good sense and he is, for example, one of the few writers to give any guidance on ensemble style and manners.

The publishing history of tutors for the violin and other string instruments displays a tendency for them to feed upon each other as teachers use the same material to develop their own 'improved' version. In Playford (1651) through Simpson (1659) and forward to Prelleur (1731), for example, there is a direct line as the same basic instructions are recycled and improved. Read about the unpublished English violin tutor (1694) by Lenton in Boyd (1982). In the 18th century, Leopold Mozart (1756) pays tribute to Tartini with various details from the Italian master's treatise which was in circulation before its publication in 1771. Quantz also has a definite presence in the Leopold Mozart treatise. Three great violin teachers Leopold Mozart, Tartini and Geminiani are worth comparing for common ground and differences of opinion. Details will be found in various sections of this book, particularly in the technical sections.

Sometimes reading original sources can be positively misleading: C. P. E. Bach warns (1753) that the explanations of ornaments as published in his sonatas are wrong (the Huffner edition of 1744), and were published without his consent or knowledge. Common sense dictates that specific rules written by any composer should only be strictly applied to the music of the writer and his immediate circle of followers. Geminiani wrote clear and very specific instructions for the performance of his music, but how far this guidance can be applied to the performance of music by his contemporaries is a matter requiring careful consideration, as he is now generally regarded as having been a violinist with a somewhat eccentric style, although a great teacher who had significant influence. The general background level of performance conventions for any period or location needs to be understood before specific instructions can be laid over the basic style of the musical period in question. Neumann points out that Quantz and C. P. E. Bach disagreed on many important principles even though they were closely connected with the same musical establishment at the court of Frederick the Great.[21]

The terminology used by authors of different treatises needs to be carefully examined. Signs and symbols for bowing and the higher positions in particular may be confusing. Some authors (Prelleur, Leopold Mozart and Tartini) call second position the 'half position' or 'half shift', and third position the 'whole shift'. Geminiani uses the familiar modern terminology for the various positions (see table on p. 81).

Bowing instructions appear variously as:

    Down bow   t (tirer), N (niederzug), I, d, g (giu)

    Up bow   p (pousser) A (aufzug), V, u, s (su)

How should we react to criticism by an author of a habit or convention which the writer of the treatise considers to be in bad taste, or incorrect? Should the player of today interpret this as positive evidence of the existence of such a practice, and so imitate it? If the practice described is obviously one to avoid, such as bad intonation or ludicrous facial expressions, then this evidence may safely be ignored. Other practices such as the use of vibrato or excessive ornamentation, are a matter of taste. Most performers wish to perform music of any period in the best possible way. If bad tuning and style existed then, this does not mean that we should attempt to recreate a badly out of tune and tasteless performance.

---

[21] (1967) p. 318

Attitudes to rules

In order to understand contemporary attitudes towards the treatises it is helpful to read what the treatise writers themselves wrote about rules.

Quintilian:

> Rules are helpful so long as they indicate the direct road and do not restrict us absolutely to the ruts made by others.
>
> II. xiii. 16

Agricola:

> It must be, and in fact it is, highly necessary that the youths who begin to learn, be not overwhelmed and deterred with many superfluous words and rules, enticed and allured to study.
>
> (1528) quoted in Riley (1954), p. 16

St. Lambert:

> A good teacher ... teaches a general rule as if it were without exception, waiting for an occasion to produce this exception before speaking about it, because he knows that thus it is better understood, and that if he had discussed it at first, it would have hindered the impression of the general rule.
>
> (1702) tr. Harris-Warwick, p. 6

St. Lambert's idea is that taste provides

> ... the freedom that musicians give themselves to transgress their own rules.
>
> (1702) tr. Harris-Warwick, p. 45

In other words, rules are for beginners, and an understanding of the rules should form a basic framework from which to depart should the occasion arise. Dupont in his *Principes de violon par demandes et par reponce*:

> Q. Is one obliged to observe all the rules of bowing?
>
> A. Yes, when one is learning, because it is easier to play the airs in good taste; but when one is advanced, one takes such license and liberties as one judges to be proper.
>
> (1718) quoted in Riley (1954), p. 104

Another translation of this passage[22] gives 'but once you are acquainted with the style' in place of 'but when one is advanced'.

However, a glimpse of the strict regime maintained by the Lullian orchestral school is provided by Muffat:

> Only apprentices, ignoramuses and incompetents in all countries disobey the rules.
>
> (1698) tr. Cooper and Zsako, p. 223

The grey area where rules and good taste meet is dealt with by Loulié in his *Eléments ou Principes de Musique* (1696) with a comment about the use of ornaments:

> It would not be possible to provide rules for the placement of the *agréments*, because only those with taste can make rules, and those who have none would almost never know how to apply them.

Maugars criticises the French rules of composition declaring that he preferred the freer Italian manner of composition:

> To tell the truth, it is not so necessary to amuse ourselves by observing the rules so rigorously that it makes us lose track of a fugue or the beauty of a song, in view of the fact these rules have been invented only to keep young schoolboys under control and prevent them from emancipating themselves before they have reached years of discretion.
>
> (1639) quoted in MacClintock, p. 117

---

[22] Mather, p. 175

6.3 Reading the treatises

Praetorius:

> There are many matters of this kind where the impression can be given that there is only one right way of doing something. So, for instance, some keyboard players are held in contempt for not using some particular fingering or other. This is ridiculous, in my opinion. If a player can fly up and down the keyboard, using the tips, mid-joints, or the backs of his fingers—yes, using his very nose if that helps!—and either keeps or breaks every rule in existence, so what? If he plays well, and plays musically, it matters very little by what means he does so.
>
> (1618) tr. Crookes, p. 53

Charpentier 'on the beauties of music' sums up the prevailing feeling amongst the above writers about rules:

> Experience teaches more than all the rules.
>
> (1698) in Cessac, p. 410

PRACTICAL APPLICATION

The famous 'rule of down-bow' comes in for a great deal of criticism from mid-18th-century writers since the universal application of this dance-style bowing must have held sway as a natural bowing rule since the violin first appeared. By the middle of the 18th century, the principal violin tutors all recommend practising pieces with reverse bowing to counteract the down-bow hierarchy which was inappropriate in much music which did not demand regular bar accentuation, which by this time was considered crude. However, Quantz in Berlin still favours beat and bar-line emphasis after the (old fashioned?) French style. The bowing rules as written down by Muffat in the late 17th century[23] however, show a strict regime of bar-line emphasis appropriate for the music of Lully and his followers to which these rules refer. Several examples of rules not applying in fast tempi may be found: the re-take loure bowing of Muffat and the prolonged appoggiatura rule of Quantz are both ruled out where a fast tempo would make the application impractical.

In reading the treatises it is important to pick out universal musical truths from the mass of specific information, about the performance of ornaments or choice of fingering for example, in order to absorb the good taste of the particular style in question. Try to play music by the authors of the various treatises in order to understand the application of specific details. Then look for similar contemporary applications of the points illustrated in the texts. Learn and practise the material from the treatises in order to sense the approach from a technical and stylistic point of view. After a period looking at other areas of the repertoire, return to the treatise and you may find that points which have been previously over-looked or considered as of little importance may now be more clearly understood in the light of experience in playing more of that particular repertoire, or other music in a contrasting style.

Finally, a word about translation. It should not be taken for granted that the translations currently available are the last word. Some well-used modern editions were made before the present more informed state of performance practice arrived. Many details that might have been assumed by translators fifty years ago may have been misunderstood, and in the light of more recent discoveries about the way music was performed in the 17th and 18th centuries, some details may need further investigation.

The possibilities of language can give us a variety of interpretations, and if at all possible, players should examine the treatises in the original language in order to make their own decisions about dubious areas of terminology or emphasis. Many editions admit the possibility of various readings and give a word, or in some cases the complete text in the original language. It is illuminating (and sometimes shocking) to compare different translations of the same passage (Dupont example given above).

---

[23] (1698) tr. Cooper and Zsako

A list of the principal historical treatises and tracts quoted in this book:

1523 Venice	Sylvestro Ganassi, *Regola rubertina*
1529 Wittenberg	Martin Agricola, *Musica instrumentalis deudsch*
1553 Rome	Diego Ortiz, *Trattado de Glosas sobre Clausulas otros generos depuntos en la Musica de Violones*
1556 Lyons	Philibert Jambe de Fer, *Epitome musical*
1589 Paris	Thoinot Arbeau, *Orchesography*
1597 London	Thomas Morley, *A Plaine and Easie Introduction to Practicall Musicke*
1601 Venice	Giulio Caccini, *Le Nuove Musiche*
1618 Wolfenbüttel	Michael Praetorius, *Syntagma musicum, De organographia* parts I & II
1620 Wolfenbüttel	Michael Praetorius, *Sciagraphia*
1636 Paris	Marin Mersenne, *Harmonie Universelle*
1639	Andre Maugars, *Response faite à un Curieux, sur le sentiment de la musique d'Italie*
1645 Milan	Gasparo Zannetti, *Il Scolaro per imparar a suonare di violino, et altri stromenti*
1659 London	Christopher Simpson, *The Division-viol*
1660-72	*The Burwell Lute Tutor*
1674 London	John Playford, *An introduction to the Skill of Musick*
1676 London	Thomas Mace, *Musick's Monument*
1682 London	Nicola Matteis, *The False Consonances of Musick*
1687 Paris	Danoville, (first name unknown) *L'Art de toucher le dessus et basse de viole*
1687 Paris	Jean Rousseau, *Traité de la Viole*
1694 London	John Lenton, *The Gentleman's Diversion*
1695/8 Augsburg/Passau	Georg Muffat, *Florilegia* [the author's foreword to the gracious amateur]
various London	contained in *Roger North on Music*
1701 Passau	Georg Muffat, *Auserlesene Instrumental-Music*
1702 Paris	Monsieur de Saint-Lambert, *Les Principes du Clavecin*
1711	Johann David Heinichen, *Der General-Bass in der Composition*
1716/17 Paris	François Couperin, *L'Art de Toucher le Clavecin*
1731 London	Peter Prelleur, *The Art of Playing on the Violin*
1738/82 Paris	Michel Corrette, *L'Ecole d'Orphée: methode pour apprendre facilement à jouer du violon dans le goût françois et italien. L'Art de se perfectionner dans le violon*
1739 Hamburg	Johann Mattheson, *Der Vollkommene Capellmeister*
1740 Amsterdam	Hubert Le Blanc, *Defense de la basse de Viole contre les entreprises du violon et les prétensions du violoncel*
1741 Paris	Michel Corrette, *Methode, théorique et pratique. Pour Apprendre en peu de tems le Violoncelle dans sa Perfection*
1751 London	Francesco Geminiani, *The Art of Playing on the Violin*
1752 Berlin	Johann Joachim Quantz, *Versuch einer Anweisung die Flöte traversiere zu spielen*
1753/1762 Berlin	C. P. E. Bach, *Versuch über die wahre Art das Clavier zu spielen*

6.3 Reading the treatises

1755 Paris	Michel Corrette, *L'Ecole d'Orphée: méthodes pour apprendre à joüer de la contre-basse à 3. à 4. et à 5. cordes, de la quinte ou alto.....*
1756 Augsburg	Leopold Mozart, *Versuch einer gründlichen Violinschule*
1760 Padua	Giuseppe Tartini, *A letter from the late Signor Tartini to Signora Maddalena Lombardini*
1761 Paris	L'Abbé le fils, *Principes du violon pour apprendre le doigté de cet instrument, et les différens agrémens dont il est susceptible*
1771 Paris	Giuseppe Tartini, *Traité des Agréments de la Musique*

GLOSSARY

Check index for further information.

Affekt (Ger)	Word used to describe the affect emotions have on the body. Used in Baroque music to describe particular emotional states represented in the music.
Affetti (It)	17th-century Italian ornament. Usually marked on minims, means use bow vibrato to play pulsing quavers in imitation of the tremulant stop of an organ.
Arcata (It)	Long bow-stroke used in Italian style playing
Archet (Fr)	Bow. *Coupe d'archet*: bow-stroke.
Arpeggio (It)	Broken chord. In string music, an indication to break the written chord into continuous rhythmic figures.
Band(e)	Term commonly used for the early form of orchestra. Any instrumental ensemble.
Bariolage	Breaking a harmonic figure across the strings, often using the same note stopped and open string.
Bass viol	Bass member of the viol family with 6 or 7 strings, flat back and frets.
Bass violin	Bass member of the violin family of various sizes with 4 or 5 strings and a variety of tunings.
Basse de violon (Fr)	Bass violin.
Bassetto di viola (It)	Small bass instrument of the violin family.
Basso continuo (It)	Bass line with figures to indicate harmony.
Bastarda	see Viola bastarda.
Buono (It)	Good. In bowing terms, down-bow on a strong beat.
Bourdon (Fr)	Lowest string or drone.
Bow vibrato	Pulsating bow stroke imitating the tremulant stop of an organ. Achieved by varying the pressure of the bow with the hand.
Broken consort	A consort composed of members of more than one family of instruments, e.g. viols and violins.
Cadence	Harmonic progression indicating the end of a phrase.
Cadenza (It)	Literally means cadence. Opportunity for an extemporised flourish by a soloist, usually on the penultimate note of the cadence.
Caesura (It)	Pause.
Catline	A gut string made like a rope with several threads entwined.
Cattivo (It)	Bad. In bowing terms, up-bow on a weak beat.
Cello	Small bass instrument of the violin family. Usually with 4 strings.
Chanterelle (Fr)	Literally 'the singer' or top string of an instrument.
Chiffrée (Fr)	Figured, as in *basse chiffrée* (figured bass).
Concertante (It)	Containing a small group of solo instruments.
Concertino (It)	A small group of solo instruments, as *concertante*.
Continuo (It)	A bass line with figures to indicate the harmony. May be played

GLOSSARY

	by one melodic or chordal instrument or by a group.
Coulamment	Smoothly, legato, flowing.
Coulé	Legato, slurred.
Coup d'archet (Fr)	Bow-stroke.
Croches (Fr)	Quavers.
Da camera (It)	Chamber.
Da chiesa (It)	Church.
Dessus (Fr)	The treble part.
Division viol	A small form of 17th-century bass viol used for playing divisions.
Divisions	The variation of a tune by dividing it up into smaller notes, or elaborations on an harmonic pattern.
Double	A written out ornamented repeat of a dance or section of music, usually with continuous quick notes.
Egale(s) (Fr)	Equal, as in notes *égales* or *croches égales* (equal quavers).
Extempore (It)	Made up.
Fermata (It)	Pause.
Figured bass	A bass line with figures to indicate harmony.
Full stops	Full double stopping or chords.
Generalbass (Ger)	Figured bass.
Giu (It)	Down-bow, used by Geminiani.
Graces	Ornaments, usually the small type indicated by signs.
Ground bass	A melody or sequence of chords repeated with variations, usually 4 or 8 bars in length.
Gruppo (It)	Cadential ornament used in early 17th-century music.
Handgrip notation	A form of notation indicating where the fingers should be placed, rather than as the music sounds, to facilitate playing in different tunings.
Haute-contre (Fr)	In string music used to indicate the highest viola part (usually the 2nd part down). Also means a high tenor voice.
Hemiola	Greek for sesquialtera. Cadential figure implying a long bar of 3/2 across two bars of 3/4.
Inégal(es) (Fr)	Unequal. Used in French music where pairs of notes moving in step-wise motion are played with the first longer than the second, in varying degrees.
Lira da braccio	An early instrument, of the violin type played on the arm, with a flat bridge and many strings, including *bourdon* strings off the fingerboard. Used to accompany the voice.
Lirone	A bass version of the *lira da braccio* with many strings, including *bourdons* and a flat bridge to facilitate chordal playing. Used to accompany the voice.
Loure	A dance (see section 2.5)
Loure	Slurred
Lourer	Pairing of notes where the first played longer; may mean slurred in pairs as well.
Mean	Term used for the middle strings. Playford (1674) calls the violin A string *small mean* and the D string *great mean*. Term used by Playford for the viola.

GLOSSARY

Mean-tone	An early tuning system where the 3rds and 6ths in the most commonly used keys such as C and F are very well in tune at the expense of the less used ones which use more accidentals.
Messa di voce (It)	Literally 'placing of the voice'. Used to describe the effect of swelling and diminishing the sound on a long note.
Notes inégales/égales (Fr)	Play unequal/equal notes where appropriate. See section 3.2.
Obbligato (It)	Compulsory, or necessary. Applies to written out independent parts. Used to describe a written out keyboard part, instead of figured bass.
Partia (It), Partie (Ger)	A form of suite or set of variations.
Partita (It)	A form of suite.
Passions	Used in the 17th century to mean 'emotions' and their physical affects.
Pedal (point)	A continuously held or repeated bass note.
Petit choeur (Fr)	Little choir, or concertino group.
Poussez (Fr)	Up-bow.
Quinte (Fr)	In string music describes a viola part, usually the lowest or 3rd viola part.
Quinton	A 5-stringed instrument combining the range and characteristics of the violin and par-dessus de viole, tuned in 4ths and 5ths with frets. See Herzog.
Rhetoric	The oratorical manner of speaking (or performing) used to persuade the listener into a certain emotional state.
Ripieno (It)	The rest. The large group which form the tutti of a concerto grosso.
Scordatura (It)	Mis-tuned. Used to describe any tuning which differs from the one normally used.
Secco (It)	Dry. Describes the practice of playing short notes or chords in Italian-style recitative.
Sesquialtera (Lat)	'The whole and the half' or a ratio of 3:2.
Spiccato (It)	Short, detached strokes lifted from the string, not continuously sprung as in modern usage.
Stile concitato (It)	Agitated style. An early instrumental style, used by Monteverdi.
Su (It)	Up-bow, used by Geminiani.
Tablature	A notation system in which signs or numbers show the player where to put the fingers rather than the pitch of the note. The number of lines on the 'stave' corresponds to the number of strings. The top string may be at the top or the bottom of the stave.
Taille (Fr)	The middle or 2nd viola part.
Tasto solo (It)	Single key. Instruction for the player to play the bass line without harmony.
Temperament	Tuning system. In an unequal temperament the more frequently used 'home' keys are more in tune than the less used 'distant' ones.
Thorough bass	Bass line with figures to indicate harmony.
Tirez (Fr)	Down-bow.

GLOSSARY

Tremolo (It)	Usually means trill, or vibrato with the left hand in early string music. Monteverdi used it to describe a measured repeated semiquaver figure. Unmeasured bowed tremolo is not used in Baroque music.
Tous (Fr)	All or tutti.
Viol	A family of bowed instruments with flat backs and frets, usually with 6 or 7 strings.
Viola (It)	The alto or tenor member of the violin family. Also a generic prefix for many bowed stringed instruments.
Viola bastarda (It)	A small form of bass viol designed to play a virtuoso repertoire characterised by florid embellishment. Also used to describe this style of music.
Viola da braccio (It)	Viola held on the arm. May be used with reference to all the members of the violin family, including the cello.
Viola da gamba (It)	Viola of the leg. Applies to all the members of the viol family.
Viola d'amore (It)	Viola sized bowed instrument played on the shoulder with a flat back and often sloping shoulders, but without frets. It has 6 or 7 strings with additional wire sympathetic strings running through the bridge and underneath the fingerboard. Various tunings.
Viola pomposa (It)	A 5-string viola played on the arm.
Violetta (It)	A small viola. Used early in the Baroque period for the viol or violin family.
Violino piccolo (It)	Small violin, usually 3/4 size usually tuned a 3rd or a 4th higher than normal.
Violoncello (It)	Small bass instrument of the violin family.
Violoncino (It)	Small bass instrument of the violin family, the same as violoncello.
Violone (It)	Bass instrument (may be small or large size) of the viol or violin family.

BIBLIOGRAPHY

Books and articles, including tutors cited in the text

L'Abbé le fils	*Principes du violon pour apprendre le doigté de cet instrument, et les differens agremens dont il est susceptible* (Paris, 1761, 1772 facs. Geneva 1976)
Agricola, Martin	*Musica instrumentalis deudsch* (1529, Wittemberg, tr. & ed. William E. Hettrick, Cambridge, 1994)
Allsop, Peter	*The Italian 'Trio' Sonata* (Oxford, 1992)
	'Da camera e da ballo - alla francese et all' italiana: functional and national distinctions in Corelli's sonate da camera', *Early music*, vol. 26 (1998), 87-96
Apel, Willi	*Italian Violin Music of the Seventeenth Century* (Indiana, 1990)
Arbeau, Thoinot	*Orchesography* (1589 tr. Mary Stewart Evans, New York, 1967)
Ashworth, Jack and O'Dette, Paul	'Basso Continuo', chapter 14 in Carter, ed. (1997)
Bach, C. P. E.	*Versuch über die wahre Art das Clavier zu spielen* (Berlin, pt. 1, 1753, pt. 2, 1762, tr. & ed. W. J. Mitchell, New York, 1949)
Bachmann, Alberto	*An Encyclopedia of the Violin* (New York, 1925, facs. 1975)
Baines, Frances	'What Exactly is a Violone?' *Early music*, vol. 5 (1977), 173-176
Banks, Margaret Downie	'The violino piccolo and other small violins', *Early music*, vol. 18 (1990), 588-596
Barnes, John	'Bach's keyboard temperament. Internal evidence from the Well-Tempered Clavier', *Early music*, vol. 7 (1979), 236-249
Bianconi, Lorenzo	Eng. trans. David Bryant, *Music in the Seventeenth Century* (Cambridge, 1987)
Bonta, Stephen	'From Violone to Violoncello: a question of strings?' *Journal of the American Musical Instrument Society* (1977), 64-99
	'Terminology for the Bass Violin in 17th Century Italy', *Journal of the American Musical Instrument Society* (1978), 5-42
Boyd, Malcolm and Rayson, John	'The Gentleman's Diversion, John Lenton and the first violin tutor', *Early music*, vol. 10 (1982), 329-332
Boyden, David	*The History of Violin Playing from its Origins to 1761* (London, 1965)
	Catalogue of the Hill Collection in the Ashmolean Museum, Oxford (Oxford, 1979)
	'The Violin Bow in the 18th Century', *Early music*, vol. 8 (1980), 199-212
Brossard, Sébastien de	*Dictionnaire de Musique* (Paris, 1703 facs. ed. H. Heckmann, Hilversum, 1965)

BIBLIOGRAPHY

Brown, Clive	'Bowing styles, vibrato and portamento in 19th-century violin playing', *Journal of the Royal Musical Association* (1988) p. 97-128
Buch, David J.	*Dance Music from the Ballets de Cour 1575-1651 - Historical Commentary, Source Study, and Transcriptions from the Philidor Manuscripts* (New York, 1993)
Buelow, George J.	*Thorough-Bass Accompaniment according to Johann David Heinichen* (Lincoln, Nebraska, 1986)
Burnett, Henry	'The Bowed String Instruments of the Baroque Basso Continuo (ca 1680 - ca 1752) in Italy and France', *Journal of the Viola da Gamba Society of America*, vol. VII (1970), 65-91
Burney, Charles	*Dr. Burney's Musical Tours in Europe* ed. Percy Scholes (Oxford, 1959)
	A General History of Music, from the earliest ages to the present (1789, New York, 1957)
	tr. see Tartini, Giuseppe *A letter...* (1760)
Burwell Lute Tutor, The	(*c.* 1660-72, facs. Leeds, 1974)
Butt, John	*Playing With History. The Historical Approach to Musical Performance* (Cambridge, 2002)
Caccini, Giulio	*Le Nuove Musiche* (Venice 1601), ed. H. Wiley Hitchcock (Madison, 1970)
Carse, Adam	*The Orchestra in the XVIIIth Century* (Cambridge, 1940)
Carter, Stewart	'The String Tremolo in the 17th Century', *Early music*, vol.19 (1991), 43-59
Carter, Stewart (ed.)	*A Performer's Guide to 17th-century music* (New York, 1997)
Cessac, Catherine	*Marc-Antoine Charpentier* (Paris, 1988, tr. E. Thomas Glasow, Portland, Or.,1995)
Cicero, Marcus, Tullius	*De Oratore* (*c.* 55 CE, tr. Sutton & Rackham, Harvard, 1942)
Corrette, Michel	*L'Ecole d'Orphée: méthode pour apprendre facilement a jouer du violon dans le goût françois et italien. L'Art de se perfectionner dans le violon* (Paris 1738/1782, facs. Geneva, 1972)
	Methode, théorique et pratique. Pour Apprendre en peu de tems le Violoncelle dans sa Perfection, (Paris 1741, facs. Courlay, 1998)
Couperin, François	*L'Art de Toucher le Clavecin* (Paris 1716, 1717, tr., ed. Margery Halford, Port Washington, 1974)
Cowart, Georgia, ed	*French Musical Thought 1600-1800,* (Ann Arbor, 1989)
Cyr, Mary	'Basses and Basse continue in the orchestra of the Paris Opera 1700 - 1764', *Early music*, vol. 10 (1982), 155-170
Danks, Harry	*The Viola d'Amore* (Halesowen, 1976)
Danoville, (first name unknown)	*L'Art de toucher le dessus et basse de viole* (Paris 1687, facs.Courlay, 1997)
David, Hans T. & Mendel, Arthur (eds.)	*The Bach Reader - a life of Johann Sebastian Bach in letters and documents* (New York, 1945)
Descartes, René	*Les Passions de l'Âme* (Paris, 1649, tr. J. Cottingham et al, Cambridge, 1985)
Dickey, Bruce	'Ornamentation in Early-Seventeenth-Century Italian Music', chapter 13 in Carter, ed. (1997)
Dilworth, John	'The Violin and Bow - origins and development' (Chap. 1 in *Cambridge Companion to the Violin*, ed. Stowell 1995)

Dixon, Graham	'Roman Church Music: the place of instruments after 1600', *The Galpin Society Journal* vol. 34 (1981), 51-61
	'Continuo Scoring in the Early Baroque: the role of bass instruments', *Chelys* vol. 15 (1986), 38-53
Donington, Robert	*The Interpretation of Early Music* (London, 1963)
Dreyfus, Laurence	*Bach's Continuo Group* (Harvard, 1987)
Finson, Jon W.	'The Violone in Bach's Brandenburg Concerti', *The Galpin Society Journal* vol. 29 (1976), 105-111
Feuillet, Raoul-Auger	*Chorégraphie ou L'Art de Décrire La Dance* (Paris 1700, facs. 1968)
Ganassi, Silvestro	*Regola rubertina* (Venice, 1523, tr.?)
Geminiani, Francesco	*The Art of Playing on the Violin* (London, 1751, facs. ed. D. Boyden, London, 1952)
Haynes, Bruce	*A History of Performing Pitch. The Story of "A"* (Lanham, 2002)
	The End of Early Music. A period performer's history of music for the twenty-first century (Oxford, 2007)
	'Pitch Standards in the Baroque and Classical Periods' (unpub. diss., Montreal, 1995)
	'Beyond temperament: non-keyboard intonation in the 17th and 18th centuries', *Early music*, vol. 19 (1991), 357-381
Hefling, Stephen E.	*Rhythmic Alteration in Seventeenth- and Eighteenth-Century Music* (New York, 1993)
Herzog, Myrna	'Is the quinton a viol? A puzzle unravelled', *Early music*, vol. 28 (2000), 9-31.
Hilton, Wendy	'A dance for kings: the 17th-century French Courante, its character, step-formations, metric and proportional foundations', *Early music*, vol. 5 (1977), 160-172
	'Dances to music by Jean-Baptiste Lully', *Early music*, vol. 14 (1986), 51-63
Holman, Peter	*Four and Twenty Fiddlers: the violin at the English court 1540 - 1690* (Oxford, 1993).
	Henry Purcell (Oxford, 1994)
	Dowland: Lachrimae (1604) (Cambridge, 1999)
Houle, George	*Meter in Music 1600 - 1800* (Indiana, 1987)
Jardine, Lisa	*Ingenious Pursuits - building the scientific revolution* (London, 1999)
Johnson, David	*Scottish Fiddle Music in the 18th Century* (Edinburgh, 1984)
Kircher, Athanasius	*Musurgia Universalis*, (Rome 1650, facs. undated)
Le Blanc, Hubert	*Defense de la basse de Viole contre les entreprises du violon et les prétensions du violoncel* (Amsterdam, 1740) tr. Barbara Garvey Jackson, *Journal of the Viola da Gamba Society of America*, vol X (1973), 11-28, 69-80; vol. XI (1974), 17-58; vol. XII (1975), 14-37
le Huray, Peter	*Authenticity in Performance: Eighteenth-Century Case Studies* (Cambridge, 1990)
Lenton, John	*The Gentleman's Diversion* (London, 1694)
Little, Meredith & Jenne, Natalie	*Dance and the Music of J. S. Bach* (Indiana, 1991)
MacClintock, Carol	*Readings in the History of Music in Performance* (Indiana, 1979)

BIBLIOGRAPHY

Mace, Thomas	*Musick's Monument* (London, 1676, facs. Paris, 1977)
Marais, Marin	tr. & ed. in *Marin Marais translated: an English translation of the playing instructions in Pièces de Viole by Marin Marais*, Ian Gammie (5 books 1686, 1701, 1711, 1717, 1725, Harpenden, undated)
Mather, Betty Bang	*Dance Rhythms of the French Baroque* (Indiana, 1987).
Matteis, Nicola	*The False Consonances of Musick* (1682, facs. Monaco, 1980)
Mattheson, Johann	*Der Vollkommene Capellmeister* (Hamburg, 1739, Eng. tr. E. C. Harriss, 1969)
Maugars, André	*Response faite à un Curieux, sur le sentiment de la musique d'Italie* (1639 tr. H. Wiley Hitchcock, Geneva 1993)
Mersenne, Marin	*Harmonie Universelle* (Paris, 1636, facs. Paris, 1963)
Milandre, Louis	*Méthode Facile Pour La Viole d'Amour* (Paris, 1782, facs. Geneva, 1979)
Morley, Thomas	*A Plaine and Easie Introduction to Practicall Musicke* (London, 1597, facs. London, 1952)
Mozart, Leopold	*Versuch einer gründlichen Violinschule* (Augsburg, 1756; Eng. tr., E. Knocker, London, 1948).
Muffat, Georg	*Georg Muffat on Performance Practice. The texts from Florilegium Primum, Florilegium Secundum ans Auserlesene Instrumentalmusik*, ed. and tr. David K. Wilson, (Bloomington, 2001)
	'Observations on the Lully style of performance', *Musical Quarterly* vol. 53 (1967), 220-45. Eng. tr. Kenneth Cooper & Julius Zsako
Neumann, Frederick	*Ornamentation in Baroque and Post-Baroque Music* (Princeton, 1978)
	'The Use of Baroque Treatises on Musical Performance', *Music and Letters*, XLVIII (1967), 315-324
New Grove	*The New Grove Dictionary of Music and Musicians*, 20 vols., ed. S. Sadie (London, 1980)
Newman, William S.	*The Sonata in the Baroque Era* (N. Carolina, 1966)
North, Roger	*Roger North on Music*, ed. J. Wilson (London, 1959)
O'Dette, Paul	see Ashworth, Jack
Ortiz, Diego	*Trattado de Glosas sobre Clausulas y otros generos de puntos en la Musica de Violones* (Rome 1553, Kassel, 1936), tr. Ian Gammie
Parrott, Andrew	'Transposition in Monteverdi's Vespers of 1610', *Early music*, vol. 12 (1984), 490-516
Playford, John	*The English Dancing Master* (London, 1651, facs. London, 1957)
	An introduction to the Skill of Musick (London, 1674 facs. Ridgewood, N.J. 1966)
Praetorius, Michael	*Syntagma musicum II: De organographia* parts I & II, tr. & ed. David Z. Crookes (Wolfenbüttel 1618, Oxford, 1986)
	Sciagraphia (Wolfenbüttel, 1620) in *Syntagma* (Oxford, 1986)
Prelleur, Peter	*The Art of Playing on the Violin* (London 1731, facs. London undated)
Price, Curtis (ed.)	*Music and Society: The Early Baroque Era* (Basingstoke, 1993)

Quantz, Johann Joachim	*Versuch einer Anweisung die Flöte traversiére zu spielen* (Berlin 1752; tr. E. R. Reilly as *On Playing the Flute*, London & New York, 1966)
Quintilian, Marcus Fabius	*Institutio Oratoria* (95 CE), tr. H. E. Butler, (Harvard, 1920)
Riley, Maurice W.	*The History of the Viola* (Ann Arbor, 1980)
	'The Teaching of Bowed Instruments from 1511 to 1756' (unpub. diss., Michigan, 1954)
Ritchie, Stanley	*Before the Chinrest. A Violinist's Guide to the Mysteries of Pre-Chinrest Technique and Style* (Indiana, 2012)
Rousseau, Jean	'Traité de la Viole' (Paris, 1687, tr. & ed. R. A. Green, unpub. diss., Indiana, 1979)
Sadie, Julie Anne	'Charpentier and the early French ensemble sonata', *Early music*, vol. 7 (1979), 330-335
Sadler, Graham	'The Role of the Keyboard Continuo in French Opera 1673-1776', *Early music*, vol. 8 (1980), 148-157
Saint-Lambert, Monsieur de	*Les Principes du Clavecin* (Paris, 1702, tr. & ed. R. Harris-Warrick, Cambridge, 1984)
Sartori, Claudio	*Bibliografica della Musica Strumentale Italiana* (Florence, 1952)
Sawkins, Lionel	'Doucement and Légèrement: tempo in French Baroque music', *Early music*, vol. 21 (1993), 365-374
Schröder, Jaap	*Bach's Solo Violin Works. A performer's guide* (Newhaven, Yale, 2007)
Schröder, Jaap and Hogwood, Christopher	'The Developing Violin', *Early music*, vol. 7 (1979), 155-165
Schwarze, Penny	'Two Aspects of Baroque Violin Technique, Part I: The Frog Hold'. *Journal of the Violin Society of America: VSA Papers*, Vol. XX, no. 2, pp. 189-206 (Summer, 2006)
	, 'Two Aspects of Baroque Violin Technique, Part II: The Low Hold'. *Journal of the Violin Society of America: VSA Papers*, Vol. XXI, no. 1, pp. 185-202 (Summer, 2007)
Segerman, Ephraim	'Strings Through the Ages', *Strad*, vol. 99 (1988), 52-55, 195-201, 295-299
Seletsky, Robert E.	'New Light on the Old Bow', *Early music*, vol. 32 (2004), pp. 286-301 and 415-426
Shute, John D.	'Anthony a Wood and his manuscript Wood D. 19(4) at the Bodleian' (unpub. diss., 1979)
Simpson, Christopher	*The Division-viol* (London, 1659, facs. London, undated)
Smith, Mark	'The Cello Bow Held the Viol-Way; once common, but now almost forgotten', *Chelys*, vol. 24 (1995), 47-61
Snyder, Kerala J.	*Dietrich Buxtehude organist in Lübeck* (New York, 1987).
Steblin, Rita	*A History of Key Characteristics in the Eighteenth and Early Nineteenth Centuries* (Rochester, 1981)
Stowell, Robin	*Violin Technique and Performance Practice in the Late Eighteenth and Early Nineteenth Centuries* (Cambridge, 1985)
Stowell, Robin (ed.)	*The Cambridge Companion to the Violin* (Cambridge, 1992)
Strunk, Oliver	'A Comparison between the French and Italian Music', *Musical Quarterly*, (July 1946)
Strunk, Oliver (ed.)	*Source Readings in Music History: The Baroque Era; The Renaissance* (New York, 1950, 1998)

BIBLIOGRAPHY

Tarling, Judy	*The Weapons of Rhetoric, a guide for musicians and audiences* (St. Albans, 2004)
Tartini, Giuseppe	*A letter from the late Signor Tartini to Signora Maddalena Lombardini* (Padua, 1760, tr. Dr. Burney; supplement to *Traité des Agréments* . . . Celle, 1961)
	Traité des Agréments de la Musique (Fr. tr. P. Denis 1771; Eng. tr., ed. E. R. Jacobi, Celle & New York, 1961)
Topham, John	'Tree Ring Analysis Applied to English Instruments' in *The British Violin* (proceedings of a symposium held by the British Violin Making Association, April, 1998)
	'A Dendrochronological Survey of Musical Instruments from the Hill Collection at the Ashmolean Museum in Oxford'. *The Galpin Society Journal*, Vol. 55 (April, 2002), pp. 244-268
	'A Dendrochronological Survey of Musical Instruments from Three Collections in Edinburgh, London and Paris'. *The Galpin Society Journal*, Vol. 56 (June, 2003), pp. 132-146
Tosi, Pier Francesco	*Opinioni de' cantori antichi e moderni* (Bologna, 1723); tr. J. E. Galliard as *Observations on the Florid Song* (London, 1743; facs. 1967)
Trichet, Pierre	*Traité des Instruments de Musique* (Paris, c. 1640; ed. F. Lesure, Geneva 1978)
Walden, Valerie	*One Hundred Years of Violoncello - a History of Technique and Performance Practice*, 1740 - 1840, Cambridge (1998)
Walls, Peter	'Strings'. *New Grove Guide to Performance Practice*, vol. 2, ed. Howard Mayer Brown and Stanley Sadie (London, 1989), 44-79
	'Mozart and the Violin', *Early music*, vol. 20 (1992), 7- 29
	'Performing Corelli's Violin Sonatas, op. 5' *Early music*, vol. 24 (1996), 133-142
	'Iconography and early violin technique', *The Consort*, vol. 54 (1998) pp. 3-17
Wasielewski, Wilhelm Jos D.	*The Violoncello and its history*, tr. Isabella S. E. Stigand (London, 1894)
Watkin, David	'Corelli's op. 5 Sonatas: "*violino e violone o cembalo*"?' *Early music*, vol. 24 (1996), 645-663
Webber, Oliver	*Rethinking Gut Strings: a Guide for Players of Baroque Instruments* (King's Music, 2006)
	Real Gut Strings: Some New Experiments in Historical Stringing. *The Consort*, vol. 55 (1999), 3-29
Wessel, F. T.	'The Affektenlehre in the Eighteenth Century' (unpub. diss, Indiana, 1955)
Wilson, J. (ed.)	*Roger North on Music* (London, 1959)
Zannetti, Gasparo	*Il Scolaro per imparar a suonare di violino, et altri stromenti* (Milan, 1645; facs. Florence, 1984)
Zaslaw, Neal	'The Compleat Orchestral Musician', *Early music*, vol. 7 (1979), 46-57 & vol. 8 (1980), 71-2
	'The Italian Violin School in the 17th century', *Early music*, vol. 18 (1990), 515-518
	'Ornaments for Corelli's Sonatas, op. 5', *Early music*, vol. 24 (1996), 95-115

Audio examples commentary

The audio examples are selected from recordings made by The Parley of Instruments (director Peter Holman) for Hyperion Records, between 1987 and 1995. The choice of tracks has been influenced by the fact that there are many widely available recordings of the more popular 18th-century works referred to in the book, whilst the earlier repertoire often presents more problems in performance as a result of its relative unfamiliarity. Many players already accustomed to using period instruments have difficulty in identifying the functions of violins, violas, and bowed bass instruments in the 17th-century string orchestra. Knowledge of these practices and styles form the building blocks of the performance of 18th-century music by composers such as Bach. The emphasis on English music is the natural result of Peter Holman's research into English string music of the period, which has revealed a rich and varied early repertoire for instruments of the violin family. More information about music for the early violin band, its players and composers is revealed in Professor Holman's book *Four and Twenty Fiddlers, the violin at the English Court 1540-1690*.

The Parley of Instruments was the first group in modern times to assemble a matched set of 'Renaissance' violins, violas and bass violins, the whole ensemble using all gut strings and short bows. Through the experience of using these instruments, the players have gained valuable insight into the performance of music written for the early violin family, and have adapted their technique and style to suit the music. The Parley's use of these early model violins extends from the first known repertoire for instruments of the violin family, to Locke and Purcell. The violin was in a process of continuous evolution during the 17th century, so a certain amount of overlap in the use of new and old style instruments must have taken place. The use of these instruments has shown that, when making the decision whether to use 'Renaissance' or 'Baroque' instruments, the older style instruments are suitable as long as the range stayed in the lower positions (up to a semitone higher than first position: c^3 on the violin, f^2 on the viola). All the items use Renaissance instruments except those by Finger, Corbett, Stradella and Purcell which were recorded using Baroque instruments. The bass violin (a large type of cello) is used throughout as the orchestral bass instrument, with the tuning $B^\flat, F, c, g$, a tone below the normal cello tuning.

Tracks 1-2	Almand, Pavan and Galliard of Albarti
Scoring	Renaissance instruments: 5 part single strings 1 violin, 3 violas, bass violin, lute continuo, drum
Pitch	$a^1 = 440$
Temperament	115 comma mean-tone
Edition	Arundel Part-Books (c1560). Musica Brittanica, Elizabethan Consort Music

The middle pavan movement is more solemn in character than the outer two dances, which are more lively. Note the tempo relationship from pavan to galliard. Simple decorations of the division type are added on repeats and at cadences. The ensemble moves with the same emphasis in all the parts and the rule of down-bow is used for accentuation of main beats. The principal function of the viola parts is one of harmonic padding. The main melodic interest is in the violin part.

Audio examples commentary

Tracks 3-4	Orlando Gibbons (c1583-1625), Fantasia a 3, no. 7 and 8
Scoring	Renaissance instruments: 2 violins, bass viol, organ
Pitch	$a^1 = 440$
Temperament	1\15 comma mean-tone
Edition	Performers' Facsimiles (parts only), New York. Northwood Music, Urbana, Illinois (modern score and parts)

The fantasies are written with three equal voices which maintain a singing contrapuntal style. The organ doubles the parts. Ritardandos are avoided at passing cadences. A constant beat is maintained through various sections. The absence of bar lines encourages a free flow of rhythmic and melodic ideas. There is no time signature at the beginning. Where triplet crotchets occur in the final section there is a 3\1 sign to signify 3 notes played in the time of a minim beat. The rule of down-bow is used only to emphasise the character of the individual points, and these constantly cross over, imitating each other in all parts in a conversational manner. The harmony is the result of the voices crossing or agreeing, usually coming together at cadences. The parts are called: altus, tenore and basso. Range: in no. 7 both the upper two parts reach a^2, but in no. 8 the middle part maintains its middle role. Suitable for viols or violins. See part 3.6 on consort style and pp. 252-253 playing from facsimile.

Tracks 5-6	Robert Johnson (c1583-1633), The Prince's Alman and Coranto
Scoring	Renaissance instruments: 5-part Renaissance violin band: 4 violins, 2 violas on each of 3 parts, 3 bass violins, 1 great bass viol. Continuo: 2 lutes, theorbo, harpsichord
Pitch	$a^1 = 440$
Temperament	1\15 comma mean-tone
Edition	Brade's 1617 collection *Neue liebliche Branden* ed. B. Thomas, Musica Rara

A general rule of down-bow is used to emphasise the strong bar-lines. The whole group follows the same emphasis which is dictated by the harmony. There is not much overlapping of parts except for passing notes in inner voices. Free ornamentation is not added in orchestral playing except at cadences. If single players were being used, more ornamentation might have been added in the violin part. The mood of the gentle alman is contrasted with the more lively coranto.

Track 7	Francesco Rognoni (d. before 1626), Passaggi on Lassus's Susanna un jour 'per il violone over trombone alla bastarda'
Scoring	Bass violin (tuned in B♭) and virginals
Pitch	$a^1 = 440$
Temperament	1\15 comma mean-tone
Edition	*Selva di Varie passaggi secondo l'uso moderno* (Milan, 1620). London Pro Musica

The 'bastarda' style of writing is demonstrated in this set of *passaggi*. The bass instrument plays elaborate written out divisions while the keyboard part plays the original madrigal tune and harmony. The fast notes run from the very top of the instrument down to the bottom open string (B♭). Most of the fast notes are played with separate bows, only some slower melodic notes are slurred in pairs as marked. See pp. 38-41 on the division style of ornamentation.

Tracks 8-9	Thomas Morley (155718-1602), Southerne's Pavan and Galliard
Scoring	Renaissance instruments: single 5-part strings: 1 violin, 3 violas, bass violin, lute continuo
Pitch	$a^1 = 440$
Temperament	115 comma mean-tone
Edition	Pavan unpublished (Kassel MS). Galliard reconstructed by Peter Holman from a Galliard by Morley in the Fitzwilliam Virginal Book

These dances are written in contrapuntal style with simple division type ornaments added on the repeats. This is more private chamber music than public dance music. The sections use different material which is developed in the consort style, setting 'points' with varying characters which are passed around the group equally. The 3rd section of the pavan is more lively especially in the inner parts, with the violin sustaining a slow *cantus firmus* over the top. The livelier triple galliard follows the solemn pavan. Simple cadential ornaments are added. See pp. 108-109.

Track 10	Angelo Notari (1566?-1663) Variations on the Ruggiero
Scoring	Renaissance violin, lute, theorbo and harpsichord continuo
Pitch	$a^1 = 440$
Temperament	115 comma mean-tone
Edition	Paul O'Dette (unpub.)

These written out divisions on the ground bass *Ruggiero* are elaborate and virtuoso in character. The Italian flavour in the composition seems to need in turn both an extrovert and rhapsodical singing manner of performance. A variety of ornamental devices are specified, roulades, trills, syncopated rhythms, and fast notes marked both separate and slurred on different occasions. Some shocking (Italian style!) intervals occur in contrast to the plain harmony of the repeated bass, and are emphasised. See pp. 103, 114-115, 182 for ground basses.

Track 11	Francesco Cavalli (1602-1643), Canzona a 3
Scoring	Renaissance instruments: 2 violins, bass violin, organ
Pitch	$a^1 = 440$
Temperament	114 comma mean-tone
Edition	King's Music

This sonata is the typical 'patchwork' structure made up of many short contrasting sections which need to flow continuously to give the work unity. The sections are linked, and carried by a basic pulse which is common throughout, with only the final ground bass section detached by a short pause. Typical canzona-type entries are doubled by the organ. Cadential ornaments are added by the players. The three parts participate equally in the musical material. The second section is slightly free and rhapsodic in character developing different moods until moving seamlessly into a section with quicker notes. The final cadence of this section is allowed a slight pull up before commencing the last 4-note descending ground bass movement, which is in pathetic mood with many different falling figures. The extended closing cadence in duple time emerges without a sudden break or change of tempo. Many trio sonatas by mid-17th-century composers use this form in continuous, unbroken linked sections using a common pulse with changes of mood and material. They include Legrenzi, Buonamente, Fontana, Castello, Buxtehude, Purcell and Blow. See section 3.5 for more performance information about the Italian 17th-century sonata.

Audio examples commentary

Track 12	Alessandro Stradella (1644-1682), Sonata a otto Viole con una Tromba
Scoring	Baroque instruments: Trumpet. Choir 1: violin, 2 violas, bass violin. Choir 2: violin, 2 violas, bass violin. Continuo: theorbo, great bass viol, organ
Pitch	$a^1 = 415$
Temperament	Vallotti
Edition	Arno Volk Verlag, Koln. Complete instrumental music of Stradella

Another work in short sections which should hang together by using related tempi. The rich eight part texture is split into two choirs which answer and compliment each other in short phrases before joining together for a resolving cadence. The basic style is full, singing, and harmonically based. The harmony often lurches suddenly in a cadence-avoidance exercise, before resolving normally. In the canzona-like section listen for trills starting on the note in the rising figure. The work ends with a cheerful triple section with many short answering phrases.

Tracks 13-17	Gottfried Finger (d. 1730), Sonata in C major
Scoring	Baroque instruments: Trumpet, violin, oboe. Continuo: bass violin, organ
Pitch	$a^1 = 415$
Temperament	Vallotti
Edition	Musica Rara

A sonata in through-composed Italian style consisting of many short sections, some of which run freely into one another. The three solo instruments introduce various contrasting figures which get passed around the group. The violin then changes the character to a reflective mood which develops into a cadenza-like passage (the bass becomes static) leading to a 'song' theme which is taken up by the trumpet and oboe. A canzona in triple time leads to a new more lively conversation between the trumpet and oboe. The violin interrupts this in a dramatic outburst, leading to a robust swaggering allegro where the three instruments finally agree, ending on a humorous note. The characters of the instruments and their musical material are well defined to make the most of the contrasting points which are developed before the next new idea is presented. Strict tempo sections are set against freer rhapsodic passages for the violin. The style of composition is similar to that of the sonatas of Biber and Schmelzer, with free passages over a static bass set among sections with continuous fast notes, and others of a more contrapuntal canzona-like style, where all parts participate equally.

Tracks 18-24	Matthew Locke (1621/2-1677), Suite of Brawles in B♭ First Brawl, Second Brawl, Leading Brawl, Gavott, Corant, Saraband, Conclusion
Scoring	Renaissance band: 4 violins, 2 viola 1, 2 viola 2, 4 bass violins
Pitch	$a^1 = 440$
Temperament	Vallotti
Edition	facsimile of *The Rare Theatrical* music for London Entertainment ed. Peter Holman

The first three dances form a continuous sequence, with the mood changing for each section. The rule of down-bow is much used for emphasis, as the cross-rhythms are complicated and lively. French style small graces are added by the performers for ornamentation, particularly at cadences. All the parts move together in harmonic intention, without much independent part writing, except for passing notes in the inner parts. When the inner parts fulfill the role of being the written out continuo, as in large dance bands of this type and in theatre music, chordal continuo instruments are often omitted. A poised gavott follows the Brawls, then comes a graceful corant and a fast (as was the custom in the 17th century) saraband which leads seamlessly into the up-beat conclusion.

Tracks 25-28	Matthew Locke, Suite in C major 'The Broken Consort' no. 4. (1661) Fantasy, Corant, Air, Saraband
Scoring	Renaissance instruments: 2 violins, bass viol. Continuo: 3 theorbos, organ (doubling)
Pitch	$a^1 = 440$
Temperament	115 comma mean-tone
Edition	Musica Britannica, Matthew Locke chamber music vol. II

After the introductory chords, the fantasy moves into full contrapuntal style. There are many contrasting sections, in free and strict tempo, all introducing new points which are characterised. The three parts participate equally in this exchange. The fast corant has lots of echo effects (indicated). French ornaments are added. The air is reflective with the two upper parts conversing sadly in agreement. In the second section an angry mood appears with larger intervals and more pointed rhythms. The ending returns to the calm mood. The fast wild saraband has tantalising cross-rhythms and dotted figures which are pointed and playful. See pp. 98-99 on the 17th-century suite, and part 3.6 on consort style.

Tracks 29-31	John Jenkins (1592-1678), Fantasia Suite in E minor. Fantasia, Alman, Saraband
Scoring	Renaissance instruments: 3 violins, bass viol, organ
Pitch	$a^1 = 440$
Temperament	115 comma mean-tone
Edition	Peter Holman (unpub.)

The rich sonority of three violins is quickly established with the three entries. The three violins and bass viol take an equal share in the part writing. The fantasy develops slowly before new faster lively figures are introduced. The tempo remains the same. Points are shaped in each individual part without regard for bar-line position. After the main cadence the harmony is expanded with slow material for the richness of the final close. The alman is lively with lots of imitation of small points in the 2nd section. The cadential close is re-iterated before the repeat is taken. The fast saraband again passes round small figures between the parts before they unite for cadences. See pp. 98-99 on the suite and p. 118 on the saraband.

Track 32	William Corbett (d1748), Overture from Suite in D major
Scoring	Baroque instruments: 2 trumpets, 2 oboes, bassoon, string orchestra 4 violin 1, 3 violin 2, 2 violas, 4 bass violins, continuo harpsichord.
Pitch	$a^1 = 415$
Temperament	Vallotti
Edition	Peter Holman (unpub.)

The up-beat quaver is played as written, i.e. without over-dotting or shortening. The dotted quaver-semiquaver rhythms are lively. This practice is carried through the first section. The fugue is commenced without ritardando. Listen for the variety in the performance of the two-note up-beat figure in the fugue theme, and for cross-beat hemiola figures. See section 3.4 Dotted notes.

Audio examples commentary

Tracks 33-35	Henry Purcell (1659-1695), Music in 'The Double Dealer'. Overture, Hornpipe, Minuet.
Scoring	Baroque instruments: 2 violins, viola, bass violin, continuo theorbo, harpsichord
Pitch	$a^1 = 415$
Temperament	116 comma mean-tone
Edition	Purcell Society; facsimile parts available from Jacks Pipes and Hammers, or Performers' Facsimiles

Note the strong/weak harmonic emphasis in the first duple section of the overture, and how the fast notes fit gracefully in between the main beats without being aggressively overdotted. There is no ritardando before the fugal section. Note the change in the character of the material half way through the fugue after a series of cross rhythms where equal full quaver upbeats start to appear. The transition to the sweet closing section is relaxed before the fugue is repeated. The final cadence has a French-style appoggiatura added in the viola part. The Hornpipe is in a very steady three with well-defined phrasing by the whole group. The minuet has slightly *inégales* quavers. French style trills, *tierces coulé* and appoggiaturas are added. See part 3.4 dotted notes; 2.5, dance, and 3.2 alterations to written rhythms in the French style.

Track 36	Henry Purcell, Music in 'King Arthur'; or, 'the British Worthy'. Chaconne
Scoring	Baroque instruments: 4 violin 1, 3 violin 2, 3 violas, 3 bass violin, 1 great bass viol, 4 oboes, 2 bassoons. Continuo theorbo, guitar, harpsichord
Pitch	$a^1 = 415$
Temperament	116 comma mean-tone
Edition	King's Music; facsimile parts available from Jacks Pipes and Hammers or Performers' Facsimiles

Listen for unequal quavers combined with dotted notes. Trills are liberally added in all parts. The minor section is particularly pathetic and slightly held back in tempo, which picks up for the concluding major section for a happy ending with very little ritardando. The final note is not held much longer than its written value, but 'placed'. See pp. 103-105 chaconne.

INDEX

For meanings of words see Glossary.
Page numbers of musical examples are prefixed by ex.

Abbé le Fils, *see* L'Abbé le fils
Accidentals, 20, 248-249, 251
   see also Chromatic movement
Accompanying,
   level of tutti, 23-24
   ornamentation, 37-38
   Purcell songs, 215
   rubato, 31
   vibrato, 61, 62
Acoustic, 136
Affect,
   appoggiatura, 51
   bow-stroke, 17
   bow vibrato, 129-133
   communication, of 2
   dance, 98, 100
   dances, see individual entries
   dissonance, 21
   dotted notes, 92, 178
   dynamic, 18, 20
   harmony, 204-205
   intervals, 5-6
   Italian, 30, 181
   key, 7, 188-189
   meaning, 2
   national style, 158
   ornamentation, 34-35, 48, 51, 55, 56, 58
   overture, 174, 176
   rhythm, 170
   speed, 135
   tempo words, 29
   walking bass, ex. 4
Affekt, see Affect
Affetti, 131
Agricola, Martin,
   rules, 263
   tuning, 194
   vibrato, 58
Alberti, ♫
   Pavan and galliard, ex.108
Albergati, Bernadino, 211
Allemande,
   affect, 100, 101
   allemande & courante pair, 99
   tempo, 26
   J. S. Bach, ex. 101
Alman, 101
Alternativo, 99
Amati, Andrea, 238
Amati Brothers, A. & H., 226, 238
Amati, Nicolo, 239
Amen cadence, 127
Anapest, 94
Andante, 137, 167

Brossard, 30
   Leopold Mozart, 27
   North, 29
   with tempo word, 30
   J. S. Bach, ex. 16, ex. 226
Appoggiatura, 37, 51-55
Appuyé, 52
Aquila Strings, 247
A-R Editions, 259
Arbeau, Thoinot,
   dance rhetoric, 98
Arching, of violin table, 234-240
Arpeggios, 15
   Corelli, 136
   instruction, 152
   J. S. Bach, ex. 120
   Corelli, ex. 42
Articulation, 9-17
   allegro, 134
   dotted notes, 15
   emphasis, 14, 15
   repetitions, 10
   signs, for 16-17
   slurs, 142-148
Aspiration, 16
Audience, 2, 24, 26, 33
Austria, *see* Bohemia/Austria

Bach, Carl Philipp Emanuel,
   continuo choice, 209
   dotted notes, 177
   dissonance, 6
   father's,
      French taste, 168
      viola playing, 223
   ornamentation, 34, 35, 51, 56, ex. 55, 57
   speed, 135
   treatise, 261
Bach, Johann Sebastian,
   arrangements, 230
   bow vibrato, 132-133
   French taste, 168
   gigues, 110
   inequality, 168
   recitative, 219-222
   sarabandes, 119
   slurs, 144
   suite or partita, 99
   viola, 223
   Works,
      Brandenburg Concertos,
         no. 1, violino piccolo, ex. 202
         no. 3, 230

INDEX

no. 4, Presto, ex. 4, 93, ex. 154, ex. 224
no. 5, Allegro, ex. 171
no. 6, 230
double bass, 216
Cantata 202, gavotte, 110
Christmas Oratorio, 1st chorus, ex. 79, ex. 133
Concerto for harpsichord in D minor, Allegro, ex. 3
Magnificat, 'Esurientes', pizzicato, 8
Mass in B minor,
   Crucifixus, rhythm, 3
   Domine deus, ex. 53
   Et in unum, slurs & dots, ex. 16
   up-bow staccato, ex. 141
St. John Passion,
   recitative, ex. 219, ex. 222
   Erwäge, ex. 93
   final chorus, ex. 11
   viola d'amore, 230-231
St. Matthew Passion,
   recitative, ex. 220, ex. 221
   Erbarme dich, ex. 12, ex. 23
   Gebt mir meinen Jesum wieder, ex. 32, ex. 225
Sonata for viola da gamba and harpsichord, arr. Druce, ex. 257
Sonatas and Partitas for solo violin,
   Sonata in G minor,
     Prelude, ex. 41
     Siciliana, ex. 151
     Presto, ex. 139
   Sonata in A minor, Grave, ex. 154
   Partita in D minor for solo violin,
     Allemande, ex. 101
     Chaconne, ex. 152, ex. 155, ex. 156
     Corrente, ex. 144
     Sarabande, ex. 53, ex. 120
     Giga, ex. 139
   Partita in E major, Loure, ex. 112
   Partita in B minor,
     Corrente, ex. 105
     Sarabande & double, 119, ex. 120
Sonatas for violin and harpsichord,
   no. 1 in B minor, Adagio, ex. 14
   no. 2 in A major, ex. 152
   no. 3 in E major,
     Adagio, ex. 42
     Allegro, ex. 172
   no. 4 in C minor,
     Largo, ex. 121
     Adagio, ex. 6, ex. 172
   no. 6 in G major, Allegro, ex. 12
Suites for solo cello
   no. 1, Corrente, ex. 105
   no. 3, Sarabande, 120
   no. 4, Sarabande, ex.120
   no. 5, Prelude, 197, ex. 197
Suites, Orchestral,
   no. 1,
     Bourée, ex. 102
     Courante, ex. 107
     Forlana, ex. 108
     Gavotte, ex. 109
     Passepied, ex. 115
   no. 2,
     Menuet, ex. 93
     Overture, ex. 175
     Polonaise, ex. 116
     Rondeau, ex. 118
     Sarabande, ex. 37

   no. 4, air, ex. 55
Well-Tempered Clavier, 188
Baillot, Pierre, v
Ballets, *see* Dance
Baltzar, Thomas, 76, 81, 156
Bariolage, 67, 73, 136, 152, 154, 155, 197
Bar-lines, 184, 249, 252-253, 256-257
Baroque,
   instruments, 235-240
   meaning, 157
Bass-bar, 233-234, (illus) 237, 239
Bass line, *see* Basso continuo
Bass violin, 213-215, 226
   hold, 70
   tuning, 238
Bassano, Giovanni, 34, 39
Basse de violon, *see* Bass violin
Basso continuo, 180, 203-222
   choice of instrument, 208-217
Basso di viola, 212
Batteur de mesure, 30
Beams, 249
Beat, *see* Tempo, Time signatures
Bebung, *see* Vibrato
Bergamasca, 39, ex. 208
Berlin school, 35, 45, 52, 57, 261
Biber, Heinrich Ignaz Franz von,
   chords, 155
   ground bass sonata, 182
   Italian style, 181
   upward range, 67, 80
   Works,
     Battalia, 8
     Harmonia Artificiosa,
       no. 3, 198
       no. 7, 231
     Mensa Sonora, viola parts, 228
     'Rosary' sonatas,
       no. 4, Ciacona, ex. 141
       no. 10, 199
       no. 11, tuning, ex. 199
       no. 12, Intrada, ex. 198
       no. 16, Passagalia, ex. 114
     Sonatas (1681),
       nos. 1 and 2, ex. 138
       no. 6, re-tuning, ex. 200
Blanc, Hubert Le, *see* Le Blanc, Hubert
Blow, John, 169
Bohemia/Austria, 67, 79, 155, 181, 199, 214
Bonnet-Bourdelet family, 159
Bononcini, Giovanni Maria, 211, 239
Bonporti, Francesco Antonio,
   Invenzione VI, ex. 150
Borin,
   on tempo, 26
Boston Catlines, 247
Bouman, (illus) 242
Bourdon, 114
Bourée, 102
   tempo, 26
Bow,
   Baroque, 155, 194, 241, (illus) 242
   hold, 83-87, 241
     cello, 86
     double bass, 87
     underhand, 86
   position, 69
   pressure, 122, 136

INDEX

screw, 241
speed,
    affect, 3, 21
    Grave, 28
    with pressure, 124
    strokes,
        even, 91-92
        Lullian, 9
        Tartini, 134, 136
tension of hair, 86, 241
Bowers, Martin,
    violins, (illus) 237,
    bows, (illus) 242
Bow vibrato, 129-133
Bowings,
    cadences, 222
    signs for, 262
    see also
        Rule of down-bow
        individual dance entries
Boyce, William,
    minuets, 113
Bremner, Robert, 62
Brescia, 238
Bridge, 74, 123, 155, 194, 233-234, (illus) 237, 239
Brossard, Sébastien de,
    basso continuo, 203, 213
    basso di viola, 212
    bow vibrato, 131
    trillo, 50
    gigue, 110
    intrada, 112
    Italian mixed time signatures, 170
    loure, 112
    passacaille, 114
    spiccato, 134
    strings, 245
Bryant, Percy, (illus) 242
Buonamente, Giovanni Battista, 211
Buono (good notes), 19, 89, 125
    see also Cattivo
Burney, Charles, 261
    Corelli, 76, 89
    Geminiani's rubato, 31
    Vandini's bow hold, 86
Burwell Lute Tutor, 2, 164, 168
Buxtehude, Dietrich, 37, 89, 181, 209, 214, 216

Caccini, Giulio,
    trillo, ex. 50
Cadences, 203
    articulation, 10
    bowings, 222
    plagal, 127
    punctuation, 9
    recitative, 221-222
    tempo, 25
    weak, 12, 129
Cadential trill, 37, 47
Cadenza,
    at pauses, 32
    over pedal, 181
Caesura, *see* Rests
Cammerthon, 193
Canaries, 102-103, 92
Cantabile, *see* Style, singing
Canzona,
    meaning, 180
    tempo, 29
Case studies,
    alteration of rhythms, ex. 178
    anapest rhythm, ex. 94-95
    articulation, ex. 12-15
    dotted rhythms, ex. 95-97
    inequality, ex. 165-168
    Italian bowing style, ex. 95
    long notes, ex. 128
    loud rest, ex .93-94
    quick notes, ex. 138-140
    rule of down-bow, ex. 93
    slurs, ex. 144
    syncopation, ex. 94
Castello, Dario, 80, 181
La Giustiniana,
    Sinfonia a 3, ex. 256
    Sonate Concertate, Libro Secondo (1627), ex. 145
    Sonata prima, ex. 51
    Sonata seconda, ex. 131
Catlines, 245
Cattivo (bad notes), 19, 20, 89
Cavalli, Francesco ♪, 211
Cazzati, Maurizio, 99, 183, 211
Cello,
    continuo, 203-222
        France, 213-214
        Italy, 210-213
    expresses harmony, 20, 204-205
    invention, 239
    ornamentation, 37
    strings, 245-246
    thumb position, 82
    tunings, 197, 202, 214
Chaconne, 103-104
    affect, 100
    tempo, 26
    Corelli, 99
    Marais, ex. 146
    see also Passacaille
Chambonnières, J. Champion de, 43
Changing position, see Position changing
Charles II of England, 106, 168, 226
Charpentier, Marc-Antoine,
    ensembles, 213, 226
    hierarchy of beats, 88
    key affect, 7
    Rules, 264
    Te deum, ex. 228
Chiavette, 236
Chin, use of, 63-69
Chin-rest, 63
Chords, 74 149-156, 155, 158
Chorton, 193
Christina, Queen of Sweden, 182
Chromatic movement,
    affect, 6
    crescendo and stress in, 19, 206
    slides, 79
    trills, 46
Ciacona, *see* Chaconne
Cicero, Marcus Tullius, 1
Cima, Giovanni Paulo, 180, 211
    sonata (1610), ex. 212
Classical instruments, 235-237, 240
Clefs, 249
    in facsimile, 254-255

INDEX

as indications of continuo, 210
   Corelli, ex. 255
   viola, 226-228
Clip-in frog, 241
Close shake, *see* Vibrato
Colombi, Giuseppe, 182
Comic affect, 3,
   J. S. Bach, ex. 4
Consort,
   repertoire, 226
   style, 184-185
Continuo, *see* Basso continuo
Contrapuntal style, *see*
   Style
   Counterpoint
Corant, 105
   dynamics, 22
Corbett, William, ♪
Corda Music, 259
Corelli, Arcangelo, 1
   Geminiani arrangements, 229
   ground bass sonata, 182
   Muffat's inspiration, 162
   orchestral discipline, 89
   upward range, 67, 76
   no minuets, 113
   pitch, 193
   sonatas da camera, 99
   sonatas in England, 84
   style of composition, 157, 182
   Works,
      Sonatas op. 1, continuo, 211
      Sonatas op. 2, no. 2,
         Allemanda Adagio, ex. 101
        no. 5, Tempo di Gavotta, ex. 109
        no. 6,
           Allemanda Largo, ex. 101
           Corrente Allegro, ex. 105
        no. 7, Giga, ex. 111
        no. 8, Sarabanda, ex. 119
      Sonatas op. 5,
        no. 1,
           Adagio, ex. 254
           Grave, ex. 36
           Allegro, ex. 42, ex. 140
        no. 6, Adagio, ex. 128
        no. 7, Giga, ex. 23, ex. 148
        no. 10, Allemanda Allegro, ex. 102
        no. 11, Gavotta, ex. 146
        no. 12, 'La Follia', 39, 210
        ornaments for op. 5, 36, 43
      Concerti grossi op. 6,
        no. 2,
           Allegro, ex. 47
           Largo andante, ex. 206
        no. 3,
           Grave, Allegro, Vivace, ex. 95
           Allegro, ex. 170
        no. 4,
           Adagio, ex. 132
           Allegro, ex. 171
        no. 8 'Christmas', Grave, ex. 15
        no. 10, Adagio, ex. 3
        no. 11,
           Andante largo, ex. 4
           Vivace, ex. 5
Corrette, Michel,
   bow hold, (illus) 84-85

bowings, ex. 88
cello hold, 70
   invention, 239
   thumb position, 82
   tunings, 238
dances with bowings,
   chaconne, ex. 104
   corrente, 153
   entrée, ex. 107
   menuet, ex. 113
   rigaudon, ex. 117
double bass tutor, 224
duets, 260
messa di voce, ex. 126
staccato & spiccato, 134
time signatures for inequality, 163
sarabande, ex. 126
violin hold, 65
   open strings, 154
   positions used, 81
   scordatura, 200, ex. 201
   Pièces a Cordes Ravallées, ex. 201
   positions, ex. 257
   rests, ex. 252
   viola tutor, 224
Corrente, 105, 144, 153
Coulé, *see* Tierces coulé
Coulé du doigt, 56
Counterpoint,
   in double stopping, 151, 155, 156
   viola part, 224, 228
   see also Style, contrapuntal
Couperin, François,
   continuo choice, 213
   inequality, 163
   ornaments, 43, ex. 44, 48
   phrasing and articulation, 13
   on measure and cadence, 25
   slurs, 144, 146
   Works,
      Apothéose de Lully,
        Sonade en trio, ex. 165, ex. 255
        rondement, ex. 27, ex. 167
      Concerts,
        1ier,
           Gavotte, ex. 167, ex. 250
           Menuet, ex. 250
        2ième, ex. 44
           Echos, ex. 146
        3ième,
           Chaconne legere, ex. 105
           musette, ex. 114
        4ième,
           Courantes Françoise, a L'italiene, ex. 106
           rigaudon, ex. 117
        7ième, sarabande grave, ex. 210
        8ième,
           Air Léger, Air de Baccantes, ex. 14
           Air Tendre, ex. 166
           Grande Ritournele, ex. 21, ex. 256
           Loure, ex. 112
           Ouverture, ex. 165, ex. 178
           Saraband, ex. 119
      L'Art de Toucher le Clavecin, ex. 44, 261
Courante, 106-107
   affect, 100
   Couperin, ex. 106, ex. 250
   crotchet length, 176

INDEX

Locke, ex. 106
Muffat, ex. 106
tempo, 26
pair with allemande, 99
Craquer, 90, 91, 102, 106, 107, ex. 113, ex. 117
Croches blanche, *see* white notation
Croft, William, 169
Crome, Robert,
    tuning, 188
    violin hold, 66, 67

Da camera, *see* Sonata
Da chiesa, *see* Sonata
Da gamba, *see* Viol
Daggers, *see* Signs
Dalla Casa, Girolamo, 34, 39
Dance, 98-121
    common phrase structure, 11
    emphasis of beats, 20
    playing for, 33
    social function, 100
Dance bands, 100, 214, 215, 226, 260
    bow hold, 83
Dancing masters, 67, 68, 168, 241
d'Anglebert, Jean Henry, 43
Danoville (first name unknown), 56, 73
Dashes, *see* Signs
Dendrochronology, 239
Descartes, René, 2
de Selma, Bartolomeo, *see* Selma, Bartolomeo de
Dissonance,
    affect of, 6, 204
    appoggiatura, 52
    dynamic level, 21, 204
    emphasis of, 20, 36, 154, 206
    Italian style, 158
    long notes, 127
Dittersdorf, Carl Ditters von, 229
Division-viol, The, *see* Simpson, Christopher
Division-violin, The, *see* Playford, John
Divisions, 34, 38-41
    affetti, 131
    on grounds, 39
    rushing, 135
    use of 4th finger, 75
Dlugolecki, Damian, 247
Dodd, Edward, 241, (illus) 242
Doe, Roger, (illus) 242
Dots, *see* Signs
Dotted notes, 174-179
    articulation, 15, 16
    bow technique for, 95-97
    bow-stroke,
        canaries, 102-103
        entrée, loure and courante, 107
        lifted, 92
    French music, 16, 157, 167
    gigue bowings, 110
    position of little note, 92
    sarabande, 119
    siciliana, 121
    used for position changing, 77
Double bars, 249-250
Double bass, 215, 235, 240-241, 246
Double stopping, 149-156, 158
Doucement, *see* Tempo
Dowland, John, 226

Down-bow, *see* Rule of down-bow
Dragonetti, Domenico Carlo Maria, 87
Dupont, 263
Dynamics, 18-24
    bow-stroke, 23
    editorial, 248
    influence of tessitura, 6, 20
    crescendo/diminuendo, 19
    figured bass, 204
    French, 160
    for harmonic surprise, 206-207
    Italian, 160, 181
    markings, absence of markings, 21, 23
    in slur, 142
    3rd position for piano, 78

Editions, ex. 144, ex. 156, 248-249, ex. 253-254, 257-259
Eighteenth-century suite, 99-100
Eisel, Johann Philipp, 192
Elbow, position of in violin playing, 86
Emotion, *see* Affect
Emphasis, equal, 17
    harmonic, 19-20
    ornament, 35
Enfler, 126
England,
    dotted notes, 96, 168
    bass instruments, 213-214
    ensemble, 226
    inequality, 168
    Italian style in, 183
    Jigs, 111
    scordatura, 200
    17th-century violinists, 84, 156
    theatre suite, 99
Enharmonic tuning, 188
Ensembles,
    discipline, 89
    double bass in, 215
    French five-part, 226
    orchestral piano, 23
    ornamentation in, 36, 38
    vibrato, 62
Entrée, 107
    crotchet length, 176
    rhythm, 2
    tempo, 26
Equal,
    bow-strokes, 91-92
    quavers (égales), 27
    string tension, 245
    temperament, 187
Equipment, 233-247
    French/Italian, 160
Extempore *see* Ornamentation
    preludes, 101

Facsimile, 248-259
Falck, Georg,
    positions used, 81
    shifting, 79
    tuning, 191
    violin hold, 65
Fantasia, 184
    Gibbons, ex. 252
Fantasia-suite, *see* Seventeenth-century suite

INDEX

Farina, Carlo, 261
    bow vibrato, 130, 145
    pizzicato, 8
Fast bow-stroke, *see* Bow speed
Fer, Jambe de, Philibert, 260
    hold,
        bass instruments, 70
        violin, 64
Feuillet, Raoul-Auger,
    Canarie, ex. 103
    Folie d'Espagne, ex. 103
    Forlana, ex. 108
    Gigue, ex. 110
    Passepied, ex. 115
    Rigaudon, ex. 117
    Sarabande, ex. 119
Figured bass, 203-207
    unfigured bass, 204
    see also Basso continuo
Finger, Godfried, ♪, 81
Fingerboard, 194, 233-234
Fingering choice, 72-82
    counterpoint, 151
    scordatura, 197
Fischer, Johann, 168
Flackton, William, 223, 230
Flattement, 60
Flute, 100
    dynamic level, 24
    J. S. Bach, ex. 37, ex. 93
    flattement, 60
Follia, Folies d'Espagne, 39, 99, 120, 182
    Feuillet, ex. 103
    Playford, ex. 103
Fontana, Giovanni Battista, 131, 181, 211, 261
Forkel, Johann Nikolaus, 223
Forlana, 107
    Couperin, ex. 251
Forqueray, J. B., 156
Forte, *see* Dynamics
France,
    bow grip, 83-85
    bowing style, 90
    clef, 255
    continuo chamber/orchestral, 213
    courante, ex. 106
    dotted style, 174
    ensemble, 80, 226-228
    forms, 158
    gigue, 112
    ornaments, 41, 43-44, 55
    overture, 99, 174-6
    pitch, 193
    range, 158
    recitative, 26, 220-221
    slurs, 146
    style, 158-161
    tempo markings, 26-27
    tunings for cello/bass violin, 238
    viol players, 156
Frescobaldi, Girolamo, 30
Frets, 58
    violin, 60, 72, 192
    double bass, 216, 240
Fretwork Editions, 259
Frog, 241-242
Fugue, tempo, 25, 26, 29
    see also Style, contrapuntal

Fuhrmann, Martin, 37
Fux, Johann Joseph, 201
Fuzeau, 258

Gabrieli, Giovanni, 180
Galant style, *see* Style, galant
Galliard, 108
    tempo, 26
    pair with pavane, 99
Ganassi, dal Fontego, Sylvestro di, 34, 142, 236
Gauges of strings, 244-246
Gavotte, 109
    Couperin, ex. 251
    tempo, 26
Gayement *see* Tempo
Geminiani, Francesco,
    bow hold, 85
    bow technique, 86
    buono and cattivo, 98
    Composition 1a, ex. 125
    Corelli op. 5 no. 9 (ornamented version), ex. 43
    dynamics 18, ex. 79
    Essempio
        IB (hold), 66
        IC & D (position changing), ex. 76
        X (3rd position), ex. 78
        XII (fingering), ex. 74, ex. 78
        XVIII, no. 7 & 8 (swell), ex. 125
        XXI (arpeggios), ex. 152
        XXIV (even bowing), ex. 92
    mordent, 56
    positions, 81
    pupil/teacher, 62, 182, 183
    rubato when leading, 31
    slurs, ex. 143
    swell, 123, 125
    treatise, 262
    vibrato, 58, 61, 125-6
    viola solo, 228-229
    violin hold, 66, 68
Gerle, Hans, 243
Germany,
    continuo, 214
    double bass, 216
    inequality and French style, 168
    mixed style, 161
    string scoring, 228
    tempo, 27
Gibbons, Orlando, ♪
    Fantasia in 3 parts no. 8, ex. 252-253
Gig
    Corelli, ex. 23
    character, 2
Gigue, 110, 92
    affect, 100
    duple meter, 170-171
Gique, 110
Grabu, Louis, 168
Gracieux, Gracieusement, *see* Tempo
Grassineau, James, 101
Grave, gravement, *see* Tempo
Great bass viol, 209, 215
Greensleeves, 39
Ground bass,
    chaconne, 103, ex. 115
    passacaille, ex. 114
    sonata, 182

INDEX

Gruppo, 51
Guarneri, Andrea, 239
Guarneri, Giuseppe 'del Gesù', 239
Guignon, Jean-Pierre, 190
Gut strings, *see* Strings

Halle, 194
Handel, George Frederick,
    Concerti grossi minuets, 113
    inégale, 113
    Suite or overture, 99
    Works,
        Concerto Grosso
            op. 3 no. 1, ex. 154
            op. 3 no. 2, Gavotte, ex. 173
            op. 3 no. 3, Allegro, ex. 225
            op. 6 no.1,
                A tempo giusto, ex. 141
                Allegro, ex. 5
                fugue, ex. 6
            op. 6 no. 6, musette, ex. 114
            op. 6 no. 7, hornpipe, ex. 94
            op. 6 no. 8,
                Grave, ex. 4
                siciliana, ex. 121
            op. 6 no. 9, Largo, ex. 6
            op. 6 no. 10, overture, ex. 175
    Israel in Egypt, ex. 144
    Messiah,
        Overture, ex. 96
        And lo! And suddenly, ex. 221
        Comfort ye, ex. 132
        Blessing and honour, ex. 94-95
        Recit. He that dwelleth in heaven shall laugh them to scorn, 2
        I know that my redeemer liveth, ex. 11
        Pastoral symphony, 121
        Thou shalt break them, ex. 32
    Sonata in A major, Adagio, ex. 42
Hand-grip notation, 75, 197-198
Hanging dot, 253
Harmonics, 75-76
Harmony, 6, 20
    chords, 149
    cellist, 20
    chaconne, 104
    fast passages, 137, 138, 139
    rhetoric 1, 129
Hartlib, Samuel, 245
Heinichen, J. D., 7, 218
Hemiola, 11, 12-13, 109, 113, 115, 129, 249, 254
Hierarchy, 19, 20, 61, 88, 127, 164
Hill, Thomas, 210
Holding the instrument,
    violin/viola, 63-69
    bass instruments, 70
Hornpipe, 111
    Handel, ex. 94
Hotteterre, Jacques, 56
Hummel, Johann Nepomuk, 229

Imitation, 37, 159, 184
Inégales, see inequality
Inequality,
    rhythmic, 15 163-169
        allemande, 101
        bourée, 102
        case study, 178
        entrée, 107
        gavotte, 110
        sarabande, 119
    Tuning, *see* Temperament
Instruction books, *see* Treatises
Instrumental colours, 8
    affect of key, 7
Instruments, 233-241
Intervals,
    articulation between various, 15
    rhetorical affects, 5-6, 12
Intonation *see* Temperament
Intrada, 112
Italy,
    advanced school of playing, 74
    alignment of note values, 170
    J. S. Bach, ex. 119, ex. 120
    Bohemian composers, 155
    bowing style, 95, 160, 241
    clef, 255
    continuo choice, 210
    courante, 106
    dance music, early, 99
    Muffat,
        concerto descriptions, 22, 100, 161
        tempo, 30
    equal quavers, 27
    forms, 158
    gavotte, 109
    giga, 112
    gigue, 111
    inequality, 163, 165
    instruments, 236, 239
    ornaments, 43, ex. 44, 158-160, 181
    recitative, 218-219
    scordatura, 199
    slurs, 145
    sonata, see Sonata
    strings, 245
    style, 158-161, 183
    swell/long notes, 124-133
    tempo words, 26, 28, 30
    violinists see separate entries for Corelli, Locatelli, Marini, Matteis, Tessarini, Uccellini, Veracini, Vivaldi

Jacks, Pipes & Hammers, 258
Jambe de Fer, Philibert *see* Fer, Jambe de
Jenkins, John, ♫
Johnson, Robert, ♫

Key,
    affects, 6-7, 188-189
    signatures, 248, 251
King's Music, 258
Kircher, Athanasius, 180, 238
Kit, 236
Kreisler, Fritz, 246
Kusser, Johann Sigismund, 161

L'Abbé le fils,
    arpeggios, ex. 153
    bow hold, 85
    bowings, ex. 91
    cadence appuyé, ex. 52

INDEX

cadence subite, ex. 54
chin-rest, 63
duets, 260
gigue, ex. 110
menuet, ex. 113
tierce coulé, ex. 54
trills, ex. 46
violin hold, 67
Lanzetti, Salvatore, 82
Larson, Daniel, 247
Latour, Daniel, (illus) 242
Lebègue, Nicolas-Antoine, 43
Le Blanc, Hubert,
   cello, 160-161
   changing position, 77
   harmonics, 75
   Italian/French style, 159, 161
   Lullian bow-strokes, 9
Leclair, Jean-Marie,
   double stopping, 156
   Sonata V, book III, ex. 149
Legato, *see* Style, singing
Léger, Légèrement, *see* Tempo
Legrenzi, Giovanni, 183
Length of note, 3
Lent, *see* Tempo
Lenton, John, 262
   bow hold, 84
   bowing rules, 90
   ornaments, 41
   violin hold, 65, 67
   vibrato, 61
Linerol, 238
Locatelli, Pietro,
   L'Arte del Violino, ex. 81
   range, 80
Locke, Matthew, ♪
   hornpipe, 111
   Little Consort preface, 39
   Broken Consort suite in C major, ex. 32, ex. 184
      saraband ex. 118
   Suite no. 1 'for several friends', pavan, ex. 116
   Suite of Brawles, 215
Lombardini, Maddalena, 48, 122
Lonati, Carlo Ambrogio, 182, 183
London Pro Musica, 259
Long notes, 122-129
   rhetorical significance, 3
   trills, 49
Louis XIV, 100, 106, 213, 226
Loulié, Etienne, inequality, 168, 169
   rules, 263
   time signatures, 26
Loure, 112, 176
Lourer, 164
Lully, Jean-Baptiste,
   fashion in England, 183
   Isis, tremblers' chorus, 131
   orchestral discipline, 89
   orchestral style, 160
   mute, 8
   pupils, 168
   recitative, ex. 220
   speed of entrée, 26
   style of composition, 157
Lute, 100
   imitation of by pizzicato, 8
   rhetorical properties, 8

strings, 245
Lyons (strings), 245

Mace, Thomas,
   allmaines, 101
   bow hold, 84
   chords, 149
   coranto, 105
   dynamics, 18
   fashion in instruments, 233
   galliards, 108
   interval affect, 205
   key affect, 189
   metronome (pendulum), 31
   pavan, 116
   saraband, 118
   speed, 135
   strings, 244-245
   toys and Jiggs, 111
   trills, 49, 50
Maggini, Giovanni Paol, 238
Makers,
   Renaissance period, 236-237
   Baroque period, 237, 239
Malcolm, Alexander, tempo words, 30
Marais, Marin, 261
   double stopping, 156
   Pièces de Viole, 3ième livre, Sarabande, ex. 126
   Pièces en trio, ex. 47, ex. 147
   vibrato, 60, 126
Marini, Biagio, 261
   sonata op. 1, 'La Foscarina', ex. 129
   op. 8, 'd'Inventione', 199 145
Markings, *see* Signs
Matteis, Nicola,
   bow grip, 84
   bow-stroke, 122, 159
   chords, 149, 156
   dynamics, 18
   Italian style of playing, 59, 183
   loure, 112
   per far la mano, ex. 39-40
   ornaments, 35
   speed, 135
   style of playing, 159
   tempo/time signatures, 28
   violin hold, 65, 67
   Works,
      Ayrs for the Violin,
         First part, Sarabanda Amorosa ex. 45
         Second Part,
            Ricercata, ex. 149
            Sonata, ex. 145
         Third part,
            Aria, ex. 40,
            Adagio, ex. 44
Mattheson, Johann,
   affects of intervals, 5
   allemande, 101
   articulation, 9
   bow vibrato, 130
   canaries, 102
   chaconne, 103
   English dances, 111
   entree, 107
   French dots, 174
   gavotte, 109

INDEX

gigues (English) and similar dances, 110-111
intrada, 112
key affect, 7
minuet, 113
music for dancing, 100
overture affect, 175
passepied, 115
polonaise, 116
rhetorical devices, 2
rigaudon, 117
sarabande, 118, 120
siciliana, 121
temperament/tuning, 189
vibrato, 59-60
viola, 224
Maugars, Andre, 210, 263
Mealli, Giovanni Antonio Pandolfi,
    Sonata secunda, op. 3, Adagio, ex. 51
Mean-tone, *see* Temperament
Menuet *see* minuet
Merck, Daniel,
    positions used, 81
    tuning, 192, 238
    violin hold, 65
Mersenne, Marin,
    fingering divisions, 75
    intonation, 187
    invention of mute, 8
    positions used, 81
    singing tone of violin, 9
    tuning, 201, 238
    strings, (illus) 244-246
    twenty-four violins, 226
    vibrato, 58
Merula, Tarquinio, 180
Messa di voce, (swell), 21, 61, 75, 87, 123, 124-127, 129, 204
Methods, *see* Treatises
Metronome,
    Mace, 31
    Quantz, 121
Milandre, Louis, 231
Minkoff Editions, 258
Minuet, 113
    Mattheson, ex. 12-13
    Menuet,
        J. S. Bach, ex. 93
        Corrette, 201
        Couperin, ex. 250
        Purcell, ex. 250
    Purcell, ex. 168
    tempo, 26
Modère, see Tempo
Modern,
    chord execution, 149, 155
    pitch, 192
    set up for instrument, 155, (illus) 237
    tuning, 187
Mondonville, Jean-Joseph Cassenea de,
    harmonics, 75
Monteclair, Pignolet de,
    violin hold, 65, 68
Monteverdi, Claudio, continuo, 212
    pizzicato, 8
    stile concitato, 180
    tremolo, 130
    trillo, 50, 51
Mordent, 56

Morley, Thomas, ♪
    allemande, 101
    pavan & galliard, 99
    Southerne's Pavan and galliard, ex. 108
Mouvement,
    Bacilly, 25-26
    tempo, 29
Movement,
    Purcell, 28
Mozart, Leopold, 262
    appoggiaturas, ex. 52
    arpeggios, ex. 153
    bow hold, (illus) 83
    bow pressure, (illus) 123
    bow-stroke, 122, 130
    dotted rhythms, 136, 177
    dynamics, 18
    elbow position, 86
    emphasis of beats, 19
    fingering, ex. 72-75, 80
    harmonics, 75
    open strings, 74
    position changing, ex. 76-78
    position terminology, 81
    rushing, 136
    singing tone, 9
    slurs, ex. 142-143
    string thickness, 245
    tempo, 27-28
    trill, ex. 46
    vibrato, 58-9
    viola d'amore, 230
    violin hold, (illus) 66-67
Mozart, Wolfgang Amadeus, 229
Muffat, Georg,
    bow hold, 84-85
    bowing,
        rules, ex. 89-91, 263
        dances,
            Bourée, ex. 102
            Chaconne, ex. 104
            Courante, ex. 106
            Forlane, ex. 108
            Gigue, ex. 110
            Minuet, ex. 113
    double bass, 216
    French style, 168
    Lullian style, 160
    concertos, 22, 104, 228
    Florilegium suites, 100, 158
    Lully's airs de ballets, 89, 98
    style of concertos, 161
    time signatures, 26
    tuning, 192
    vibrato, 60
    viola size, 226
Musette, 114
Musica Repartita, 259
Mute, 8

National style *see* France, Germany, Italy
Neck,
    player, 64-67
    violin, 233-240
        length & thickness, 67-68
Niedt, Friedrich E., 218
Niedhart, Johann Georg, 188

INDEX

North, Roger,
    accoustic, 136
    bow vibrato, 131
    Corelli fashion, 183
    dynamics, 19, 21-22
    English fantasy suite, 98
    gavotte, 109
    Italian fashion, 158
    Italian ornamentation, 182
    Matteis, 18, 65, 84, 159
    rubato, 31
    open strings, 74
    ornamentation, 35, 36, 45, 47, 49
    Purcell, 158
    resonance, 176
    rushing, 135
    swell, 123
    tempo, 25
    tempo words, 29
    tunings, 188, 191
    vibrato, 59, 60
Notari, Angelo, ♪, 41
Notation,
    large note values, 29
    ornaments, 35
    see also White notation

Ondeggiando, 154
Open strings, 49, 72, 74, 76, 153
Oratory,
    aim of, 1
    classical sources, 1
    dance, 98
    Geminiani on dynamics, 18
    Le Blanc on style, 161 Quantz, 1
    raising the voice 2, 18, 19
    raising and soothing the passions, 2
    rhythm, 2
Orchestra, *see* Ensemble
Original instruments, 233
Ornamentation, 34-62
    appoggiatura, 37
    bad taste, 15, 36, 37, 39
    Corelli's, 254
    dances, 98
    divisions, 38-41
    essential graces, 43-56
    extempore, 34, 37, 38, 39
    French style, 158
    Geminiani-Corelli, ex. 43
    Italian style, 42-43, 158, 181
    mordent, 56
    slurs, 146
    tierces coulés, 53
    trillo, 50
    trills, 45-51
    turns, 55-56
    written out, 34, 41-43
Ortiz, Diego, 34, 261
    Divisions on a falling 2nd, ex. 38
    ornamentation, 57
    slurs, 142, 145
Overture, 99
    affect, 100, 174
    dotted notes, 174-176
    dynamic, 23
    rhythm, 2
    style, 174-176
    J. S. Bach, ex. 175
    Ballet des Festes de Bacchus, ex. 227
    Charpentier, ex. 227
    Lully, ex. 228
    Purcell, ex. 179
    see also Entrée
Ozanam, 188

Paganini, Nicolò, 183
Partia, partie, see Partita
Parties de remplissage, 168, 226-227
Partita, 99
    see also Bach, J. S., Sonatas and Partitas for solo violin
Pasquali, Nicolo, 218
Passacaille, Passacaglia, 104
    tempo, 26
Passamezzo antico, 39
Passepied, 115
    tempo, 26
Passions, *see* Affect
Pauli, 211
Pauses, 32, 10
    Italian feature, 158
    Leopold Mozart, 9
Pavan, pavane, 2, 98
    pavan & galliard, 99
Pedal point, 31, ex. 42, 127, ex. 138, 154, ex. 179, 181
Penna, Lorenzo, 211
Performers' Facsimiles, 258
Petite reprise, 98
Phantasticus style, *see* Style, Phantasticus
Phrase,
    in oratory, 1
    articulation, 9
    chopped-off phrasing, 9
    minuet illustration, ex. 12-13
    length, 14
    see also
        Articulation
        Punctuation
Piani, Giovanni Antonio,
    Sonata II, Sarabanda, ex. 21
    Sonata IV,
        Allemanda, ex. 251
        Preludio, ex. 125
    Sonata V, Corrente, ex. 166
Piano, *see* Dynamics
Pistoy, 245
Pitch, 192-195
    Italian/French, 160, 238
    cammerthon/chorton, 193
    Classical, 195
    Corelli, 193
    Dresden, 193
    French opera, 193,
    ecurie, 195
    historic, 193
    modern, 192
    perfect, 193
Pizzicato, 8, ex. 23
Playford, John, (illus) frontispiece, 261-262
    Baltzar's compositions, 81
    bow hold, 84
    bowing rules, 90
    fingering, 72
    frets, 192

INDEX

maggot, 111
positions used, 81
tablature, ex. 196
D. Purcell, chacone, ex. 115
Faronell's Division on a ground, ex. 39, ex. 103
Readings Ground, ex. 200
rests, 251
Roger of Coverly, ex. 145,
strings, 244
tablature, 196
trills, 47
tuning, 194
vibrato, 60
violin hold, 64, 65
Pochettes, 67, 236
Point d'arrêt, 50
Polonaise, 116
Portamento, 79
Port-de-voix, 51
Position changing, 72-82
    trill in 2nd position, 49
    Tartini, 66
Praetorius, Michael, instruments, (illus) 236
    rules, 264
    strings, 244
    violin hold, 64
Prelleur, Peter, vi, 261-262
    bowing rules, 90
    position terminology, 81
    pitch, 194
    positions used, 81
    shifting, 79
    tuning, 194
    violin hold, 65
Prelude,
    J. S. Bach, ex. 41
    Corelli, 102
    Corelli/Geminiani, ex. 43
    Mace, 100-101
Prinner, Johann Jacob,
    violin hold, 6
Professionals,
    de Fer, 260
    French, 100
    North, 22
Psaltery, 236
Punctuation, 10
    phrasing, 9
    instrumental melodies, 10
    Mattheson, ex. 12-13
    recitative, 218
Purcell, Daniel,
    Chacone in The Division-violin, ex. 115
Purcell, Henry, ♪
    inégales, 113
    Italian style, 158, 183
    mute, 8
    pavan, 116
    styles of composition, 157
    theatre suites, 99
    time signatures/tempo, 28
    trio sonatas, 208-209
    Works,
        Abdelazar,
            overture, ex. 175
            rondeau, ex. 118
        Chacony, ex. 55, ex. 96, ex. 168
        Dido and Aeneas, Overture, ex. 179
        Double Dealer,
            Hornpipe, ex. 111
            Minuett, ex. 168, ex. 250
            Overture, ex. 223, ex. 252
        Gordian Knott, minuett, 113
        King Arthur,
            Chaconne, ex. 96, ex. 104
            Frost scene, 131
        Song for St. Cecilia's Day (1692), ex. 147
            In vain the am'rous flute, ex. 29
        Sonnata's of III parts (1683),
            title page, 208
            no. 7, ex. 47, ex. 185, ex. 209, ex. 253
            no. 9, ex. 28, 158
Purfling, 238

Quantz, Johann Joachim, 261-262
    appoggiaturas, ex. 51-53
    arousing the passions, 1
    articulation, 9, 10, 14, 134, 176
    bourée, 102
    bowing for dynamics, 23
    cello strings, 245-246
    chaconne tempo and affect, 104
    chromatic movement, 80
    continuo choice, 215
    courante bowing, 106
    dotted notes, 92, ex. 177, 178
    double bass shadow technique, ex. 217
    dynamics,
        for affect, 20-21, 23,
        exaggeration, 22,
        for harmony, ex. 205
        varied, 24
    emotional dissembling, 2
    emphasis of harmony, 20-21
    even bowing, 92
    figured bass expression, 204, ex. 205
    final notes, 127
    gavotte, 109
    gigue/canarie bow-stroke, 102
    inequality, 164
    key affect, 7
    long notes, 125, 126
    open strings, 74, 75
    orchestral piano, 23
    passacaille speed, 114
    passepied, 115
    playing for dancers, 33
    ornamentation, 35, ex. 41, 43, ex. 51, ex. 52, ex. 53, ex. 54, 56, 57
    recitative, 218
    rhythm alignment, 170
    rigaudon, 102
    rondeau, 117
    rushing, 135
    slurs, ex. 142
    speed of repeats, 33
    tactus, 25
    tempo, 27, 29, 102
    tierces coulés, ex. 54
    trills, 45, 48, 49
    triplets, 172
    tuning, 190-191
    viola, 37, 223, 224, 229, 230
    walking bass combined with long notes, 4
Quick notes, 61, 73, 134-141, 254

INDEX

Quintilian, Marcus Fabius, 1
   rhythm, 2
   rules, 263
   speed, 135

Raguenet, François, 159, 245
Rameau, Jean-Phillipe,
   'Baroque' style, 157
   continuo, 214
   key affect, 7, 189
   ornaments, 43
   string ensemble, 213, 228
   recitative Castor et Pollux, ex. 220
   rigaudon, 117
   temperament, 189, 190
Range,
   ensembles, 80
   French, 158
   Italian, 158
   viola parts, 80
   violin, 76, 79, ex. 80
   cello, 81-82
Recitative, 218-222
   Borin on speed in French, 26
Renaissance instruments, 235-239
Repeated notes,
   bow vibrato, 16, 132
   weak, 12, 120
Repeats,
   dances, 98
   dynamics for repeated motifs, 20
   Quantz, 33, 10
   schemes, ex. 118, 249
   signs, 250, 251
Resolutions, 47, 61, 139
Resonance, 73, 74, 150, 154, 176, 239
Restoration (17th-century English), 215
Rests, 249, 251-252
   articulation, 9
   Bach's counterpoint, 151
Rhetoric, 1-8
   articulation, 9
   dance, 98
   ornament affect, 34
   see also Affect
Rhythmic alteration, *see*
   Inequality
   Overture, style
Rhythm,
   anapest, ex. 94-95
   dance, see individual entries
   fast triple, 2
   freedom, 138
   molossus (slow triple), ex. 3
   patter, ex. 5
   rhetoric, 2
   slow duple/triple, 2
   spondaic, 116
   trochaic, ex. 5
   unequal, 163-169
Ricercar, 98
Rigaudon, 109, 117
   tempo, 26
Ripienists, see Accompanying
Roger, Estienne of Amsterdam 43, 212
   Corelli, ex. 36, ex. 254
Rogeri, Giovanni Baptista, 239

Rognioni, Richardo, 34, 39
Rognoni, Francesco, ♫
Romanesca, 39
Rondeau, 117
   Purcell, ex. 118
   rondo, gavotte en rondeau, 110
Rondement, *see* Tempo
Rosin, 243
Rossi, Salamone, 211
   Sonata sopra la Bergamasca, ex. 208
Rousseau, Jean, 261
   fast craquer, 91
   la plainte, 56, 80
   key affects, 7
   tenüe, 73
   tierce coule, ex. 54
   time signatures, 26
   vibrato, 60
Rousseau, Jean-Jacques, 190
Rubato, 42, 30-31, 138, 180
Rugeri, Francesco, 239
Ruggiero, 39
Rule of down-bow, 20, 88-97, 264
Rules,
   general 263-264
   for appoggiaturas 51, 52, 57
   Muffat, *see* Muffat,
      bowing rules
      bowing dances
   Tartini, 15, 134
Rushing, 135-137
   Leopold Mozart, 27
   gavotte, 109

St. Lambert, Monsieur de, 261
   articulation, 9
   inequality, 163, 164
   ornamentation, 36, 49
   rhetoric, 1
   rules, 263
   time signatures, 26
Salò, Gasparo da, 226, 238
Sanvitali, 211
Sarabande, 99, 118
   affect, 100
   J. S. Bach, ex. 53, ex. 37
   like chaconne, 104
   Corrette, ex. 126
   Marais, ex. 126
   Piani, ex. 21
   dynamic, 23
   tempo, 26
Sartori, Claudio, 211
Schmelzer, Johann Heinrich, 67, 74, 80, 138, 155, 181, 182
   Sonata Terza, ex. 79
   Sonata Quarta, ex. 79
   Sonata Quinta, ex. 73
   up-bow staccato, 141
Schop, Johann, 39
Schütz, Heinrich, 181
Scordatura, 182 196-202
Scotland, ex. 201
Selma, Bartolomeo de,
   Canzona quarta, ex. 254
Sesquialtera proportion, 29, 246
Set-up, 234-240, (illus) 237
Seventeenth-century suite, 98

INDEX

Short notes, 3
Shoulder-rest, 63
Siciliana, 121
Signs,
    bowing, 88, 92, 262
    daggers, ex. 133
    dashes, 16-17
    dots, 16, ex. 132-133, ex. 141, ex. 166, ex. 167
    French, 256
    ornament, 34, 45
    positions, 257
    swell, 125, 126
    vibrato, 125, 126
    see also
        Dynamics
        Slurs
Simpson, Christopher, 261-262
    divisions on a perfect cadence, ex. 39
    table of ornaments, 34, ex. 40, 41
    slurs, 146
    tenüe, 73
    vibrato, 60
Singing style, *see* Style, singing
Slides, 80
Slow bow, 122-133
    Grave, 28
Slurs, 142-148
    articulation, 9, 11, 16
    editorial, 258
    gigues, 111
    position, 78
    unusual, 117
Somis, Giovanni Battista, 161
Sonata,
    a due, 180, 208, 212
    a tre, 208, 212
    da camera/da chiesa, 99, 182
    17th-century Italian, 180-183
    18th-century, 209
    slow movements, 15, 43, ex. 128-129
    trio without continuo, 212
    see also
        Purcell sonnatas of III parts
        Italian composer/violinist entries
Sonority, 78, 194, 194, 226
Sorge, Georg Andreas, 189
Sound-post, (illus) 237, 239
Speed, 135
    of bow for affect, 21
    Italian gavotte, 109
    17th/18th century dances, 99
    trills, 48
    word instructions see Tempo
S.P.E.S., 258
Spiccato,
    meaning, 134, 136
Spike (cello), 70
Spohr, Louis,
    chin-rest, 63
    duets, 260
Staccato,
    heavy staccato, 4
    meaning in Baroque use, 134
    up- & down-bow, 141
    Veracini, ex. 150
Stainer, Jacob, 239
Stamitz, Carl Philipp, 229
Stil moderno, *see* Style

Stile concitato, *see* Style
Stoppani, George, 247
Stradella, Alessandro, ♪, 182
Stradivari, Antonio, 239
Strings, 244-247
    humidity, 192
    tension, 194, 245-246
    testing, (illus) 244
    thickness, 194, 246
Strokes, *see* Bow, strokes
Structure, 10
    oratory, 1
    phrase, 11
Style,
    antico, 185
    concitato, 41, 51
    consort, 20, 31, 184-185
    contrapuntal, 20, 31, 116, 127, 158, 184-185
    French, see France
    galant, 22, 177, 261
        continuo choice, 209
        turn, 55
    Italian, *see* Italy, style
    mixed, 161
    moderno, 51
    Phantasticus, 157, 180
    singing, 9, 11, 15
Suspensions, 127, 204-205
Swell, *see* Messa di voce
Syncopation, 19, 102
    bowing, 3, 91

Tablature, 75, 196
Tactus (beat), *see* Tempo
Talbot, James,
    galliard, 109
    saraband, 119
    strings, 244
Tartini, Giuseppe, 183, 262
    articulation, 9, ex. 134
        between notes, 15
    bow-stroke, 122
    even bowing, 92
    letter, 48, 122, 134
    position terminology, 81
    quick notes, ex. 134
    rosin recipe, 243
    slurs, 143
    trills, ex. 46, ex. 48-50, 75
    turns, 55, ex. 55
    vibrato, 61
    violin hold, 66
Taste, 159
    good, 123, 164, 263
    bad 15, 35, 36, 37, 39, 182, 262
Telemann, Georg Philipp, 99, 100, 116, 157, 190, 218, 230
Temperament, 187-192
    Bach, 188
    equal, 187
    mean-tone, 187
    unequal, 6-7, 163
Tempo, 25-33,
    canzonas, 29
    choice of, 25, 29, 135, 137-138
    dances, see individual entries
    editorial, 248

INDEX

effect on interpretation, 5
England,
    Matteis, 29-30,
    Purcell, 28-29
France, 26, 27
fugues, 29
Germany, 27
Italy,
    Muffat, 30
    see also Andante markings, 248
ornaments, 36
overture, 174
tactus (beat), 25, 29
tempo ordinario, 25, 29
Tenor violin, 223, 228-229, 236
Tenüe, 73
Terminations, 50, 146
Tessarini, Carlo, 79, 81
Tessitura, 13, 95
    affect of, 5
    dynamics, ex. 6
    instrumental, 80
Theatre,
    music, 107
    suite, 99
Thumb,
    violin, 68, 69, 72
    on bow, 83, 86
    position (cello), 82
Tierce coulé, 53-54, 109
Time signatures,
    French 26
    for inequality, 163-164
    Matteis, 28
    meanings, 26-28
    mixed, 170
    overtures, 174
    Purcell, 28, 29
    related, 180
    sarabands, 9
Title pages,
    Corelli, op. 5, 209
    Geminiani, Concerti Grossi, 229
    Italian 17th-century, 211
    Purcell, Sonnata's of III Parts, 208
Tosi, Pier Francesco,
    rubato, 31
    slurs, 142
Tourte bow, 88, 96, 136, 241
Transitional,
    violin, (illus) 237, 240
    bow, 240, (illus) 242
Transposition,
    key, 194
    of the hand, *see* Position changing
Treatises, 257, 260
    list, 265
    ornament information list, 57-58
Tremolo, bow vibrato, 129-133
    left hand vibrato, 59, 61, 62
    trill, 50
Trichet, Pierre,
    violin hold, 64
Trill, 45-51
    cadential, 37
    on open string, 48, 72, 75
    speed of, 48-49
    accelerating, 41, 48

Trillo, 50-51
Trio sonata, *see* Sonata
Tromba marina, 236
Tuning, 187-192,
    cello, ex. 238
    double bass, 240
    open strings, 189-192
    scordatura, 197-202
    viola d'amore, 231
    see also Temperament
Turn, 55-56
Tutors, *see* Treatises
Twenty-four violins, 213

Uccellini, Marco, 67, 211, 261
    dance collections, 99
    Sonata decimo, book 5, ex. 80
Unequal,
    rhythm, *see* Inequality
    tuning, *see* Temperament
Up-beat, allemande, 101
    bars, 11, 61
    bourée, 102
    forlana, 108
    passepied, 115
    rigaudon, 117

Vague, 163, 168
Vandini, Antonio, 86
van Eyck, Jacob, 39
Veracini, Francesco Maria, 183
    Cappricio Primo, ex. 43
    slurs, 145
    Sonata prima, op. 2,
    Largo e staccato, ex. 150,
        Toccata, ex. 125
    op. 2 no. 3, Allegro, ex. 146
Vibrato, 58-62, 72, 73, 125-6
    in ensemble playing, 36
    with bow vibrato, 132
Vingt-quatre violons, see Twenty-four violins
Viol, 60, 100, ex. 114, ex. 146, 184, 210, 212, 213, 214
Viola, 223-231
    meaning, 211-212
    French ensemble,
        Parties de remplissage, 226
        inequality in inner parts, 168
    obligato, 229
    ornamentation, 37
    repertoire, 230
    sizes, 80, 238-239
    strings, 245-246
Viola d'amore, ex. 93-94, 230-231 Viola da gamba, see
    Viol Violetta, 212, 226
Violino piccolo, 201-202
Violone, 215, 235, 239-241
    hold, 70
    Germany/Austria, 214
    Italy, 210-213
    meaning, 209, 238
Virgiliano, Aurelio, 34, 39
Vitali, Giovanni Battista, 183, 211
Vite, très vite, *see* Tempo
Vivace, *see* Tempo, Italy and France
Vivaldi, Antonio, 183,
    violin range, 80, 81

cello range, 81
Concerto op. 11 no. 6, Allegro non tanto, ex. 53
The Four Seasons, Autumn, Allegro, ex. 12

Wagenseil, Georg Christoph, 81
Walking bass,
  rhetorical affect, 4
  see also Andante
Walther, Johann Jakob,
  bow vibrato, 133
  chords, 155
  continuo, 211
  pizzicato, 8
  sonata in G major (1676), ex. 151
  up-bow staccato, 141
  upward range, 80
Waterhouse, John, (illus) 242
Wavy line, see Signs

Werckmeister, Andreas, 190
Westhoff, Johann Paul,
  Suite III, ex. 155
White notation, ex. 21, ex. 27, ex. 256
Wind instruments,
  articulation, 9
  fluctuation of pitch, 192
  key colour, 188
  in recitative, 219
  transposition, 195
  vibrato with diaphragm, 130
Wood, Anthony a, 76
Written-out ornamentation, *see* Ornamentation, written-out

Zannetti, Gasparo, Il Scolaro, 261
  bowings, 88
  tablature/fingering, 75, 196

Audio Examples

These examples can be downloaded free of charge from:
https://www.hyperion-records.co.uk/dc.asp?dc=D_BSP1
It is recommended that you use the Hyperion Download Manager to do this, as this will preserve the track numbers below.

CD of origin	Track	Title	Time
CDA66929	1-2	Almand, Pavan and Galliard of Albarti, from the Arundel Part-Books (c1560). JT TC PD DD MC FJ PH	2.22
CDA66395	3-4	Orlando Gibbons (c1583-1625), Fantasia a 3 no. 7 and 8. JT TC MC PH	4.48
CDA66806	5-6	Robert Johnson (c1583-1633), The Prince's Alman and Coranto. The Parley of Instruments Renaissance Violin Band	3.03
CDA66929	7	Francesco Rognoni (d. before 1626), Passaggi on Lassus's *Susanna un jour* 'per il violone over trombone alla bastarda'. MC PH	4.00
	8-9	Thomas Morley (1557/8-1602), Southerne's Pavan and Galliard. JT TC PD DD MC FJ	4.30
CDA66806	10	Angelo Notari (1566?-1663), Variations on the Ruggiero. JT EK FJ PH	5.43
CDA66970	11	Francesco Cavalli (1602-1643), Canzona a 3. JT TC MC TR	5.06
CDA66255	12	Alessandro Stradella (1644-1682), Sonata a otto Viole con una Tromba. CSP PB JT JN MC RG TC LC JC POD IG PH	7.04
CDA66817	13-17	Gottfried Finger (d. 1730), Sonata in C major. MB JT FdB MC PH	6.13
CDA66667	18-24	Matthew Locke (1621/2-1677), Suite of Brawles in Bb. JT HO WT EOD TC PD DD JN MC JWC RC HG	6.52
CDA66727	25-28	Matthew Locke, Suite in C major 'The Broken Consort' no. 4. Fantasy, Corant, Air, Saraband. JT TC MC PH POD LK FJ	6.33
CDA66604	29-31	John Jenkins (1592-1678), Fantasia Suite in E minor. JT TC HO MC PH	6.02
CDA66817	32	William Corbett (d1748), Overture from Suite in D major. MB ML The Parley of Instruments Baroque Orchestra	3.40
CDA67002	33-35	Henry Purcell (1659-1695), Music in 'The Double Dealer'. Overture, Hornpipe, Minuet. RG (director) TC JT MC EK POD PH	5.13
CDA67001	36	Henry Purcell, Music in 'King Arthur; or, the British Worthy'. Chaconne. The Parley of Instruments Baroque Orchestra directed from the violin by Roy Goodman	3.17
		TOTAL	72.26

The Players

Mark Bennett, Pavlo Beznosiuk, Richard Campbell, Mark Caudle, Theresa Caudle, Lisa Cochrane, Jane Coe, Frank de Bruine, Duncan Druce, Ian Gammie, Roy Goodman, Helen Gough, Peter Holman, Fred Jacobs, Elizabeth Kenny, Michael Laird, Jane Norman, Ellen O'Dell, Paul Denley, Paul O'Dette, Helen Orsler, Timothy Roberts, Crispian Steele-Perkins, Judy Tarling, William Thorp, Jennifer Ward-Clarke.

The above tracks have been selected from
HYPERION RECORDS

CDA66929	*'Musique of Violenze'*, dances, fantasias and popular tunes for Queen Elizabeth's violin band
CDA66395	*Music for Prince Charles*, by Gibbons and Lupo
CDA66806	*A High-Priz'd Noise*, violin music for Charles I
CDA66970	Cavalli, *Messa Concertata*
CDA66255	*Italian Baroque Trumpet Music*
CDA66817	*Sound the Trumpet*, Henry Purcell and his followers
CDA66667	*Four and Twenty Fiddlers*, music for the Restoration Court Band
CDA66727	Matthew Locke, *'The Broken Consort'*
CDA66604	*Late Consort Music* by John Jenkins
CDA67001	Henry Purcell, complete *Ayres for the Theatre* CD1 of 3 CD set.
CDA67002	Henry Purcell, complete *Ayres for the Theatre* CD2 of 3 CD set.

www.ingramcontent.com/pod-product-compliance
Lightning Source LLC
Chambersburg PA
CBHW040950020526
44118CB00045B/2826